BLAKE'S
CLASSIC
TRUE CRIME
COMPENDIUM 1

BLAKE'S
CLASSIC
TRUE CRIME
COMPENDIUM 1

Amazing True Crime Stories from the *News of the World's Sunday Magazine*, plus the stunning story of how one man smashed an international drugs cartel.

DREW **M**ACKENZIE AND
JOHN **L**IGHTFOOT

BLAKE'S
TRUE
CRIME
LIBRARY

Published by Blake Publishing Ltd,
3 Bramber Court, 2 Bramber Road,
London W14 9PB, England

First published in 2003

ISBN 1 85782 561 6

British Library Cataloguing-in-Publication Data: A catalogue record for this book is
available from the British Library.

Design by www.envydesign.co.uk

Printed and bound in Great Britain by Bookmarque

1 3 5 7 9 10 8 6 4 2

Papers used by Blake Publishing Ltd are natural, recyclable products made from
wood grown in sustainable forests. The manufacturing processes conform to the envi-
ronmental regulations of the country of origin.

Contents

SUNDAY
BLOODY
SUNDAY

To my wife Emily without whose love,
help and encouragement this book and my tennis game
would not have been possible.

And to my mother Mary MacKenzie who is only
a phone call and 3,500 miles away from giving
me some sound and loving advice.

Acknowledgements

THIS BOOK IS really a team effort. The staff at *Sunday Magazine* came up with numerous ideas and supplied endless support and encouragement. Sue Carroll and Peter Picton deserve a special mention, but words cannot express my gratitude to Martin Malin, Karisia Cooper, Angie Mulligan, Mike Davey, Mark Lomas and Daniel Taylor.

This book would have been hard to imagine without the help of dozens of detectives and prosecutors throughout the US. They gave up countless hours of their spare time to give me shocking details of these mysterious and chilling crimes.

I'd also like to give my deepest thanks to my family for their help over the years which paved the way for this book. My mother Mary MacKenzie, former deputy director of information at Greater London Council, got me out of betting shops and into the family business — journalism. My father Ian MacKenzie, retired editor of weekly papers, gave me my first job at *News Shopper*. My brother, Kelvin MacKenzie, gave me my first shifts on daily papers in England and in America. My brother Craig MacKenzie, gave me my first freelance assignments and much advice along the way.

And I cannot forget Dick McWilliams, a producer on the American TV show *A Current Affair*. He always found time to help me with my crime research despite the pressures of his own job.

But most of all my heart goes out to Terri Jeffers, whose son Danny was brutally killed by her ex-husband. Her courage, as shown in this book, is an example to us all.

1

My Crusade
for Danny Boy

THEY ARE WOMEN who share a special, bitter grief. Every one of them is a mother who has lost a little child at the hands of a murderer. The Parents of Murdered Children group, based in Houston, Texas, is battling for a compulsory death penalty for the murder of a child under six. And these grieving parents are led by a woman who has more reason than most to see child-killers executed.

Terri Jeffers, 37, was forced to listen, in horror, over the telephone as her ex-husband calmly slaughtered their three-year-old son, Danny.

The fair-haired boy had been staying with his father, carpenter Jimmy Ward, 44, for a week in August 1988, under a temporary custody deal. It was a month after Terri got a divorce from her wife-beating husband. But instead of returning him, Ward phoned Terri at her home in the quiet Houston suburb of Humble, and begged her to forgive all his brutality and come back to him.

She refused. He begged again. And again she refused. Ward began threatening to 'put a bullet in Danny's head', then kill himself. Twice, he hung up.

A panic-stricken Terri phoned up Ward's mother — and the police.

The third time Ward rang, Terri had a tape-recorder tapped into the phone to collect evidence for a battle to prevent him sharing custody of the boy. And at the other end of the line, Ward had a .22 calibre hand gun, aimed at little Danny's head.

Outside, by now, Ward's mother, Margaret, was hammering on the front door. 'Alright,' Ward told Terri, his voice calm and flat, 'Mum's showed up. I guess the cops will be here in a couple of minutes.'

'No!' Terri lied.

'Honey,' Ward told her, as the tape rolled, 'I do love you.'

'Don't kill my baby!' Terri pleaded. 'How could you threaten to kill my baby?'

'You want to tell him goodbye?'

'You're going to kill him … ?'

'Yes. I am. Here he is. You want to tell him goodbye?'

'Don't you dare!' the horrified Terri blustered.

'You made the decision,' Ward replied in the same flat voice. 'You called my bluff.'

'Don't you dare touch my baby!' the mother screamed.

But the horror was reaching its climax. 'Hey,' Ward jeered, the gun still at his son's head, 'you're the one who called in the cops. You always thought you were cool, didn't you? You did what you thought was right, huh? Think about it!'

There were two quick popping noises. Gunshots.

Terri, near collapse, managed to ring off and call the police again.

Ward had put the gun to his son's forehead, just above the little boy's right eye. And, as Danny stared up in terror at his dad, Ward fired. Then he put the gun to his own head, at the left ear, and fired again. He managed to get to the door and let his mother in before he collapsed.

Incredibly, both father and son were still alive when the ambulance came. In hospital, they were put into the same intensive care ward, just four beds apart from each other. But little Danny was already brain-dead.

He was put on a life-support system, to await the transplant team who would take his heart to save another life. Terri sat holding his hand. Danny's half-sister, Melissa, 10 — the child of Terri's first marriage — came in to say goodbye. And the killer-father was becoming conscious again . . .

He showed no remorse. 'Get me a good cup of coffee and a good lawyer,' he ordered his ex-wife. 'I might get two years for this and I'll be out in about two weeks. If I have to stay in prison longer, I'll get a college degree, and get a desk job when I get out.'

Terri, a lab technician, had met Ward through friends, in 1983. Like her, he had been married before. At first, she could hardly believe her luck. So soon after her first marriage had collapsed, she seemed to have found Mr Perfect.

'He seemed to be everything I wanted,' she says. 'A hard worker, a family man, a churchgoer. And he liked Melissa.'

Within eight months, Terri knew him rather better. 'He had a violent, uncontrollable temper. He'd say, "You are never going to leave me. I'll kill you first." He abused Melissa and me physically and emotionally. He also drank cases of beer, which made him even more vicious.'

Ward was also a jealous husband. 'He often accused me of being unfaithful. Once, he threatened to cut off my hands because he thought I was having an affair. Finally, I was forced to leave him.

'But he had therapy, to stop his raging tantrums, and I agreed to go back to him, for Danny's sake.'

It didn't last. 'His tempers started again,' Terri recalls. 'The final straw came when he threatened me with a gun and smashed my head against the headboard of the bed. I waited until he was out at work. Then I packed some clothes and moved into a battered wives' shelter with Melissa and Danny.'

By now Danny, though only three years old, was convinced his father was going to kill him. 'Danny had this premonition,' Terri says. 'But I just didn't take him seriously. I don't know why.

'Jim had sworn to kill me and my daughter — and even my

3

parents – if I didn't take him back. I just never thought he'd touch Danny. Not his own son.

'Danny kept telling me, "Daddy's got a gun and he's going to kill me." And I would tell him, "No. Daddy loves you. He's not going to hurt you." In the final weeks before Jim did kill him, my poor little Danny was terrified.'

In court, Jim Ward pleaded insanity. But he was declared fit for trial. His first wife, Geraldine Adams, mother of his two daughters, testified that his violent temper had destroyed their 11-year marriage. He once threatened to kill her, Geraldine said. 'He told me he would never spend time in jail because he'd get out on the grounds of insanity.'

Ward was convicted of murdering little Danny and jailed for life. But this year, he'll be eligible for parole. Terri plans to fight to keep him inside for the rest of his days. 'I could never forgive him,' she says. 'I believe in God, but I'm angry at a God who'd let someone like Jim go up to heaven, as long as he repents.'

Since Danny was murdered, his mother has carried the horrifying tape of that last phone call around in her handbag. It only lasts 30 seconds or so. But she uses it to try to persuade local politicians to vote through a new law that would bring much harsher treatment for those who kill children.

She wants any convicted child-murderer to be executed or at the very least to spend no less than 35 years behind bars, instead of the present 15-year minimum under Texas state law. 'I've got my whole life to think about this,' Terri says. 'It's the fire that keeps me going.'

These days, Terri carries a .38 calibre gun for protection. And she has no thought of marrying again. 'I live in a self-made prison,' she says. 'I live in fear because of Jim. And I don't think I could ever trust another man again.'

Once a month, she finds solace at Parents of Murdered Children meetings. They have made a quilt with transfer pictures of their 30 dead children. At each meeting, the Keeper of the

Quilt, Shirley Parish — her daughter Kimberly was killed by a madman — holds up the cloth. And one of the bereaved parents talks about the never-ending heartbreak of their loss.

Danny's picture is there on the quilt, of course. And in time, it will be Terri's turn again to point to her little boy and tell some grieving new member about that August day in '88. The day she picked up the phone and listened to the sound of her son being murdered.

'It helps to know that others care,' Terri says. 'But my heart has been ripped out, just the same. All the plans I had, all the love … You raise your child. You teach them, you nurse them, you stay up at night when they're sick. Danny never got to play football, He never got to see the Astros baseball team. One of my last memories of him is when he was standing there in the bathtub, saying, 'I love you, Mama, I love you.'

Terri and Melissa wrote this poem, in loving memory of their Danny:

> A million times we've missed you.
> A million times we've cried.
> If love could have saved you,
> You never would have died.

> Things we feel most deeply
> Are the hardest things to say.
> Our dearest one, we'll always
> Love you in a very special way.
> We often sit and think of you
> And think of how you died,
> To think we couldn't say goodbye

Before you closed your eyes.
No one can know our loneliness
And no one can see us weeping.
All our tears from aching hearts,
While others are still sleeping.

If we had a lifetime wish,
A dream that would come true,
We'd pray to God with all our hearts,
For yesterday – and you.
Love, Mom and Melissa.

2

Cop by Day –
Bandit by Night

HERO COP GARY Steadman, 35, got the shock of his life when he ripped the mask off a burglar he'd just shot. For it was his best friend and fellow police officer, Mike Stanewich.

Distraught Gary gently held his pal as he bled to death. He looked at Mike in disbelief and the injured man said, 'Yeah, it's me, Gary.' When the 36-year-old stopped breathing, Gary tried mouth-to-mouth resuscitation – but it was in vain.

As other officers arrived, he cried, 'I've killed my best friend. God help me, what am I going to say to his wife and kids?'

Gary and Mike had worked at the same police station in San Diego, California, for years. They went drinking together and their families were close, too. But Gary had no idea that his best buddy was a cop gone bad.

The drama began on 3 July, 1991, with a call that a house was being robbed. Gary, who was patrolling the Encinitas area of San Diego, was at the house in minutes. The burglar had beaten and threatened to kill the owner, Donald Van Ort, 32. He was handcuffed to a chair with a lighter-fuel soaked pillow over his head.

The 6' 3" crook, wearing a nylon mask and rubber gloves, warned he would turn Donald into a human torch unless he opened his safe. 'He said he was going to light my fire unless I gave him the combination,' revealed Donald. 'But I wouldn't give it to him.'

The intruder had also bound and gagged Donald's grandmother

Helen, 82, who was lying on a couch. 'He warned me, "You're going to shut up or I'll blow your brains out," ' she said. But when Mike was clumsy enough to drop a book of matches, the elderly lady overcame her fear and hid them.

Gary burst in and shouted at the thief, 'I'm a police officer, freeze!' The robber had a gun tucked in his waistband but moved towards a kitchen knife on the side of the sink. Again Gary screamed, 'Freeze!' But Mike still headed for the knife. Gary fired three rounds with his 9mm gun, hitting his friend twice in the back and once in the elbow.

Police now think Mike may have deliberately got himself shot because he was so ashamed at being caught as a common criminal. He was skilled in self-defence and had given lectures on how to handle encounters with armed and dangerous suspects. Captain Bon Apostolos said, 'Why did he make furtive movements while standing in front of a gun? Did he want to die?'

Mike Stanewich joined the force in 1981 and rose quickly through the ranks. In 1989, the father of five was commended for 'outstanding service to the community' and a year later was promoted to detective and assigned to the elite undercover narcotics unit.

Mike was well-liked at the station because of his sense of humour. And in his neighbourhood, he was a local hero who spent hours telling kids about his exploits. But there was a dark side to his character, unknown to most people.

Shortly before he became a cop, Mike was arrested in 1980 for impersonating a police officer — a fact he left off his application. A few months before he was killed he was reprimanded for the first time by his superiors, for making an unauthorised surveillance.

Mike also had money troubles. He'd been happily married to Kathy, a probation officer, for five years. They had three children — aged four, three and 22 months. Although they each earned £25,000, a new £130,000 house was draining their finances. Plus Mike had to pay £200-a-month alimony and support to his first wife and two children. His ex-wife took him to court several times after he fell behind with the payments.

Mike desperately needed cash and he knew where to get it. He was one of six plain-clothes officers who had searched Donald Van Ort's house for drugs six weeks earlier. Donald was ordered to open his safe – and all the cops had seen jewellery, heirlooms and $60,000 in cash from the sale of his grandmother's home. No drugs were discovered anywhere in the house and the police soon left.

The next day Donald saw Mike in his back yard. When confronted, the officer said he needed a urine specimen. Later Donald noticed a window had been tampered with. 'I thought he was trying to plant drugs in my house,' he said.

Soon after, Donald changed his safe combination and put most of the money in the bank. On the day of the robbery, Donald was in the shower when the doorbell rang. He opened the door to two men – as Mike pulled out a gun, his accomplice panicked and ran off.

Donald screamed, 'It's a robbery!' – alerting his girlfriend Carla Sawcliff who was in the back room. She escaped unnoticed through a window and called the police from a neighbour's house.

Mike's car was found nearby with the plates removed, convincing detectives he'd carefully planned the whole operation.

Donald claimed that the second thief was one of the five deputies who had swooped on his house with Mike. But the officer he picked out had an iron-clad alibi, and so did the rest of the drug squad.

Meanwhile Gary Steadman has been undergoing counselling to overcome the trauma of killing his best friend. One police official says: 'Nobody feels any compassion for a crooked cop like Stanewich. I feel a lot sorrier for Gary Steadman.'

3

Day I Faced
Dad's Killer

JOHN MUDD JNR, 22, had lived with a secret so devastating, his conscious mind blotted it out for 16 years. He was only five when his adored father was murdered at home in Wilkinsburg, Pennsylvania on 28 December, 1975.

John Mudd Snr, 28, had been watching TV with his wife Arlene and their son when the TV and lights in the living room blacked out. John went down to the dark cellar to check the fuse-box.

Moments after his father had been shot seven times, the terrified little boy clearly saw the killer. But the murder was so traumatic he had erased it from his memory. It could have vanished for ever, but the horror of that night came flooding back to him when, at 21, he was playing Trivial Pursuit with friends. He was about to hit a pal who'd made fun of his girlfriend, when John burst into tears. He says, 'I wanted to hurt him, but went into the hallway, knelt down and everything came flooding back to me.'

The drama triggered a series of clear memories which he later compared to photographic slides. But he couldn't put a name to the killer's face until police showed him a photo line-up of possible suspects.

John quickly picked out the person he'd seen after the shooting – his mother's lover, Steven Slutzker.

In 1991, he told a new inquest, 'I heard seven loud noises, then I remember being at the top of the cellar steps looking down at my dad's body. I was being held by someone.' He recalled sitting on the couch with his mum seeing Slutzker come out of the cellar.

It was enough for police to reopen the case and charge Slutzker, 41, with murder.

Back in 1975, police homed in on Steven Slutzker, who lived across the street. A friend of Steven's, Michael Pezzano, had told the police five days before the murder that Slutzker had tried to hire him to kill Mudd with a .32 calibre automatic gun, the same type as the murder weapon.

Police also learned that Steven and Arlene had been having an affair. They had even lived together briefly but Arlene moved back home for the sake of her young son.

At first Steven was charged with the killing, but as there was no proof he pulled the trigger, the charge was dropped. But he still faced two counts of solicitation to commit murder.

Arlene testified that the killer was probably a burglar who had entered the house through the kitchen and gone out through the cellar door. But the only footprints police found were at the front of the house. Steven's attorney suggested Arlene had killed her husband, or hired a hitman, whom she'd let out through the front door.

When Michael Pezzano testified that Steven had offered him $300 to kill John, he said, 'Steven wanted him killed by Christmas so that he and Arlene could have a good holiday together.'

Steven was sentenced to 23 months in jail. When he walked free after a year, he thought he'd got away with murder. But he'd forgotten about the boy he thought was asleep on the fatal night.

In 1976, Arlene lost custody of John Jnr, who went to live with his aunt, Maureen Perri, near Wilkinsburg. He had no contact with his mum and grew up believing Slutzker was involved in his dad's death.

After his moment of recall, John was to get revenge on the witness stand. Psychologist Russel Scott said it was not unusual to have recall after 16 years. 'When people face trauma, it can get locked in the memory but be triggered by a later event.'

A surprise last-minute witness, Steven's daughter Amy, clinched the jury's verdict. Steven claimed that he and Amy had spent the night of the murder with friends.

Amy, who was six at the time of the killing, said this was a lie. She also said she had seen Steven take a gun from their dresser at home. She hadn't come forward earlier because she was terrified of her father. As a child she remembered him pulling a gun on her mother.

Arlene, called by the defence, exercised her legal right to refuse to answer questions that might incriminate her. It was revealed that Steven was an electrician, who'd installed a light in the Mudds' living room. At the time of the crime, this was the only fuse that wasn't in place; it was unscrewed.

Slutzker was found guilty and got life. The victim's sister Maureen said, 'We finally got the justice due to us.'

4

A Cold Killing

THE LAST WORDS Edward Sherman said to his pregnant wife were: 'I love you, too.' But a little girl who was eavesdropping on the phone thought there was something very strange about the call.

Two days later the body of Ed's wife Ellen was found in their bedroom, which was freezing cold because the killer had turned the air-conditioning up to maximum. Ellen, 38, who was five months pregnant, lay naked on the bed and had been brutally strangled with her own bikini panties. The unborn baby was also dead.

Ellen's balding husband, then 42, was ruled out as the prime suspect at the beginning because he had a concrete alibi. For Ed, a college lecturer with a genius IQ of 165, was out at sea, sailing off the coast of Maine with four friends, at the time.

When he was quizzed by the cops, he said: 'I didn't kill Ellen. I'm not capable of doing such a thing. I am not a violent person. I've never hurt anyone. I just couldn't use violence on anyone.'

The police began to look elsewhere for the vicious killer, but the investigation always seemed to lead back to the unfaithful husband. Police discovered that the Shermans, who had been married for 16 years, had been having angry rows over his eight-year affair with pretty Nancy Prescott.

Nancy had even given birth to Ed's daughter Rachel eight

months earlier. When heartbroken Ellen found out about her husband's love-child, she got pregnant as well. Although they already had a 13-year-old daughter Jessica, Ed did not like kids, and Ellen had aborted his baby seven years earlier.

Nancy had also aborted Ed's child two years before she had Rachel.

Detectives also learned that Ed and Ellen had briefly separated a few weeks before the murder and then reconciled when he'd agreed to stop seeing his mistress. Ellen had threatened to kick Ed out of the house if he saw Nancy again, and warned him she'd take him to the cleaners in divorce court.

The couple were joint owners of a small advertising agency, Ad Graphics, but because she had the controlling interest and did most of the work, she'd get it if it came to a divorce battle.

On the day she was last seen it appeared that the Shermans had finally solved their marital problems because Ellen gave him a card for his 42nd birthday and a milkshake maker for a present. However, she did not know that a few days earlier Ed had tried to convince Nancy that she should leave the door open to resume the relationship 'if things ever changed'.

Within weeks of Ellen's death, he'd moved in with Nancy, and soon they bought a home together. Three years later, police were called to the house after he kicked her in the face. Knowing he was a murder suspect and had claimed he was not a violent person, they took photos of the bruises covering her face.

Police subsequently discovered that in 1978 Sherman had an affair with another woman whom he'd pushed into a door and then knocked down. He also tried to choke her, but she hit him over the head with a frying pan. And before he met Ellen, he was briefly married. But his first wife got an annulment after he assaulted her.

Police also found a computer disk containing the manuscript of a chilling murder mystery Ellen was writing. The plot was eerily similar to real life – a wife is murdered and although her husband is the prime suspect, he was out of town at the time.

The circumstantial evidence was mounting up against Ed but, just like in the book, he had an iron-clad alibi. Then the police heard about a TV movie called *Blackout* that Ed had seen three days before Ellen was found.

The homicide squad realised that the film probably solved their own murder case. It was a thriller about a businessman named Ed who murders his wife and then turns the air-conditioning up before going out of town.

The idea was to slow the decomposition of the body so that cops were confused about the time the wife was killed. Had Sherman also put the air-conditioning on maximum at his house in East Lyme, Connecticut, to preserve the body and mask the time of death?

The police began to think he had. They believed he'd killed Ellen early on a Friday evening and then joined his friends for a weekend sailing jaunt. The chances of proving it, however, seemed remote.

But, nearly five years after the callous crime, the police finally got their big break when Kristin McDuff mentioned to her father Henry a phone call she'd overheard around the time of the murder.

Fifteen minutes after Ed had kissed goodbye to his wife on 2 August, 1985, he stopped off to pick up Henry, who was going sailing with him. Sherman asked to use the phone so he could call his wife to tell her to shut off the battery to a sailboat they owned. Kristin, who was then eight years old and had a habit of eavesdropping, picked up the phone to make a call – unaware Sherman was using an extension in another room.

She told police: 'He said, "I love you, too" as if someone said, "I love you" first.' But all Kristin could hear on the other end was a ringing telephone.

Blonde-haired Kristin, now 15, also heard him say: 'If you need anything, go to the neighbours. I have to go now.'

She was ashamed about listening in on the call and for years had been afraid to tell her mother about it. 'I used to listen in on my mother's conversations, then I'd feel bad,' she said. It was obvious that Ed had made a fake call to his wife to help prove she was still alive when he last saw her. Sherman had also called Ellen in a ship-to-shore call, planning to tell her when he might be back and to remind her about the battery. But nobody answered. He tried again on Sunday, but still no reply.

He managed to get through to his wife's friend Barbi Lane from the ship, and asked her to check on his wife and to tell her to turn off the battery – even though he'd already told his wife that.

In March 1990, Sherman was finally charged with murder. If the foetus of his child had been three weeks older, he would also have been charged with capital murder, an offence punishable by death. The prosecution claimed he killed Ellen because she wanted him to stop seeing his lover and he faced a costly divorce if he didn't.

And the baby boy whom Ellen was carrying would have meant that he would have to spend more time at home, and thus less with Nancy and Rachel. State Attorney Robert Satti pointed out that as a Mensa member he was an intelligent person, as well as shrewd and manipulative, and was capable of planning and carrying out a murder.

Forensic tests showed that her last meal was linguini and clam sauce – which was still in her stomach, indicating she'd died from within minutes to two hours of eating on Friday night.

But the most damning evidence came from Kristin McDuff and country singer Barbi Lane, who testified that she'd spoken on the phone to Ellen on Friday morning. Lane said that Ellen was so upset about another crisis in her marriage that she couldn't talk – especially since her husband was there.

Barbi called again at 8pm that night and nobody answered. She kept on calling repeatedly for the next two days. 'I was extremely upset,' said Lane. She knew Ellen's daughter Jessica was away at summer camp and that Ed was off sailing, so Barbi went to Ellen's house to see if she was okay.

Lane banged on all the windows, screamed out Ellen's name and then, fearing the worst, went to get a mutual friend, Len Fredericksen, to break into the house. He recalled that the bedroom was freezing cold 'like a refrigerator'. He said: 'I heard the air-conditioning going, so I broke in. When I got into her bedroom, it was a horrifying picture I'll never forget.'

Sherman was found guilty of murder. And jury foreman Donald Arthur said: 'I think it was a crime of passion and when it was over it was over.'

Rose Cooper, Ellen's mother, said: 'It's not bringing my daughter back, but at least there's justice.'

He was sentenced to 50 years behind bars, but from the dock he continued to protest his innocence.

He said: 'I want to say that I stand by my testimony. I did not kill Ellen. I don't know who killed Ellen. But I want to apologise to the woman I promised to love, honour and cherish. Each and every day for the last six years I've apologised to Ellen for the lifestyle I led. I loved Ellen but apparently I did not honour our relationship. She certainly deserved a better life than the one she lived with me. For that I'll be eternally sorry. Had we lived a better life, perhaps Ellen would have been alive today.'

Then he addressed Ellen's mother, saying: 'I, too, want someone punished for this crime.' He also apologised to Nancy Prescott and their daughter Rachel.

He also turned to Jessica and, with tears in his eyes and a crack in his voice, said: 'As I look at you, Jess, I see many of the beautiful characteristics that remind me of your mother. May God bless you.'

5

Dad Forgives Daughter for Family Slaughter

LOVELY BRENDA WILEY was the apple of her father's eye. The blue-eyed beauty was a bright, loving child, who never caused any trouble. And that's what made it so much harder for Mark Wiley when police told him that his wife Bonnie, 40, and son Keith, 14, had been murdered. For the unspeakable crimes had been committed by his 15-year-old daughter Brenda. Furthermore she had planned to kill her father as well.

The trouble began when Brenda suddenly blossomed into a beautiful buxom blonde. It was not long before she had a steady boyfriend, 18-year-old Keith Santana.

Three months later Brenda's lust for Keith was out of control. She'd leave her window open so he could spend passionate nights with her.

However, her parents were woken by banging noises and caught them in the act. Her dad threw Keith out of the house, in America's New Jersey, took Brenda's door off the hinges and ordered her to end the relationship. But she saw him in secret and, as a result, got grounded.

On the morning of 8 November, 1990 – the last day of her grounding – Brenda's anger suddenly boiled over.

She was cleaning the house, her brother was folding the laundry while her mother was working outside. Then her brother started calling her a sneak. She finally flipped and hit him over the head with a Pepsi Cola bottle. As he was still conscious, Brenda picked up a 10-inch-blade carving knife and attacked him in a frenzy. She stabbed him nearly 20 times, piercing his liver, heart, neck and abdomen. His last words were, 'I won't tell, I won't tell.'

She locked the door while she cleaned up the blood, and could hear her mother banging on it, trying to get in. Says Brenda: 'I took this bar as my mother went round the house banging on windows. I unlocked the door and she came in. I hit her on the head. Then I took the same knife and kept hitting her. And she was dead.'

Bonnie's last words to her daughter were, 'What did I ever do to you?' She had 30 stab wounds and her skull was crushed by the blows.

Brenda put her brother in a sleeping bag and put a rubbish bag over his head. She mopped up before phoning Keith and telling him what she had done. Keith arrived with his friend Brian Adams and three girlfriends. While the girls waited outside, Keith and Brian went in. When they saw the grisly mess, Adams asked her why she had done it. She said she loved Keith. Then Brenda jumped into her mother's car and drove off. But her friends called the police and she was stopped.

At her trial, her lawyer Frank DiChiara claimed she was either suffering from temporary insanity or diminished capacity when she killed.

Two psychologists and a psychiatrist testified for the defence, saying she had a 'severe depressive disorder' that prevented her from acting 'knowingly or purposefully'.

The court heard how Brenda's problems with her parents intensified when her 17-year-old brother Tim left home to enter a drug detoxification clinic.

Psychologist Dr Edward Dougherty said: 'All the energy that had centred on Tim was now on Brenda.' He also revealed that before killing she had twice tried to kill herself, but the gun had only fired blanks.

In her confession, Brenda said she had also planned to kill her father, but he was working at Acme's supermarket that day and so was spared.

Brenda's boyfriend testified that four days before the killings she rang him up begging him to help murder her parents. He said, 'No way.'

Dr Irwin Perr, a psychologist for the prosecution, claimed that although Brenda was 'thinking crazy' she was not insane.

But Brenda, claimed she was out of her mind at the time. Nonetheless, she was found guilty and sentenced to life in prison, without a chance of parole for 30 years. Her distraught father launched an appeal. He said: 'She killed her own mother and brother and she was in the right frame of mind? I just can't buy that.

'Brenda is amazed I am standing by her. But I love her as much as I loved my wife and son.'

6

Blind Robbery

Probing with a white stick in his hand, 42-year-old Bob Toe would step out of a taxi and carefully tap his way across the pavement to the bank entrance. Usually the security guard would open the door for him and then Bob would feel his way to a queue in front of a teller. When it came to his turn, Bob would hand the teller his calling card. It read: 'I have a gun. Be quick, be quiet or you're dead. Put all the cash in the bag.'

Seconds later Bob would retrace his steps out of the bank and hail a taxi. Because he was blind, one would usually stop for him right away. He'd tell the driver: 'To the airport and step on it.' Blind Bob had struck again.

Incredibly, 15-stone Robert Vernon Toe robbed 24 banks . . . despite being unable to see what he was doing. Life has been nothing more than a blur to Bob for years – but it hasn't stopped him living a successful life of crime.

Bob was born with an incurable eye disease known as retinitis pigmentosa – which meant as a child he could not see in the dark. Over the years his eyes gradually got worse until he became almost completely blind. 'My eyes got so bad I was forced to become a crook,' says Bob.

He staged his first hold-up in 1974 – just minutes after being released from prison after serving five years for a mail fraud. 'I'd always wanted to be a bank robber,' says Bob. 'My heroes were Jesse James and Bonnie and Clyde. While I was in the slammer other cons told me there was a bank nearby nobody had ever hit, so I decided that would be my first job.

'The prison got me a cab to leave and I told the driver to wait while I picked up some money.' He certainly did – and walked out of the bank with £4,000 in a brown paper bag. He didn't even have a gun.

Three years later in New York, Blind Bob hit again. Some money he'd made as a child selling stolen fish worms vanished from his account, probably due to an accounting error. Bob was furious and got his revenge on the bank by holding it up for £1,500. 'The bank guard even opened the door for me because he could see I was blind. I hopped in the waiting cab and told the driver to take me to the airport. I like New York because as soon as you stick out your hand for a cab, one stops.'

Over the next few months, Bob hit another seven banks – twice he robbed two on the same day. 'I'd never rob banks on a rainy day, though, because you can't catch a cab then,' he says.

Barely able to make out shapes, Bob would follow people into the bank and stand in line. 'Young people walk too fast so I'd always follow older ones.' He'd then pass his calling card to the teller – a one-eyed jack with the message demanding money on the back.

'One time a woman started screaming in panic, so I left. I didn't want her to suffer undue stress. I pulled out my cane, walked a few blocks and robbed another bank. Then there was the time a red dye bomb went off all over the money 30 seconds after I left the bank. I was so mad I got the cabbie to take me to another of their branches and robbed that, too.'

Bob was finally nabbed in 1977 by a million-to-one chance. As he unfolded his cane, he stumbled into armed guards delivering money to the bank. They were moonlighting cops – he had literally walked into the arms of the law!

Sentenced to 18 years in an Alabama jail, he was sent back to New York in 1983 for parole. But there was no halfway house that would take him, because of his handicap, and he faced another 11 years in jail. Then he got a huge break when the authorities couldn't decide where to place him so he walked free. It was the third time Bob had left prison before his sentence was finished – only the first couple of times he'd escaped.

During his first prison term, he cut through iron bars in the cell, smashed the window, cut a hole in a fence and climbed over a second barbed-wire fence. He was out for nine months before police caught up with him in Hollywood, where he'd starred in three porn movies and acted as a pimp to eight prostitutes.

'Weeks before I was finally arrested again, the FBI showed me a picture of myself and asked if I recognised this man. I couldn't see a thing so I told them I knew him but didn't know where he lived!'

After Bob was freed from jail for a third time he celebrated in his usual style – by robbing a bank. 'This time I hid a Coke bottle under my coat to make it look like a shooter,' says Bob, who never carried a real gun. 'I got $9,000 and flew to Las Vegas.' While living it up at night with leggy show-girls, Bob would commute to New York by day to do his 'job'. 'I flew to New York so often I even got a frequent flyer discount from Pan Am,' he laughs.

Once a little old lady tried to jump the queue Bob was standing in. 'I told her to wait her turn. She wouldn't, so I said, "Dammit, lady, I'm robbing this bank." '

However, Bob's luck ran out in 1983 when he changed his routine. Instead of going back to Las Vegas, Bob went to his old neighbourhood. 'The taxi driver recognised me from a wanted poster in his cab and after he dropped me off he called the cops. I was taking a stroll round my old haunts when cops armed with shotguns started following me. The first I knew about it was when they jumped on me. I crashed to the ground, shouting, "Help, help, muggers are trying to rob a blind man!" But it was no good.'

Sentenced to another 17 years behind bars in Lompoc Federal

Penitentiary, a maximum-security jail outside Santa Barbara, California, Bob made one more escape attempt in 1987.

'I climbed over two fences but set off an alarm. The guards started to come after me, so I ran — and crashed head-first into a tree, knocking myself out.'

The heavily tattooed Bob admits to being a lifelong thief. He was a gang member at eight, a shoplifter at 10, a burglar at 12 and a con man at 16. 'I grew up dirt-poor because my father hardly ever had work.' Although he's the black sheep of the family, Bob says he's not all bad. In fact, he considers himself a modern-day Robin Hood.

He claims he's given large sums of stolen money to charities such as the Special Olympics and donated heavily to research into the eye disease retinitis pigmentosa. He's been paid over $17,000 for the film rights to his life story and has given it all to the RP Association. 'I also get two per cent of the film's profits and plan to keep that. I'm hoping Robin Williams will play me, because I'm told we look alike and he mixes drama and comedy so well.'

7

'Small Sacrifices'

IT WAS A fatal attraction with a horrifying twist. Spurned Diane Downs was totally obsessed with her hunky lover Lewis Lewiston and was shattered when he ditched her.

To win him back, the 35-year-old divorcee drove her car down a deserted, wilderness road, pulled out a .22 gun and blasted away … at her three children sitting helplessly in the back seat.

Her seven-year-old daughter Cheryl died instantly from head wounds. Her son Danny, three, was shot in the back and is paralysed for life, and eight-year-old Christie suffered a stroke after losing several pints of blood from bullet wounds to the chest.

Dishy Diane, who was once paid $10,000 as a surrogate mother, tried to wipe out her family because Lewis hated children so much that he had a vasectomy at 21 and didn't want to be a father to her kids.

After 'mommie dearest' shot herself in the arm to make it look like someone else had done it, she drove her 'bleeding babies' 10 miles to the hospital to get help – for herself.

The busty blonde mail carrier told police in Eugene, Oregon, that a 'deranged, shaggy-haired hitch-hiker' had shot the children. But they suspected her right from the start after she giggled in the hospital while asking them: 'Is my car okay? It's brand new.'

Although Christie sometimes suffers from paralysis in her arm, she recovered enough to take the witness stand a year later and testify against her murdering mother.

Evil Diane was found guilty and sentenced to life in prison. Now her shocking story was turned into a blockbuster mini-series, *Small Sacrifices*, starring sexy superstar Farrah Fawcett with her heart-throb boyfriend Ryan O'Neal playing her screen lover Lewis.

Downs's ex-husband Steve, who is the father of the two older children, was enraged when he saw the four-hour movie. 'She should have been given the electric chair – that's how it should have ended,' said the dashing former model. 'I'd gladly pull the switch personally.

'Dead, she'd just be a bad memory, but alive she's still a living hell that could surface and hurt the children some more.'

His bitterness is an eternity away from the days when they fell in love as teenagers while going to the same school in Chandler, Arizona. Leggy Diane could not wait to leave home because she had been sexually abused by her father since she was 12. He used to take her on long, terrifying drives in the desert, while her mother was working.

Diane and Steve were married when they were both 18 and in the beginning everything was great – especially the sex.

'She was attractive with a great body, and she had the personality to match,' says Steve. 'And her appetite was basically insatiable – she could not get enough – with me or anyone else. Twice a night was nothing to her – she needed it much more than that. I'd go to work and I'd be beat to death. I'd wake up in the middle of the night and she'd be on top of me, going at it. Then she went on for hours on end.

'I'm not trying to make myself look a stud or anything, but my sexual appetite grew along with hers.' However, their marriage started to come apart after they had had two children. He decided he didn't want any more and had a vasectomy, but the operation failed and she got pregnant again.

After he ordered her to have an abortion, she went into a deep depression, realising that she desperately wanted another child. Then Steve had a second successful operation, and she decided to seduce mailman Russ Philips at the Chandler Post Office, where she worked, and have his baby instead. But her husband literally caught her in the act. 'She was such a planner,' Steve says with disgust. 'She dropped the kids off the night before with the babysitter because, she said, she wanted to be alone with me.

'I woke up in the middle of the night and she was gone. A friend at work had told me that he'd heard my wife was fooling around with some guy in a nearby town.

'I drove down to the area and saw my wife's car there. I walked in the front door of the nearest house, which was unlocked, and began checking bedrooms. And, lo and behold, the first one I came to my wife was there naked – pumping this dude. I guess I screwed things up for them. I kicked her out of my house, but she kept begging me to come back and, for the sake of our children, I let her.'

She got pregnant by 19-year-old Russ and had his baby Danny, but kind-hearted Steve loved and treated the child like one of his own.

'I found out later that she'd had affairs with scores of men during our marriage. She went through half the mailmen where she worked, especially the married men.'

Although she was an unfaithful wife, Diane appeared to be a loving mother. 'The children adored her,' adds Steve. 'They had a special attachment to her. She put up a complete façade of being a nurturing mother.'

But there were early signs that Diane, who had slashed her wrists as a teenager, was a time-bomb waiting to explode.

'She could be pretty weird at times. She would turn against herself and scream her lungs out. She'd get so tense that she would just lie on the floor and be as stiff as a board. She'd scratch her face with her nails while being careful not to draw blood or scar herself. That always kind of scared me. Who would do that to themselves?

'But I was not a professional, so there was no way I could tell that I'd married a monster in the making. We finally got a divorce when she got my oldest daughter to lie about where she was while she was out having an affair.'

After they split, Diane moved into a mobile home and was desperately short of cash. She saw a TV show about surrogate mothers and offered her services to a local agency that paid $10,000 a birth.

But at first she was rejected as being mentally unstable because she showed signs of psychopathic behaviour, and it was feared that she was unlikely to give up the child.

On the second attempt, doctors gave her a clean bill of health and she was inseminated with sperm from a donor, in the next room.

She gave birth to a healthy baby girl and gave her a big hug before signing away all rights to the child. Nobody knows if the girl's parents are aware that the real mother of their child is a sick, sex-mad child-killer.

It was about this time that she fell in love with lusty Lewis at the post office, where she wore cut-off T-shirts and no bra to turn him on. He said: 'Our affair began when she told me she was afraid of having any more affairs with married men because she'd get pregnant.

'I asked her why she didn't have an affair with someone who wouldn't get her pregnant. She said, "Like who?" and I said, "Like me."

'I expected a short-term, easy-going thing like the flings I had during my first marriage, but it went on and on. My wife Nora wasn't home till five, so I had lots of time in the afternoon. She suspected something, but I lied to her all the time and told her nothing was going on.'

He finally dumped Diane after he found out that she'd given

him venereal disease. He told his wife all about it and she forgave him. 'I took Nora, on my birthday, to a clinic for treatment. It was so humiliating.'

Although Diane had seduced many men, she was now besotted with only one, and wasn't going to let go of him easily. She found more ecstasy in their lovemaking than she'd known with any of her lovers. So she bombarded Lewis with love letters and poems, and begged him to leave his wife. When he refused, she moved with her children to Oregon, thousands of miles away, hoping in vain that he would follow her. As the months went by, she grew more convinced her children were to blame for the break-up.

Says Steve: 'She told me a number of times that Lewis hated kids. She said that, if she didn't have kids, there wouldn't be a problem between them.'

In the months after the shooting, as police built their case against her, she began hitting the bottle hard. In her diary, she wrote: 'I've been drinking a lot in the past few days. I just wish I could be dead, but I had a great idea. Tell ya later if it works.'

Because she dearly missed the children she had shot in cold blood, she wanted to get pregnant again. In a drunken stupor, she called an old friend, Matt, and invited herself over. An angry Matt says: 'She walks in with a six-pack of beer and says, "Guess what? I'm on birth control pills now." I guess I was a damn fool. I was set up. It wasn't a seduction; it was a manipulation. She was using me.'

But Diane was overjoyed with her sixth pregnancy and proudly told a TV interviewer at the time: 'You can't replace children but you can replace the effect they give you.

'They give me a reason to live and a reason to be happy. And that's gone. They took it from me. But children are so easy to conceive.' She was eight months pregnant when she was finally charged with the horrendous crime of shooting her own children.

Her baby Amy Elizabeth was taken away from her by the State immediately after the birth and given up for adoption. Her other two children, Christie and Danny, were adopted by Fred Hugi, the prosecutor who sent her to jail for life. Their real fathers have not seen them in six years. Steve, 35, who is happily remarried, says: 'I really miss them and love them, but I couldn't afford their health bills.

'It was better that Fred took them. He's a wonderful man, and they are now in safe hands. He'll never let my ex-wife harm them again.'

Diane has always professed her innocence, not flinching from her story about the hitch-hiker who shot her kids because she wouldn't give him the car keys. But she was found guilty on all counts and jailed at the minimum-security Oregon Women's Correction Centre, which she escaped from three years ago.

After she'd climbed over the fence and done a runner, a massive dragnet was launched while her children were in protective custody 100 miles away. It was 11 days before the FBI tracked her down to a seedy little house less than half-a-mile from the prison.

Three men were arrested for harbouring an escaped convict – one of whom, Wayne Seifer, was the husband of Diane's cellmate Louise. She broke down and wept in jail as he admitted on TV that he'd fallen in love and slept with Diane in their short time together.

Said Wayne: 'I've told her, "I'll take care of you and when you feel you have to leave, you have to leave." Diane was the most honest woman I've ever known.'

Her murder trial had gripped the north-eastern states and the public fully expected that fertile Diane would be pregnant by Wayne. To her disappointment, she wasn't.

Diane is now in a maximum-security prison in New Jersey and is not due for parole until 2014. Farrah, who plays Downs in the mini-series, at first turned down the role because she was sickened by the thought of playing such a despicable woman.

'For a woman to kill is unbelievable,' says the real-life mother of Ryan's child Redmond. 'For a woman to kill her children is unspeakable. I really didn't want to do it. I didn't like the woman and didn't think I could do it justice. Diane was diagnosed as being histrionic, narcissistic and a sociopath. I'm not used to playing a character that I don't identify with in some way. But something drew me to her, although she was in no way vulnerable or sympathetic. And in the end I thought it was my best work. For the first time in my career I could be uninhibited. It was easy for me because, except for the crime, Diane was a good-time girl who liked to party, to drink, and liked men.'

8

The Nastiest Nice Guy of All

WHEN VIETNAM VET Arthur Shawcross pedalled down the street on his bike, people would wave or stop him for a chat. He was the neighbourhood nice guy who baked pies and cookies for the elderly and gave out gifts to friends, especially women. He once handed out clothing to a family whose house had burned down, and he cheerfully ran errands for his wife. But little did the locals know that the soft-spoken Shawcross was still on parole after spending 14 years in jail for raping and killing an eight-year-old girl. And so it came as an even bigger shock to the community when he was suddenly charged with being a brutal mass murderer.

His wife Rosemary, who'd been his prison pen-pal and knew of his violent history, has refused to see him since his arrest but his mistress Carla Neal still loves him — although she could have one day become one of his victims. 'No matter what happens, I'll be there for him,' says the 58-year-old cook, who had an affair with him for two years. 'I'm too deeply in love to do anything to hurt him. He may have done wrong, but he treated me better and he treated me with more respect than my children's father ever did. They'll send him back to prison but, with God's help, I'll go see him, wherever he goes.' Mother-of-ten Carla is angry at his wife for not sticking by him or going to see him. 'She hasn't written him a letter or even asked how he's doing.'

She revealed to the cops that Shawcross would express outrage at the killings when he was reading about them in the local paper and he would warn her to be careful. 'He'd say: "When is this going to stop? Every few days they find a body. I don't want you to be out on the streets alone." '

Police in Rochester, New York, a town of 240,000, grilled the 58-year-old grandmother about Shawcross, but she says: 'I told them all I know because I didn't know anything bad about him.' Her help, however, was crucial in linking him to the slaughter. She took cops to Shawcross's favourite fishing haunts along the Genesee River and it turned out that several murdered women were found in the same remote area, not far from the local red-light district. The police also found an earring in Carla's car that matched an earring worn by one of the victims. She added that when she asked him during the jail visit why he did it, 'he just looked at me with passionate eyes and said, "I don't know." '

But Shawcross was always a violent person – at school he beat up smaller kids. He was often in scrapes with the law and was arrested for shoplifting and starting a blaze at a milk plant where he worked. After he served in Vietnam, he was jailed for two years on burglary charges and was paroled in 1971. The next year, he was convicted of strangling eight-year-old Karen Hill and dumping her body under a bridge. He returned the day after killing her and ate an ice-cream near her body. He also admitted the horrifying murder of 10-year-old Jack Blake, who vanished from his home during a robbery. Shawcross told a psychiatrist that he killed Karen because she reminded him of his younger sister Jeannie, with whom he'd had sexual relations as a child. He said: 'One day I was fishing and I was thinking about Jeannie and this girl showed up. It was at that moment that I didn't hear nothing around me, and daylight got brighter, and I just grabbed this girl. All I could see was Jeannie. And I strangled her, and I raped her.'

When he was paroled in 1987 after 15 years in jail, Shawcross went back to New Delhi, in New York State, but a furore erupted among townsfolk who feared for their children's lives. The same thing happened when he moved to nearby Binghampton. Police hassled him every day until he finally moved to Rochester with his prison pen-pal Rose, whom he took for his fourth wife even though he was already carrying on an affair with Carla at the time.

When killers are freed from jail, statistics show that they are highly unlikely to kill again – only a one in 20 chance of that happening. So it was no surprise that Shawcross's parole officer did not suspect him of the shocking string of murders that began in March the next year – especially since he only rode a bicycle. He was viewed as a paedophile, not a man who attacked call girls.

'Serial killers are extremely ordinary and blend in very well,' said Dr James Fox, a US university criminologist and author of a book on mass murder. 'They're not glassy-eyed lunatics.'

The balding and paunchy Shawcross took a night job as a three-dollar-an-hour salad maker for a food wholesaler and spent his spare time fishing. Unknown to his wife he took up another hobby … going to hookers. He was a popular customer, giving some of them bags of fruit or potatoes and paying $15 more than their usual $35 rate. Then they started disappearing, one by one. But police did not admit to the press that a 'Yorkshire Ripper'-style killer was at large until two months before Shawcross was arrested.

He'd pick them up in Carla's car and take them down to the river for sex. Afterwards he'd strangle or suffocate them or just beat them to death. Some of them he killed after they ridiculed him because he appeared impotent. He cut open one victim, 20-year-old June Stott, from her neck to her pelvis and covered her with pieces of carpet to hide the body. One woman was murdered after telling Shawcross that she was not a prostitute and, in fact, was a virgin. Another was killed when she accidentally damaged the knob on the gear stick of his girlfriend's car. He also killed a second mistress in a rage after she punched him while they were swimming in the river. Police claimed that he had planned to kill 59-year-old Dorothy Keeler anyway after she'd threatened to tell his wife about their affair. He cut off her head and police were not able to identify her body until Shawcross was charged. His other victims were Dorothy Blackburn, 27, Patricia Ives, 25, Frances Brown, 22, Anne Steffen, 27, Darlene Trippi, 32, Maria Welch, 22, Felicia Stephens, 20, Elizabeth Gibson, 29, and June Cicero, 34.

His two-year reign of terror came to a sudden end with an incredible stroke of luck. Three alert state troopers were flying in a helicopter over dense woods, hunting for a missing hooker, when they spotted a man eating a salad lunch while sitting in a Chevrolet car on top of a bridge. When they also noticed a woman's body under the viaduct, they followed the car to a nursing home where Shawcross's wife worked. He was questioned briefly by police on the ground and released until the next morning, when another prostitute was found dead just two miles from the bridge. He admitted all the killings and even told police where they could find three more bodies. During his confession, he said he killed one after she bit him, another for being too loud during intercourse, another for trying to steal his wallet, and a fourth for calling him a 'wimp'.

In a letter to a psychiatrist, full of bad spellings and missing words, sinister Shawcross said: 'I should be castrated or have an electrode placed in my head. I'm just a lost soul looking for release of my madness. Please God, let someone help me.' He claimed at his trial that he was innocent – by reason of insanity because he was braindamaged and had multiple personalities, including himself as a child, his mother, his sister Jeannie, and a man from a former life. The jury was shown a shocking video of Shawcross under hypnosis, during which he told horrifying stories of cannibalism, mutilation, child abuse and incest. Sometimes crying as he spoke, he said he was sexually molested as a child by his mother, who stuck a broom up his backside or gave him enemas for being naughty. He said his mum burned his fingers on the stove as a punishment for stealing, and threatened him with a knife when she caught him playing with himself.

Identifying himself as his mother Bessie, he took on a falsetto voice and said: 'I keep trying to get him to stay away from these girls and he won't listen. They ain't nothing but trouble, but he never learned.' He suggested that his mother had somehow taken control of him during the murders, but the prosecution claimed he was modelling himself after Norman Bates in the *Psycho* movie to avoid jail.

As himself under hypnosis he described how he killed June Stott, a friend whom he'd often met for coffee. On the day she died, she asked Shawcross to show her how to make love but then threatened to tell police he had raped her. 'Then some sensation came over me,' he recalled. 'I start sweating like crazy, and the daylight around me got brighter and brighter, and I didn't even hear the birds or anything around me. I'm there but I'm not there. I just grabbed her around the neck, but it was like I was standing there watching someone else do it. I don't hear nothing – not a bird, not an insect, not a plane, not even the wind. And I'm soaking wet.' When he killed June Cicero, he again felt like someone else was carrying out the heinous act. 'I get a feeling in me that I'm not alone in the car with her. Then I feel like I'm floating away. I'm not even in the car, but I can see in the car.'

He claimed that he ate parts of two women he killed and that he also cannibalised two Vietnamese women while in Vietnam. Police denied he ate his victims and the army said he had a non-combat role in the war and so was unlikely to have had a chance to eat corpses. Under hypnosis, he also took on the personality of a friend called Ariemes from a previous life, who had watched over him since he was nine. Saying he first learned to eat flesh during medieval times in England, he said that Ariemes was with him when he killed Jack Blake. His defence lawyers claimed that Shawcross had a hole in his brain and that he suffered from post-traumatic stress disorder caused by severe child abuse.

But the prosecutor alleged Shawcross dreamed it all up and the jury agreed with him.

They found him guilty of first degree murder and he was sentenced to 250 years in jail. Karen Hill's father Robert was delighted, saying: 'They should have hung him in 1972, I now hope they put him in an electric chair with double voltage and amperage because that's what he deserves.' However, they do not have the death penalty in New York State, so Shawcross will rot in jail for the rest of his life. But Carla will be able to see him once a month.

'I'll be there,' she vows.

9

Die, Daughter, Die

GROCER ZEIN ISA, 60, and his wife Maria, 48, were sure they could get away with murder when they repeatedly stabbed their rebellious daughter to death. But, unbeknown to them, they were being recorded by government agents who were investigating them as possible spies.

The savage couple were furious with their 16-year-old daughter Tina for sleeping with a black man, staying out late and working in a fast-food restaurant.

When her boyfriend, 20-year-old Cliff Walker, walked her home at midnight one evening, it was the last straw and her parents decided to kill their wild child.

Hidden bugs linked to tape recorders picked up the shocking last minutes of Tina's life, as she kissed Cliff goodnight and went inside.

'Where have you been?' screamed her mother. Tina told her she had been working her first shift at Wendy's restaurant. 'We don't accept you working,' yelled her father.

The bitter conversation grew louder and louder as her parents raged about Tina taking a job and having a black boyfriend.

'I know you're trying to throw me out, aren't you?' said Tina. Her father called her a she-devil and she said she was going to leave home.

Zein said: 'Do you know that this is your last day? That you are going to die tonight?'

Then on another chilling tape, picked up by a bug in another room, there are sounds of a struggle. Tina is heard screaming again and again – each time sounding more desperate. But her father just says, 'Keep still, Tina.' Between her shrieking and crying, Tina begs, 'Mother, please help!' Maria replies, 'Are you going to listen?' Tina, 'Yes, yes, yes I am.' Maria yells, 'Shut up.'

Seconds later Zein says, 'Die, die quickly. Die, my daughter, die.' Her screams then slowly subside, turning into barely audible groans and laboured breaths before Tina finally becomes silent.

Tina died of six to eight stab wounds in the chest from a black-handled boning knife. Her father called the police, telling them he had acted in self-defence after his daughter had demanded £2,500 and attacked him with a knife.

Zein knew his wife and his three other children would support him and he fully expected to go free. But he hadn't bargained on the tapes.

He was a Palestinian from the trouble-torn West Bank in Israel and had come to America looking for a better life. He married Brazilian beauty Maria and they had four daughters. And although Maria was a Catholic, he brought up the children in his strict Islamic faith.

Zein eventually became an American citizen and opened his own successful grocery store in St Louis, Missouri. But the FBI believed he was working for the Palestine Liberation Organisation and planted electronic monitoring devices in his home. They had been bugging his house for three months before that fateful night on 7 November, 1989.

As Zein and Maria spoke poor English, the recordings had to be translated from his Arabic, his wife's Portuguese and the little English they both knew.

The FBI handed over the shocking tapes to the police. Zein tried to have them suppressed from evidence by claiming they were unlawfully authorised under the Foreign Intelligence Surveillance Act. And, although he had been to Israel three times

44

in the past five years, he claimed he had no links with the PLO.

But Judge Robert Gibson said: 'The court was convinced that overwhelming support existed for issuing a surveillance order.' The FBI have refused to comment on what their investigation of Zein revealed.

The Isas were charged with murder and while Zein stuck to his defence claim, his wife alleged she was trying to protect Tina.

But once again the hidden tapes – this time of their telephone conversations – were their downfall. They revealed that the Isas had plotted to kill Tina in revenge for her disgracing the family honour.

Although Maria was a Catholic, her three older daughters, Fatima, Soraia and Azizah, had stuck to the ways of Islam. But Tina, whose full name was Palestina, rebelled against the rigid Arab family rules.

She wore tight jeans and put on make-up when she went out with her hunky, black boyfriend.

The clash of cultures led to violent family fights, with Tina going to school with black eyes and her body covered in bruises.

At the murder trial, Zein's lawyer told the jury: 'Tina had developed an absolute hatred of her father and had threatened him several times.'

Zein took the stand and testified in Arabic that the bugs dotted around his house hadn't picked up his daughter's demand for cash to leave home. He also explained that he told her she was 'going to die tonight' because she 'already had the knife in her hand'. He said, 'I then directed the knife towards her to stab her until she fell down.' Zein said that Tina got the knife, not him. 'I didn't attack her. She went to the kitchen and came back so fast.'

Isa said he'd struggled with Tina on the floor and at one point put his foot in her mouth to muffle her screams and stabbed her some more.

He pointed out that he'd once had to call police to his store after Tina tried to hit him with a can and threatened him with a meat cleaver. 'She never showed me any respect,' he said. 'If I asked her to bring me a cup of coffee or a glass of water she would kick me in my bad leg.'

Zein alleged that he had never objected to Tina having a black boyfriend and that he'd even offered them money to help get them started in married life. But prosecutors maintained that tapes from the bugged phone revealed it was not a self-defence or spontaneous killing.

For months before the murder Zein told friends and relatives that Tina was beyond redemption and had discussed different ways of killing her without him being charged with murder. On one tape, he said: 'For me this has become a burned woman, a black whore and there is no way to cleanse her except through the red colour that cleanses her. '

And when his married daughter Fatima Abdejabbar called to urge him to be strict with Tina, he said: 'If God makes my wish, I'll put her in the grave. I'll put a knife in her hand after she falls down, of course.'

Fatima even offered a curse of her own for Tina. 'May God pain her, may God make her sleep and not get up. She is a whore. She will never enter my house.'

The next day his other married daughter Soraia phoned to suggest that Tina be chained up in the basement and her passport be sent to the homeland. Zein replied he'd have to send Tina 'home in a box'.

Soraia told him if he killed Tina the family would defend him, saying that he had acted in accordance with the ancient laws of his homeland.

Defence lawyers claimed that the only crime that Maria committed was being married to Zein, who during his testimony begged the court to have mercy on his wife. 'Punish me the way you want,' he said. 'My wife has nothing to do with it.'

But prosecutor Robert Craddick proved that she took an active part in the killing by pointing out that Tina was 'a 6' 4" strong, vigorous young woman'. She was about the same size as her father, and he needed his 15-stone wife to pin their daughter to the floor while he killed her.

Medical evidence showed that Maria held Tina down by her hair, although she said she was just trying to pull her away in the struggle. But pathologists pointed out that without Maria's help, Zein wouldn't have been able to stab Tina repeatedly in the chest. His daughter would have fought and been stabbed in other places.

Although the FBI tapes showed Maria had often sided with Tina in domestic disputes, the prosecution argued that she'd helped kill her because of the black boyfriend.

Tina's school guidance counsellor Pamela Fournier testified that after a stormy meeting with Maria, she had told the headmaster that the family 'was going to stone that girl'.

Fournier also said that Maria told her she was keeping Tina from school as punishment for going out with Walker, whom she'd been seeing for nine months.

Walker told the jury that when he walked Tina home that night, she told him that she expected a family fight. 'She told me that if I heard screaming she would come back out. But she never did and I left.'

But it was the gruesome tapes of Tina's murder that convinced the jury of the Isas' guilt. Zein and Maria were found guilty of first-degree murder and the jury recommended that they be executed.

10

Double Jeopardy

LANDLORD RUSSELL SWART shocked a packed courtroom when he confessed to strangling his sexy tenant Julie Everson. He dropped his bombshell just as his best friend Keith Bullock – who pleaded guilty to killing Julie – was about to be sentenced for the hideous crime.

After Swart made his confession, he walked out of the court as free as a bird. The charges against Bullock were quickly dropped and he was also a free man.

Two men had admitted to killing Julie, but nobody would ever go to jail for it. Swart and Bullock had reason to rejoice, but only one of them had reason to laugh at the law. For he'd just got away with murder. The sensational case shocked the whole of America and left Julie's angry family wondering whether there was any justice in the world.

The Eversons' nightmare began on 28 December, 1990 when Bullock was arrested for assaulting Julie, his 29-year-old girlfriend. Swart paid Bullock's bail so he remained free until the trial.

Everson and Bullock were living together in an upstairs flat of a large house at 3027 Clinton Avenue, Minneapolis, which was owned by Swart. Their relationship had often been stormy, with many fights. Julie also had several angry rows with her landlord, who lived downstairs, and she once called the police to have Swart removed from her flat after he'd refused to leave.

On 29 December, Julie did not show up at the supermarket where she worked as a cashier. Then the battery charges against Bullock, 28, were dropped when she failed to appear in court to testify against him.

After Julie had been missing for a few days, her distraught mother Joan went to the police. Believing a frightened Julie had run away from Bullock, the missing persons bureau said there was little they could do.

Mrs Everson tried to get into Julie's flat to see if there were any clues to her whereabouts, but Swart refused to let her in. He even threatened to have her charged with stealing her daughter's belongings.

As days stretched into weeks and then months, mother-of-six Joan finally went to the homicide division and begged detectives to investigate the case. She pointed out that Julie had been having bitter arguments with both her boyfriend and her landlord just before she'd disappeared. Armed with a search warrant, detective lieutenant Charlie Miles and a team of officers went over Swart's house with a fine-tooth comb. But they found nothing.

Then the cops looked in the backyard, where they noticed there was a large mound of dirt as well as a depression in the ground. There, buried three foot down, was Julie's nude body. Her mouth and nose were covered with duct tape and her head was covered with plastic. Her legs and hands were also wrapped in tape – and she had been strangled.

Swart and Bullock were arrested and charged with second-degree murder with intent. But under Minnesota state law, they had to be tried separately. Swart, who claimed he was innocent, was set for trial first. He was tried just before Christmas, when jurors are notoriously more interested in buying presents than serving justice.

The jury decided that there was insufficient evidence to find Swart guilty 'beyond a reasonable doubt' of killing Julie. And he went home a free man.

Five months later it was Bullock's turn in the dock. But prosecutors managed to talk him into accepting a plea bargain — admitting to second-degree murder committed during a felony offence. By pleading guilty to a lesser charge, he would have served 12 years in jail — or eight years with parole. If he'd been convicted of murder with intent, he'd have faced 30 years in jail — or 20 years with parole.

Bullock told relatives he believed there was a good chance he'd be found guilty of murder with intent because he'd beaten Julie up the day she'd disappeared. Also, Swart had already been found innocent and, therefore, Bullock was the only other person who was likely to have killed her.

The prosecution, however, should have known his confession was false. For Bullock claimed he'd smothered Julie with a pillow, which police knew could not be true. She had died of strangulation, not asphyxiation.

After being granted immunity from further charges, Swart agreed to testify on behalf of the prosecution at Bullock's pre-sentence hearing. But instead of helping to put his friend behind bars for a long time, Swart helped Bullock to go free as well. At Swart's own trial he'd professed his innocence but at Bullock's trial he admitted killing Julie. Swart, a burly six-foot nightclub bouncer, told the court that Julie had planned to move out after her fight with Bullock, and he went upstairs to check if she'd left.

He said: 'When I got to the top of the stairs, I saw Julie in the bathroom. She started hollering at me to get out and leave her alone. She flipped out. She caught me off-guard. She cut me on the hand.

'I grabbed her with my left hand by the throat. She was berserk. I picked her up to restrain her and then she was dead. My only intent was to restrain her. I didn't realise that I would kill her.'

He carried her body into the garage where he left it for four months, until the ground outside thawed and he could bury her in a shallow grave. When he ended his confession, Julie's sister Jill suddenly sprang out of her seat and screamed: 'You son of a bitch. You killed her and you got off. Someone ought to kill you.'

Because Swart had already been acquitted of killing Julie, he could not be tried for her murder a second time. Under the US Constitution it's the law to prevent what's known as 'double jeopardy'.

Famed American civil rights attorney William Kunstler said: 'Swart could have come out of that courthouse following his acquittal and screamed to the high skies that he was guilty, and there's not one thing that anyone could do against him then or now.'

Richard Frase, University of Minnesota law professor, said: 'The point of this law is to protect the accused from having to defend themselves over and over again. If prosecutors are allowed repeated attempts to try the same case before one jury after another, there's a likelihood they will find a jury willing to convict.'

Pete Connors, the county attorney who prosecuted both Swart and Bullock, was furious with the confession, even though it meant an innocent man had escaped jail. He said: 'Sometimes our system of justice lets the guilty go free. Our founding fathers recognised that. We are happy about finding the truth, but are we happy about Mr Swart walking free? Absolutely not.

'I hope in the end there will be some form of justice for the Eversons. I recognise that Julie's family and friends are devastated to find out Swart is the killer.'

Connors said he was 'convinced' that Swart's story was the truth and that he had not concocted a lie with Bullock to have him cleared as well. But Julie's sister Jill believes Swart lied when he said that he'd killed Julie in self-defence. Said Jill: 'I think he went up there to kill her. He wanted her dead.'

Julie's father Gerry said: 'It's a travesty of justice. I knew Swart was guilty the whole time. This man admitted he killed her, yet he gets off without any punishment. It's the most outrageous and ridiculous thing I've ever seen. If I arranged for someone to kill him for murdering my daughter, I'd be put in jail for a very long time.'

And Julie's mother Joan added: 'There's something wrong with the system. Is the loss of a kid so very hard to understand?'

The mother-of-six added that she had talked to lawyers about bringing a civil suit against Swart. 'We have to do something because of what's going on in this country. Maybe a lawsuit will set a precedent. Maybe it will help other people in a similar situation.'

But the Bullock family was delighted. 'It was like winning the lottery,' said his father Douglas, adding that the family planned to 'baby' Keith for a while. Bullock had spent 10 months in jail waiting for trial. Keith's sister Kathy Long said that the fact he was learning disabled led to the false statements her brother gave to the police about how and when Julie had died.

She said: 'Keith couldn't see the whole picture. His capacity for understanding events as they happen is not what other people have.' His brother Mark said that Keith, a restaurant busboy, was so naive that he was 'convinced there was enough evidence to put him away'.

Mark added: 'We told him we didn't want him to go away for 30 years, and to take the plea bargain. We believed him innocent, but we wanted him home in eight years.

'Keith told me, "I'm going to go with the plea bargain, but I don't want you to think I did it because I'm saying I did it."'

Swart's attorney Peter Wold said that his client had 'always wanted' to tell the truth about how Julie died but wasn't willing to do so unless he was granted absolute immunity.

Wold explained that although Swart could not be tried for murder again, he could be prosecuted under federal law for violating Julie's civil rights. Wold said: 'I had to make sure his rights were protected. When he was given immunity, he testified to the whole truth.'

Double jeopardy means Swart is literally getting away with murder. But an editorial in the local paper, the *St Paul Pioneer Press*, believes that justice will eventually be served.

It said: 'At the very heart of the American criminal justice system lies this principle: it is better for the guilty to go free than the innocent to be punished. Mr Bullock is restored to his family and his life. While Mr Swart cheated justice and should be in prison, we take comfort in the knowledge that conscience is a more tireless pursuer.'

11

Mr **Bigamy**

WOULD YOU MARRY this man? Well, 105 women said yes, putting Giovanni Vigliotto in the *Guinness Book of Records* for bigamy. He was so carried away with his new loves, he forgot to divorce their predecessors. Or was he?

His career took him right round the world. And netted him a fortune. The 'Italian Stallion' walked 105 women down the aisle – an average of one every four months. There were weddings in 26 American states and 15 other countries. He used 50 aliases – so it's not surprising he couldn't remember them all. 'I didn't keep score,' he explained.

Giovanni's only legal wife is believed to have been Joan Bills, whom he married in Korea in 1949, when he was 19. Three years later the bigamy spree got under way ...

A couple of ceremonies at Houston, Texas, in 1952 turned Ann Hendrix and Margie Lang into the first of the bogus Mrs Vigliottos. Next year Giovanni was back in Korea, wedding Mi Wha Hann Chuchon. A few months later he married Shizuko Yamaguchi in Japan. Then it was on to Hong Kong and the charms of Sue Ming.

Giovanni got hitched twice in London in 1966, to Betty Hume and Dinah Smathers. In 1968, he plucked four more 'wives' off one loveboat cruise on the SS *Mariposa*.

Vigliotto was tall, distinguished and seemingly rich. But, 'As a stud, he was a dud,' said wife 104 Sharon Clark. 'Although he could charm the tail off a rattlesnake.'

The supercharmer claimed: 'I'm in love with life, women, marriage.' But he was much more in love with money. The love 'em, loot 'em Lothario prowled flea markets, eyeing up the stall-holders or shop owners. He wined and dined them, talked them into a quickie wedding and asked them to let him handle their money. Then he vanished.

'Giovanni promised me love and devotion,' said Joan Bacarella, 50, of New Jersey, who met him after her marriage failed. 'He seemed so sensitive. He wrote me poetry and bought me big bunches of flowers.'

Joan was one who didn't 'marry' Giovanni. But she was ripped off for £20,000. She sold her house and her clothes store – then let him drive off to sell her belongings, leaving Joan and her three kids destitute.

His final victim, No 105, was estate agent Pat Gardiner, 50, of Mesa, Arizona, who lost £18,000. 'He became the husband I wanted,' she said. 'He'd wake me in the night and say sweet things.'

Pat, too, sold her house for Giovanni. They also loaded everything into a van and drove to Palm Springs, California. There, he abandoned her in a motel with her dog, Mindy, while he went off to sell the goods for her. 'I'll never trust any man again,' Pat said.

Just before meeting Pat, Giovanni married divorced antique dealer Sharon Clark in 1981. 'He excited me,' she said. 'He had style. But he was a kinky, weird lover. He asked me to rip off his clothes because they were given to him by other women. He called me a witch.'

After a hippie-style wedding in the Tennessee hills, Giovanni persuaded Sharon to sell her house – and her mother's too, then hand him the money to invest. She also let him drive off with antiques worth £25,000.

But Sharon swore revenge. She and a man friend went on a

hunt, following a map on which Giovanni had marked flea market towns. 'I kept coming across my things that he'd stolen,' she said. After six months, in Panama City, Florida, Sharon saw him getting out of a car. 'My friend slashed his tyres and I called the police. They came just in time.'

Giovanni – police say his real name was Frederick Bertram Jipp – was jailed for 34 years in 1982, for bigamy and fraud. 'I hope he dies inside,' a bitter Pat Gardiner said.

In February 1991 she got her wish. Giovanni died of a brain haemorrhage in Arizona State Prison. None of his 100-plus widows went to the funeral. But there was still a woman at his side: private eye Pat O'Connor, who'd fought to free him. 'He was a genius,' she said. 'No wonder so many women fell in love with him.'

12

Cold Comfort

HOUSEWIFE IRENE AVILA was devastated when her beautiful teenage daughter Missy was found brutally murdered with her hair hacked off. The divorced mother-of-four needed someone's shoulder to cry on, someone whom she could pour out her heartache to.

Missy's best friend Karen Severson saw the intense emotional pain Irene was going through, and so two weeks after the killing she moved in with the Avila family to help console them. Karen, 17, who lived just down the street, stayed for nearly two months — sleeping in Missy's bed. She even joined the Avilas for their first Thanksgiving dinner without Missy.

'She was there to comfort me,' said 47-year-old Irene. 'She used to see me every day and saw what hell I was going through. She became like part of the family. She was close to me like another daughter.'

Severson also appeared to be deeply affected by the loss. She often took flowers to the cemetery, wrote letters to Missy and brought a Christmas tree to the grave. She also carved a note on a tree near the murder scene saying: 'Missy & Karen 4 Ever'.

They were very close, though to look at they were exact opposites. Slim and pretty, the vivacious 17-year-old Missy, 5ft 2in tall and weighing under seven stone was popular with boys and made friends easily. Karen, on the other hand, was unattractive and overweight, and she was known to have a big mouth and was always getting into fights.

After the murder, she really packed on the pounds, ballooning to 14 stone. 'She started drinking a lot,' says Irene. 'When I asked her why, she said it was because she'd lost her best friend.'

Laura Doyle, another of Missy's friends, also seemed to have trouble accepting the fact that she was never going to see her schoolmate and neighbour again. She broke down in tears at the funeral and sent Irene a touching sympathy card. 'It said that she was heartbroken about what happened to my daughter. That not only was I Missy's mother but hers too.

'She came over to my house all depressed. She said she wanted to commit suicide because she was the last person to see Missy alive.

'Laura had picked Missy up the afternoon she died. They were laughing and joking. My daughter ran out in a real good mood. Her last words were: "We're going to the park. I'll call you at eight." At 6pm Laura called and asked to speak to Missy. I said, "What are you talking about? She's with you." She said, "No, I left her at the park." '

Irene waited up all night for Missy. 'At two in the morning, I thought to myself, "Boy, is she going to get it." But I was scared. I knew something had happened to her. I just knew it.'

The next morning a distraught Irene called the cops in Arleta, a suburb of Los Angeles in the San Fernando Valley, and a search was launched. Laura told police she'd dropped Missy off at a park while she put petrol in her car. But as she drove off, she noticed Missy talking to two young men in a blue Chevrolet Camaro. When she came back they were gone.

Two days later, hikers found her body in a picturesque creek running through a forested area of Big Tajunga Canyon in Angeles National Forest. Missy's lovely, long brown hair had been chopped off in clumps and her head had been held under six inches of water until she'd drowned. Her killer, or killers, had placed a large log on top of her body in a feeble attempt to hide it.

Recalling the bitter day she learned the tragic news, Irene said: 'It was like a bad dream, and I kept hoping I'd wake up.

'It was really rough at Christmas because I'd go shopping and I'd see the back of a girl that looked like her. And I'd think, "Oh my God." '

Irene, who has three grown sons, was not just traumatised by her daughter's death, she was also upset that she didn't know who'd killed her. But she could always turn for support to both Karen and Laura, who were willing to rush over if she needed anything or just someone to talk to.

Karen often told Irene that she wanted to avenge Missy's death. 'She'd always tell me, "The minute we find the animal who did this I will be sitting right next to you in the courtroom." '

Frustrated by the homicide squad's failure to find suspects in the case, Irene carried out her own manhunt for drivers of blue Camaros.

She said: 'I would stop guys in the street at 11 at night and make them get out of their cars. Karen would be right next to me the whole time. I harassed innocent guys.'

Karen and Laura helped out with Irene's murder hunt, even going down to the police station for her to get the latest information on the case. Karen also gave Irene the names of Missy's boyfriends who may have had a reason to kill her. But the leads came to nothing.

For three years, the heartbroken mum went to bed each night praying that police would catch the killers. But when cops did finally make an arrest, the identity of the suspects was more than she could bear.

'It was like someone punched me in the stomach. I was shocked. I walked to my room and passed out.'

Karen Severson and Laura Doyle were charged with killing Missy in a jealous rage because she'd slept with their boyfriends.

'Now I know why Karen was here so much,' says Irene. 'She wanted to be one step ahead of everyone else. She and Laura made fools out of all of us. And I trusted Karen so much. We all trusted her. She was my daughter's best friend. They grew up together. That girl was part of this family.'

The deadly duo would have got off scot-free except for a guilt-ridden friend of Missy's who was with the girls that fateful October day. Eva Chirumbolo, now 23, had been haunted by the murder, but told police she was too frightened of the killers to come forward earlier.

'I was afraid for myself, that my life would be in danger,' she said, adding that Laura and Karen warned her they would blame her for the murder. Eva decided to speak up after her 18-year-old brother's suicide made her realise the grief Irene and her sons were feeling.

At the trial, Eva testified that after Karen had picked her up, they met Missy and Laura. Then they drove in both cars to their canyon hideaway, where they often went to drink beer and smoke pot. Eva told the court Karen said she was going to 'scare' Missy. And when they arrived at the creek, Karen and Laura began taunting Missy about all the boys she'd been to bed with, including their boyfriends.

At one point, Laura grabbed Missy by the hair and accused her of having slept with Victor Amaya, Laura's boyfriend. While still sitting in the car, Missy was crying when Laura suddenly grabbed her by the wrist and said: 'Let's go for a walk.'

The four of them walked down to the creek. Laura then stepped into the water and Karen pushed Missy towards her. Laura grabbed Missy by the wrist again and pulled her into the water.

Eva was so scared things were getting out of control that she ran back to her car. She said: 'Then I heard a scream – so loud. I just froze. I could not go back down that hill. I just sat there between the cars and just waited.'

Minutes later the other girls joined her – without Missy. Karen quickly drove off, leaving Eva to go home with Laura. 'She was laughing and crying,' said Eva, 'and she was saying, "Ha, ha, ha. We killed Missy." '

Laura said Missy deserved to die because she had slept with her boyfriend Victor. Asked why she didn't stop the fight, Eva replied: 'I don't know. I just didn't know how far it was going to go.'

But Laura's lawyer Charles Lloyd claimed that Chirumbolo only came forward after rumours began to spread linking her to the murder. He also pointed out that Eva's boyfriend John Avril had a crush on Missy and the girls had had a bitchy row only weeks before the murder. 'It's obscene that Chirumbolo is not charged with this killing,' said Lloyd.

Severson's attorney Harold Vites said: 'If Karen and Laura had this elaborate plan to kill Missy, why would they take Eva along if she was not part of the plan? That doesn't make a whole lot of sense.'

But Deputy District Attorney Tamia Hope said: 'Eva is not an accomplice to this crime. If she was really involved, why didn't she just keep quiet?'

Victor Amaya, 23, swayed the jury, however, when he testified that Laura had threatened to kill Missy six weeks before the murder. Then Irene revealed that Karen had visited her house to talk about a problem with Missy. 'She started to tell me a bunch of dirty things about my daughter. She said Missy took everybody's boyfriends and that she was a big flirt. I just told her: "If you're not going to talk properly, just get out."'

Irene also recalled that Missy and Karen often had big rows 'over boys' and at the time of her death they had not been talking for a month. 'They had an argument over this guy Karen was living with, Randy Fernandez. My daughter used to go out with him first.'

Severson and Doyle, who were tried as adults although only 17 at the time of the crime, were charged with first-degree murder. But the jury was not convinced the killing had been planned and had trouble believing Eva's testimony. Instead they convicted both of them of second-degree murder.

One juror said: 'There just wasn't any proof that it was

premeditated. We thought they got carried away and didn't know when to stop. And Eva was probably holding something back to protect herself.'

Severson and Doyle, were sentenced in 1990 to at least 15 years in jail, but will be eligible for parole in 1997. Both women have appealed.

Freelance reporter Karen Kingsbury has written a book about the case, which is now being turned into a TV movie.

Irene, meanwhile, says she'll never recover from her daughter's murder.

'My life has been shattered for ever because of this cold-blooded and senseless act. They cut off Missy's hair to make her look ugly. That was their way of torturing her. And they left her to die in the woods like an animal. I keep thinking that Missy will finally be able to rest in peace. But for me, it will never be over. You can't get over losing a child. That just doesn't happen. When they killed her, they killed a part of me.'

13

The Perfect Teacher

JOHN GARRIS WAS perfect for the teaching job. He was bright, well-dressed, and spoke eloquently. His references were impeccable and he had two college degrees. But, deep down, he was keeping a dark secret from thousands of schoolchildren – he was a convicted killer on the run from the law after escaping from prison.

The education department of Fairfax County, on the outskirts of Washington, DC had desperately needed good teachers and Garris fitted the bill to a T. Garris, 38, was offered a position as a substitute teacher, and had an excellent chance of getting a full-time post.

Although he specialised in maths and science, he was asked to teach a variety of subjects at a dozen secondary schools because he had a vast all-round knowledge. He soon took up a regular position at Whitman Intermediate School, where he turned up every day in smart suits and expensive ties.

The headmaster, Garris's colleagues and especially the kids all gave him top marks. That was, until the FBI came to the school one afternoon and arrested him.

Hundreds of students and teachers watched from classroom windows as Garris was led away in handcuffs. The gossip soon spread through the school corridors that he was a fugitive killer.

'The children were never in any danger,' says Garris, who once hit a jail guard on the head. 'At no time did I bring them any harm.'

And Whitman's headmaster Eugene Jordan said: 'Kids were very upset about the fact that he's not going to be a substitute here any more.'

After a few minor offences as a teenager, Garris was sentenced in 1974 to 45 years for brutally beating, robbing and strangling a 71-year-old man.

'I got involved with a couple of bad guys I hardly knew,' he maintains. 'I was only 20 at the time. We got involved in a minor robbery that escalated into a murder.'

In June 1991, Garris escaped from a car that was taking him back from his work-release programme at Rosewood State Hospital to the Maryland House of Correction in Jessup, near Baltimore.

He said: 'Because I'd been in jail for so long, the only thing I'd learned was that when you get a chance to escape you go for it. I had a propensity for negative behaviour.'

Prisoners on work-release programmes are allowed to carry £30 in their pocket and Garris used the money to track down friends who helped to hide him. While working on various jobs as a labourer, he kept moving between three different flats – one in Virginia, another in Washington and the other in Maryland.

He also found himself a girlfriend. 'She was a mother of two kids, and the first time we had sex it was unbelievable. I hadn't made love for 18 years.'

After his arrest, Garris shocked FBI men by claiming that during his year as a fugitive he worked in the White House. He told them that 'influential friends' on Capitol Hill got him a job, with full security clearance, painting President Bush's basement for two weeks.

Garris said he had a great time helping the kids at Whitman get an education so they wouldn't end up in jail like him.

'They looked up to me. I gave them things I always wanted to hear as a kid. They need people like me who really care. I took a job as a teacher so I could do something worthwhile while I was out. It was my responsibility to help them understand the subject matter. Most of them weren't very up on their lessons.

'My students often said they liked me, that I was teaching them the way it was supposed to be done. They were so impressed with my methods that they often told me about problems in their personal lives to see if I could help out there as well. One of the things that I would do was let them know that they were much better people than they often thought they were, and better than what other people said about them. I remember in one class students were passing around a piece of paper. I confiscated it. But it was a petition to the principal, demanding that he permanently assign me to the school. I gave the petition back to the kids and they handed it to the principal. I was waiting to find out whether I was going to get a full-time job when I was arrested.

'I later confiscated another piece of paper on which the kids said things like they loved me and they thought I was the best teacher. I was so badly treated as a kid that I wanted these children to be the best that they could be. Not only did I teach them the subject, I taught them things about life. I often acted as a counsellor and we developed a close and trusting relationship. I treated them all equally and loved them so much. I really miss them.'

On his job application, Garris said he'd never been convicted of any offence, which he admits now was a blatant lie.

But he also claimed he'd received a Bachelor of Science degree in applied psychology from Coppin State College, where he said he graduated in 1978. He did, in fact, have a degree from the college but he never attended the graduation ceremonies.

Garris was behind bars at the time and got his degree through a correspondence course. He also passed another degree in human services through the mail. He even taught other prisoners.

Fairfax County education supervisor Alan Leis said that Garris's personal references, which included a letter from Senator Charles

Robb's office, were genuine and contained 'very high marks and very good comments'.

But Leis didn't bother to look into them or his college education because he thought there was nothing more he could learn about Garris by double-checking. A simple phone call, of course, would have revealed that Garris got his degree while doing his homework in jail.

'He was interested in working and he was anxious to work so we called him often,' said Leis. 'Who would think an escaped convicted murderer would apply for a substitute teaching job?'

But Garris was tired of doing various exhausting bluecollar jobs and aspired to be a white-collar worker. So he wrote in for a job as a substitute even though it only paid £30 a day.

'When I applied, I never tried to hide anything. I wanted them to know I was who I said I was.' And up to a point that was true. He gave his real name and correct address. If county officials had bothered to check on his address, they would have found it was a shelter for homeless men which he stayed at now and then.

To become a substitute, Garris had to have his fingerprints taken and he freely obliged. Schools in Virginia have required fingerprinting since 1988 when a school psychologist was arrested for molesting children.

At the time Garris applied, Fairfax County officials did not wait for the results of fingerprint checks before teachers started work.

It takes up to 10 weeks to get them back and there is such a huge turnover of teachers that there could be a staffing shortage.

But Garris was certain his prints would not show up on Virginia's criminal files. He'd got a job working at the White House part-time without any trouble and thought it would be easier to pass security checks for a teaching job.

However, he did not realise that his fingerprints were then passed on to the FBI to see if he had served time or was a fugitive from elsewhere in the nation.

About 30 applicants a year are found to have criminal records.

Two months after Garris had started working, the FBI discovered he was a wanted man. When he had escaped, Garris had only a few months left to serve in jail before he was paroled.

He told the FBI that he ran off because he'd been falsely accused of sexually abusing a mentally disturbed man at Rosewood State Hospital, where he was working as a counsellor. Garris, who has spent more than half his life behind bars, is now facing another 10 years in jail – which could be added on to his murder sentence.

Fairfax County, which needs 93,000 substitutes a year, has now changed its teacher-hiring policy. It now refuses to let teachers start work until their prints have been cleared by the FBI.

Garris, meanwhile, is looking forward to the day when he finally gets out of jail: 'I know what I want to be now – a teacher.'

14

Marianne Alexander

THE PEEPING TOM crept down the dark hallway into sultry student Marianne Alexander's bedroom. He pulled back the blankets, slowly lifted her nightgown and pulled down her knickers to her knees. But she suddenly woke up and screamed in terror. To silence her, he hammered poor Marianne over the head repeatedly with a heavy object.

That was the blood-curdling beginning to a 10-year murder mystery that terrorised a university campus and a small American town. It was only after a crack cop handled the chilling case as a last resort that students and local residents could go to sleep at night feeling safe in their beds – without being afraid that the sick killer would strike again.

The 22-year-old brunette was found four hours later, still breathing, by her roommate Susan Hoyt, who'd left the front door unlocked when she went out earlier that night. She thought her friend was making strange noises so she turned on the light to see what was wrong, and to her horror she saw Marianne's face was covered in blood and there was blood on the curtains and the ceiling.

The nursing student at Lowell University in Massachusetts died of massive brain damage the next day, with her parents and her two sisters by her side. 'She never regained consciousness,' said her father David, a retired design engineer for General Electric. 'The doctors gave us no hope – all we could do was hold her hand until she died. Marianne was a wonderful child. We never had a moment's trouble with her. She was such a happy kid. She was a quiet, straight-A student and had never had a date in her life. She would have made a great nurse.'

Police were baffled by the gruesome murder on that freezing February night in 1980. The possibility that Marianne had had a row with her three flatmates was ruled out after Susan took a lie-detector test along with students Catherine LeBourdais and Eileen Maloney, who had both been away on a skiing trip. A robbery motive was dismissed because nothing was taken, but a rape attempt was likely because her clothing had been tampered with. Police chief Len Macphail said at the time: 'Whoever killed Marianne knew the victim and her flatmates or knew that four young women were living in the apartment.' But that's all they had to go on – except for a 'suspicious-looking person' who was seen by Hoyt in the vicinity that night carrying an unidentified object. He turned out to be a neighbour and was immediately dubbed the 'prime suspect' by the cops. But his alibi that he was buying stereo equipment at the time of the murder was soon confirmed by witnesses.

Police quizzed several boyfriends of Marianne's flatmates, but came up with no new clues to the callous killer. And despite searching a mountain of garbage at a landfill with a metal detector, cops were unable to find the murder weapon, at first believed to be a hammer.

The investigation dragged on for years until eventually the massive file was stored with other cases of unsolved murders in the tiny mill town of 130,000 people. Frightened students at Lowell kept their doors firmly locked, while nervous neighbours like Louise Podanoffsky lived in fear of the murderer in their midst. She said: 'We never knew if he'd come back one day and do it again.' And Marianne's heartbroken mother Harriet said: 'I never thought I'd learn what really happened to my daughter – who killed her and why.'

Then a new police chief dusted off the file and handed it to top cop David Tousignant, who was named Lowell Officer of the Year in 1988. He spent four months poring over reports and at first he was puzzled, too. 'There was no clear-cut reason why this girl should die,' he said. 'None of the normal scenarios in a murder were present.'

His investigation took him full circle – back to the original prime suspect, bizarre bachelor Roland Douglas Phinney. The detective discovered that Phinney was a troubled loner with a kinky fascination for taking semi-pornographic photos of young women, mostly without their knowledge by zoom lens. The 47-year-old technician, a small bespectacled man who'd been a lifelong member of the local baptist church choir, had lived almost his entire life with his parents right next door to the murder house.

Tousignant first came across his name when he began questioning Marianne's flatmates again. One recalled that two weeks before the murder a pair of panties had disappeared from her room. Phinney's mother Doris had returned them, saying her son found them after they'd blown over the fence while they were being hung out to dry. But none of the girls had ever hung clothes out on the line. Next the officer learned that Phinney was known as the local peeping Tom because he was often spotted by neighbours sneaking into backyards to grab photos of women sunbathing.

The obsessive cop also noticed that the one letter of sympathy that the Alexander family had received from a stranger was written by Phinney's mother. Then a friend of Phinney's, Josep Amaral, revealed that during a conversation about the murder Phinney muttered something about 'proof' – adding that the cops 'ain't so smart'.

Amaral said: 'Phinney loved pornographic videos, particularly ones that depicted women in bondage. He had a very negative attitude towards women, never rated them and often referred to them in a vulgar manner.' Another friend of Phinney's, Roland Bartell, said: 'He would rant on and on about the girls living next door to him, what a good view he had of the girls from his upstairs window.'

Amaral, 72, also told police that Phinney had a favourite hand-held camera flash that he used constantly before the murder, but two days after the brutal beating he noticed that it was dented. He asked Phinney about it and the voyeur amateur photographer replied that he'd smashed it in a fit of anger when it wouldn't work. Tousignant said: 'I began looking at old metal flashes and realised they were similar to a hammer. I took a facsimile one to the pathologist and asked him if it could be the weapon and he said yes.' Then when he checked on Phinney's alibi, he learned that it was not as airtight as he first believed. Phinney had been at the stereo store much earlier than he'd previously claimed.

Phinney also appeared to be a perfect match to a profile of the killer drawn up eight years earlier by the FBI. It said that the killer would live close to the crime scene, only had a high-school degree and had never been arrested. The profile also said that the killer probably engaged in peeping Tom activities and the theft of ladies' underwear. He would be a quiet person who had difficulty dealing with members of the opposite sex.

Tousignant believed he now had enough to bring Phinney in for questioning. While the suspect was still at the police station, Tousignant went to his home armed with a search warrant. In his room, the police found a collection of pornographic video tapes and nearly 10,000 photos of women. Some were dressed in swimsuits, some in miniskirts, and some were naked; while other photos consisted of close-ups of breasts, buttocks, legs and vaginas. He'd destroyed photos of Marianne and her flatmates but there were pictures of other women who'd lived in the house that were taken while they were sunbathing in bikinis in the back garden. Incredibly, the police also found the murder weapon – the Yushika flash, which was badly bent out of shape. 'He could not bear to throw it away – or maybe he wanted to hold on to it as some type of trophy,' said Tousignant.

When he was told the Yushika flash was intact, the dogged detective stepped up the questioning and finally after nine years of silence Phinney cracked under the strain, admitting he'd killed Marianne after she woke up while he was trying to take a nude picture of her. He said that after he'd looked through Marianne's window and saw she was asleep, he entered the unlocked apartment and made his way down a dark corridor to her room. In his hand-written, four-page confession, he continued: 'I had just gotten her underwear down when she woke and saw me. I could see she was frightened. I grabbed the camera and started hitting her with it. I saw her bleeding from the head so I took off.' He ran home and threw away his blood-stained clothes.

Phinney told Tousignant that he did not have to kill her but he panicked because he was afraid of what his domineering mother would do if she found out. She had already threatened to kick him out of the house if she found him watching pornographic videos or stealing panties again. In the end, Tousignant almost felt sorry for him. 'He was a loner whose world revolved around his camera and photographs. That was his way of interacting with women. It was the closest he felt he could get to them.'

Phinney claimed at his trial that he made up the confession following hours of gruelling interrogation. 'I figured the police weren't going to let me go until I said something.' But he was found guilty and was sentenced to life in prison without parole.

Marianne's mother was delighted with the verdict, saying: 'Her soul will finally be at rest now. And so will mine, knowing that her killer is behind bars for ever. We can now get on with our lives and finally put this thing to rest.'

15

Poetic Justice

IF DAVID SCHOENECKER'S plans had succeeded, 55 people would be dead. But after the first murder he left a giveaway clue to be read.

He wanted to enjoy the last laugh by leaving an amusing little poem near his wife's corpse. And then David Schoenecker, 50, intended to go rampaging on the orgy of violence he'd planned. But it was Judge Robert Fitzgerald who laughed the longest, after sentencing the killer with a short ditty of his own.

Schoenecker, a chemical engineer from Anaheim Hills, California, had drawn up a 'hit list' of 54 relatives and former friends he had grudges against, including his first wife. Many of these were from Milwaukee, Wisconsin, where he used to live. He had tried to explain his feelings to his second wife, Gail, but she was horrified by the thoughts going round in his head. Schoenecker decided he had to do away with her before she gave his vicious plan away.

His evil scheme began with a romantic, candlelit dinner on 5 May, 1989. After it, Gail, a 40-year-old schoolteacher, fell asleep. Then the voluntary Sunday school teacher shot his wife in the head with a .357 Magnum.

Afterwards, Schoenecker left his sick little rhyme on a table in clear view, for the police to find. The verse he had written was a perversion of the well-known Christmas song, Santa Claus Is Coming to Town.

'I made my list, I'm checking it twice. I'm going to find out who's naughty, not nice. All I seek is real revenge. And I want it made very clear they have taken from me things that I've held very dear. This plan has taken three years to prepare. I've hidden weapons and money everywhere. I'll come in the night, I'll come in the day. I've chosen for each their own special way. All on the list will go to their grave, all with the help of friendly old Dave.'

Armed with his copy of the hit list, his Magnum and $4,000 in savings, Schoenecker headed for Montana, where his next victim lived.

However, Schoenecker could not resist bragging about his plan and his poem. So he wrote to his favourite columnist on the local paper – Bob Emmers of the *Orange County Register*. A chilling excerpt from Schoenecker's rambling letter, which also gave details of his hit list, reads:

'Last Friday I killed my wife. There is a very strong possibility that no one has discovered her body so I suggest you have the police check 7871 East Amanda Circle. There was no hatred. I loved her – but the action was necessary because I have a purpose – one that cannot have any interference. Over the past few years I have had images that I know what is going to happen before it occurs.

'At first I simply dismissed these sensations, but when I started to see certain events very clearly, I knew there was more to this than just daydreams or nightmares. What I was seeing were events in my life involving people that had done wrong or evil against me. The feeling is that all will be made right and I will be the force to make it right.'

The paper contacted the police, who broke into Schoenecker's house and found his wife's rotting body. She had been dead for five days.

When the police notified potential victims, some on the list said that they'd never heard of Schoenecker.

David Nuss, who appeared on the hit list and had played with

Schoenecker on the school football team, said: 'I didn't sleep well until they captured him.' And Schoenecker's ex-wife Kathy, to whom he was married for 15 years, recalled, 'I was scared to death. I panicked.' But she couldn't remember him ever being violent.

'He loved to be in control and I didn't want anyone running my life. I guess the other people on the list felt the same way as me.'

Her daughter Traci, 22, added: 'I can't believe that my own father has killed my stepmom and wanted to murder my mother. I was petrified.'

Schoenecker admitted later that it might have been a 'bit foolish' to send a letter to the paper saying where he was going, but he thought he would have plenty of time to escape. Except a flat tyre let him down – and once he had abandoned his car and started hiking towards the scenic Hoodoo pass, across the 7,000-foot snow-capped peaks of the Bitterroot forest mountain range, on his way to Idaho, it was only a matter of time before he was caught.

Schoenecker claimed he'd suffered temporary insanity when he killed his wife and wrote the bizarre poem. But Sheriff Chet Barry said: 'He didn't suddenly snap. It was all thought out over at least three years.'

The final nail in Schoenecker's coffin was the evidence that he had cancelled all postal deliveries a day before the killing. 'He wasn't going to be there and he planned that she wasn't going to be there either,' said prosecutor Chris Evans. In August 1989, a jury found David Schoenecker guilty of murder in the first degree. When he was sentenced two months later, Judge Robert Fitzgerald recited his own little rhyme.

'You won't kill in the night, nor kill in the day. All on your list can go on their merry way. You killed your sweet wife who loved you so dear. For that you're being punished, let me make that fact clear. The sentence I've chosen to you may seem cold. You'll pay, and you'll pay all the while you'll grow old. One day you will die, a funeral your warden will hold. For you will serve your entire natural life and not be paroled.'

Although Fitzgerald has been criticised in some quarters for his frivolous delivery, many feel his sentence has ensured more than poetic justice. Schoenecker will end his days in Chino State Jail.

16

How Many **Did One Single** Shot **Kill?**

THE CALLOUS MURDER of petrol-station hand William 'Petey' Norwood wasted a young life. But when his mother carried out his last wish, for his body to be used to help others, she set off a chain reaction of fear and death all over America. For, unbeknown to her, Petey had the deadly AIDS virus. Over six years later, how he caught it is still a mystery. And his killer stays free.

Quiet, carefree 22-year-old Petey Norwood gave his mum a shock when he disclosed a premonition – that he'd die young. How could he have known that a week later he'd be shot dead by a bandit during a robbery that went tragically wrong? Or did he know something about his health that he never revealed to a soul … that he had AIDS?

A single shot from a robber's gun killed William Norwood. But that one murder is now being blamed for death after death. Because Petey left all his organs for transplants. Each of them carrying the HIV virus.

Norwood was working nights at a petrol station in the Virginia farming town of Dinwiddie when the robber aimed a gun at him and demanded money. Petey wasn't quick enough. So the bandit shot him in the head, grabbed $100 from the till and fled.

The dying man was taken to Petersburg General Hospital – now renamed the Southside Regional Medical Center. There, after a vain 12-hour fight to save him, his mother, Bessie Rathbone, gave permission for all his organs to be used for transplants. Only a week earlier, in August 1985, he'd told his mum to donate his organs when he died.

Before any organs were taken, Norwood's body was given routine tests for AIDS. He was found to be 'clean'. Not that anyone would have suspected him of carrying the HIV virus, as he wasn't known to be in any of the high-risk categories: homosexual, drug user, or a haemophiliac needing blood transfusions.

All usable organs were taken out and fresh-frozen like peas. Sterilising them first might have spoiled the organs. Not sterilising them left the unsuspected AIDS virus very much alive.

The organs were soon requested by a non-profit organisation called LifeNet and shipped off within hours to 30 hospitals all over the United States. Hospitals where desperate patients waited for the chance of a life-saving transplant. Bessie Rathbone might have lost a well-loved son. But at least, she thought, she'd done her bit for others. She could not have been more wrong.

In 1986, the man who was given Norwood's heart died of AIDS. Two years later, the patient given one of his kidneys also died of AIDS. In 1990, the man who got Norwood's other kidney went the same way. The patient who received the liver died of 'complications after surgery'. The one who was given the pancreas has never been traced.

The scandal erupted when an elderly woman in Colorado, who'd been given one of Norwood's hip joints, tested positive for HIV. Health officials first thought she had caught the AIDS virus from a blood transfusion. But when they checked they found her bone graft had been done without a transfusion.

Despite this discovery, Colorado's state medical authorities did not warn LifeNet, who handle around 30,000 human organ donations every year.

And it was not until later that the alarm went out. LifeNet tested cells preserved from the murdered man. And discovered he had AIDS. Hospital officials all over America began searching for 50 more people who had been given various kinds of tissue from Norwood's body. Tissue grafts including bone, tendons, ligaments and skin are used for a wide range of surgical procedures such as dentistry, cancer surgery and dealing with athletic injuries. At least, three people given grafts from Norwood have caught the AIDS virus.

People who got skin or bone grafts may be luckier than others. Skin and bone tissue is exposed to radiation, or treated with Ethyl alcohol, to kill off germs before being freeze-dried. But the safeguard is not foolproof.

'We can't be 100 per cent certain that it kills the AIDS virus,' says a Food and Drug Administration official. 'But it does reduce the risk.'

Norwood's bone marrow had been sent to the US Navy – but it was recovered before any of it had been used. Two people given the corneas from his eyes were also lucky: tests showed they didn't have AIDS. And tests on a handful of other potential victims have also proved negative.

'This case is tragic, unfortunate,' says LifeNet official Doug Wilson. 'But we were not at all negligent. The science simply was not there in 1985. And the likelihood of this happening today is slim-to-zero.'

Petey's auntie, Emma Norwood, who is Bessie Rathbone's sister, says: 'It made us feel so much better arranging for transplants. After Petey died, my sister and I said, "What we'd love to know is who got his heart because that would make us feel he was still alive." All we wanted was to help somebody else out.'

The sisters were upset to find out how many of Petey's organs had been taken for medical use. 'It was bad enough that he was murdered,' Emma says. 'But all this AIDS thing has brought it back. It's like Petey died all over again.

'And Bessie was mad as hell, because she thought the doctors were saying they would only remove her son's heart, kidneys and spine, and then she heard about all those other things that were taken and sent all over the United States.'

LifeNet's president Dr Richard Hurwitz has called for all state health departments to report on transplant-AIDS cases immediately, in future. But the baffling, vital question still remains: how did Petey Norwood catch AIDS in the first place?

Friends and relatives all remember him as a carefree, normal young man who loved to go out boozing, fix up cars and cruise the back roads in his blue Ford Ranchero wagon. He was no stranger to trouble, they admit. But, they insist, definitely not gay. And not into hard drugs and needles.

Petey's petrol-station colleague, Steve Shifflett, says, 'It was a real shock when I heard he had AIDS.'

And Walter Reese, who managed another petrol station not far from Petey's, declares: 'He was ordinary enough, seemed happy-go-lucky. He and my stepson went out drinking and to the bowling alley, just like other kids that age. My wife, Pat, was so upset when he was shot, that she set up a reward for catching the killer.'

Despite Petey's legion of loyal supporters, some people in the community have been wondering whether he was a secret homosexual, or had a hidden drug problem. But his best friend, Chip Wright, is outraged by such rumours. 'It's a smear campaign,' he says. 'Nobody even wonders whether it might have happened in the hospital.'

One unnamed woman friend said, 'I miss Petey a lot. He always made me laugh.'

Waitress Mary Harlan, who worked across the street from Petey's Exxon station, says, 'The only way I can figure it is that Petey caught AIDS in hospital, from transfusions when they were trying to save him.'

But some health officials wonder if the hospital tests of 1985 – far less sophisticated than today's – just failed to pick up the virus. Dr Harold Jaffee, AIDS department director at the government's Centre for Disease Control, says: 'Norwood probably got the virus just before he was shot. So it didn't show in tests.

'If you're going to use organs for transplants, there's a small chance you're going to miss someone who's been infected so soon before death that he has not yet produced antibodies against HIV.

'Routine AIDS tests register only the antibodies, not the virus itself. So there is this "window" of infection that can last between four weeks and a year, without being traced.'

Virginia Health Department chief Dr Martin Cader says: 'We're investigating the possibility that Mr Norwood was infected by a transfusion. But it's a remote chance, because the tests run on blood donors are very reliable – if not 100 per cent.'

Among those for whom that chance could mean life or death are four cops under Dinwiddie Sheriff Benny Heath, who heads the murder hunt. They carried the dying man from the petrol station and fear his blood may have given them the deadly virus.

These days Petey's mum is still outraged that her boy's killer has never been arrested, despite a $5,000 reward put up by his employers.

'The police are not interested in catching the person who murdered my son,' Bessie Rathbone claims. 'They are only interested in him because of the AIDS. Yet before he got shot he was never sick.

'They've told me over and over again that they know who the killer is, but don't have enough evidence to charge him with murder.

'I call the sheriff's office every now and again and give 'em hell. Because whoever is walking round out there has got off scot-free.'

17

The Three Wives of Doctor Strangelove

NORMAN LEWISTON HAD a lot on his plate. The 52-year-old doctor had three wives to keep happy. In an extraordinary juggling act, Lewiston kept secret from the three women — who incidentally knew each other — the fact that he was married to all of them at once.

And as Norman flitted from one wife to another, his weight ballooned to over 17 stone and pushed him to an early grave. Not surprising — since he often ended up eating two or three big dinners in an evening just to keep the three Mrs Lewistons happy.

Wife No 3, Robyn Lewiston, 42, said, 'I know for a fact that he had three turkey dinners one Thanksgiving Day.' And wife No 2, Katy Lewiston, 44, said, 'Norman was so overweight, he was eating all the meals three wives were feeding him.'

His first wife, Diana Lewiston, 51, recalls they had lunch 'every Friday' — the same day Katy swears he regularly had lunch with her.

Incredibly, Norman juggled his wives while holding down a stressful job as a professor of paediatrics at the Stanford Children's Hospital, in Palo Alto, northern California. He also headed a cystic fibrosis clinic and helped to develop the first heart-lung transplant programme for child sufferers of the deadly disease. But, despite his six-figure salary, he owed £40,000 on his credit cards after trying to support three homes. Norman was paying the mortgage on two houses, rent on a small flat plus his three kids' college tuition fees.

On 5 August, 1991, Norman had dinner with Katy before dashing off to the hospital, where he supposedly often stayed the night. Katy let him sleep there because 'He snored so loudly that I couldn't sleep. I let him come to bed with me whenever he wanted but he slept at the hospital.'

That night, as usual, he drove to Diana's house. While in bed with her Norman died of a heart attack brought on by high blood pressure. Katy got the terrible news the next day from the hospital. 'In one call, I learned my husband was dead and the woman who brought him in was also married to him.'

She got an even bigger shock when she went to Norman's office. Katy found photos of her husband with Diana and Robyn. She recognised Robyn immediately as they had both worked with the bearded doctor. Katy found Robyn's number and called, suspecting the worst. Robyn told her: 'Norm and I married two years ago. He said he'd divorced you.

Says Katy, 'It was awful – I lost 12lbs in seven days, I couldn't eat or sleep. I loved him so much and thought he was an extremely loyal man. But it's turned into a nightmare. It hurt, not just the financial problems, but the betrayal, too.'

Robyn added, 'I believe he loved all three of us, but was incapable of letting any of us go. Once you had a relationship with Norm, you had it for life. And there was a strong sexual attraction. Just because people don't spend the night together doesn't mean they don't have sex.'

Although the unmerry widows say they still love him, they also hate Norman for the lies he told over the years. It all began when Norman walked down the aisle with Diana when he was 21.

They had three children – David, 27, James, 24, and Pamela, 20. But by the '70s he was cheating on his wife, usually with women from the hospital. Robyn was a nurse, Katy an administrator.

At a Christmas party, Robyn was one of several women who queued up as a joke to kiss Dr Lewiston. He declared Robyn the winner. Within days they were dating each other.

Norman showered her with gifts and took her to Europe on holiday. She even met his mum. Diana found out about the affair but accepted that she and Norman were leading separate lives. She even called Robyn and said, 'As long as he does not divorce me, he can do anything.'

Five years later, Robyn gave Norman an ultimatum – divorce Diana and marry me or it's over. He showed her divorce papers but she had them checked and was told they were forged. So Robyn moved 800 miles away to San Diego. Later Norman moved in, claiming he'd quit his job and planned to marry her.

The next six months were the happiest of Robyn's life. But then Norman told her he'd only taken a sabbatical from work. 'It was obvious he'd gone back to his job and also Diana. That was very hurtful,' said Robyn.

Although Norman was back with Diana, he was up to his old tricks. He bumped into Katy and asked her out. 'I thought he'd divorced Diana as I knew he'd been living with Robyn.

Norman and Katy got engaged but, says Katy, 'When I mentioned the wedding, he'd change the subject.' She stepped up the pressure after they bought a house in Los Altos, just 10 miles from Diana's home. Her dream came true on 6 November, 1985, when they were married. But the wedding night was a disappointment. 'Norman left for the hospital to work while I painted our living room for the reception.'

Katy became his public wife who attended office functions and parties. Even when they bumped into Diana, who was giving demonstrations in a shopping mall, he brazened out the introductions. Katy thought she was meeting his ex; Diana always turned a blind eye to his other women.

Meanwhile, Robyn had married a dentist and had a daughter. But they split up after two years together. Norman had kept in contact with her and wrote: 'Katy and I are growing distant. It won't be long before one of us gets itchy feet.'

After Robyn's divorce, Norman began flying to San Diego at weekends, telling his two wives he was doing research there. Robyn says, 'I assumed he'd divorced Diana because he'd married Katy. And when he told me he'd divorced Katy, I believed him as they were together such a short time.'

In September 1989, Norman and Robyn were married. The devious doctor told his bride that he had to continue living up north for two more years so he'd be eligible for his pension. Robyn believed he was sleeping at the hospital every night. He even rented a room near the hospital – conveniently situated between Diana's and Katy's homes – so they could be together when Robyn visited.

Says Katy: 'I never once thought he was cheating on me. He didn't call me Robyn or Diana or use general names like darling.'

But eventually the dirty doc's luck ran out. Robyn came north to a hospital do. Norman introduced her to a colleague, who said, 'I met you at a party a while back.' Robyn replied, 'I haven't been to one with Norm.'

He said the colleague had mixed up her dates. But Robyn searched his briefcase and found a letter addressed to him at Katy's house. 'I knew deep down I had to say goodbye. It's hard to admit there are some marriages you walk away from.'

She called in a private eye, who found out Norman was a bigamist. Robyn's lawyer demanded £10,000 to settle the marriage and she got a cheque in three days.

Six weeks later, Norman died before signing the annulment papers. Diana, the sole beneficiary in his will and executor of his estate, is suing Katy for half her house. Katy is suing his estate for fraud, in an attempt to hold on to the house and get a share of his pension.

Robyn jokes, 'The only thing I want to inherit are his frequent flyer air miles.' The revelations about his tangled love life led to an investigation of a research fund he handled. Auditors suspect he used £5,000 of it to settle debts.

The three wives have been considering offers of Hollywood movie rights to the Lewiston story. And Katy is writing a book about him.

'It's easy to fantasise about the fun Norm had but I think it was hell for him,' said a colleague. 'He was in a complete mess and didn't have the character to get himself out of it.'

18

Please! I Didn't Kill My Baby.

TO SEE YOUR tiny baby fall sick and die is horror enough. But, for Patti Stallings, that tragedy turned into the nightmare of a murder charge. Only the sadness of a second sickly child saved her from a lifetime spent behind bars.

Patti Stallings cuddles her son David, distraught that he was born with a dangerous illness. Yet she also knows it was only the discovery of that illness which proved her innocent of murdering his brother.

For Patti, now 26, and her husband Dave, the nightmare began on 7 July, 1989. Their first-born, three-month-old Ryan, had never been able to keep his bottle-feed down. And suddenly, that morning, he lay obviously in pain in his cot, breathing unnaturally.

Patti rushed Ryan to hospital. After three days of tests on him, his parents were taken to the local police station in St Louis, Missouri.

The tests had shown ethylene glycol – used in anti-freeze – in the child's blood. And the police suspected the parents of poisoning him. Detectives grilled Patti and Dave separately. Patti was asked if she'd suffered post-natal depression or been jealous of the attention her husband paid to the baby?

Dave was asked if they'd been fighting a lot – and if he, rather than Patti, had been jealous of the baby. They told him his wife had failed a lie-detector test. That, itself, was a big lie. He nearly fell for it. 'But,' he says now, 'my senses came back and I thought, "They're crazy!"'

After 12 days in hospital, baby Ryan recovered. But he was put into foster care. The heartbroken parents were only allowed to see him for an hour a week. And they were forbidden to feed him.

But on one visit, Patti was briefly left alone with her son – and a bottle of baby-milk. A little later, when others were in the same room, she fed Ryan his milk.

Five days later, the baby was back in hospital, diagnosed as having ethylene glycol poisoning. Patti was arrested at once and charged with assault. Her husband kept watch by their son's hospital cot. 'He was lying there with tubes in his arms and throat, blowing up like a balloon,' Dave recalls. 'I couldn't stand it.'

On 7 September baby Ryan died in his father's arms. At the Stallings' home, police found a bottle of anti-freeze. Patti was charged with first-degree murder.

'I couldn't sleep,' she says. 'I lost a huge amount of weight. Only my husband's support, and my Buddhist religion, kept me from going insane.'

After a month held in jail, Patti discovered she was pregnant. The new baby, David Junior, was born in February 1990. He was taken from his mother and put in a foster home. Not for the first time, Patti Stallings broke down and wept.

Within days, Patti was told her new baby had been vomiting and breathing unnaturally. 'They were the same things that had been wrong with Ryan,' she says. 'I went into shock.'

Tests showed that David Junior had a rare genetic disorder called methylmalomic acidemia, or MMA – which can create its own poisons. It affects one in every 48,000 babies, and few live beyond eight years old.

Patti's lawyers called on the prosecutors to look into the possibility that baby Ryan had died of the same ailment. Patti was let out on bail while the police investigated.

But the murder trial went ahead. Doctors claimed that whether or not Ryan was born with MMA, what killed him was a dose of anti-freeze.

Patti went on trial in January 1991. Doctors and scientists testified that the human body could not make ethylene glycol. The defence tried to show the similarities of Ryan's and his brother's symptoms. Judge Gary Kramer would not allow that evidence because no experts were called to back it up.

Police and social workers claimed Patti seemed cold and uncaring when told her son had died. But the most damning testimony came from tests showing that the bottle Patti had used on her visit to Ryan in the foster home contained traces of ethylene glycol – even though it had been washed and filled again since her visit.

A tearful Patti told the jury she had not worn a coat or carried a handbag on her visit, so would have had nowhere to hide any poison. 'I don't know how they think I did it,' she said. 'I'm just as confused as anyone else in this room.'

Defence lawyer Eric Rathbone suggested that another relative might have killed Ryan – or that poison could have got into his body by some other mysterious means. The jury debated the evidence for 10 hours. Then they found Patti guilty. She was jailed for life, with no parole.

Even then, the nightmare was not complete. Social workers decided to take baby David Junior away from his father, on the grounds that Dave Stallings had 'abandoned' the child. In fact, Dave said, lawyer Rathbone had advised him not to see his baby.

Patti appealed against the jury's verdict, claiming that Rathbone had made a mess of her defence. The State ruled that she had been let down by her lawyer and ordered her to be freed on $60,000 bail, to await a fresh trial. And a senior university scientist who had been reading about the case also took a hand.

William Sly, chairman of St Louis University's biochemistry department, suspected that baby Ryan, like his brother, might have been born with MMA – and could have died from it. Sly arranged for tests to be done on frozen samples of Ryan's blood serum. They showed that the original reports of deadly amounts of ethylene glycol in the blood had been incorrect.

More tests were done by Yale University genetics professor Dr Piero Rinaldo. He proved that MMA had indeed killed Ryan.

The make-up of poisons produced by the disease, he explained, is similar to that of ethylene glycol. But the earlier findings were 'grossly inaccurate and probably preconceived'. Rinaldo said, 'I've never seen such lousy work.'

Patti Stallings was freed. State prosecutor George McElroy made a public apology. 'We can't undo the suffering the Stallings have endured,' he said, 'but I hope they will be happier in the future.'

Patti, a former shop assistant, and Dave, a plate engraver, have launched multi-million-pound lawsuits against two hospitals, three doctors and a laboratory firm. But, Patti claims, she is not bitter. 'The anger and rage and all that – it's ugly,' she says. 'I want to move on. We just want to quietly go on with our lives.'

And there is still the uphill battle of sick little Dave Junior. Patti has to feed him by a tube into his stomach. That takes special patience because the MMA makes it hard for him to digest proteins. And he's so frail, even a cold could kill him.

'Taking care of David is going to be a whole new fight,' Patti says. 'But we are used to fighting.'

19

Murder they Wrote

Bloodbath in Beverly Hills

THE BRUTAL MURDER of Jose and Kitty Menendez shook their wealthy Beverly Hills community to its core. Seven months later, parents rich and poor were united in shock at the two sons' arrest. Had Erik and Lyle slaughtered their parents for money?

Hollywood scriptwriters would have been hard pressed to come up with as shocking a case as the 'Murder They Wrote' scandal that rocked America. On the balmy night of August 20, 1989, multi-millionaire movie mogul Jose Menendez, 45, and his ex-beauty-queen wife Kitty, 44, were cold-bloodedly gunned down in the library of their beautiful Beverly Hills mansion.

The handsome, hardworking couple were relaxing in front of the TV, eating strawberries and cream, when they were blasted with pump-action shotguns at point-blank range. Jose, in shorts and sweatshirt, almost had his head blown off when shot from behind with a 12-gauge shotgun. The crazed killers pumped four more slugs into him to make sure he was dead – one of them through his mouth. His wife Kitty, still in her jogging clothes, was riddled with 10 wounds from another shotgun, leading police to believe that more than one person was involved in the shocking outrage. She had been shot all over, but the four blasts aimed at her face left her unrecognisable.

At first police suspected that Mafia hitmen or even Fidel Castro's henchmen were responsible for the awful slaughter – Jose had dealt with a video company linked to the Mob, and the Cuban-born tycoon was known to hate the dictator's regime. But homicide experts soon rejected the theory of professional assassins, as the murder was too messy.

After seven months, the victims' two sons Lyle, 22, and Erik, 19, both college tennis champs, were suddenly arrested and charged. The dashing duo weren't even major suspects at first, even though Erik, with Lyle's help, had penned a screenplay called *The Perfect Murder*. It involved the farfetched tale of a sadistic 18-year-old who kills his rich parents to inherit a $200 million fortune.

Police discovered the amateurish 61-page script during an intense manhunt for the vicious killers. It had been carefully written just two months before the real-life murders and, in a bizarre twist, Erik's mother had helped to type it. It described how 'The door opens, exposing the luxurious suite and Mr and Mrs Cromwell lying in bed. "Good evening, Mother, good evening, Father." Hamilton's voice is of attempted compassion but the hatred completely overwhelms it. Their faces are of questioning horror as he closes the door gently. The scene fades and the murder is left to the imagination of the audience.'

Murder investigators were at first unwilling to suspect the boys, as they found it hard to believe that the 'loving' but often wayward kids could have committed such a horrific and callous crime. The Menendezes owned a sprawling $3 million eight-bedroom mansion on Elm Drive, Beverly Hills, and the luxurious home, complete with its own swimming pool and tennis court, could count Elton John, Michael Jackson and also Prince as former occupiers. The couple's happiness and wealth had made them the envy of Tinseltown and their gory deaths came as a brutal shock.

Beverly Hills police chief Marvin Iannone said: 'I have been in this business for 33 years, and I know of few murders that were more savage. But who knows what goes on in families? It seems the boys may have acted out their screenplay for real.'

There was no evidence of burglary at their heavily fortified mansion which had the latest in high-tech security alarms.

The boys said they found the fortress-like iron gate open and the front door unlocked. 'They shot and killed my parents,' wailed Lyle, between sobs, to the emergency number as Erik made the chilling screams in the background. 'I don't know what happened. Didn't hear anything. I just got home. Erik, shut up. Get away from them.'

Lyle and Erik, who were as thick as thieves, claimed they'd gone to see the Bond movie *Licence To Kill* on that fateful night but couldn't get in and went to see *Batman* instead. They did not have any ticket stubs. Then they visited a Santa Monica food festival where they rang a friend. No trace was ever found of the call.

The two sons at first seemed to be heartbroken and had help from Jerome Oziel, a psychologist, to get over the trauma. Said Erik, 'I've never seen anything like it, never will see anything like it. They looked like wax. I've never seen Dad look so helpless, it's sad to think he ever would be. He came to the US from Cuba when he was 16, without his father – at almost the same age when Lyle and I don't have a dad.'

But there was a hint from their shrink's notes that everything was not all rosy. 'My dad really could not do something well enough,' said Lyle. 'It was very hard for Erik and me – I had arguments with him all the time and I rarely won.' Yet within a few weeks their mourning seemed to be over as the boys lived it up on a $3 million life insurance policy taken out by their dad. Lyle bought a $40,000 red Porsche Carrera convertible car, a $1,000,000 apartment and a $10,000 Rolex watch. His shopping sprees included five silk shirts snapped up in several minutes. Lyle then quit Princeton University in New Jersey and paid $300,000 for a local restaurant, called Chuck's Spring Street Cafe.

Renaming it Mr Buffalo's, he planned to form a nationwide chain and also dabbled in real estate and showbiz. He tried unsuccessfully to become a promoter of a Soul II Soul concert.

Meanwhile little brother Erik, once a top US tennis junior, turned down a chance to go to the prestigious University of California and tried to make it as a tennis pro. He moved into an elegant apartment and hired a full-time private coach at $30,000 a year.

The Menendez sons' spending alerted the police. What they uncovered were two spoiled rich kids who would lie, cheat and steal to get all they wanted. At 17, Erik was arrested for breaking into two houses in LA and stealing a safe from one and $55,000 worth of cash and jewellery from the other. He got off with probation after his father paid damages to the victims. Lyle was suspected of involvement but Erik took the rap as he was a minor and so likely to get off with a light sentence. Big brother was just as bad. Lyle was suspended for the year in his first term at university when his class report was nearly an exact copy of a classmate's. He flaunted his wealth at high school and was know as 'Lyle the Loanshark', cruising clubs and showing off his red Alfa Romeo. He was also suspended twice from driving as he hadn't paid his parking tickets, so he was chauffeured in a luxury limousine at Dad's expense.

Their best mate Reed Newhall remembers they were 'very competitive'. He says: 'Erik was verbally aggressive. If he didn't get his own way, Lyle would swear or bat a ball over the wall in disgust, a bit like John McEnroe in one of his tantrums.'

Soon after the murders, Erik said: 'There was a lot of pressure to become great. We are prototypes of my father – he wanted us to be exactly like him. My father hated Fidel Castro with a passion and wanted to spend the rest of his life getting him out of Cuba. He probably would have done it and probably would have been assassinated somewhere down the line.

'My brother wants to become President of the US but I want to be Senator, and be with the people of Cuba. I'm not going to live for my father, but I think his dreams are what I want to achieve. I feel he's in me, pushing me.' The boys were driven to succeed by a father who rose from dishwashing to get through college to a young, successful businessman and a mother who was a national swimming champ.

When Jose won a scholarship to the University of Illinois, he met Kitty Anderson, a former beauty queen of a nearby town. Jose got a degree in accounting and quickly made his fortune. After working for RCA, where he signed Duran Duran and the Eurythmics, he moved to the subsidiary of the company that produced the *Rambo* films with Sylvester Stallone. Friends included Barry Manilow and Kenny Rogers.

Jose was so rich, he was spending $10 million on doing up his new mansion on elegant Mulholland Drive, which is down the road from Marlon Brando and Jack Nicholson, while he still lived in his old house. But his co-worker Ralph King said, 'Despite the pressures of work, he always had time for his children.'

His executive job took him into some dodgy deals with tough tycoons. One firm that sued him was a distributor of porn films with Mafia ties, while the owner of a record chain bought by the company was a convicted extortionist. Homicide cops thought the killings were linked to Jose's recent takeovers, but soon Erik and Lyle were nailed to the nightmare on Elm Drive by circumstantial evidence and confession tapes.

Although the police had read Erik's screenplay, the first real break came when a shotgun shell casing was found in Lyle's jacket. Then cops discovered that a file reference to a new will had been erased 'by mistake' on Jose's home computer by Lyle. The old will left the $9 million estate to his sons. A police spokesman said: 'We believe the parents were going to cut them out of the will because they were out of control, and that's why they were killed.'

Erik's friend Craig Cignarelli then claimed that Erik had confessed to the murder in private – Erik denies this. The murder weapons were never found but two 12-gauge shotguns were bought at a nearby store two days before the massacre under the name of Donovan Goodreau, once a roommate of Lyle's, who'd had his driver's licence stolen.

Erik was charged on his return from a tennis tournament.

20

Presumed Innocent

A wife-killer's tears that fooled the world

WHEN WEALTHY CHARLES Stuart was pulled out from his car with a serious bullet wound, his pregnant wife dying beside him, America was outraged by the brutal attack. Months later the horrific truth was discovered – yuppie Stuart was a man so bent by money and ambition that he slaughtered his own family.

'My wife's been shot – I've been shot!' These chilling words marked the beginning of a gory murder that mystified and horrified America. The dashing yuppie Charles Stuart was speaking to police on his car phone, telling them that his pregnant wife Carol had been shot next to him and he was bleeding to death from a horrific stomach wound.

Driving through the streets, looking for help, Stuart was able to remain on the phone long enough for police patrol cars to track him down and save his life – only for him to kill himself two months later.

Stuart, a 29-year-old manager of a posh fur shop in Boston, claimed that a 'black mugger wearing a track suit and baseball cap' had hijacked their car just as they were leaving their pre-natal classes. The gravel-voiced gunman had supposedly robbed them of jewellery and cash – then opened fire and left them in their car for dead.

Although Carol died within hours of a massive gunshot wound to the back of her head, her baby, Christopher, was delivered by Caesarean section, born eight weeks premature and weighing only 3lb 13 oz. After clinging to life for 17 days, the tragic tot also died and the nation wept once more. Although he was still in agony following two life-saving operations, Stuart insisted on being taken to another hospital to cradle baby Christopher in his arms as he died.

Stuart's touching farewell message to Carol was read out at his wife's funeral, to some 800 mourners, including the Massachusetts Governor – Michael Dukakis. 'Good night, sweet wife, my love,' it said. 'Now you sleep away from me. I will never again know the feeling of your hand in mine, but I will always feel you.

'I miss you and I love you. God has called you to His hands, not to take you away from me but to bring you away from the cruelty and the violence that fill this world.'

Two months later, just as it looked like a cold-blooded psychopath was about to get away scot-free, the terrible truth behind the double murder suddenly emerged.

Greedy Charlie, who enjoyed every luxury that his $80,000 salary could afford, had killed his wife to get his hands on even more money – several six-figure insurance policies. One of these had been taken out just weeks before her death.

With police on the verge of arresting callous Charlie, he parked his flashy new car on the Tobin Bridge in Boston and plunged 200 feet to his death in the murky River Mystic. The suicide note he left in his car said simply: 'I love my family. The last four months have been hell.'

Amazingly, the real-life drama was caught on film when a TV crew working with the Boston police just happened to be on the scene when the Stuarts were being pulled from their car. The press were also on the scene, having followed the police patrol cars trying for 15 minutes to trace their Toyota Maxima. Charles had claimed that he could not see the street signs because he was too weak from loss of blood to turn the car lights on – even though they were only under the steering wheel.

While the Stuarts were being rushed to the hospital, he asked over and over again, 'How is my wife?' But the heartless killer only wanted to make sure that she was dead.

Former altar-boy Stuart was never a suspect in the investigation until the day before his death. Says Boston District Attorney Thomas Mundy: 'It might seem unusual for a mugger to jump into a car and shoot two people. But then it's even more unbelievable that a man whose only vice is playing hockey on Wednesday nights, who works 52 hours a week and makes a large salary, who friends said was enthralled with his wife and baby, would shoot her. And then shoot himself so seriously that the bullet would almost kill him.' Stuart was in intensive care for 10 days followed by six weeks in hospital with damage to his bowels, gall bladder and liver – he had to wear a colostomy bag after his operations. Police think that Stuart panicked and shot himself in the stomach by mistake while aiming for his foot.

In the wake of Stuart's death was left a city seething with racial tension because innocent black men had come within hours of being charged with the murders. And tension was already high in the weeks after the brutal crime as hundreds of black men were stopped by police and questioned in an attempt to prevent more murderous attacks.

Stuart's suicide prompted an investigation into his personal life that soon revealed his sordid history of devious lying, cheating and also womanising. He'd even bragged to his friends on nights out that he'd had an affair with pretty university graduate Deborah Allen, although she has since denied it.

'There will never be any evidence of romantic involvement between us,' she said in a statement through her lawyer.

Smoothie Stuart came from the nearby wealthy town of Revere but had lied when he'd talked his way into a job at the top people's store Kakas by claiming that he went to a good university on a sports scholarship. After Stuart's death plunge, and on learning of his lies, the owners of Kakas checked the safe and found that a .38 snub-nose revolver was missing. There has never been any concrete evidence that Chuck, as he liked to be known, pulled the trigger that ended two lives, but circumstantial evidence is now overwhelming.

The man who turned Stuart's image from heroic victim into heartless villain was his own younger brother, Matthew, who had helped hide vital evidence – including the apparent murder weapon. Stuart took his life the day after he learned that paint-mixer Matthew had told police what he really knew about the grisly events on the night of October 13, 1989.

After a dry run the day before, Chuck met his brother at a prearranged place in the Boston neighbourhood of Mission Hill to carry out an 'insurance scam' – for which he would be paid $6,000. Chuck pulled up and threw Carol's Gucci handbag, containing her wallet and jewellery, and a .38 calibre gun, into Matthew's car. Matthew drove off and hurled all the incriminating evidence into the Revere River, but kept Carol's expensive engagement ring – which he later gave to police to prove his terrible story.

Matthew says that he did see something in the seat next to his brother but didn't realise that it might have been Carol and that his brother was wounded. He claims that he knew nothing of his sister-in-law's murder until later that same night. Under an old Massachusetts law, he can't be charged with trying to conceal the crime as it was carried out by a member of his own family. He only went to the police when, 71 days after the murder, a black man called William Bennett, who had a long history of armed robbery, was about to be charged with the killing. Chuck had hoped to frame Bennett by picking him out of a police line-up saying that he 'most looked like' the gunman he'd seen.

'The line-up pushed Matthew over the brink,' says his lawyer.

'He had agonised over it for weeks.' Ironically, Bennett's picture in the paper was recognised by one of his real victims and he was charged for robbing a shop at gunpoint.

A police probe revealed that for months Chuck had been plotting to kill his wife. He had even tried to hire an old friend, David MacClean, to do the murderous job. 'He asked me, "Can you take care of my wife – you know, kill her?" ' says MacClean. 'It was very business-like, almost like a board meeting. He didn't want to spend the rest of his life breaking his back for somebody else. His wife refused to have an abortion and he was afraid that she would not return to her job when the baby was born.'

Stuart also allegedly arranged with Matthew to break into his house and make it look like a robbery had been committed, so he could kill her and blame it on burglars. A few days before the murder the calculating killer had even dropped into a local restaurant to confirm a reservation for a party, setting up his image as the devoted husband. The Driftwood restaurant owner Jim Hogan remembers: 'He sat there talking about how he was going to have a Christmas baby, and how excited they were about coming to the party – and all the time he knew she wasn't going to make it. She was going to be dead.'

On 13 October, Chuck took Carol for a romantic break at a charming country inn in Connecticut so that they could celebrate their fourth wedding anniversary. They acted like young lovers but Chuck had already set the wheels in motion to end what friends and family thought was the perfect marriage, with one gunshot.

The couple met and fell in love in 1980 when Chuck was a short-order cook at the Driftwood and Carol got a part-time job as a waitress. With similar working-class backgrounds and with dreams of a better life, they bought themselves a beautiful four-bedroom house in the well-to-do town of Reading, where he was a very popular man in the community. There was no hint that behind the façade lay a merciless killer. 'My children loved having Chuck over to baby-sit,' says a neighbour.

Their $100,000 mortgage kept the couple on a tight budget but Carol desperately wanted a baby and she was overjoyed when she got pregnant. Carol told her family, 'I know it's a boy. It's Christopher.' Still, the only real crack in their marriage appeared to be Chuck's boozy nights out with the lads on a Friday. Maureen Vajdic, their bridesmaid, says, 'Carol told Chuck, "Don't you have any concern for me at all? I'm pregnant. These late nights will have to stop when the baby's born."'

There was also an unconfirmed report that Stuart was taking money from his company, and even a suggestion that he had gone into a clinic to fight a cocaine problem. But on the surface, everything seemed fine.

What drove Stuart to kill his wife? His friends think it was overwhelming ambition that drove him to work so hard and that, ironically, also drove him to kill the people he should have loved most. The prospect of a baby in the family had made him fear for his lavish lifestyle. Until he became a home owner, the exceedingly vain Stuart wore $500 suits and dyed his hair. He dined at the best restaurants, and went on expensive holidays with his wife. David MacClean reveals, 'He dreamed of owning his own restaurant and realised that he could not afford it on his income alone.'

The whole truth about the private world of this cold-hearted killer may have gone down with Stuart to his watery grave, but the closest thing to a confession of guilt could be his farewell letter to Carol. 'We must know that God's will was done. We must forgive the sinner, because He would.'

Actor Ken Olin sees Stuart as a terrible symbol of the insatiable greed inherent in the yuppie culture of the '80s. 'He just took it to the extreme. And then he outlived the decade by just four days.'

21

Over the Top

THE PANORAMIC VIEW from the clifftop overlooking the ocean was spectacular. Bride-to-be Deana Wild, 20, looked on in wide-eyed wonder for a few minutes. Then she took a few careful steps forward and peered over the edge at the waves crashing on to the granite rocks 400 feet below.

It was Big Sur at its most beautiful – one of America's seven natural wonders. This picturesque stretch of northern Californian coastline, with its huge surfer waves, thick redwood forests and mountainous range, attracts thousands of tourists each year.

One second Deana was enjoying the scenery, overlooking Seal Beach, and the next she was hurtling to her death. One of her high-heeled shoes was found on the top of the cliff while the other was discovered 50 feet below on a narrow ledge just before a sheer drop to the Pacific Ocean. Did she jump? Did she trip? Or was she pushed?

Her future in-laws, Virginia, 55, and husband Billie Joe McGinnis, 53, heard Deana's screams and the sickening thud as her body bounced like a rag doll when she hit rock bottom. They told police they didn't see what happened because they were walking back to their car. But they gave police 12 snapshots they had taken moments before Deana's plunge, including one photo with Billie Joe's hand on her back.

The spot she'd fallen from was known locally as 'lover's leap' because many distraught people had jumped to their deaths there. After police conducted an exhaustive investigation, they ruled Deana's death on 2 April, 1987, a tragic accident – even though the coroner's report left the verdict as 'pending'.

But Deana's mother Bobbie Roberts couldn't believe that her retarded daughter, who had the IQ of a 10-year-old and was naive and trusting, would kill herself or even risk her life by stepping too close to the edge. After all, according to the McGinnis duo, she had everything to live for.

After a brief marriage, Deana had fallen head over heels in love again, and was engaged to James Coates, Virginia's son by her first marriage. This was despite the fact that Deana had not finalised her divorce, and her intended was in prison for second-degree murder. Deana had been staying with the McGinnises at their home near San Diego, California. They appeared to get along fine. So well, in fact, they'd taken that fateful trip together 500 miles up the coast.

Bobbie Roberts had taken out a £1,500 burial policy on Deana to pay for funeral bills, just in case of a tragic accident. But after her daughter's death, she had trouble claiming it. So she turned to an old family friend, lawyer Steve Keeney, to get to the bottom of it. 'I promised Bobbie I would find the truth,' says Keeney. 'Right from the start, nothing fell into place. First the case did not pass the 'smell test' of the coroner's office, which never gave a cause of death.

'And the more we learned about Virginia's background the more we learned about the case facts.'

Over a period of two years he uncovered a shocking catalogue of potential crimes in Virginia's past – including the possibility of murder – that had gone virtually unnoticed by police. Over two decades, Virginia had made seven insurance claims for fire, all suspected arson cases. One claim paid out £80,000. She'd lived in houses in Kentucky, New York and California that had all burned down.

Virginia met her first husband, neighbour Richard Coates, when he was watching a fire at her parents' barn in New York. But he divorced her after two more mysterious fires at their homes. In 1985, Virginia insured a truck she had rented while moving house. It was stolen along with many items from her home. The truck was later found burned out. Keeney discovered an even more shocking secret buried in her past. In April 1972, Virginia's three-year-old daughter Cynthia died in an accident in Louisville, Kentucky. She was playing on top of a tractor in a barn when she jumped off, hanging herself on some loose twine. Virginia told friends that she got £600 in insurance after Cynthia died.

In 1974, Virginia's second husband Sylvester Rearden died of cancer. But police have discovered that Virginia was nursing him and giving him medication. Three months later a blaze burned the house down.

A few months before Deana fell, Virginia's mother, Mary Hoffman, died – officially of a heart problem. But Virginia, who lived with her, was helping to give her insulin for diabetes. A family friend told police that Virginia had talked about how insulin could be used to kill somebody without raising any suspicion. The friend also said Virginia had told her Mary had talked one day about 'not living very long'. The next day she was dead.

Police are also probing her death. 'We are looking into any death that Virginia has been present at or associated with,' said an official.

Bobbie Roberts believed hers was the only insurance policy on Deana's life. But Keeney unearthed another one. On 1 April, 1987 – the day before the tragedy – the McGinnis duo took out an insurance policy on Deana's life.

State Farm insurance agent Mac McCain told Keeney that he had an uneasy feeling about Virginia. As she was leaving the office she turned and asked, 'Does this policy cover accidental death?' Deana signed the policy, not knowing she was virtually signing her death certificate. Virginia paid the first premium of £40.

McCain knew that Virginia had made several claims against his company and balked at approving the policy. So he sent it to head office to let them decide. A company spokesman said: 'What could we tell Deana? "We can't insure you as we believe there's a possibility you're going to be murdered!"'

Two weeks later Virginia came back to the office, tossed the policy on the desk and said, 'She's dead.' The signature of Deana's neighbour had been forged on the £22,000 policy. The major beneficiary was Deana's jailed fiancé James Coates. The other beneficiaries were Virginia and Billie Joe, who later divorced.

Tests show that Deana had taken the anti-depressant Elavil, for which Billie Joe had a prescription at the time. Deana's mum says, 'Physically, it could make a person very drowsy, so Deana wouldn't have been aware of what was going on.'

The mounting circumstantial evidence was enough to convince police to charge the couple with murder. But while awaiting trial, Billie Joe died in prison of AIDS.

District Attorney Luis Aragon said in his opening statement that 'this was murder, not an accident'. He claimed the couple drugged Deana and gave her a shove over the cliff. The insurance policy was 'the smoking gun' that tied the plot together.

But defence attorney Albert Tamayo said: 'There are bound to be suspicions where an insurance policy's bought one day and a fall occurs on the next. But it doesn't prove murder.' He claimed Deana had somehow slipped in her high heels.

During the seven-week trial, a makeshift courtroom was set up on the majestic cliff overlooking Seal Beach so that the jury could get an idea first-hand of what happened. Tamayo said, 'It was a unique experience. The judge said it was a most spectacular courtroom and I tend to agree with him.'

Juror Peter Young said the bus trip from the Monterey courtroom to Big Sur was crucial in visualising what happened that day. Juror Jim Allender reckoned it was unlikely that a person could have slipped from the point where Deana fell.

Virginia McGinnis was found guilty of murder in the first degree. She was also found guilty of conspiracy, insurance fraud and forgery. She was sentenced to life without any chance of parole.

Deana's mum said, 'I'm elated. This is the best day I've had in five years.' Virginia may also face murder charges connected to the death hanging of her daughter Cynthia.

22

Rivals in Love -
One had to Die

FARMER BILL BUSS, 26, couldn't believe his luck when two beautiful women – one a princess, the other a queen – battled for his hand in marriage. But the dream turned into a nightmare when 21-year-old dairy princess, Lori Esker – heartbroken by Bill's rejection of her after a year-long affair – strangled homecoming queen Lisa Cihaski, 21.

Lovely Lisa's lifeless body was found by her distraught mother who'd gone looking for her when she failed to come home late at night. The grisly murder horrified residents of tiny, tightly knit farming communities Birnamwood and Hatley in Wisconsin – the dairy heartland of America. They were terrified a madman was on the loose and, for the first time in their lives, locked their doors at night.

But eight days after the killing, on Wednesday, 20 September last year, they were in for an even bigger shock. The newly crowned dairy princess was charged with her former classmate's murder. To add to the heartache, Lori and Lisa's mothers had gone to school together and were 'best of friends'.

At first Lori denied the murder, but after being quizzed three times by cops she confessed that she'd killed Lisa 'by accident' while begging her to give Bill up. She said that a life-and-death struggle broke out between them when Esker suggested that she was pregnant by Buss. As they wrestled, Lori claimed that she grabbed a belt from the back seat of the car, wrapped it round Lisa's neck and tightened it. When Lisa's body went limp, Lori took out a mirror from her rival's bag and held it to her face to see if she was breathing. 'When I realised that she wasn't, I thought to myself, "Oh my God, I killed her." I didn't mean to hurt her. I know Lisa knows that.' Nevertheless she pulled a ring off Lisa's finger because she thought 'maybe Bill gave it to her'. When police asked Bill if Lisa had any enemies, he replied 'only Lori'. The police – who didn't believe it was a case of self-defence – claimed Lori's fatal attraction for Bill led to her hatching a deadly plot.

Blonde-haired Lori, president of the local Future Farmers of America organisation, was the first woman in rural Marathon County history to be charged with killing another woman. The packed trial was told that Esker was so infatuated with Bill, that when he told her he was engaged to Lisa, she refused to believe it was over and begged him to marry her instead.

Bill had been dating Lisa for three years when she told him she needed 'some space'. He began seeing Lori and admitted, 'I loved her and I really cared about her. We had a romantic and sexual relationship.' But when his ex-girlfriend found out, she became jealous and wanted him back. Bill obliged. The day he saw Lisa again, a devastated Lori rang him in a rage, saying, 'How could you do this to me?'

Buss told the court that although she looked like a fragile beauty, Lori had grown up on a 350-acre farm and was strong enough to handle tough farm chores. The implication was that she was strong enough to strangle another woman. The last time they had spoken by phone was just three days before the murder. Lori told him, 'I just want you to know that I have accepted the fact that you and Lisa are back together, now I'm going to leave you alone.'

But that telephone call was her first step in an evil murder plot. The day of the murder, Lori left a message on a friend's answerphone saying, 'I just called to talk. I'm going to the library to study.' The prosecutor said it was a weak attempt to create an alibi. Lori drove to where Lisa worked and waited until she came out.

The jury took seven hours to find Lori guilty of pre-planned murder. She was sentenced to life in prison but could be paroled by the age of 34. When sentenced, she broke down and wept as she said: 'If I could trade places with Lisa, I would. I'll be punishing myself for as long as I live.'

23

Debts Drove Dad
to Drown Kids

IT HAD BEEN a tiring day. Mum and Dad trailing the four kids from one furniture store to the next, checking the prices of beds for the new house. For Larry DeLisle, 30, it had gone on too long and he was glad that now at last they were heading home.

In the back of the 12-year-old car, the two older kids – Brian, eight, and Melissa, four – ate their ice-creams on that hot August day in 1989, chattering and laughing away with their little sisters – Kathryn, two, and eight-month-old baby Emily.

But all of a sudden those screams of laughter turned into screams of terror as their car roared out of control, smashed through a dead-end barrier and plunged into the river.

Larry DeLisle struggled free and swam to safety. So did his wife. But the children all drowned.

In the working-class Detroit suburb of Wyandotte, the public flocked to dead-end Eureka Street to lay bouquets next to pictures of the victims, devastated by the tragedy.

'To have four beautiful babies one minute and the next they're gone,' Larry DeLisle told local TV. 'If you think about that all the time, you might as well put on a straitjacket.'

But how did this tragedy happen? DeLisle, a store manager, explained to police that his accelerator pedal had stuck and, at the same moment, he had suffered cramp in his leg. His 33-year-old wife Suzanne, he added, had tried to turn off the ignition and take the car out of gear.

Police ran routine checks and soon discovered a sinister background of financial and emotional troubles. Larry DeLisle was up to his eyes in debt. On credit cards alone, he owed $10,000. Though he took home around $300 a week, he had to hand over 90 per cent of that to Suzanne.

To help solve his money worries, DeLisle's uncle Bill had given them a rent-free home. But Suzanne just spent all of their money on things for the house, including new beds.

Detectives also discovered that the family's 12-year-old car had been left to Larry 18 months earlier by his father ... who had shot himself in its front seat. Blood stains from the suicide were still there.

The car was tested for mechanical failure. Out of 20 trial runs, the accelerator did stick – just once. But why had DeLisle turned down that dead end anyway? And, even if the accelerator was sticking and the driver did have a sudden cramp, why didn't he try braking? Or swerving the wheel right or left, instead of charging straight down into the river?

Police came to the conclusion that DeLisle had attempted to murder his entire family and commit suicide – but that he chickened out of his own death at the last moment, never considering the possibility that Suzanne might swim clear too.

DeLisle agreed to a lie-detector test. 'I had a little leg cramp,' he said. 'I just couldn't seem to slam on the brakes. I didn't want to. I don't know why.'

But then he began what sounded like a confession ... 'I just wanted to scare my wife enough. Slam on the brakes, come to a standstill. Get her all upset so that she'd forget about beds for a couple of days and just let me be. I couldn't stop the car accelerating. I didn't want to stop it.

'I didn't mean to hurt my babies. I love my wife. I didn't even realise they were in the car. My mind went blank. I really hate that car. My father blew his brains out in it. And he didn't even say goodbye . . .'

DeLisle's job, too, had got on top of him. 'I just wanted it to be over. The constant repetition. Same thing, day after day. I wanted to be closer to my wife. I don't deserve to live. Gas chamber, electrocution, hang me. I don't care. Just throw away the key.'

DeLisle was charged with four murders, and sympathy for him soon turned to hatred. During pre-trial hearings other parents screamed, 'Killer! Scum! Drown the man!'

Suzanne DeLisle stuck by her husband. 'If I thought for a second he was guilty,' she declared, 'I'd be screaming louder than anyone to convict him.' Giving evidence, she tried to explain away the fact that the car had not turned away from the river. She said that she was pulling the wheel to the left – and her husband was trying to pull to the right.

But her testimony contained a damning giveaway. Though she had told police her husband's foot had stayed jammed to the floor, she now said that a split second before the crash, he took it off the accelerator.

Also, the night before the tragedy, and again earlier on the day of the alleged murders, DeLisle had been seen driving along Eureka Street. So he knew it was a dead end.

DeLisle was found guilty. Judge Columbo sentenced the bereaved father to life in jail, with no parole. DeLisle has appealed for a new trial, claiming that police 'hypnotised' him. And wife Suzanne plans to stand by him to the bitter end. 'He's not guilty,' she weeps. 'I think about him every minute of the day.'

24

Slaughter of the Innocents

SOBBING AND SCREAMING, the panic-stricken mother dashed into the hospital, her small son in her arms. 'He's stopped breathing!' she shrieked. Doctors rushed four-year-old Jose Antonio Lumbrera into the emergency room of St Catherine's Hospital. But an hour later, the child was dead.

The boy's mother, 32-year-old Diana Lumbrera, seemed inconsolable. She broke down and, between bouts of helpless sobbing, blurted out a tragic tale. All her other children, she told the nurses, had also died young. All five of them.

On the day of Jose's funeral, as his mother wept piteously at the graveside, a pathologist back at the hospital in Garden City, Kansas, was doing a post-mortem on the boy. Jose, the expert decided, had probably been suffocated by someone.

The police began to look into Diana Lumbrera's past. She had not lived long in Garden City. Her home had been the tiny farming town of Bovina, in neighbouring Texas. It was there, on 30 November, 1976, that Diana – then 18-year-old Mrs Garza – ran into Parmer County Hospital carrying the lifeless body of three-month-old Joanna Garza, her second child by husband Lionel Garza. Doctors certified death by 'strangulation due to convulsive disorder'. There was no post-mortem.

Fifteen months later, in February 1978, she turned up at another hospital – the West Texas Medical Center in Lubbock –

carrying her small son, Jose Lionel Garza. He was 10 weeks old and, she said, 'very sick'.

Jose Lionel was treated successfully for pneumonia. And after three days he was well enough to be moved out of the intensive care unit. But before he could be transferred, there was sudden drama in the unit. Diana Lumbrera came rushing out, screaming that something had happened to her baby.

Jose Lionel was dead. Dr John Rankin, who had been treating him, ordered a post-mortem. But it failed to pinpoint how the baby had died. Jose Lionel was marked down as a victim of Sudden Infant Death Syndrome – cot death.

'Two or three nurses were on duty in the unit,' Dr Rankin says now. 'But because of the layout, patients were not fully within sight at all times. It was a bit unusual to have a patient who's been improving, with no fever, suddenly stop living. But I had to accept it at the time, on the objective evidence.'

And, of course, Jose's mother had conveniently not told Dr Rankin about the equally sudden death of little Joanna.

About eight months later, it happened once more. Into Parmer County Hospital rushed Diana Lumbrera, yet again, this time with her three-year-old daughter Melissa. The child was already dead. Again doctors performed a post-mortem to try to discover the exact cause of her death. Their paperwork lists the cause as 'asphyxia due to aspiration of stomach contents' – she had choked on her own vomit.

Hospital officials did realise that another of Diana's children had died there too. But they wrote it off as just one of those tragic coincidences in life.

Husband Lionel Garza was less easily satisfied. He had been viewing the remorseless death-roll of their babies with growing suspicion and worry. On the very morning Melissa died, he had been playing with her before he went to work. Yet half an hour after arriving there, he got a call to say his little girl was dead. Without even waiting for funeral number three, he quit home – although Diana was pregnant with their fourth child.

It was almost exactly two years later that she had a fourth child's death to announce. This time it was not one of her own. She swept into West Plains Medical Center at Muleshoe, near her home town of Bovina, carrying the body of six-week-old Ericka Aleman, whom she had been babysitting for her cousin Benita. Ericka was dead on arrival.

A post-mortem was ordered. But, whatever the report said, it somehow disappeared. Officials were left with the recollection that, according to Diana Lumbrera, Ericka had just 'quit breathing'. More attention would certainly have been paid if she had mentioned the three previous deaths.

But the toll was far from complete. On 17 August, 1982, Diana regretted to report the death, at home, of her two year-old daughter Melinda. A pathologist ruled out crime. He decided she had heart disease and died of 'acute heart failure'.

Diana, by now divorced and using her maiden name Lumbrera again, took Jose Alvonis as a lover. On 10 October, 1983, she gave birth to his son, Christopher. Just short of six months later, on 28 March, 1984, his mother carried him into West Plains Memorial Hospital at Dimmitt, near Bovina. The story, this time supported by Diana's aunt Maria Aleman and sister Virginia Bribiesca, was that little Christopher turned purple while being fed.

Dr Brian Lee diagnosed septicaemia, a fatal blood infection. 'There were no signs of foul play. Infants can get infections and die very quickly. They're very susceptible to them ... the only other action I could have taken would have involved a post-mortem. But there is no pathologist at West Plains.'

By now, Diana was getting rather too well known at hospitals in her own area. And the headstones of her five dead children stood side by side in the Bovina Cemetery. So in 1985 she moved over the state border, to Garden City. Soon afterwards she gave birth to her sixth child, Jose Antonio, another Alvonis baby. Considering whom he had for a mother, this second Jose lasted a comparatively long time. But after four years, on 1 May, 1990, he died.

After the post-mortem, Bovina Police Chief Gary Coleman investigated the deaths. And Lumbrera was charged with Jose Antonio's murder. She claimed she had been cursed by a 'curandero' – a witch. Her friend Maria Antillon said, 'She used to tell me her mother-in-law had cursed her.'

At her trial, District Attorney Ricklin Pierce claimed that she murdered Jose Antonio for three reasons: she'd inherit a lump sum if her son died, she was heavily in debt – and she was psychologically disturbed.

Diana wanted to collect on a $3,000 insurance policy, he said, just as she had done with her three daughters. In answer to this, defence lawyer Mike Quint pointed out that $2,000 went on Jose's funeral. The prosecutor suggested that she probably planned the funeral when Jose was born and only needed to make a small profit.

The second motive alleged was that Diana, up to her eyes in debt, needed to cut down on expenses. She had to shell out $25 a week, for instance, to a childminder while she worked at a meat-packing warehouse. Lastly, he claimed, Diana was a 'sympathy junkie'. The jury heard of a mind disease called Munchausen's Syndrome, which drives people to fake illnesses to gain sympathy. In this case she did it 'by proxy', killing her son so that she could star as the grieving mother.

Diana had also lied to friends to gain their sympathy. She told them her father had died in a car crash and that Jose had leukaemia and she needed money for his chemotherapy.

Although the jury were not told of the other deaths, they convicted her of killing Jose. She was jailed for life. Under a plea-bargaining arrangement in Texas, to save taxpayers' money on a lengthy trial, she admitted killing three more of her children and was given further life sentences.

In Bovina, police chief Coleman is still baffled. 'I can't understand why people weren't suspicious.'

25

Candid Camera Killers

A CHRISTMAS PARTY video is meant to be a happy memento of the festive season. For one family, a home movie brings back only memories of horror.

In front of a twinkling Christmas tree a man brandishes a gift-wrapped package and flashes a toothy smile for the video camera. A highly seasonal home movie. Until you look closer – and see the gun peeping out of its holster at his waist.

The movie was shot while two murderous thieves waited for their victims to arrive at a three-storey holiday cabin in the snowbound hills near Salt Lake City, Utah. The man with the gift was Von Lester Taylor, 26. Behind the camera was his accomplice, Edward Deli, 22. Both were petty crooks on parole. The prey they lay in wait for, three days before Christmas 1990, was the Tiede family from Humble, Texas. They were rich businessman Rolf Tiede, 50; his wife, Kaye, 49; daughters Linea, 20, and Trisha, 16, and Mrs Kaye's handicapped, partly blind mother, Mrs Beth Botts, 72.

Rolf Tiede had taken the family Christmas to Salt Lake City. Overnight, the killers moved in. They helped themselves to drinks, tried on Rolf's clothes and opened presents.

Kaye Tiede, her mother, and her daughter Linea were first back. They were ambushed by Taylor, who had a .38 calibre pistol, and Deli with a long-barrel .44 hand gun. The pair demanded cash. 'We'll give you the money!' Kaye cried. 'Anything!'

But, as the women pleaded for their lives, the robbers started shooting. Blood sprayed everywhere. Kaye Tiede was hit once in the back with the .44 and twice in the neck with the .38. Her mother was shot once in the head, twice in the chest.

Daughter Linea sobbed and prayed. 'That's not going to work,' Taylor sneered. 'I'm a Devil worshipper.' She was tied, gagged and thrown into a cupboard. Hours later, her father and Trisha returned.

They too were ambushed, this time in the garage. Rolf handed over all his money. 'Not enough,' said Taylor. He ordered Deli to shoot Rolf. Deli didn't fire. So Taylor did it. But the blast didn't kill him. He played dead.

The killers decided to burn the house. They poured petrol around – and all over Rolf, who moved slightly. They noticed, and Taylor fired into Rolf's head. Yet still he did not die.

Taylor and Deli rounded up the two girls, set light to the petrol and fled in two of the snowmobiles with their captives. Once they had gone, Rolf struggled to his feet and stumbled around, looking in vain for his wife and mother-in-law. He stamped on the flames – and became a ball of fire.

Blinded by blood, seared by flames, he ripped off most of his clothes and staggered out of the blazing building, into the freezing cold. He drove the second snowmobile two miles to where his brother Randy waited to be picked up, to join the family for Christmas.

Randy hardly recognised bleeding, blistered Rolf. He called the police by car phone and within minutes, the killers' vehicle was spotted. They were off the road and were arrested. Mercifully, the two sisters weren't hurt.

In court at Coalville, Taylor admitted first-degree murder. He was sentenced to die by firing squad or poison injection. Deli denied both murders and blamed Taylor for all the shooting. One juror held out for second-degree murder, with no death penalty, so Deli got life.

Rolf Tiede, despite the horror, has had the cabin rebuilt. 'I just think of Taylor and Deli as animals, stalking their prey. They were without emotion, other than feelings of cruelty. But there's no sense dwelling on it. We're going to enjoy the cabin, I'll hear my wife's laughter there again and know she's watching us.'

Will they gather at the cabin this Christmas? 'No,' says Rolf. 'Not for Christmas. Not ever again.'

26

I Was an Undercover Lover

BRUNETTE BEAUTY KIM Paris finally found herself the perfect job. She quit her spot as a topless go-go dancer at Caligula One to work two doors up the street at the Clyde Wilson private detective agency. As an undercover private eye, every day was riddled with danger. But the 29-year-old from Houston, Texas, had no idea it would mean she'd have to become a cold-blooded killer's lover.

Kim's very first assignment as a super-sleuth meant she had to go back to taking off her clothes, this time at a nudist club in California.

'It took me four days before I finally took off all my clothes,' says Kim. 'I was so embarrassed. It wasn't like topless dancing at a bar where you cannot see the customers' faces because of the bright lights.' She was on the trail of a young mother at the centre of a child custody case and her evidence helped the husband win the tug-of-love battle.

She also worked on suspected insurance scams, proving that 'invalid' employees really were healthy enough to work. Curvy Kim would ring claimants' doorbells and ask for help changing the tyre of her car. Few men could resist the beautiful damsel in distress and as they set to work, a hidden camera took pictures which led to charges of fraud.

But it was the way she helped crack the mysterious murder of a wealthy couple that turned her into a local hero. It was this startling story that was turned into a movie – *Love and Lies*.

It all began a couple of years before Kim joined the detective agency in 1984. Two masked intruders burst in on millionaire attorney James Campbell, 55, and his wife Virginia, 50, as they lay in bed, and shot them dead. Their grandchildren, Michael, eight, and Matthew, seven – who'd been lying in sleeping bags at the foot of their bed – were woken by gunfire and found themselves splattered in their grandparents' blood.

Among those interviewed by the police were the murdered victims' daughter Cynthia Ray, 35, and her boyfriend David West, 34. And suspicions were aroused immediately when they gave each other perfect alibis. Her three sisters also suspected Cynthia because she'd once boasted that she was going to kill her parents for their money. The dishy divorcee, who had given her two kids to her parents to bring up, bragged to a friend she'd killed them. But the police had no proof.

For three years the chilling case went unsolved, until it was time to divide the inheritance. Then one of the sisters, Betty Hinds, turned to the Clyde Wilson detective agency in a last-ditch attempt to stop Cynthia getting a penny from the will.

After the killings, Cynthia soon dumped her partner in crime David West, and the plan was for Kim to become his undercover lover and charm the true story out of him.

'I knocked on his door and pretended I had the wrong address and asked to use the phone,' explains Kim, who changed her name to Theresa while on the assignment. 'David was out when I called but his friend invited me in and then asked me to go for a drink. When David joined us at the bar he didn't suspect a thing. He struck me as a gentle, chivalrous man, so it was quite easy for me to forget I was working.

'He asked me out and on our first date I knew I was on to something when he told me that he was going to open a business as an old girlfriend was coming into some money. He told me that both her parents had died in a car crash and the estate was about to be settled.'

By the third date West was so infatuated with Kim that he asked her to marry him. She naturally turned him down, but to try and get him to open up she said she was only interested in macho men.

He quickly admitted that he'd done some shameful things but he wouldn't say what. For 10 weeks Kim kept up the charade, seeing West five days a week and speaking to him every day on the phone. 'Although we were together constantly, I never slept with him or even kissed him,' says Kim. 'There were times when he tried to kiss me and I'd pull away, but he was content to be close to me whatever the conditions. If we'd had sex I would have been dirty in his mind and that's not what he wanted. He was starting a new life and he wanted to forget his past. He worshipped me and it didn't matter that I wouldn't go to bed. And I really did enjoy his company – he was smart and he made me laugh.

'David was preoccupied with Cynthia. Always talking about their sex life. She would lay in bed and call him Daddy. She convinced him that her father had raped her when she was a child. He finally admitted he was hiding something about his life with Cynthia but it was "perfectly legal".

'I worked on persuading him he could trust me. When I felt he was ready to crack, my boss and I went to the police.' After police 'wired' her with a hidden microphone in her purse, Cynthia embarked on the most frightening 48 hours of her life. As she sat in the car with the callous killer, police listened from a van around the corner.

Kim told West she'd sleep with him and wanted to marry him and have children. But only if he was completely honest. This was enough to get David to confess all ...

David said, 'All right, I killed both of her parents. Cynthia begged me to do it, and I wanted to do it, frankly. And she offered me a lot of money and I said great. And the thing was that I made her stand there with me when I did it. I didn't have the belly for it. I made her go in there with me and stand right by the bed as I shot each of them three times. I didn't do anything wrong as far as I'm concerned.'

Kim was devastated at West's confession to the callous killings. 'I wanted to clap my hand over his mouth and scream, "God, please don't tell me! You just don't know what you're doing to yourself." '

She was forced to see him again the following night because the police wanted enough evidence for Cynthia and David to get the death penalty.

'I was terrified, I thought he was going to kill me because now I knew about the murders.'

But the unsuspecting West was more concerned about Kim than himself when he was arrested. He only found out how he'd been set up a few days later when it was revealed on the news.

'After his arrest I was shown 40 slides of his brutal handiwork,' says Kim. 'To see these photos was to experience the victims' agony.'

Deadly Dave had his sentence reduced to life imprisonment in return for giving evidence against Cynthia. She was found guilty of conspiracy to murder.

Kim is now married with two kids. And although now working as a radio reporter, she still moonlights as an undercover private eye. 'The danger is just like a drug,' Kim smiles.

27

Killed by His
Baby Katy

GEORGE TELEMACHOS NEVER knew what hit him. The gun-powder burns on his eyelids showed he was fast asleep when a bullet was pumped into his brain at point-blank range.

The blast knocked 60-year-old George's dentures out of his mouth and shattered his skull. But the killer handed the gun to one of his two accomplices and said, 'If he moves, shoot him again.' George's dog Cocoa, who usually barked at strangers, had not warned him of the danger. Not even a growl. After checking his pulse to make sure he was dead, the killers ransacked his home. Before they fled, they stole £400 and a Movado watch.

George's friends thought he was lucky to die instantly. For if he'd survived and found out who had masterminded his murder, life wouldn't have been worth living.

A wealthy former restaurant owner, the lonely divorcee had bought a tobacco shop rather than spend time alone in his comfortable house in Fort Lauderdale, Florida. The only person who meant anything to him was daughter Katy, 19. He'd always spoiled her because she'd been born with a liver disease. The doting dad feared she would die young like her brother Tony, who succumbed to the same disease when he was five. At 10, Katy's liver started to fail as well and she had to have an emergency transplant operation. But 10 months later her body rejected the organ and she needed a second liver swap, which was successful.

Her father paid medical bills totalling £30,000 out of his own pocket because her illness was not covered by his health insurance.

Over the years Telemachos had been such a devoted dad to Katy, he had little love left over for his wife Mary, and they divorced. He was devastated when, at 17, Katy had to fight for life again after her kidneys gave out. Katy's mother donated one of her kidneys.

While Katy was sick, George, a hard-working Romanian immigrant, brought her dinner from a different restaurant every night so she would not have to eat bland hospital food. The day she was released from hospital he bought her a new, red Ford Probe sports car worth £10,000. And for her 18th birthday he splashed out on a gold necklace. He also gave her the master bedroom at home so she'd have enough room for her clothes and the stuffed animals he'd given her. George bought her a cellular phone and beeper so he could contact her at any time.

She was a little rich girl who had everything. Katy's friend Caroline Hesford said, 'Spoiled! She got everything she wanted.'

After her second organ transplant, however, Katy began to change. And, with the change, her life began to go to pieces. She shaved the right side of her head and combed her ringlets to the left. She had two abortions and took drugs. She even smoked hash in her dad's shop. Katy, who thought George was a millionaire, started borrowing large amounts of cash from him and was seen carrying a small gun in her handbag. She was also known to keep a .38 calibre gun in her car, and told friends she was acting as 'middleman' in drug deals between New York and Miami. In her diary she talked about 'shipments' and 'Ks' – referring to kilos of cocaine. She also wrote a mysterious note saying: 'Get Danny to kill David C.'

While working in her dad's shop in the spring of 1990, Katy met stocky Puerto Rican Erik Delvalle, 24, who'd dropped out of school to be a construction worker. Soon they were madly in love. But she was from an affluent suburb with everything Daddy could afford to buy her, while he was a small-time drug-dealer from a very poor area of town.

Nevertheless, within weeks, Erik had given her his grandmother's ring and asked her to marry him. And she'd said yes. But her furious father called Erik 'a blue-collar worker' who was not good enough for his daughter. He also said Erik was a 'walking drug attack'.

George grew more concerned when money went missing from his shop – up to £350 a time. After it had happened several times, he had to face the truth – his little princess was robbing him blind.

He confronted Katy and her fiance and screamed at them, 'Get out and don't come back!' He took away her shop and house keys. So Katy and Erik leased an apartment and rented a yellow van to move their stuff, enlisting the help of his friend Vinnie Magona, 21.

Katy now hated her father so much for interfering in her life that she and Erik plotted to kill him and live on her inheritance. Erik even boasted to a friend, Cheryl Lamb, 19, about the plan, saying, 'Katy, Vinnie and I are going to kill her dad. She's going to be coming into a lot of money and we'll be set for life.'

Katy had calculated that her dad was worth about £3 million but the true figure was only about £200,000. And they might have got away with their callous plan if it had not been for eagle-eyed cop John Posson.

On the night of 21 July, 1990, he was patrolling in Cooper City when he spotted a yellow unlocked van with the licence plate covered up. In it he found three cold bottles of Budweiser beer, a latex surgeon's glove, a woman's wallet containing several credit cards and a driver's licence belonging to Katy. Suspecting something was going on, Posson pulled his car into the shadows and waited. A few minutes later, three figures came running down the road towards the van.

Katy, Delvalle and Magona said they had been visiting a friend on the next street. The officer was still suspicious but let them go after taking their names and addresses. When a neighbour found George's body next day, the police knew where to go. Magona broke down after 20 minutes of questioning, admitting that Delvalle 'went over to the bed, told me to look outside then shot him'.

He said Delvalle had offered him £200 to come along as a lookout. Magona admitted, 'I said okay. I guess it was peer pressure.' He also said it was Katy's job to keep the dog quiet.

Delvalle broke down and confessed after five hours at the police station. He admitted carrying the gun but insisted Katy pulled the trigger. But police discovered that after the murder he'd bragged to Cheryl Lamb that he'd pulled the trigger.

While in prison Delvalle wrote to Katy saying he still loved her. 'We are not over and we will never be,' it said. 'We have the rest of our lives to be together. We just got to wait it out.'

He also used the letters to discuss an alibi with Katy, unaware that they would be examined and used in evidence against him. Delvalle and Magona pleaded guilty to murder charges but Katy denied it.

At her trial, Delvalle had a change of heart and said he shot George to stop him wrecking his marriage plans. 'Katy reacted badly when I told her I'd killed her dad,' he said. 'I pleaded with her not to say anything.'

Delvalle testified that after drinking a few beers and smoking some pot, he and Magona sneaked into the Telemachos house and shot George in bed. Proclaiming her innocence, Katy supported her fiancé's statement and said she knew nothing about the murder plan.

'I always loved my father,' she said. 'I knew everything he did was for me. I couldn't believe Delvalle was so much in love with me that he could take my father away.'

And she said she didn't need her dad's money. 'If I wanted more money during the week, my father would give me whatever I wanted.' But the prosecutor claimed Delvalle was so much in love with Katy he was willing to lie for her.

Magona testified that Katy had masterminded the murder, and the jury were convinced she was involved. Her gun was used and police found .38 calibre hollow-point bullets, the type that had killed George, in her car.

Katy was found guilty of murder and will serve the rest of her life in jail. Delvalle was sentenced to life, with parole possible after 25 years, while Magona got four years.

28

The Hiss of Death

WAYNE POPE, 38, got a gruesome idea for a murder — and it involved an unusual weapon. Cruel Wayne wanted to get rid of his adoptive mum with a lethal snakebite. And the sweet-natured old lady knew nothing about the evil thoughts of the son she had brought up as her own.

Wayne first hatched his plan when he got chatting to a stranger, Keith Davis, in a restaurant in Pensacola, Florida. Davis told Pope that his hobby was hunting snakes, and instantly Pope, who had by then been mulling over the idea of murdering his mother for three years, dreamed up the venomous plot. 'You're just the man I'm looking for,' he told David. And, although he didn't explain his deadly mission, he showed a keen interest in the poisonous reptiles. The following day his motive became horribly clear. Pope explained to Davis that he'd been thinking of 'getting rid' of someone. He later offered David $150 to kill Kathleen Etheridge with a deadly rattlesnake. This would be followed by more money once his ill-gotten inheritance came through.

But Pope had picked the wrong man. Keith Davis went straight to the police. 'I knew if I didn't go through with it, he'd just get someone else,' he said. 'His mother's life was in danger.'

Davis was used as a stooge by the cops so they could catch Pope red-handed. They gave him a killer four-foot rattlesnake, which Davis told Pope he would use on his mother. 'I agreed to hold the snake while it bit her in the neck twice and in the arms a couple of times.'

Kathleen, meanwhile, was totally unaware of her son's lethal plot. He had always been a well-behaved, loving child, who doted on his grey-haired mum. 'He was always so polite,' she says. 'He brought a lot of sunshine into my life.'

But Pope couldn't hold down a job and had turned to petty crime to support his ex-wife and two kids. So when police called to see Kathleen, she thought he was in the usual sort of trouble. 'What has Wayne done now?' she asked. The cops had to break the news of his wicked plan to astounded Kathleen.

'My heart was broken, it was very shocking,' said Kathleen, who had adopted Wayne when she was with her first husband Clifford, now dead. The couple couldn't have children of their own and they took in Wayne when he was seven.

'He used to call every weekend to see how I was doing and he'd say "I love you dearly". But he'd got behind with his bills. I suppose he wanted my little house and car, and what I inherited on my mother's death. This is the payback I get for 30 years.'

Pope wanted Davis to hold the snake so it bit the artery in her neck several times while she took her afternoon nap. Then Pope would drag the body outside to make it look like the old lady had disturbed a snake resting in her garden.

But the cops were waiting when he and Davis arrived with the snake in a sack. 'He never said a word,' said Kathleen. 'But I'll never forget the expression on his face. He didn't even look human.'

District Attorney Wade Drinkard called Pope 'a sick individual', and the jury took less than 10 minutes to convict Pope of conspiracy to murder. He was sentenced to 30 years behind bars, but could get out in 10.

His mother still has forgiveness for the son she loved as her own.

'I still love and care for him,' she says. 'I had a miserable

Christmas without him. I was always used to having him home — the first few days after his arrest I'd listen for him to come in, just like he always did.'

29

The Good Twins who Turned Evil

WHICH TWIN IS the evil one? That is what heartbroken mum Robbie Good is desperate to know. Then one of her baby-faced identical twin sons, Craig and Timmy, can be cleared of a gruesome double murder. They were just 15 years old when their father William and grandmother Cleo were shot dead at point-blank range in their trailer home at Lake Murray on Saluda Island, South Carolina.

During their trial the boys blamed each other for pulling the trigger of the .22 calibre rifle. The jury took four hours to find them both guilty of the brutal slaughter.

Now their cancer-stricken mother is praying that her dying wish will be fulfilled. She wants one of them to admit he committed the murder single-handed, so an innocent twin can go free and be by her side for her last days. And she has her suspicions as to who the bad twin is.

'I love them both,' wept Mrs Good. 'But I honestly don't think Timmy did it. I'm convinced it was Craig who shot them. He once told me he might as well tell the truth and get it over with. But he won't own up because he wants his brother in jail to keep him company.'

She believes Craig lied to the police: 'He says he was out feeding the dog and Timmy says he was shaking the rug when it happened. But I've always known whether they're telling the truth or not.'

The ordeal has left Robbie, 37 – she is undergoing chemotherapy for her life-threatening cancer – a physical and emotional wreck. 'I can't sleep or eat anything. I have nightmares. I keep on seeing them in prison. Jail is not for children,' said the distraught mother. 'I think one of them was robbing my ex-husband and the gun went off,' she explained. 'I don't think they meant to hurt anyone.'

Pranks have been part and parcel of the twins' lives, says the mum, who lost custody of her twins after a bitter divorce. Afterwards her husband had gone on the run from a drug charge and she had not seen or heard from her boys in years. She did not even know where they lived until she read the headlines about their arrest. The Good boys had been double trouble ever since they were born on 23 April, 1973. They shared the same tiny bedroom and did everything together, from doing homework to doing drugs. They were so similar they even appeared to share a psychic connection. A close relative, Anne Jones, said: 'They could look at each other and instinctively know what the other was thinking.'

They would swap classrooms and pretend to be each other to confuse the teachers. But their shared fun and games eventually turned to the headier and finally deadly thrills of sex, booze and drugs.

By the time they were nine, they were already selling dope for their dad. Craig's lawyer Steve McCormack blamed their poor upbringing for their lack of discipline.

'Their father let them do whatever they wanted,' he said. 'If they wanted to go out at night, they went out at night. He knew they did drugs and drank alcohol. He didn't care. If they didn't want to go to school, they didn't have to. In fact, he pulled them out of school so they could help him build their house.'

In one year Craig missed 46 days from Irmo Middle School,

while his twin missed 27 days. 'Me and my dad had an arrangement,' said Timmy. 'I done what I wanted and he done what he wanted to.' Even when the twins did manage to get to school, they were often suspended for smoking reefers, setting off the fire alarm or getting into fights.

Neighbour Dale Hewlett recalled, 'There were occasions when the boys got out of control. Their father was more like a friend to the boys than a disciplinarian.

He added that William, a 36-year-old electrician, had given his sons rifles for Christmas just before he was killed. The twins ran around with such a bad crowd that one official was prompted to say William and Cleo died so the boys could 'party with their drug-smoking, school-cutting, beer-drinking friends'.

The day after the horrific murders, schoolgirl Jill Tucker played truant to spend the day with Timmy, smoking pot and having sex, while teenager Tim Scott sold Cleo Good's rings – pocketing most of the money.

William Good and his 60-year-old mother, Cleo, whose wedding and other rings had been ripped from her fingers and stolen along with her chequebook and pick-up truck, were murdered on 20 February, 1989. But it was five days before the bodies were discovered by a neighbour who had become concerned about their Doberman pinscher moping around.

At first police thought a psycho killer was on the loose and scoured the nearby woods, expecting to find the bodies of Craig and Timmy. However, to their horror, they soon realised that the Good boys had joined forces with evil and a nationwide hunt was launched. Three days later they were arrested in their grandma's van, near their mum's home in Nashville, Tennessee.

They were broke and had been living in a cavity above the foundations of the laundry room of an apartment building. Both were high on drugs and were charged with possession. They had sold off Grandma's jewellery, paid a friend to forge her signature on $500 worth of cheques and had then gone on a drugs spree.

Craig told cops: 'Most of the money we got we used to buy drugs. We stayed high all the time until we were arrested.'

The twins were tried as adults. To find them guilty, jurors had to believe that both were actively involved in the decision to kill or in the killing itself.

Craig had a juvenile record including drug possession and burgling his grandma's home. But the jury could not be allowed to hear that evidence unless he took the witness stand. He refused to testify but in a 47-page statement claimed he'd seen his father and grandmother 'fall' but hadn't seen Timmy pull the trigger. Craig's lawyer told the court his client was guilty of nothing more than 'looking for his brother'.

However, Timmy, who'd also been busted on an earlier drug rap, testified that his twin fired the fatal shots. Although his lawyer admitted Timmy was an accessory after the fact, he added, 'I think the only other thing Timmy is guilty of is not turning his brother in.'

But District Attorney Don Myers, holding the murder weapon that had been covered in both boys' fingerprints, said: 'It doesn't make any difference whatsoever which one pulls this trigger. They're both guilty. When two people conspire and aid and abet each other, it's just like both hands being on that trigger.'

Myers later revealed that detectives on the case have changed their minds several times about who was the lesser of the two evil twins. 'But it doesn't matter who did it. Our position is that it was two people with one mind – one purpose.'

The bad Good boys confessed that on the day of the murders they had both been drinking stolen alcohol. Craig also passed the time by shooting holes in the trailer skylight while waiting for their dad and grandma to return to be murdered.

For four hours the jury struggled with the possibility that one of the boys did the killing while the other took no part. In the end they found both equally guilty of murder.

When the verdict was announced, Craig screamed defiantly at

TV cameras, 'I'll be back!' while Timmy shouted, 'I'm innocent.' Their mother broke down and had to be half-carried, sobbing, from the courthouse.

But prosecutor Myers said, 'It was sickening to have to sit and listen to these twins talk casually about the murders as if they were nothing. They think this is a big joke and they have absolutely no remorse. Their only regret is having got caught.

'They thought they were something big because they cut school, only caused trouble when they did go to school and did the things that they wanted to – most of which were criminal acts. But they're only punk potheads who murdered in cold blood. Acting big just flushed their lives down the sewer. They were both destined for prison. It was just a matter of time.'

And time is something Robbie Good doesn't have much of. Craig and Timmy, sentenced to life imprisonment for murder and 65 years each for armed robbery and stealing an automobile, could be paroled in 20 years. Too late for their dying mother, who is fighting to prove that one of the twins did it by himself.

'Then maybe I can have one of my boys back,' she said wistfully. 'But no matter what happens, and whatever they did, I'll always love them.'

30

Double Trouble

JOHN CASSIDY'S WIFE wept like a typical bereaved widow while convincing a coroner that her distraught husband had killed himself with a shotgun. But the father-of-nine haunted his wife Mary from the grave, by proving she was the one who pulled the trigger after plotting his murder with her toyboy lover.

Mary, 29, told police she was in the upstairs bedroom when she heard a gunshot and found his body on the living room couch with a shotgun next to it. He had a large hole in his head where his chin should have been. She said that on the night before he died, her despondent 33-year-old husband had talked about killing himself. He was racked with guilt because, apart from the five children he had with his wife, he had four children with his wife's sister Bonnie McKinley.

Mary's tale about her suicidal husband was confirmed by her brother Edward Hill, who had also heard him talk about ending it all on the day of his death.

'John said he put my two sisters through too much misery and hurt them, so he wanted to alleviate the pain,' said Hill. 'I told him, "John, this is not going to solve any problems except to leave two women without a husband and a lover, or whatever, and kids without a father." '

For years, John had been having an affair with 37-year-old Bonnie, who lived with them in the same house in Monongahela,

Pennsylvania. They would have sex when his wife was out shopping or working at the local corner store, or he'd creep into Bonnie's bed when Mary was asleep.

His wife finally found out about the affair and knew that her sister was having her husband's kids, but she would not leave him because of her own children. They had bitter arguments about the affair and eventually Mary split the house into two self-contained units, hoping that would stop it. The Cassidys would live in one half while Bonnie and the rest of her husband's kids had the other half. But John and Bonnie carried on with their romance in spite of the new sleeping arrangement.

The complications of having two women in his life – and in this case both sisters living at the same house – had seemingly taken their toll on him. There were even rumours around town that he had a secret second lover and that she'd had his baby.

So it came as no surprise to his friends and family that John had taken his own life. But police were not sure it was suicide because most people kill themselves with a shot through the head or mouth, not the chin.

However, coroner Farrell Jackson ruled that a tormented Cassidy had died by his own hand on February 12, 1991, and police called off their investigation into a possible homicide. But two weeks later Bonnie McKinley made a shocking discovery – a tape recording proving Mary was a killer.

With Bonnie's help, Cassidy had bugged his own phone the day before he died because he thought his wife was being unfaithful, although he was not certain who with. Tragically, John never listened to the gruesome tape or he might have been able to save his own life. He might also have been amazed to discover that her lover was David Bowers, a 17-year-old student who Cassidy often went hunting and fishing with.

After a stunned Bonnie heard the recording, she called a family meeting with her brother Edward Hill, her other sister Rose Marie Smith and Rose Marie's husband Orlando.

She told them about the tape and explained that if they went to the police, Mary would probably go to jail for a very long time. After a lot of soul-searching they all agreed to do the right thing and inform the cops.

State trooper Roy Fuller played just 15 seconds of the damning 90-minute tape to Mary before she cried: 'That's enough. Turn it off.' Fuller said: 'I asked her, "You killed your husband, didn't you?" She dropped her head, started to cry and then slowly nodded her head.'

Cassidy's body was dug up and the red-faced coroner changed the verdict on the death certificate to murder. Coroner Jackson said: '99 per cent of what Mary Cassidy told me was true except the part about who pulled the trigger. It makes you feel like a goon.'

Mary was unaware that under a state law a wiretap is inadmissible evidence when it is made without the knowledge of one of the parties being taped. This would have meant that she had a good chance of getting off scot-free in a trial because the evidence against her would have been purely circumstantial.

Although Mary confessed to the brutal killing, she claimed that she did it in self-defence because she was a battered wife. She told police that when her husband fell asleep on the couch after one of his drink and drugs benders, she stared at him with a mixture of hatred and fear. Officer Fuller said: 'She was thinking about all the things that had happened in the past, all the abuse, the bad experiences. I guess she'd had it with him.

'Then she got the shotgun. She knelt down beside him and thought again about her past life. She picked up the shotgun and laid the barrel on his chin. She held her hand on the trigger. She said that she thought he was going to kill her if he awoke. She was afraid. She pulled the trigger once. She screamed. The shotgun fell.'

But officials said that Mary killed her husband because she was madly in love with hunky Bowers, who went to Thomas Jefferson

High School. They found cards from her addressed to 'Dave' and signed 'Love Mary with Xs and Os'. A search of his home uncovered her class ring as well as letters and cards from her. He'd also sent her a bunch of flowers and they had spent his 17th birthday by having a sizzling romp at Seven Springs Resort, not far from their homes. District Attorney John Pettit claims that her young lover had urged Mary to murder Cassidy, and without his encouragement she would have never done it.

Mary married her bearded husband in 1973 when he was 20 and she was just 16, and they began having children almost right away. The marriage quickly went downhill because he couldn't hold down a steady job and turned into a violent, two-timing alcoholic who loved to snort cocaine.

They eventually stopped having sex, and were more likely to share a bedroom with their children than each other. Although John and Mary briefly separated, they got back together for the sake of the children, but the bitter arguments continued. Police were called to their house more than once to settle their violent fights that one time ended up with Mary claiming that he almost tried to kill her.

'He had me by the throat against the wall and was going to choke me,' she said. 'Instead he grabbed me by the hair and he had a knife in his hand and he just cut the top of my hair off. The next day when he got up he remembered what he did, but his reasoning was, "Well, it's better your hair than your throat."'

But Cassidy's mother Dolores claimed her son had never beaten his wife. 'There may have been verbal abuse but I never saw black and blue marks on her,' she said.

'He loved his children. She asked him for a divorce and he wouldn't give her one because of the kids.'

His mum also blamed Mary for not putting an end to his relationship with Bonnie. 'If you love a man, you're not going to share him with another woman, especially your sister.'

Mary pleaded guilty to third-degree murder charges under a

plea bargain in which she agreed to evidence against her lover.

After an investigation by child welfare, her kids were handed over to the care of her relatives. Bowers was held under house arrest for several weeks after the murder and had a teacher come to his house every day to give him lessons. But he was eventually sent back to school to await trial on charges of soliciting a murder.

31

He Bumped off
his Buddies

It seemed like harmless fun – two young boys playing war games. Except that when 13-year-old Richard Bourassa invited his best friend Jeffrey Bush – also 13 – to his house to play after school on 12 September, 1986, the gun he gave him was real.

Coolly, Richard brought out two guns that belonged to his father. He gave the .22 calibre rifle to Jeff while he kept the 12-gauge shotgun. They had a mock shoot-out until eventually they stood face-to-face, aiming the two loaded guns at each other as if they were toys.

Suddenly the gun-barrels touched and the shotgun went off, spraying the room with buckshot. The pellets hit the door and window and several riddled Jeff's head and body. He died the next day.

Richard sobbed as he called the police and explained what had happened. But later he managed a sick smile – as he was photographed with arms, legs, his shorts and T-shirt covered in blood. He told the police Jeff loaded the guns himself because he didn't know how. With no witnesses, the coroner ruled that this was a case of accidental death.

Four years later, on 24 May, 1990, Richard, by now 17, called another friend, 17-year-old Christian Wiedepuhl, over to play Nintendo at his house in Anaheim Hills, California.

Incredibly, in the same room and at the same time of day – just after 4pm – more deadly gunplay took place. This time the police found Christian lying on the floor, dying from a single wound. A bullet had smashed one lens of his glasses and entered his head above his eyebrow.

Bourassa told the detectives that Christian had been searching through the house and had discovered a .38 Smith & Wesson revolver in the headboard of his stepfather's bed. He had then pointed the weapon at Richard's head.

'I told him to give me the gun,' said Bourassa. 'Then he told me it wasn't loaded. But I asked him again to give me the gun. He handed it to me and then looked down to get the holster. And that's when it went off. There was a loud explosion and my ears were ringing.'

He claimed Christian had loaded the gun, as he knew little about firearms. Asked why he'd had his finger on the trigger, he replied, 'I don't know – I have no idea.'

Bourassa's story of the shooting had a chillingly familiar ring to it, coming after the one he told four years earlier. It was left to the police to decide whether he was a coldblooded killer or just a victim of hideous bad luck. After an intense four-month investigation, they charged Bourassa with murder.

When Christian's parents learned that Richard had killed before, they were horrified. 'If I had known,' said his heartbroken father, Ricky Wiedepuhl, 'then I wouldn't have allowed my son to go to Richard's house.'

For four years Jeff Bush's father, Dale, had believed his son's death was a tragic accident. But when he heard of Christian's killing, he changed his mind.

'Richard is sick. How many deaths will it take to show he's a killer?' he said.

Forensic tests did show that the lack of gunpowder on Christian's face indicated the shot that killed him wasn't fired at close range. Also, the ballistics tests stated that 'no way could the trigger have fired without direct pressure'.

The prosecuting lawyer, Kathy Harper, claimed that Richard had found the gun, which his dad had left loaded, then used Christian as target practice in a grotesque game of Russian roulette in reverse. He took out one bullet (police found it on his bed), then fired at Christian to scare him. Richard had then expected the empty chamber would come up next. But he had miscalculated the direction in which the barrel would rotate. He fired the gun and killed Christian. This constituted murder under Californian law because of his wilful disregard for life. The prosecutor also claimed the murder was premeditated. 'The killing involved a high degree of planning,' he said.

The biggest flaw in Bourassa's story was that he'd said he had no knowledge of guns. He was, in fact, fascinated by them. He'd written a project on infantry weapons at school and he also collected spent 12-gauge shotgun shells.

'Richard liked to take the .38 out and point it at people to scare them,' said Kathy Harper. 'He liked to load it and pretend to shoot at people. Enemies, burglars – even friends.'

Three of Bourassa's friends also testified that he had pointed guns at them in the past, including the shotgun that blasted Jeff Bush. A close friend, Tony Cordova, revealed that Richard had twice brought out the deadly .38 while he was over at Bourassa's house, and he'd removed the bullets.

'Sometimes he pointed the gun at the wall,' said Tony. 'A few times he pointed it at my head. He'd say: "Do you trust me? Do you trust me? Then he'd go, 'Boom!"

'He was fooling around but I was very, very scared and it caused a rift in our friendship. I thought it was weird. I used to be over at his house every day after school – I still can't get over thinking that it could have been me he'd shot.'

Another school pal, Jesse Jobe, recalled a shock he got when he was first invited to Richard's house soon after the first killing. 'He was showing me all the bloodstains. I don't know if he was proud of them, but he didn't seem very bothered about blowing his best friend away.'

Richard's love of firearms was picked up from his stepfather, Thomas Baldwin, a 51-year-old pilot. Baldwin was so attached to his shotgun and rifle that he still kept them even after Jeff's death – claiming he needed them, for his own protection'.

Christian's father, Ricky, blamed Baldwin and Richard's mother, Nancy, for the killing as much as he blamed the boy himself. 'It was negligence,' said Ricky. 'A cheap gun lock would have prevented a killing. They'd already had one death and that should have been enough for them to have learnt a lesson. They shouldn't have kept those guns, but at least they could've kept them locked up.

'My son was so full of life. I'm still trying to come to terms with his death. Nothing can bring him back, and I don't want revenge, but I hope this makes people more responsible with their weapons, especially if they have kids of their own.'

The investigation into Bourassa's past uncovered a troubled, trigger-happy child obsessed with death, guns, wrestling and the army. Diagnosed as dyslexic – word-blind – at the age of seven, he was a year behind at school and was often in trouble. When he was only nine, Richard's father, 39, died of a heart attack. The young boy was heartbroken as he'd idolised his dad, who helped design the military Apache helicopter.

Richard's greatest ambition was to join the army like his sister and brother-in-law. He said he wanted to become a soldier, so as to 'get paid to shoot people'.

Richard, just 13 when he first killed, had grown up into a 5ft 10in, 14-stone hulk by the second shooting. He jogged regularly and also pumped iron daily to train for his favourite sport, wrestling, at which he excelled. In his room he had trophies and photos of himself in the school team.

In sharp contrast Christian was six feet tall but weighed just eight stone and was considered a wimp by his classmates at Canyon High School. But they backed off teasing him when Bourassa became his friend and personal bodyguard. Ironically, after giving him the protection he needed, it was Richard who went on to kill his schoolmate.

Bourassa's lawyer, Edward Hall, claimed it was all a horrific coincidence, but added, 'A lot of people feel he must never have access to guns again.'

The day before the trial was due to start, Richard shocked his lawyer by pleading guilty to second-degree murder. He admitted 'knowingly' pointing the gun at Christian.

Hall was 'flabbergasted'. He had expected his client to serve a short sentence for manslaughter. But this surprise murder plea suddenly opened the way to a much heavier penalty – 15 years to life.

32

The Tragic Tale of Derrick Jones and Amy Smith

TEENAGERS DERRICK JONEs and Amy Smith were like a modern-day Romeo and Juliet. Because he was black and she was white, their undying love for each other faced an uphill struggle from the start. Both sets of parents were dead set against the romance. Her father Dennis – a policeman for 20 years – did not want to meet her boyfriend and refused to have him in the house. But Amy, 16, and Derrick, 17, continued to secretly see each other. And, just like Shakespeare's teens, their relationship ended in heartbreaking tragedy.

Her father shot Derrick dead after finding him inside his home in the middle of the night. Derrick's family claimed their son had been gunned down in anger when Smith caught his daughter with a black man.

But Dennis Smith was never charged with murder. Instead there was an incredible twist in the case that stunned conservative politicians in nearby Washington, DC.

The tragic tale began at 3am on 3 July, 1991, when Smith and his wife Mariaelena say they woke up to find an intruder in their bedroom. The six-foot burglar, wearing rubber gloves and a ski mask, stood over the bed in the dark holding a gun, handcuffs and a kitchen knife. He gave the handcuffs to Dennis, 46, and ordered him to put them on. After Smith handcuffed one of his wrists, the intruder clamped the other cuff to the bedpost.

Then the gunman walked around the bed towards a naked Mariaelena, waved the gun at her husband and shouted: 'I have no problem killing a cop!' After telling her to lie on the bed and stay put, he left the room to grab silverware and $357 in cash. He came back three times to check the Smiths had not moved.

At one point he found the keys to Mariaelena's car and said to her: 'I got your car – what are you going to do now?'

Mrs Smith told police: 'I told him I didn't care. It was like I wasn't afraid of him any more. I knew I was going to die. I didn't care.'

She was more concerned for her stepdaughter's safety in the next room. 'I was scared he was going to hurt her.' Her fears were ironic in the light of what would happen later. After he'd finished looting the house, the gunman handed the knife to Mariaelena and ordered her to stab her husband to death.

She recalled: 'At this point I asked God to forgive my sins and to receive me now.' When he again told her to stab Dennis, she said: 'No way.'

It was at this point that Smith – who had loosely handcuffed his wrist – broke free from his cuffs and charged the intruder.

Smith wrestled with him in the bedroom and down the hallway while screaming at his wife – who still had the knife – to 'stab him, stab him'. But she was unable to bring herself to do it.

The cop and the burglar ended up struggling in the bathroom, where Smith pushed him in the tub. As he fell backwards, the thief dropped the weapon. While Mrs Smith was picking up the gun and handing it to her husband, the burglar sprang up and ran downstairs to the front door.

Instead of running out, he ran back up the stairs and charged towards Smith. The officer shot him once in the chest and once in the head. Smith pulled off the mask. The man was black and Smith had never seen him before.

Meanwhile, a terrified Amy had heard the struggle and called the police. The operator said to her: 'What's the problem, ma'am?'

Amy replied: 'We have a prowler in the house and he's trying to kill my parents.'

The operator said: 'Does he have a gun?'

She said: 'No, I mean yes.'

Then there was a popping noise in the background. 'What was that?' asked the operator.

Amy: 'That was my dad's gun.'

After she hung up, she ran out to see if her parents were alive. When she saw the intruder lying on the floor, covered in blood, she broke down and wept.

Her father comforted his hysterical daughter until the police arrived at their four-bedroom house in Prince George's County, Maryland, a middle-class suburb of Washington. What looked at first like a simple robbery to the cops turned into a shocking case of attempted murder most foul.

Detectives found a front door key in the burglar's pockets, and in a shopping bag left by the front door they found a sketch of the inside of the house.

The map showed where Smith kept his handcuffs and 9mm semi-automatic service pistol, which the burglar had been using. And it showed the kitchen where he got the knife.

It was not long before police learned the intruder's identity – Derrick Jones, who had been going out with Amy for just three months. And police soon found that it was Amy's handwriting on the map. Police also uncovered several hand-written notes between the lovers in which Amy told Derrick to shoot her in the shoulder before leaving the house.

Police arrested Amy, a student at Friendly High School, and charged her as an adult with attempted murder and conspiracy to commit murder. They said she was supposed to survive a robbery during which her parents were to be killed.

Her father said that when he and his wife were told Amy had been arrested for trying to kill them, 'We almost fell right out of our chairs. We were stunned. It was unbelievable, unreal.'

The Smiths refused to pay £25,000 to bail her out of jail because they were afraid that she might try to kill them again if she lived in their home. Brunette Amy, a heavy-set girl whose mother died in a car crash when she was a baby, spent a month in a psychiatric centre before her father picked her up to return her to jail.

'You don't know what it's like, bringing your daughter to a place where you've been bringing prisoners for 20 years,' said Smith. 'It's the hardest thing I've ever done in my life.'

But Derrick's family and friends – who live in the middle-class town of Fort Washington – believed the shooting was not self-defence but motivated by Smith's hatred of blacks. Elbert Jones, Derrick's dad, said: 'The wrong person is on trial. It should be Amy's father. My son has never, never in his whole life had any contact with the police. Never in any trouble. Never.'

Jones, who worked on the Washington subway system, added that Derrick went to Amy's home that night just to make love with her. 'Him being a young man and her being a young woman. It was a sexual thing.'

Derrick's friend Antoine Base said: 'I think Smith shot Derrick because he didn't want a black man to be with his daughter.'

Another friend, Greg Drew, added: 'The father probably came in and saw Amy with a black guy and didn't like it so he probably shot him.'

Amy, who opted for a non-jury trial in front of Judge Hovey Johnson, did not testify but claimed through her lawyer that there was no plot to rob and kill her parents.

Her attorney Elvira White alleged that her father had shot Jones in a rage after catching him in the house with his daughter. White suggested that Smith shot Jones in the head as he lay motionless on the floor and then invented the robbery story to justify the shooting.

But the prosecutor Beverly Woodard said: 'This is a crime that no parent wants to believe could happen. But the evidence shows it did.'

Greg Drew, who was also a friend of Amy's, testified that she had once remarked to him that she wanted her father dead. She also told Drew that her dad was 'too strict' and 'wouldn't let her do a lot of things'. Smith especially didn't like her dating black youths.

And teenager Tony Harding told the court that Amy had tried to buy a gun a month before the shooting 'so she could kill her parents'. He thought she was joking at first but eventually realised she was serious.

Mariaelena's dramatic testimony of the shooting convinced the judge that there was a robbery-murder plan.

But Derrick's dad Elbert said: 'Mrs Smith gave a stellar performance. She must have been directed by Steven Spielberg or somebody.'

Nevertheless, it was Amy's own words that were the most damaging to her. When she called the police at the time of the shooting, she was asked: 'Does he [the intruder] have a gun?'

Although she was in her bedroom, she replied: 'No, I mean yes.' She knew that Jones had her father's gun and that he was probably using it at that moment to kill her parents.

When the operator heard the gunshot, he asked: 'What was that?' Amy replied: 'That was my dad's gun.' How would she know it was her dad's gun – unless she had plotted to kill him?

After a two-day trial, Judge Johnson said there was 'no doubt' in his mind that Amy enlisted Jones to kill her parents and make it look like a robbery. He said Jones took a subway train and a bus to Amy's house and climbed in through a window that she had left open. After robbing the house, he was supposed to kill her parents and then escape in her stepmother's car, following Amy's directions to a nearby highway.

Johnson said: 'For two teenagers to go to this length boggles the mind.' After he gave his guilty verdict, one of Derrick's uncles screamed at Dennis Smith: 'You're a murderer, you're a murderer, and you let your daughter take the fall.'

Amy was sentenced to 15 years for planning to kill her father. But Smith stated: 'We love our daughter and we have forgiven her. She's still just a child inside. When she is ready to see me, I plan to visit her in jail and be there for her when she goes free.'

Derrick's family, however, is not convinced justice has been done, and they have hired a private eye to conduct their own investigation.

33

Programmed to Kill

THE OFFICE NEEDED a clearout. The man who used to work there had left in disgrace and would not be coming back. As US Marine sergeant William Kane set about the job, he noticed a computer disk on the desk.

In case it contained important information, he popped the disk into a computer and called up the list of files it contained. One was entitled Murder. Intrigued, Sgt Kane opened the file on screen. And was startled by what he read.

'How do I kill her? ... What to do with the body? Make it look as if she left ... Check in library on ways of murder ...'

Last on this disturbing check-list: 'Blame it on her own kind.'

The man who had written that list was former Marine captain Robert Russell, aged 34. His office at Gulfport, Mississippi, was being cleared because he had been thrown out of the service for theft and drunkenness.

The Murder file could have been just some bizarre computer game. But Sgt Kane was worried. He recalled Russell once asking: 'If you drop a hairdryer or TV into a bathtub, can it really kill somebody?'

When Russell was dishonourably discharged, in 1988, he had been married for just a few months to a fellow captain, 29-year-old Shirley. It was an unlikely match. Twice-married Russell was white and a loudmouthed racist. His bride was black. Which gave a special meaning to that last line on the Murder file: 'Blame it on her own kind.'

The balding Russell himself was ready enough to blame his wife's colour for his lack of promotion. He once remarked to a colleague, 'I wonder what they'll think when they find out who I'm married to.'

Sgt Kane was alarmed enough to report the murder disk to his commander – and to call Shirley at her new married officers' quarters in Quantico, Virginia, to warn her, 'Be very careful.'

But the Murder file was dismissed as some kind of computer game. And Shirley, still the new young wife, shrugged off the warning. Her disgraced husband – sharing her Marine quarters now as the civilian spouse of a serving officer – got a teaching job at North Stafford High School, in Alexandria, just on the outskirts of Washington, DC. Almost straightaway, Russell began a steamy love affair with a curvy colleague, brunette Sandy Flynt. They often used to sneak back to Russell's married quarters for lunchtime sex – on 15 occasions, Sandy later admitted. Once, wife Shirley came home unexpectedly while Sandy was dozing on the couch. The teacher escaped unseen. That night, on the phone, she and Russell joked about it.

'Close, eh?' Russell said. Sandy replied, 'You're not kidding. Oh Lord, I'll know now not to fall asleep on your couch again.'

'No sweat,' her lover assured her.

But he was forgetting that he had bugged his own phone with a tape-recorder because, in spite of all the womanising and race-hate talk, he was desperately possessive of his wife. That exchange with Sandy was duly taped. Later on, Shirley found it.

A year after the move to Quantico, Russell began threatening to kill her. That, on top of his womanising and bigotry, was the end for Shirley. She moved in with a relative. On 4 March, 1989, she returned to clean out the place, before the next couple moved in. She was never seen again.

Russell raised the alarm. He told police and Naval Investigative

Service officers that Shirley went to buy paint at a store five miles away, and had not returned. He assumed, he said, she had deserted the Marines.

For months, the navy and FBI searched for clues, sure that Shirley had been murdered. Her husband had bought a .25 calibre gun two days before she vanished. Russell claimed he had given it to her, for her own protection.

Investigators also discovered his wife-murder threats, made to several people. He had paid a surprise visit to his parents in neighbouring Pennsylvania – a chance to agree on an alibi. And he had cleaned a store room at home with an acid known for its power to erase bloodstains.

Shirley's body was never found. But law officers decided they had enough evidence for a murder charge without it.

In court at Alexandria, the jury heard how, apart from bugging his own phone, Russell had hidden a tape-recorder under his wife's car seat – and after she walked out, even raided her relative's house and put another recorder under her bed.

Lover Sandy Flynt told of the time Russell said, 'I'm going to kill her. They'll never be able to prove it. I'll blow her up and make it look like a terrorist act. Or I'll poison her.'

Sandy testified, 'He seemed serious. I just hoped he was joking.' But, she added, she got a big shock when Russell showed her a six-inch metal tube and asked, 'Have you ever seen a home-made silencer?'

Russell's lover also told how she had spent some lunch dates just helping him to follow his wife. Once, she, said, while Shirley was jogging, he jumped out of his car and chased her.

The accused man's brother, Ronald, a miner, told the jury that Robert once asked him to get some dynamite, to 'blow up Shirley'.

Russell's first wife, Pamela, gave weight to a theory that the body might have been cut up and dumped in rubbish bags down abandoned mineshafts. 'He knew that area like the back of his hand,' she said.

Shirley's mother, Annie Sumpter, said her daughter wanted to cut Russell out of a $30,000 life insurance policy, because of his many threats.

Marine lieutenant Tommy Maris dismissed the claim that Shirley had deserted. 'She was a super officer,' he said. 'Shirley had a high degree of integrity, courage and reliability.'

Defence lawyer Fred Fanelli insisted that Shirley was alive. He produced four people to say they had seen her after the alleged murder. As for the computer-disk file that the prosecution called a 'Recipe for Murder', the defence claimed it was all to do with writing a novel.

Robert's loyal mum, Patricia Russell, told the jury that she and her son had been writing a book about the death of a US Marine officer's wife. 'We never determined whether she was going to be killed by a gang, or by accident,' she said. 'I was helping with the feminine aspect of a character – where a woman would hide the jewellery, that sort of thing.'

So where was the manuscript of this alleged novel? 'I threw it away,' Patricia explained.

The prosecutor, Lawrence Leiser, claimed that Patricia and her husband – another Robert – had lied in evidence to protect their son.

An ex-girlfriend, Doreen Evans, swore Russell had borrowed books to help write a novel. But the prosecutor suggested she was still in love with him. Leiser went through the computer's Murder list of things to do, such as '10: Write a nice letter', a reference to a note that Russell actually left saying, 'Shirley, where's the paint? I love you.'

Then there was '17: Vacuum floor and tidy up a bit.' Russell had done that too. He had also washed his car the day after the alleged murder.

It took the jury 16 hours to decide that Russell was a killer; he was given a life sentence.

34

The Mastermind Murderer

GEORGE TREPAL IS a computer wizard with a genius IQ, a member of Mensa, which puts him among America's top intellectuals – but George also has an extremely poisoned mind.

So much so that the man who loved scripting murder mystery weekends plotted a warped attack on his neighbours that left one woman dead, two teenage boys partially paralysed and four others horribly sick.

And all because the bright boffin, an avid Agatha Christie fan, has a lethal fascination with poison.

George and his wife Diana often organised murder mystery weekends for fellow members of the high-IQ Mensa society, in which the players were given a script and acted out the plot. The victims met several sticky ends – shootings, drownings, beatings and strangulations – but at least half were from poisoning, George's favourite murder most foul.

Says Ernest Prince, who took part in the crime puzzles, 'If someone was going to be poisoned, George would find out what symptoms they'd get and how much it may be investigated. He was always very thorough.'

But his quest for perfection didn't cross over into real life, for when George put his poisoned murder plan into action for real, he made some very simple mistakes that meant his crime didn't remain a mystery for long.

In October 1988 in Bartow, Florida, the seemingly mild-mannered Trepal, 42, struck down his next door neighbours with poisoned bottles of Coca-Cola. Peggy Carr, 41, died a slow and painful death five months after the attack. Her son Duane, 19, and stepson Travis, 18, were left partially paralysed. Her husband Parealyn and three others, including a two-year-old girl, luckily only suffered sickness, from which they fully recovered.

An eight-pack of 16oz Coke bottles found in their kitchen had been laced with thallium nitrate, a rare colourless, odourless poison outlawed since 1965. Just one gram of it is enough to kill a full-grown man.

The FBI was called in, but tampering at the plant was soon ruled out. Then attention turned to Trepal and his wife Diana — because they were the only possible people with a motive to harm the Carrs.

Even so, at first George Trepal was not a suspect. He was interviewed only in order to eliminate him from the enquiry. Then several clues began to point to him as the killer.

For the six years that they were neighbours, the Trepals had numerous run-ins with the Carrs. George complained they played their radio too loud and drove their jeeps over his property.

The last argument occurred on October 17, 1988 — when Diana and Peggy rowed over the Carrs' loud music blaring out. Two days later, Peggy Carr began suffering nausea and aching joints. Within a fortnight, Peggy and her sons were in hospital.

Peggy was racked with pain, her hair fell out and she clung feebly to life for only another four months. Within two months she had slipped into a coma from which she never recovered. On March 3, 1989, her family took the tragic decision to switch off the life-support system.

Three months earlier, the Carrs had received a chilling typewritten message that read: 'You and all your so-called family have two weeks to move out of Florida for ever or else you die. This is no joke.'

When police asked George who could want his neighbours dead, he calmly replied, 'Someone probably wanted them to move out.' A cool response that had chilling overtones after the threatening note. Then, when the police began to look into George's past, they uncovered a stunning and hideous history.

The chemistry buff had a history of trying to poison pets and had even tried to secretly drug his flatmates at college, 20 years before. To keep them from eating his food, he smeared his doorknob and the fridge door with a hallucinatory drug. He once injected drugs, possibly amphetamines, into biscuits during a trip and handed them to unsuspecting people.

He also tried to poison his wife's dog by feeding it Valium and, whenever they rowed, he frequently threatened to poison her pet cats.

Then it was discovered that George had served two and a half years in jail in 1975 for helping to run a $4 million illegal metharnphetamine (commonly known as crack) manufacturing operation. The elaborate process uses the very dangerous poison thalliurn nitrate. The evidence was still circumstantial, however, so undercover cop Susan Goreck, 35, was put on the case. She joined in one of George and Diana's Mensa murder weekends and befriended the couple. It soon became apparent that George was the type of person who would commit that type of poisoning murder.

'A person who might do something like this can't deal with situations directly,' says Bill Hagmaier, an agent at the FBI Behavioural Science Unit in Virginia (the unit featured in the hit movie thriller *The Silence Of The Lambs*). 'They deal with conflicts in a cowardly way.'

Susan Goreck found George to be a charming man, interesting to be with and very amusing. But she had to be careful. 'If we went out to dinner and I had to leave to go to the bathroom, I wouldn't eat anything I'd left at the table. I had to be very aware of it at all times.'

In December 1989, George and Diana moved to Seabring, Florida, so that Diana, an orthopaedic surgeon, could open a new practice. They were delighted to rent their old house to their new friend. It was then that their house was thoroughly searched. Not only did police uncover a phial containing thallium nitrate, but also a copy of Agatha Christie's *The Pale Horse* – a tale about a pharmacist who kills by putting thallium nitrate into food and medicine.

Those who knew George were amazed at the findings. Whodunit pal Ernest Prince says, 'I find it so unbelievable. He was a great guy. He seemed so nice and friendly.'

At his trial, Trepal pleaded innocent to the charges and even tried to accuse his wife of the grisly deed. But district attorney John Aguero told the jury: 'This is the most diabolical man you will ever see before you in your life. What we have here is a man who thought he was so smart that he could commit the perfect crime. But he was not so smart. '

In just six hours, the jury brought back a guilty verdict and, as Carr family members watched in the courtroom, the judge sentenced George Trepal to die in 'old sparky' – the electric chair.

Peggy's sister says she wants to be the one to turn on the electric current personally. 'I believe in an eye for an eye, a tooth for a tooth,' she says.

But Susan Goreck thinks Trepal killed not so much from hatred or rage but for sheer intellectual pleasure. 'I think it was a game to him,' she says of the man she found both extremely charming and pleasant to be with. 'He really thought he had committed the perfect crime.'

35

Daddy's Girl

TWO-TIMING COMPUTER tycoon David Brown thought he'd found the perfect way to murder his wife – and he very nearly got away with it. He brainwashed his 14-year-old daughter Cinnamon into killing her stepmum Linda, so he could marry his secret mistress – his wife's teenage sister, Patti Bailey, who was also a conspirator in the murder.

Brown, a $100,000-a-year computer boss, had bombarded both girls with his evil thoughts to get rid of his 23-year-old wife Linda, mother of his seven-month-old daughter. The evil schemer persuaded them to kill for him by constantly telling them, 'If you love me, you'll do it for me.' Brown, who loved Agatha Christie thrillers, told them he could not do the dirty deed himself because he was a sickly person who 'did not have the stomach' to kill his wife of three years.

He convinced them that Linda and her twin brother Alan had ties to the Mob and were planning to kill him and take over his growing computer business. His reasoning was so effective that Patti had even gone to her sister's bedroom one night and aimed a gun at her. But when it came to it, Patti couldn't pull the trigger. 'I couldn't do it,' she said. 'She was my sister, I loved her.'

So it was left to Cinnamon to do the dirty deed. The gruesome murder took place in the early hours of 19 March 1985, in a quiet house on a suburban street in Los Angeles. After weeks of secret plans, Brown woke Cinnamon and her stepmum's young sister Patti to say, 'Girls, it has to be done tonight.' Cinnamon took a .38 Smith & Wesson, given to her by Brown, wrapped a towel round it and crept into Linda's bedroom. To muffle the sound of gunfire even further, she stuck it in a pillow and then shot her stepmother as she lay sleeping.

But the shot made the baby cry, and then Linda gave an awful gasp. Cinnamon screamed, 'She's not dead!' and ran back in the room and pumped another shot into her.

The second silver-tipped bullet in the chest was enough to kill her. Cinnamon quickly scribbled the suicide note which Brown had made her practise countless times before. 'Dear God, please forgive me,' it said. 'I didn't mean to hurt her. '

It was meant to look like a murder, followed by attempted suicide. Cinnamon would swallow a 'safe' dose of pills – she firmly believed she wouldn't die from taking the tablets her loving dad had given her. But it was only due to good luck that she didn't – her father deliberately gave her a lethal dose.

Conveniently, Brown had gone out just before the shooting to give himself the perfect alibi. He went to a nearby store and bought groceries.

When the police arrived at his house hours later, he told them he went out in the middle of the night because his wife and daughter were having a flaming row. He appeared to be a genuinely grief-stricken husband – shaking and crying, but he was also too 'scared' to see his wife's body.

Meanwhile, police found Cinnamon in the backyard lying in her own vomit – lucky to be alive.

She was rushed to hospital, where she fully recovered, but she refused to believe that her father had planned to murder her as well. 'I was willing to kill Linda because I loved Dad,' she says. 'I didn't want to lose him. I trusted him. Why would he tell me to do something that wasn't right?'

Young Cinnamon – who had been assured by her dad that she

wouldn't go to jail – was devastated when she was found guilty and sentenced to life in prison, with possible parole at the age of 25. But for nearly four years she never once implicated her father in the shocking crime. And yet while she rotted in a juvenile jail, Dad began to live it up with the money he got from insurance policies taken out against his wife's death – two of them drawn up weeks before she was killed, making a total of $500,000.

Then he quietly married his secret mistress Patti, and within a year they had a daughter, Heather.

But not even his new wife was safe. After Brown was finally arrested as the murder mastermind, the father of three also plotted to have Patti killed, along with two American district attorneys, Jay Newell and Jeoffrey Robinson. It was Newell who was sure that Cinnamon had not acted alone and visited her in jail, hoping she'd give him the full story. Finally, after five years, she did.

The turning point came when Newell informed her that Brown and Patti had become parents and had been on a wild spending spree. Cinnamon, now 20, was outraged. Feeling badly betrayed, she finally decided to tell shocked detectives the true twisted and terrifying tale.

'I was mad and angry because David and Patti didn't tell me of the affair,' Cinnamon wept on the witness stand. 'And I felt so hurt because they just left me and it seemed like I was not important to them any more. They killed Linda just as much as me.'

She revealed that, months before the killing, the three of them had plotted several murder methods – including pushing Linda from out of a moving van, running her over and hitting her over the head.

'My father told me that I was too young to get into trouble and they'd simply send me to a psychiatrist and then send me home. He made us feel guilty to get us to co-operate,' Cinnamon explained when forced to accept the truth – the man she worshipped had used her.

After Cinnamon confessed to the police, Patti also decided to come clean. She, too, gave evidence against Brown, who was branded a 'diabolical manipulator' and a 'paranoid liar' by prosecutors.

One of 11 children, Patti grew up in poverty with an alcoholic mother and an older brother who molested her as a small child. Single-handed, her mum Elaine was struggling to bring up her family on welfare payments when con man Brown came into her life. Then in his 20s, the son of a mechanic, he told her that he was dying of cancer and had six months to live. He asked Elaine whether any of her daughters could help clean his house.

And before very long Brown, who had already been married a couple of times, began dating Pam Bailey – Linda and Patti's sister. He soon dumped her for leggy Linda. After getting her mother's signature on a wedding form, they married in Las Vegas when Linda was 17.

Her brother Alan remembers: 'David was always a guy who liked being with young girls. That and money were what he was after.'

Brown went to a trade school to study computers and picked it up so well that he soon opened his own firm, helping to retrieve lost data. He began to rake in a fortune.

Linda started working for him and soon knew the business as well as he did. Soon the pressure of living and working together took its toll and they divorced, but then got back together again and remarried.

During this time, Brown's young daughter Cinnamon, from a previous marriage, had been living with her mother but then moved in with her father and Linda. Shortly afterwards Patti Bailey, who was 11, moved in as well.

'I felt like I finally had a family,' explained Patti, now 22. 'I always felt like I was the black sheep at home but David treated me special. He'd go out and buy me clothes and make me feel good about myself.

'David was everything to me. He was my family. If I thought he was going to be taken away that would be like pulling the plug.'

She told the packed courtroom that she 'wanted to keep David to myself'. And she was so completely under his spell that it was not hard for her to believe that her sister planned to steal his business.

Admitting that she had helped to kill in order to 'protect David', she was sentenced to three years in a reform school.

When Brown was finally arrested in 1988, he wrote dozens of letters to both Patti and Cinnamon begging them not to testify against him, saying that he'd kill himself if he was convicted. He told his daughter: 'I can't survive in jail. Don't tell them the whole truth. I would kill myself before I let myself die a slow and painful death in a cell.'

And to Patti he wrote: 'You should know that neither one of us has bad things to say about the other – only good. We can have our trial together if you want.'

When his pleas didn't work, he even planned to have Patti assassinated in jail. When he was behind bars he got friendly with burly convict Richard Steinhart and hired him to get rid of Patti, as well as the two district attorneys Newell and Robinson. But another inmate overheard them plotting and he went to the authorities with the gruesome tale.

Steinhart was then persuaded to wear a hidden tape recorder, and hours of conversation between him and Brown were recorded. The police also recorded Brown's chat with a policewoman posing as an inmate from Patti's prison. His plan was to pay the 'prisoner' to come forward after Patti's death to say that Patti had admitted to her that she'd made up the story against him. 'I'll take care of you,' he promised the undercover officer. 'I do take care of people – that's how I get ahead.'

At his arrest Brown claimed that the murder plot was 'all just a joke'. He said, 'It was meant to be a game. I was shocked Linda was killed.'

But the tapes were enough to convince the jury that Brown was the brains behind the murder. They took just seven hours to find him guilty. While Cinnamon is set to be freed in a deal worked out with prosecutors, Brown, faces the death penalty or jail for life.

Linda's brother Alan hopes Brown 'rots in jail for the rest of his life'. But the victim's 59-year-old mother, Elaine, wants a more severe sentence than that.

'He took my daughter's life. I want him to hang,' she says.

36

Cindy's Candlelit Dinner Was Never Meant To Be

CHRISTMAS IS A time for living and giving, and for pretty blonde newly-wed Cindy Apelt, that was exactly what she planned to do. She carefully wrapped her thoughtfully chosen presents for her husband in red ribbons and bows, and laid them out under their huge, lavishly decorated tree.

Cindy, 30, was eagerly anticipating the very romantic candlelit Christmas dinner at an exclusive restaurant that she'd planned with hunky husband Michael, the dashing young German millionaire she had married after their whirlwind three-week courtship. They had been married for 56 blissful days, and now, thought Cindy, they would share a truly memorable Christmas together.

But on Christmas Eve, Cindy's horrifically mutilated body was found 200 yards from the road in the Arizona desert. She had been brutally murdered – stabbed five times, her throat savagely slashed from ear to ear, and her lovely face gruesomely stamped on by her vicious killer in an attempt to make her body unrecognisable.

Festivities were over for Cindy, her horrified family, and for her distraught husband Michael, who was inconsolable when told the tragic news.

Back at her elegant flat, police began the task of piecing together the seemingly meaningless killing. They found several expensive presents for Cindy's smooth-talking husband, but strangely there was not one — not even a stocking filler — from him to her. It was the first of several clues that finally led police in the dusty town of Mesa, Arizona, to suspect the blond 6ft 7in hulk and his equally striking brother Rudi of the callous killing.

And the most incriminating evidence against Michael, 26, was the fact that Cindy, at his insistence, had taken out a life insurance policy for a staggering $400,000. It cost her $305 a month, an amount she could ill afford on her meagre $10,000-a-year earnings, which is all her work as a nutritionist and part-time waitress brought in. But why would Michael or Rudi, 30, need the money? After all, they had boasted they were worth millions. But an investigation by Interpol showed they had extensive criminal backgrounds and had also both served prison sentences.

The Apelt brothers came to San Diego in August 1988, with Rudi's wife Suzanne and also Anke Dorn, a glam 27-year-old hairdresser who'd been a lover of them both. They toured California and Mexico before arriving in Arizona, where they convinced everyone they were stinking rich.

Sultry Cindy Monkman was swept off her feet by Michael when she met the pair at the hottest nightclub in Mesa. Dripping with gold jewellery, they bragged about their wealth, saying they were international bankers. Cindy's sister, Kathy, recalls: 'Michael was a Casanova. He was playing the right game and saying all the right things. He was putting his hands all over Cindy, telling her, "You're the woman of my dreams." '

Cindy's friend Annette Clay fell head over heels for Rudi, which meant they were soon going out on foursomes together. But Annette became suspicious of smoothie Rudi's line of patter and talked Cindy into following them home one night. The brothers claimed they were staying at a ritzy hotel, but the girls trailed them to a cheap motel, and when Annette knocked on the door, Anke Dorn answered. A fight erupted, with the girls demanding to know just who the mystery woman was and why the two brothers had lied.

Brunette Annette carried on: 'The next day Rudi started screaming at me, calling us stupid and saying that he and his brother had lost their well-paid jobs because their security cover was blown. We were absolutely convinced by them. We even felt responsible.' They even believed the brothers' line that they were financially supporting Anke while her husband was in a nearby hospital. So, as besotted as ever, and just 20 days after they met, Cindy married Michael in Las Vegas.

At 2am on Christmas Eve, Michael called the cops to report that his wife had got a mysterious phone call earlier that evening and had rushed out, saying only she could handle it. Cindy allegedly told her husband she'd meet him for a romantic dinner later, but hadn't been seen since.

Two weeks after Cindy's body was found, the Apelts, along with Anke, were hauled in for questioning. Under an intense grilling, Anke broke down and admitted Michael had murdered Cindy for the insurance money, while Rudi stood guard.

A bloodstained pillowcase and a receipt from a knife shop were both found in Michael's flat. And although he claimed he was at home when she disappeared, a camera situated at an automatic bank machine recorded his picture at the time.

After a 17-month investigation, it took a jury seven hours to convict him of first-degree murder. Saying that 'This was a cold-blooded murder,' Judge Robert Dean then sentenced Michael to die in the gas chamber. His brother was found guilty at a second trial and is still awaiting sentence. Now Germany, which is firmly opposed to the death penalty, wants the Apelts extradited to serve their sentence in Germany.

But for Cindy's grief-stricken family, there is no escape from the horror of her murder. 'Nothing can make anything right,' sobbed her sister Kathy. 'Christmas won't ever be the same without Cindy.'

37

A Deadly Obsession

THE KILLER SPRANG out of the shadows as dishy mum Dianne Hood was leaving a meeting for victims of a deadly rare disease. Wearing a ski mask, gloves and heavy army fatigues, the gunman attempted to wrestle Dianne's purse from her and then shot her in the chest at point-blank range. As her friends watched in horror, Dianne tried to run for safety while screaming for help. But the bandit chased her down the street and fired two more shots into her back. While the mother of three lay on the ground bleeding to death, the cruel killer grabbed her purse and fled into the night.

A few hundred yards away, the pint-sized gunman frantically pulled off the camouflaged clothes and threw them into a park rubbish bin. And then, as the murderer ripped off the black ski mask, her beautiful blonde hair suddenly cascaded down her back. Her gloves came off next, revealing her slender, long fingers and beautifully polished nails. Breathing heavily, her ample bosom pounded against her tight sweater as she made a quick phone call, then jumped into her car and drove home to tuck her kids into bed.

The cold-blooded murder led to a state of panic in the small town of Colorado Springs, with fears that a thrill-killing madman was on the loose. Terrified women refused to go out, believing he'd soon strike again, while police were flooded with calls from people reporting suspicious noises or strangers wearing fatigues. But within days, the shocking truth came out and families were able to feel safe once again. Tension eased when it was revealed that the killer was a stunning beauty posing as a man to throw police off the scent of a deadly love triangle.

Dianne's 'heartbroken' husband Brian told newsmen the day after the killing: 'She was a Christian, and she's at home in heaven now. And she is rejoicing with the Lord.' However, in many people's eyes, she's more likely to be turning in her grave.

The chilling case quickly began to unravel when police got a telephone tip that hunky Brian was having an affair with sexy flower-girl Jennifer Reali. She soon confessed to the gruesome murder but pinned the blame on Brian, saying he brainwashed her into doing it. Hood invoked the Fatal Attraction defence, claiming she acted entirely on her own. He hoped to convince a jury that she was totally obsessed with him and had convinced herself that his wife was the only thing stopping them from being together for ever. Police, however, argued that while she may have done it for love, he did it for the £50,000 insurance policy.

Incredibly, although a mountain of evidence pointed to him plotting the whole thing, his wife's family believed he was the victim of Jenny's deadly obsession. Dianne's brother David Moore said: 'I think Brian is innocent. I think everyone in my family thinks he's innocent, and the truth will come out. We're 100 per cent behind him. The cops have based their prosecution on the testimony of a woman whose mental competency hasn't been established. There's some serious doubts.'

Brian and Dianne were considered by their closest friends at one time to have a dream life – a perfect marriage, three wonderful children and a comfortable house with a spectacular view of the Colorado mountains. The couple met during a chemistry class at the Angelo State University in Texas, and found that they had a perfect chemistry of their own. 'It was love at first sight,' he said.

The 6ft 2in well-built athlete was the typical all-American boy. He was a star football player on his university team, while she was the beautiful blonde cheerleader type. After they graduated, they married on 12 December 1980, and moved to Colorado, where he got a job as an insurance agent. While he went to work she was happy to play the dutiful wife and homemaker to their three kids – Jarrod, nine, Leslie, seven, and Joshua, two. But things began going downhill when she became a born-again Christian. He seemed to follow her spiritual lead and took the family to the Fellowship Bible Church every Sunday. But, on the side, he secretly started performing ungodly acts with dishy Jeannie Deboe.

Admitting she still felt 'awfully close' to Brian, Jeannie said: 'He wasn't in love with his wife, but he didn't want to get a divorce because he might lose his children, since it was against his wife's beliefs as a Christian.' She told a court hearing that he once suggested to her that she should kill Dianne by running her car off the road. But at the time Jeannie didn't think he was serious.

Brian's marriage took another turn for the worse when his 32-year-old wife came down with a sudden mystery illness. She was finally diagnosed as having the sometimes deadly disease called lupus, which weakens internal organs, usually the kidneys, heart and central nervous system. Some patients lead normal lives, but it can cause immense pain of the joints and extreme fatigue. To help get through the suffering, she joined a local women's lupus support group and prayed regularly at home, using a prayer book she kept at her bedside. Outwardly, her husband acted like the devoted husband and father, helping out around the house and looking after the kids. But inwardly he wanted out of the marriage and started having another affair.

To escape from his ailing wife, fitness fanatic Brian regularly went to a local gym, the US Swim and Fitness Club. It was not long before the smooth-talking salesman was pumping iron alongside shapely Jenny Reali, who worked at a nearby florist's shop. They were soon working out regularly together … in bed. Right after they became lovers, Brian approached a friend, Michael Maher, about murdering his wife.

Maher said: 'He told me that he couldn't kill her, and she couldn't kill herself because he wouldn't get the insurance that way. He said he needed to find a third person to act as a trigger. I didn't think he meant it, but I got real nervous and told him that wasn't the road he should be taking, and that he needed some help. Then I left the room.' Maher added that Hood gave him the impression that it would be a mercy killing, because his wife was dying a slow and painful death. But when Maher saw her a week later she showed no signs of the illness.

In August last year, Hood bought a .45 semi-automatic pistol 'for protection', from gun dealer Dallas Salladay. He paid for it with gold and silver coins given to him by Jeannie Deboe, whom he was still seeing on the side while supposed to be madly in love with Jenny Reali. Salladay told a court hearing that Hood asked if he had any ski masks. 'I said no, and he asked if we had any Halloween masks. I said, "What are you going to do, rob a bank?" We laughed about that.'

The gun that Brian bought was not the one that killed Dianne. Reali used an antique, four-calibre .46 Colt revolver from a valuable gun collection belonging to her husband, army captain Ben Reali. She also borrowed a pair of his old army fatigues and gloves to disguise herself. Her husband, who'd got wind of the affair, became suspicious when she asked him to put the gun in the armoury at Fort Carson because she didn't like it around the house. After he went to the police and forensic tests proved it was the murder weapon, his wife was arrested. They are now separated, and he has custody of their two children.

Reali, 28, claims she was so spellbound by Brian that he was easily able to 'brainwash' her into committing the brutal murder. She told police that she'd tried once before to kill Dianne, but could not go through with it. Police detective Steve Wood said, 'She told us that Hood was very angry. He accused her of not loving him enough.' Jenny also alleged that Brian told her he'd made dangerous turns in his car, hoping another vehicle would kill his wife by ramming her side. But he eventually gave up on the idea when he realised he could also be killed.

'He convinced me that it was God's will that his sick wife should die so we could be together,' Reali said. The 5ft 5in, 9-stone beauty added that it was his suggestion that she dress up like a man and make it look like a robbery. So at 8.30pm on 12 September, she lay in wait outside the Otis Park Community Centre to ambush Dianne as she left her weekly lupus meeting. That night Dianne pinned a corsage to her jacket to show that she was the hostess for the evening. A couple of hours later it was covered with blood.

Whenever Jenny wanted to talk to Brian, she'd call him and then hang up when someone answered. He'd know to call her back when he had the opportunity. But on the day of the murder, she says the call was their signal that the dirty deed had been done.

Jennifer Reali was sentenced to life, without parole, and Brian Hood was also found guilty.

38

Lethal Dose

THIS ASTONISHING PICTURE captures that terrifyingly awful moment when 35-year-old beauty Paula Prince bought her own death. Paula, a pretty blonde air hostess, is paying for a bottle of painkillers at Walgreens drug superstore in Chicago, unaware that the pills are laced with cyanide.

Lurking nearby is James Lewis, the man who holds the key to the murder of Paula and six other victims. Caught on a security camera, he gleefully watches her every move.

Paula had just returned from a three-day, long-distance trip and told a friend she had a splitting headache, so she picked up a pack of Extra-Strength Tylenol capsules. When she got home, Paula called her best friend, 28-year-old Jean Regula, and left a message on her answering machine, saying, 'I've some exciting news to tell you.' Nobody will ever know what that news was.

She went into the bathroom and took two Tylenol pain-relief capsules for the headache. She had been out of town – and she felt too tired to bother with TV or radio. Otherwise, she might have caught up with the warnings being issued: 'If you live in Chicago, don't touch Tylenol.'

Two days later, her worried sister, Carol, found her body curled up on the bathroom floor.

Paula Prince was the seventh, and last, person to die from the poisoned pills within 48 excruciating hours. Lewis, now 45, was never charged with the murders because police could not prove he committed them. But he has served eight years in jail for trying to blackmail the manufacturers of Tylenol.

The slaughter started at 6.10am on 29 September, 1982. Schoolgirl Mary Kellerman woke with a runny nose. It was a bout of flu. 'Daddy,' she said, 'I don't feel so well. Could you give me something to make me feel better, so I can go to school?'

Her father, Dennis, gave her a red and white Tylenol capsule and a glass of water. Within seconds of swallowing the pill, she collapsed. In two hours, she was dead.

That same morning, 27-year-old postal worker Adam Janus had a chest pain. Sitting in the kitchen with his children — Kathy, four, and Tommy, two — he took a pill. By the end of that afternoon, he was dead. When Adam's 25-year-old brother Stanley came to the house with his wife Theresa, 19, to comfort the family, each, unsuspecting, took two Tylenol capsules as a sedative.

Stan collapsed first. And Theresa — baffled and terrified — clutched hold of him. 'Don't you die as well!' she screamed.

Then she collapsed. Hospital doctors fought in vain to save the couple.

The next victim was 27-year-old Mary Reiner, who three days earlier had given birth to her fourth baby, Joshua. She complained of an awful migraine and took a Tylenol instead of an aspirin in case it made her breastfed baby sick. Ten minutes later, in front of her horrified children, she had convulsions and was doubled up in agony. Mary quickly slipped into a coma. Within hours she, too, was dead.

That evening, 31-year-old Mary McFarland, divorced mother of two, was working at the Phone Center Store in Lombara, Illinois. She went to the ladies' room to get some water to wash down the Tylenol she was taking for her headache. She didn't come out alive.

By now, the Tylenol connection was being made. A nationwide alert went out. And drug giant Johnson & Johnson, who own the makers of Tylenol, McNeil Consumer Products, tested every bottle in Illinois. In 75 pills, spread among eight containers, cyanide was found.

Tests revealed that the killer, wearing gloves, had taken capsules from each bottle, pulled them apart, emptied out all the contents and replaced them with cyanide crystals. Then he put the pills back on sale.

The FBI launched a massive manhunt for the person who had spiked these popular painkillers. They followed up thousands of leads and questioned 10,000 people. But they found no real clues that could lead them to the killer responsible.

Two weeks later, Tylenol makers McNeil got a blackmail letter saying that if they wanted an end to the cyanide killings, they must wire $1 million to account no 84-49-97 at the Continental Illinois Bank.

But the writer had not bothered to wear gloves. A fingerprint on the letter led police to James Lewis, who was on the run from fraud charges in Missouri.

In 1978, Lewis had also been charged with killing 78-year-old Raymond West and carving up the body. But he had been acquitted of this charge. Lewis – born Theodore Wilson, in Memphis in 1946, had been adopted, with his three sisters, by Lloyd Lewis, who often mistreated him. When Lloyd died, his widow remarried – to a man Lewis hated so much he was twice arrested for beating him up. Eventually Lewis was sent to a mental hospital.

Later he graduated from Missouri University, where he'd met his wife, Leann. He worked as an importer, then a tax consultant ... and tried to cash in on his clients' accounts.

As the murder hunt went on, Lewis wrote to newspapers from his New York hideout, denying he was the Tylenol killer. Police issued a photograph of him, with the beard, and also an Identikit picture without it.

Two months later, Lewis, a bespectacled six-footer, was spotted in the New York Public Library by one of the staff. After his arrest he revealed that he (wrongly) blamed Johnson & Johnson for the death of his five-year-old daughter, Tony, who had Down's Syndrome and had died after open-heart surgery in 1974. She had been taking a medicine made by the drug company. Families of the poison victims blamed the makers for their own agony – and sued McNeil. The firm denied negligence, but the case was settled out of court.

39

Confession of a Killer

ROBERT AND MARILYN Reza were the couple who had it all. During 22 years of a blissful marriage they'd had two lovely daughters. He'd built up a flourishing medical practice where his wife worked at his side. Every Sunday they'd walk arm in arm to the New Life Community Church in New York, where they were respected worshippers.

Only one problem dogged the dashing doctor. How to get rid of his wife so he could be with the woman he secretly loved, church organist Kathy Senese.

The couple had been making sweet music for months and now Romeo Reza wanted his devoted wife out of his life. But he didn't want it to cost him a penny in a divorce settlement.

So he cold-bloodedly hatched a brutal plot to dispose of her. The devious doc bought a rifle and decided to murder her while he was supposed to be 400 miles away at a conference in Washington, DC.

His plan worked and Marilyn, 47, a nurse at Reza's Suffolk County Lung Association Clinic, was found dead in her bed, having been shot through the head and strangled.

Police were quickly on the case, believing it to be a bungled burglary at Reza's $400,000 home. But the 'perfect' crime had a fatal flaw and the doctor's alibi soon collapsed.

Reza knew the game was up and admitted the gruesome murder in a 12-page confession. This is how he said he carried out his crime:

'I was so frustrated with my life I decided to buy a gun and kill Marilyn. But I didn't know anything about guns so I contacted a church member who was into them. He took me shooting and I asked him what would be a good gun to use to shoot indoors. He said a .22 rifle.

'I discussed buying one with Marilyn and we ended up arguing. She didn't want a gun in the house, but I told her it was only fair for me to buy myself a Christmas present as she was getting an exercise bicycle.

'She gave in and I bought a pump-action rifle for about $370. When Marilyn saw the gun she didn't like it and wanted me to change it for another, but I didn't.

'I wrapped the rifle in red Christmas paper and put it away in a closet in the attic. Later I secretly took it out, ripped off the paper and hid it behind a filing cabinet in my daughter's room so that it would be easy to get hold of when I came home the next week to kill Marilyn.

'I was due to go away to a medical conference for four days that week and had already decided it would provide a good cover for the murder. When I picked up my plane tickets I bought an extra one but paid cash. I showed the travel agent a credit card for identification and he wrote Mr R. Reza on the ticket.

'I hadn't set a definite date to kill Marilyn during the week. I decided I would play it day by day while I was away and see how it worked out. On the day I left, we had breakfast together before I drove to the airport to fly to Washington. The morning after I arrived, I woke up and realised that was the day to fly back and kill her.

'I called Marilyn at 7.10pm and she said she was going to make a nice woodsy fire and write Christmas cards. I lay on the bed for 20 minutes to gather my thoughts. This was the best opportunity to commit the murder because it was in between meetings and I had until 10am the next day to get back before being considered missing.

'I took only my briefcase and left my suitcase in the hotel. I put the "do not disturb" sign on the door of my room so the maids wouldn't go in the next morning. As I walked by the Sizzler restaurant I saw a friend – I don't know if he saw me. I walked to the Metro and went to the airport. I took the 9pm shuttle using the extra ticket. I arrived in New York one hour later and immediately picked up my car from the parking lot.

'I drove directly home and parked in the driveway. I entered by the kitchen door. Marilyn was in the kitchen. It was about 11.05pm. She was wearing street clothes and writing Christmas cards by the fire. She was very surprised to see me when I walked in. But we didn't argue. We chatted briefly and decided to go to bed. She slipped into a nightie and took half a sleeping tablet before turning in. I got in beside her and waited till she dozed off.

'After an hour I was sure the sleeping tablet had taken effect and she was sound asleep. I carefully got up and fetched the rifle from its hiding place. I didn't bother putting the lights on as there was enough illumination from the Christmas candles that she had put in the window.

'The rifle was already loaded and ready to fire. I wanted to kill Marilyn quickly by putting a bullet through her brain. She was sleeping on her back and I just walked up to her side, pointed the gun at her head and pulled the trigger.

'The gun went off with a loud bang and I knew I had killed her. She just lay there completely still. I checked for a pulse but there was nothing. I put the rifle down and quickly dressed in jeans and a shirt – I had to make her death look like a burglary.

'I turned out the drawers and messed up the room. Then, to make it look as if she had been strangled, I fetched a tie and tightened it around her lifeless neck.

'I grabbed the gun, went downstairs and opened the east side door, and left it ajar to make it look like the point of entry. I left via the kitchen door, taking the gun with me, and drove off in my car with the lights switched off.

'I had to get rid of the gun and drove to a nearby creek. I hurled the rifle over the bridge and then drove back to the airport to leave the car.

'Rather than fly back to Washington again, I caught a cab from the airport to the train station and caught the early morning express. I managed to get back to my hotel at 9.30am before anyone had noticed I had been gone – the "do not disturb" sign was still on the door.

'I am giving this statement at police headquarters and have read it. I swear it is the truth.'

After the killing, Reza coolly continued with the conference until he telephoned his office later in the day, to be told the 'tragic' news that his wife was dead.

The devious doctor immediately flew back to New York. When he returned home he was besieged by an army of reporters and camera crews. Standing with his arm around his daughter Elizabeth, 20, for comfort, he told them: 'I just want to say this family is in shock.' He added he was impressed with what the police were doing.

Reza was even more impressed by the police a week later – when he was arrested! The skilled surgeon was a clumsy murderer. His plan was riddled with holes:

- The rifle he'd tried to hide in the creek was recovered.
- His name was on the ticket for the flight the night of the murder.
- The house's alarm was off, indicating his wife knew the killer.

The clever man was a fool for love. Despite Reza's attempt to protect his lover by leaving her out of his confession, Kathy Senese went to the police and blabbed her part in the grisly saga.

Two days after his arrest, Senese came forward and publicly admitted sleeping with Reza. She said she believed he had killed his wife because of their torrid affair.

It transpired their romance had first blossomed at a wedding when he sat next to Senese. Reza, an elder at the church, had fancied her and slipped her a piece of paper with his phone number on. He told her to ring if she needed anything.

When she did call, she asked for help in getting a pay rise from the church where she had been an organist for 19 years. Reza saw his chance to ingratiate himself and arranged the increase. He then began showering her with gifts. He took her out and encouraged her musical career. After they began having sex she left her husband and kids, expecting him to divorce his wife and marry her – but he had other murderous plans.

He even revealed to her that he'd had a dream that his wife had died. Later he said: 'If anything happens to Marilyn, don't feel guilty. I may look distraught but I won't be.'

She said: 'I believe he killed his wife because he was having an affair with me. Nothing will bring Marilyn back but I'm sorry for the affair.'

Bizarrely, Reza, a part-time professor at New York State University, rarely talked to Senese about his wife – except to say that she was perfect!

Relatives and friends were shocked by the savage killing. 'It's amazing,' said one. 'They had a really good relationship.' They said Reza had never hinted at any marital problems. Nor did he show any signs of difficulty in coping with success – which he claimed was the motive for the murder.

One long-time business associate, who refused to be named, said he was stunned when he saw the news flashed up on television. 'They announced that a woman had been killed in Bayport and I said to my wife: 'I only know one woman there.' Then they said it was Marilyn. My God, I was shocked.

'Then when Robert was arrested we all reacted with disbelief. There were no indications of trouble in the marriage. They worked well together and she loved him. She was a lady. A saint. Marilyn had class and he treated her with respect.'

Pastor John Smith, who'd known Marilyn for 10 years, agreed. 'In her faith and personal life she came as close to Christian perfection as you can come,' he said. 'She was a real servant. She helped people out, responded to friends, and nobody would know about it.'

Reza faces the rest of his life behind bars.

40

Flashback

AT JUST EIGHT years old, Eileen Franklin watched in stunned horror as her best friend Susie Nason was viciously raped and murdered. The shock locked the macabre scene into the hidden recesses of her mind until, 20 years later, a flashback hammered home the terrible truth. The callous killer of the pretty, freckle-faced, redheaded child was Eileen's own perverted father.

When she was only 27, Eileen looked into the eyes of her five-year-old daughter and found herself back on a roadside, crouching by the family van. Daughter Jessica, who bears a striking resemblance to the victim, turned to look at Eileen. And her sparkling blue eyes suddenly unlocked the horrible truth that Eileen had managed to blank out for so long. She saw the shocking image of a menacing man hovering over little Susie, holding a huge rock above his head. That man, she said, was her father, George Franklin.

And, in a landmark case in California, the wealthy 51-year-old has been sentenced to life imprisonment on her evidence.

The memory of the hideous crime that Eileen had witnessed came flooding back in gory detail. Eileen and Susie had grown up together in Foster City, California, a charming waterfront suburb of San Francisco, and played together virtually every day. But their friendship was tragically cut short on 9 September, 1969, when Susie was last seen walking from her home to a schoolfriend's house. It was only a quarter of a mile trip, but it was long enough for the cruel killer to strike.

Eileen later remembered driving along the road with her father in their Volkswagen camper van. They saw Susie and offered her a lift, and the girls began playing gleefully on a mattress kept in the back of the van.

'We were bouncing around in the back and my father got out,' says Eileen. 'He climbed in the back and started innocently playing with us. I got into the front passenger seat. Then when I looked round, Susie was on the end of the mattress and my father was holding her hands above her head. He was on top of her, his pelvis against her. Susie's legs were apart. I think she said, "Stop" and "Don't". Next thing I remember, we were outside the van, Susie crouching beside me.

'Then I saw the silhouette of my father with the sun coming up behind him. He had his hands above his head – he was holding a rock. I did something which caused Susie to look up at me. I think I yelled or screamed but I'm not sure. She looked up and met my eyes, then turned her head to look at my father and brought her hands up to cover her head. I turned away. I heard a second blow. Susie's hand caught my eye. She had a ring on her finger and it was smashed in.

'He said, "It's over now. Forget about it." He told me I was a part of it as I'd wanted Susie to get in the van, and if I told anyone they'd put me away. He threatened to kill me.'

When Eileen got home, she ran straight to her bedroom, terrified and badly shaken. By the time she went back to school after the holidays, she had managed to block out the whole incident. All she could remember was 'being unable to function properly, not being able to learn'.

Susie's body was discovered by Ephne Bottimore, a caretaker for the local water company, in a ravine two months after the killing. The murder remained unsolved, until Eileen's startling revelations.

At first the adult Eileen, who was seeing a therapist to try to patch up her failing marriage to Barry Lipsker, thought she was going crazy. But as her memory grew stronger, she eventually told her husband and he took her straight to the police.

When the police investigated George Franklin, they discovered he had paedophile preferences. Eileen's sister Janice, 31, later testified that she'd always suspected her alcoholic father of the murder. She revealed that he'd sexually assaulted both her and Eileen and subjected them to physical and emotional abuse. She'd told police of her suspicions six years earlier, but Franklin had been ruled out because of a mix-up over the time he had been seen that fateful day.

As George Franklin was sentenced, Eileen admitted that, despite the horror, it was still hard for her to hate her own father, and difficult to turn him in. 'I don't like the idea of him going to jail,' she admits. 'I've always loved him and I still have strong feelings for him. But I owe it to Susie to put him away for life.'

It's not unusual for a child's mind to blank out all memory of a dreadful experience, says Dr Lenore Tarr. 'If something unusual and terrible happens in ordinary life, it would be remembered,' she says. 'But kids who go through traumatic experiences have a way of saying, "I'm not seeing." An intense reminder gets them to recall.'

41

Randy **Rev** Robbed
for **Lust**

LIFE SEEMED TO be heaven on earth for the Reverend Roy Yanke . . . a very sexy heaven. Because the 27-year-old pastor, who was a pillar of his community, certainly didn't practise what he preached. The randy rev robbed banks to pay for raunchy romps with call girls.

This man of the cloth enjoyed the pleasures of the flesh so much he stole more than $25,000 from 14 banks to satisfy his appetite for sex – and none of his parishioners ever guessed he was the Bearded Bandit terrorising their local banks.

'I wish I could say the Reverend Yanke spent all the money that he stole from the banks on his church,' says shocked FBI agent John Anthony. 'But he told us he spent it on illicit sex – from local street prostitutes to high-class hookers. He admitted he just had to satisfy his enormous appetite for sex.'

At least four times a week, the Rev Yanke would visit call girls in the wealthy town of Beverly Hills, Michigan. Sometimes he picked up a girl twice in one day – and all the time, Yanke was still making love regularly to his poor, unsuspecting wife Deborah. But while he was out supposedly doing God's work among his wealthy flock, the sex-crazed vicar of the Covenant Alliance Church was frolicking in seedy motels with hookers he found through a sleazy telephone escort service.

Wife Deborah was terrified her husband had caught AIDS and

passed it on to her … but incredibly she stuck by him. And so did his parishioners.

'I understand Yanke's wife is very worried about catching AIDS,' says police chief William Dwyer, who investigated the bank raids. Even so, on the Sunday after Yanke was arrested, his wife tenderly nestled her head on his shoulder as they sang hymns with the congregation. Then she thanked members of her husband's church for their support.

'We're both overwhelmed by the expressions of love we've received from people in our community – our friends, our family and much-loved congregation,' she said, between tears. 'We're deeply grateful and ask that everyone will continue to pray for us in the days ahead.'

Nevertheless, the rich community was stunned by the scandal. Despite the fact Yanke had given hundreds of sermons attacking sinners during his eight years with the church, he was one of those who'd fallen.

The police and the FBI, too, were shocked when they collared the villain known as the Bearded Bank Bandit and discovered he was a holy man.

The respected reverend's double life began in September 1989 when he robbed a small bank just three doors away from his church. Says FBI agent Anthony, 'In each robbery, the Bearded Bandit walked up to the terrified teller, passed them a large manila envelope and a hand-written note demanding money.' Although he only once showed a weapon, he kept one hand in his pocket to make it look like he carried a gun.

Anthony says Yanke disguised himself slightly by dyeing his hair red and wearing make-up to darken his skin. He also painted a scar on his face and sometimes wore glasses. He was often caught on the bank's video cameras – but what gave his holy terror game away were his getaway cars.

Several witnesses noted his number plates, and the cars were traced by a local rental company who then revealed the hirer was none other than the local vicar. On his last robbery Rev Yanke calmly parked the car in the church car park, where it was discovered by the police.

'He matched the description of our bandit to a T,' says an officer. Yanke, who has a 10-year-old daughter Heather and is active in the local Parent Teacher Association, was charged with robbing one bank of about $500 and another of $700. Then he admitted he was the stick-up man at 12 other banks in the area. The minister had netted around $25,000 and had blown the lot on his sex habit, which cost him up to $75 an hour or $10 for a briefer encounter. He'd also just taken out a $7,500 loan on his house, leading police to believe his addiction to sex had already decimated his family savings.

The reverend resigned from his pulpit – but continued going to Sunday services. In the first week after his arrest, the church elder Alex Hoover made it clear he should be forgiven for his sins of the flesh.

'Brothers, if someone is caught in a sin, restore them gently,' he told the close-knit congregation. 'I think it would be wholesome for our church, for those of you led by the Lord to stand and acknowledge that you have the spirit of forgiveness for the ones who really need it.'

Along with many others in his flock, the Rev Yanke wept quietly while his wife sobbed aloud. For 40 minutes after the service the 130-strong congregation gathered round to hug the couple. 'Roy knows he's loved here,' said one. 'It's probably the best place for him to come.'

Yanke's friends at the nearby William Beaumont Hospital, where as chaplain he'd often comforted the sick and the dying, were also shocked at the not-so-reverent revelations. Nobody had suspected their kind-hearted minister of such seedy hanky-panky – and it seems that's why most people are sticking by him and blaming darker forces for his sordid deeds.

'This is the Devil's work,' says one churchgoer, June Badder.

'I'm sure that's what's behind it – the Devil. This doesn't change what we stand for. Men fail. God doesn't.'

Fellow pastor the Rev John Steiner immediately sprung to Yanke's defence, saying, 'He's an impeccable citizen, a good minister and a very good father.' Yanke's neighbour adds, 'I still can't believe it. He seemed a nice, quiet person.'

Many experts are saying that Yanke's antics suggest he wanted to be caught so he could get help for his sex habit. They think a church minister who robs banks without a mask and spends the loot on prostitutes is crying out for help.

Dr Paul Schubert says: 'Sometimes, ministers will take risks when they're really calling for help – and do something shameful to contrast with their expected role in society.' He says renting getaway cars and driving them to church were signs Yanke wanted to be caught.

'Most people aren't aware of the pressures ministers are under and the expectations they live with.' He reveals that Yanke's sex habit could've been caused by deep emotional problems. 'A sex addiction can mean there are unfulfilled personal needs acted out sexually.'

Yanke was sentenced to seven years in jail and must repay $37,500. 'God be with him,' says the ever loyal and forgiving church elder.

THE
SPANISH
CONNECTION

FOR KATH, MUM AND DAD

With acknowledgement to the people who
assisted me when I needed help. They are too many to
mention individually, but they know who they are.
Thanks to Christian and Sylvie Traineau. Also to
Sentley Wilson, my lawyer, who continues
my campaign for justice.
Especial thanks are due to all my family, without
whose unflagging support and belief this book would
not have been possible.

42

A Day in the Life

IT WAS HOT, with an early afternoon temperature in the upper 90s. The sun was streaming in mercilessly, accompanied by a hot onshore breeze, the north African wind coming over the Mediterranean bringing no relief from the stupefying heat. Wearing summer bikers' gear of shorts, white tee shirt, desert boots, mirror sunglasses and an open-faced Chips-style helmet I was sitting astride my candy-apple red Goldwing motorcycle listening for the 'Go' message on the built-in CB. I could feel the tops of my legs burning even though they had been weathered against the tropical summer heat of Spain's Costa del Sol.

I was waiting on a small spur alongside the busy, dusty dual carriageway between Fuengirola and Marbella, near to the Banana Beach turn-off, about a mile from the Marbella Clinic. I was hot and sweaty, and with the passage of time I was becoming increasingly pissed off. Something had gone wrong again. I had been here for more than an hour and felt as obvious as a pimple on a page-three model's bum.

Two police jeeps went cruising past. Their occupants, the Guardia Civil, remote and blank faced behind their dark sunglasses, had already given me a good visual checking out. Those guys weren't regular traffic cops, they were multitasked specialists with on-board radio equipment that would enable them to check a

British registration plate in seconds by cooperation with NCIS, the National Crime Intelligence Service, based in Croydon, England.

High tech was at last being used by the Spanish authorities to crack down on the ever growing illegal narcotics trade from north Africa to Europe, which, despite the efforts of European-wide policing and enforcement agencies, was still growing at a rate of 15 per cent per year. The available profit to successful smugglers was so high that wannabes were flocking to the Spanish coastline like lemmings.

A piercing scream brought me back to the present. I peered across the road into the sun over the flat, blue Mediterranean. Yep, another crazy tourist, egged on by mates and a few bottles of San Miguel beer, had decided to make the death-defying bungee jump on Banana Beach. Customers drinking at the round, thatched tables screamed their delight and waved bottle-clasping hands towards him as he bounced up and down at the end of the elastic rope. I noticed he wasn't screaming back his delight at them.

My shirt was sticking to my back, and I was quickly developing a stress headache. I wiped the sweat from my face with the back of my leather glove and climbed off the bike. Rummaging around inside the top box I found a couple of dodgy-looking Brufen tablets, which I quickly swallowed with a drink of tepid mineral water from a plastic bottle.

Just as I closed the box lid my mobile twittered. I snatched it from the Velcro holding straps. 'Hello,' I answered testily as I climbed back aboard, careful not to touch the hot metal parts with my bare legs.

'John, it's Rog,' a breathless voice said. 'Have you seen them yet?'

'No sign of them. Don't tell me they've got lost again. They must know the route by now,' I answered. Something's going wrong here, I thought, as Rog pondered on this latest setback.

'They better not be pissed again. You stay cool and wait for them,' he instructed and hung up before I could respond.

Great, I thought, I get to sit here melting in the sun, while he's playing Mr Organization, sitting in his air-conditioned pad drinking cold beer and telling me to stay cool. Suddenly I heard the faint sound of helicopter rotors beating the thin air. Squinting up into the sky I could see a chopper coming along the coast over Marbella. If it landed at the Marbella Clinic it would be OK, just an air ambulance ferrying another car crash victim. If it carried on towards Fuengirola it could be a Guardia Civil or Aduana (Customs) chopper, and that could spell trouble for us.

It didn't land at the clinic. As it came closer I could make out the definitive black and white markings on the fuselage and see the Nightsun spotlight hanging below its belly. It was a police chopper, and I watched as it steadily beat its way up the coast roads towards Fuengirola and Torremolinos, watching the traffic and the deserted areas of coastline for unusual road-traffic or maritime activity. I knew they were in contact with the ground forces.

Those choppers were state of the art, utilizing digitally encrypted voice communications and containing look-down radar and thermal-imaging camera equipment slaved to video cameras. I knew they could downlink real-time imagery direct to police control vans during pursuits and infrared images in darkness. The first convictions had recently been secured against smugglers where the use of video imagery had been a key piece of the prosecution evidence. The odds were slowly but surely mounting against the smugglers.

The CB crackled to life, and Phil's excited voice came over the air.

'John, we're coming through the town now, is it clear?' I could hear the car stereo playing, and someone talking excitedly in the background. Dickheads, I thought. Probably high on speed, they had thrown their own plan out of the window again.

I pressed the talk button and said, 'Go.' Just the one word said everything I had to impart. It was a waste of time trying to explain the problems to the idiots now. That could wait until later, if there was a later. I turned on the ignition and pressed the start button, the alloy six-cylinder engine purred comfortingly into life. I settled my sunglasses more comfortably, smoothed the thin leather gloves and kicked up the side stand, feeling the centre of gravity change between my thighs as the bike balanced upright. Checking the mirror I waited for a gap in the traffic and pulled quickly on to the road. Easing into the fast lane I kept to a steady 50 mph, our previously agreed speed.

A massive tour coach with dark-tinted windows started pushing me from behind, but I had no room to move in. He edged closer and flashed his lights. The driver was probably feeling a bit jealous, wishing he could change places with me rather than driving his big bus load of cackling tourists. I think all Spanish drivers secretly covet the opportunity to drive speed bikes rather than any other more mundane form of transport.

I flicked him the finger over my shoulder and dabbed the brakes to slow him. These drivers were lethal, and unperturbed by my flashing brake lights he didn't back off. My rear view was cut off by the coach, so, desperate to see behind and catch sight of the car I was supposed to be baby-sitting, I slowed quickly, indicated and cut in front of a Seat Uno dawdling in the slow lane. The bus roared past with a blast from its roof-mounted air horns. I felt the sting of grit flung from his wheels on to my bare legs as he passed. The tourists in the Uno were gawking and pointing at the bike as I pulled back into the fast lane.

I flicked on the stereo and listened for a moment to 100 watts of Meatloaf pounding 'Bat out of Hell' through the speakers. I grinned to myself. This was the life. Momentarily thoughts of the operation drifted away as I felt the blast of powering up the road. I waved at the tourists in the Uno who seemed to be trying to climb through the windows to get a better view. Clicking the handgrip-mounted PA button I spoke over the helmet mike: 'Hi, guys, having a good holiday?' My voice boomed from the four speakers and the PA system over the intervening roadway.

An American-built fully dressed bike with a 1500cc engine, the Goldwing is the biggest production bike in the world, and, as the ultimate touring machine, it's a showstopper, much admired by bikers and non-bikers the world over. Other road users were always completely knocked out when I talked to them from the bike on the road. It sounded as clear as if I were sat in their car. The waving increased frenetically, and the driver pipped the horn. I let go my air horns and nodded back at them. Posing, I grinned and waved at them and thought how it always impressed them, even the staid blue-rinse brigade smiled and waved back at me.

My reverie was interrupted as suddenly the stereo stopped and Phil's voice cut in on the CB, 'John, I can see you, move over I'm coming through.'

I looked in the rear-view mirror. Sure enough there was Phil in the Mondeo coming up fast in the outside lane. I pressed the CB switch. 'Slow down, let me lead,' I said. Too late, he covered the few hundred yards in no time, and as I pulled in he flashed past me doing a good 80 mph.

Dropping a gear I pulled out again and accelerated easily up behind him. I flashed the lights at him, while Mike in the back seat waved, grinning like an idiot. Phil pulled over a few feet, and I edged past with a gap of less than four feet between me and the central concrete divide barrier.

According to the plan I had to maintain a minimum one-mile gap between us so I could warn them of any police activity ahead. I gunned the bike to more than 100 mph and quickly left them behind. Within seconds I was back up behind the tourist coach, which was still hogging the fast lane.

Without slowing I switched the headlights on main beam and went through on the inside lane. The driver hadn't seen me come up behind him and must have had a coronary when I screamed past his inside, bursting into view of his windscreen at 100 mph plus. He blasted the horn again. Too late, mate. Luxuriating in the moment I deliberately turned three-quarters way round in the seat, smiled and gave him a good slow V-sign.

Hammering up the hot tarmac for a quarter of an hour I left Marbella way behind as I passed through wooded areas concealing camp sites on both sides of the road in the largely undeveloped coastal area of Los Pinellas. I could smell the clean, evocative scent of the pine trees coming from the hundreds of acres of virgin land nearby. I motored on until I saw a Repsol filling station a few hundred yards ahead, a usual police parking spot. I quickly scanned for police, and sure enough there was a jeep parked just off the road in front of a couple of cheap-looking truckers' bars.

Slowing rapidly I saw them staring at me. No problem, I thought, they're just watching the bike. Nevertheless I radioed back. 'Phil, there's a jeep parked in front of the garage before Calahonda. Take it easy.' This shouldn't have been a surprise to him. We had recced the route several times, and I had pointed out several likely hiding spots for police and radar cars.

I slowed way down and pulled off at the next exit to watch. From the top of the slip road I had a bird's-eye view. Ignoring my warning the Mondeo came tearing down the hill towards the police jeep. He braked more or less in front of it and then was past, still doing 70 mph. I saw the red and blue light bar flicker on, and the police jeep immediately jumped forward to give chase.

'Go! They're after you, dickheads. I told you not to go too fast,' I shouted into the CB.

The operation was starting to go to ratshit. I went across the exit ramp and joined the opposite slip road. The Mondeo shot past me at high speed. The problem now wasn't so much the Nissan patrol police jeep behind them as their colleagues they would call in by radio. I shot on to the main road and gave chase.

Flying along I went past Calahonda at a ripping pace and saw another police jeep coming to join the chase. I was in the clear. They couldn't catch me in a speed chase, and they didn't usually bother about bikes unless you were speeding in the town streets. In any case my papers were in order, and I wasn't carrying.

On the other hand the Mondeo was a stolen car and had two gun-packing crazies on board delivering 50 kg of cannabis resin into Fuengirola, part of a shipment that had arrived the night before from Morocco. Now having abandoned the prepared plan and tearing along the main Marbella highway they were in the shit. Spanish police always loved a good chase, which I suspect increased their sense of machismo. If they felt they were losing the speeding car they would call in for help.

Obviously the Mondeo would now have to be dumped. It had only been used on this trip and had cost Rog more than £2000 with a set of false papers. He wouldn't be very happy. Such thoughts were academic, because first they had to escape from their pursuers. Their only chance really was to get into the town and off the main road.

Because I was travelling at speed I didn't hear the helicopter return, but I did see it. It must have heard the call for assistance from the first police jeep. Rounding a bend giving on to a beautiful view over the ocean, I came face to face with the chopper, hovering a few hundred feet in the air, just off the side of the road, the pilot and passenger clearly visible as they watched the traffic below them. I waved at them, just a happy tourist, and shouted into the mike. 'There's a police chopper just before the Fuengirola camp site near the bends, slow down and drive normally for Christ's sake,' I urged.

'Too late, mate, they're up my arse,' Phil screamed back, while in the background I could hear Mike shouting, 'Go, Go, Go' from the back seat.

I carried on the mile or so past Fuengirola castle on my right and took the Fuengirola exit. They needed to get into the underground car park just off the avenida Don Juan near to the vegetable market, where they could dump the car and escape by one of the many exits. Maybe if the police lost them for a few seconds, and they turned off the road without being spotted, then the car could be collected later from the parking garage, although volunteers for that collection job would be thin on the ground.

The timing was all wrong, and the initial delay in Marbella meant that now the roads were jammed with workers returning to their shops and offices after the siesta. That extra volume of traffic coupled with the mix of tourists crawling along looking for nonexistent parking spaces and getting lost made for traffic chaos in the streets. I knew it would clear in an hour, but these boys didn't even have five minutes to spare. I took the white-line route up between the traffic keeping an eye out for roaming kids whilst I watched for any police activity. Sure enough two jeeps screamed around the red traffic lights up ahead, lights flashing and sirens blaring.

'Take the back road,' I spoke into the mike. No answer. One of them had the transmit button still pressed or had inadvertently changed CB channels. Out of contact with the car I was now redundant, so I slowed way down and watched the events unfold.

Two minutes later the Mondeo came into the town engine and tyres screaming as Phil slowed to accommodate the slow-moving traffic. The car noise was accompanied by the deeper sound of the police chopper as, now in full pursuit, it had to rise to clear the tower blocks. Helicopters were no good following cars in built-up town centres. Phil drove like a madman up the centre of the road scattering cars and pedestrians alike, but he saw the temporary roadblock too late. The pursuit jeep appeared behind him off the main road, so there was no return that way. Phil veered sharply across the road and, tyres screaming, disappeared up a narrow cobbled side street. In his panic he misjudged the turn and clipped a table at a corner sidewalk bar. The lightweight aluminium and plastic chairs went skipping and tumbling across the pavement in a crescendo of noise.

The helicopter presence, the sound of breaking glass and the screams of passers-by seemed to alert everyone that a chase was taking place in the vicinity. Chaos erupted as cars turned away from the noise or stopped dead in the road. People rushed out of nearby shops and bars for a better look, and foolhardy teenagers gave chase on their go-faster striped mopeds. This confusion worked in the Mondeo's favour as the police pursuers were momentarily stalled.

By now I had stopped at the roadside, and turning off the engine I unclipped the comms lead and removed my helmet. I climbed off the bike and locked the helmet on the rack. I took my mobile from the top box and smoothed my hair down. Watching with the crowd I awaited the final outcome. To evade pursuit in a busy town you have to blend in and disappear into the crowd. Tearing around side streets in a stolen car followed by a flock of mopeds is not the way to do it. The Mondeo was standing out like a pair of tits on a bull and was about to pay the price of not sticking to the prepared plan.

I walked to a nearby bar and ordered a San Miguel from the London-accented owner. Already lost in an alcoholic haze despite the mid-afternoon hour, he seemed oblivious to the screams, sirens and chaos just outside his door. 'Having a good time then, mate?' he enquired. Amazed at his ability to be so completely out of touch with reality I nodded at him, paid a tourist price for the beer and sauntered back outside.

The show was more or less over. People were dispersing, going back to their own activities, the police were sorting out the traffic chaos, and small groups of old Spanish women were babbling away in doorways. An older man wearing Afrika Korps-style desert shorts and a hideous Hawaiian shirt was walking towards me, his brown leather open sandals and grey socks marked him down as a British expat.

'What was all that about then?' I asked.

'Oh, just some fellas in a stolen car,' he replied. 'The silly bastards crashed it in the underground car park, seems they tried to go the wrong way and drove into the front of a car coming out.'

Shit. 'Did they catch them?' I asked casually.

'The driver is still trapped in the car,' he answered, then, offering a gratuitous opinion, he added, 'They should shoot these car thieves when they catch them.'

'Yeah, they probably do here, I reckon,' I said. He nodded absently and walked on, mumbling to himself.

Feeling drained by the comedown following the adrenaline rush I walked up the road and cut across a back street towards the underground car park. There were crowds of rubberneckers in the vicinity, pointing and talking together. Police cars and bikes were scattered haphazardly across the road, and there seemed to be hundreds of policemen strutting officiously about the scene.

I pushed towards the front of the crowd just in time to see a handcuffed Phil with a bloody towel wrapped around his head being pushed none too gently at gun point into a police jeep. He looked dazed and dejected. No wonder, he knew the police would find the 50 kg of cannabis hidden behind the back seat. There was no way it would remain undiscovered. Once they found the guns it would trigger a thorough search of the car. Cannabis resin, handguns and a stolen car, it was Goodbye, Phil, I thought.

I found a payphone and called Rog, on a landline.

'Don't plan on having a drink with Mike and Phil tonight,' I said. 'They've had a crash in town, and Phil's on his way to the clinic with a police guard, I think Mike's done a runner.'

'Oh, my God,' he wailed, 'there was 50 kg in that fucking car! What's Chris going to say?' It was a rhetorical question. There was no answer required of me. Anyway Rog had bigger troubles than losing 50 kilos, but he just didn't know it yet.

'See you tomorrow at Patsy's for breakfast,' I said and hung up. I decided to phone home for a chat, and then it would be time for a shower and tea.

At 10 am the next morning I was sitting outside Patsy's Bar on the front in Fuengirola, across from the marina and small fishing-boat dock. The screaming gulls swooping around two blue-painted boats indicated they were awaiting their departure so they could feast on the gutted fish and debris floating in the dock waters. Meanwhile the tourists were up and about, the newcomers standing out like barbers' poles with their white and red striped skin. Reading yesterday's *Sun* and sipping the first of the day's many *cervezas* they waited docilely for their fried bacon and egg English breakfast special.

Patsy's Bar is typical of the thousands of small family-owned and run British bars that infest the Mediterranean coastal resorts from Portugal along the whole of Spain's coastline and islands and up as far as Greece. They are easily spotted with their amateurish hand-painted signs announcing English pub names and often sporting crude Union Jacks or British bulldogs. Too many small tables are crammed into the seating area and overflow on to the pavement, jockeying for space with tables set out by the neighbouring bar.

At this hour tables were all set for breakfast with white paper tablecloths pegged at the corners against the stiff breeze. Laid with cheap cutlery and the ubiquitous tomato and brown sauce bottles, Heinz ketchup and OK Fruity they provide a feeling of British normality for homesick tourists. Many of the bars serve breakfast specials – a glass of orange, cup of tea or instant coffee, fried bacon rashers and egg, beans and tomatoes with a couple of rounds of toast all for less than 250 pesetas, or just over £1.00. I didn't see how they could make a profit, and there again most of them don't. It is a constant round of new faces serving at the bar and tables year in and year out. Only the estate agents make money from the bars and cafes. You can spot them circling like carrion around a dying animal, awaiting the next inevitable round of bankruptcies.

I ordered a coffee and toast and awaited my contact. He soon swung purposefully around the corner and plonked himself down across the table from me. Slim, despite a hard-drinking lifestyle, sun-tanned and dressed in smart shorts and a Ralph Lauren tee shirt, he was carrying the handbag-size leather wallet *de rigueur* for the entrepreneurial set in this part of Europe. With his gold Rolex Oyster on his wrist he looked every inch the successful business-man, which I suppose he was in his world. Rog was a middle-rank-ing player in the Costa drug-smuggling fraternity.

I smiled at him. 'Morning, Rog,' I said as he signalled into the gloomy depths of the bar for a coffee. And so the game continued. I was acting my role as freelance organizer and driver ready to undertake any dodgy job for cash, and now I sat there and listened as Rog bemoaned the loss of 50 kg of gear. It was his own fault, and he knew it. A relatively straightforward transport job had been blown because he had used a few local drug-happy dickheads.

A friendly enough man with expensive tastes that were amply funded by his forays into the smuggling of illegal drugs I knew that Rog would have me killed instantly, without any hesitation, if he ever learnt that I was an undercover agent working with handlers in the Manchester office of the Drug Investigation Unit of Her Majesty's Customs & Excise. It was a bizarre experience, sitting in the hot sunshine surrounded by families of tourists with nothing more on their minds than which part of the beach to lie on or where to eat their next meal, whilst we were discussing the intricacies of delivering illegal narcotics from the Costa del Sol up to the north of England.

Anyone who has been in similar situations knows the buzz of adrenaline that comes from constantly living on the edge, mixing with vicious criminals who all share a visceral hatred of informers and nodding along with them before sneaking off to a quiet phone cabin and placing a call back to your UK-based Customs handlers. Like drugs the buzz is addictive and despite half-hearted warnings from handlers you chase the buzz like a junkie screaming for another fix; finding yourself constantly taking more and more risks and risking exposure just to beat the odds again.

Having won again the resultant high borders on the orgasmic. The sweating palms, pounding heart and gut-twisting cramps that hit at the time of maximum risk are the ignored indicators that signal the damage you are inflicting on your mind and body. You can carry on wheeling and dealing, but at the back of your mind you know the piper will have to be paid eventually.

Right now I had to convince Rog that the previous day's *débâcle* was caused by his driver's speeding, in both meanings of the word, and dumb bad luck.

'OK, so what went wrong yesterday?' he asked.

I told him what I knew, and then I said, 'I'm afraid you can kiss the gear goodbye.'

Taking a sip of coffee Rog looked at me carefully. 'Yeah, we saw them tow the car away last night,' he said, 'so the gear's gone. One bit of a result was that Mike turned up later at Frankie's Bar, when we went along late on for a chat. The twat was pissed as a fart.

'It seems they decided to call in at a mate's for some whizz. These young punks have no idea of security, only thinking of fucking birds and getting out of their heads,' he moaned. 'Anyway Mike won't be bothering with the birds for a bit. Chris was a bit pissed off at his attitude and the stupid loss of 15-grand worth of gear and the car, so he glassed him pretty good. Then he dragged him outside and worked a hammer over his wrists, fucked his hands big time.'

As he delivered this chilling tale of pain and future disablement I felt my guts quiver with fear. I lit a cigarette and was pleased to note that my hands weren't shaking.

'Serves him right,' was the best response I could come with, injecting just sufficient indifference into my voice that my lack of commitment went unquestioned.

Rog's problem now was that he had through his own stupidity lost a load of gear destined for a British buyer, who would still want either his 50 kg of cannabis or else his money back with a healthy profit on top. If he didn't deliver then Rog would soon find someone taking him outside to rearrange his skeletal structure. I thought he looked remarkably calm for someone under such a cloud.

Then Rog hit me with a big juicy one.

'It's not that important because we've just ripped off a Paddy in Torremolinos who wanted to buy 20 kg for Northern Ireland, so I can trade that. And I've already made an arrangement to buy another 50 kg off Juan tonight and ship it up to the north of England this weekend. Problem solved.'

I nodded coolly, although I could feel the first internal tremors that signalled another buzz was coming up.

'Why don't you come over tonight? We'll have a barbecue and talk. Discuss arrangements and so on. There'll be a couple of grand in it for you when the stuff gets to the UK,' he smiled.

'No way,' I said, 'I'm not having my wages depend on your wrapping skills. I'll pitch in with you, but I want paying when the gear is safely on a ferry and leaves for the UK. You can't blame me if it gets lost after that.'

He looked at me appraisingly for a long moment, 'OK,' he nodded at me and then stood up, indicating the meeting was over. Without looking backward he walked out of the seating area and disappeared around the corner. Arrogant bastard.

The young waitress from Birmingham swooped in and started to clear the table. I noticed that Rog had left me with the bill again. Cheapskate, I thought, the guy's a millionaire, and he always leaves me with the bill. Still I couldn't complain, a quick phone call, and I would put another nail in the bastard's coffin. I stretched and smiled at the waitress, saying, 'Have a nice day now.' I winked and flicked her a 2000 peseta note and left the patio, giving her probably the biggest tip she would make that day.

Shortly after lunch I walked up to the main post office, and after a swift look around I entered the telephone cabin farthest from the door. I quickly dialled the Manchester number from memory and when the operator answered asked to speak with Rob Williams.

'Hi, Rob.' After I'd introduced myself I said, 'There was a bit of bother here last night. The local police picked up a young Scottish lad called Phil in a stolen car in the centre of Fuengirola, with 50 kg of cannabis stuffed in the boot. The gear was owned by our friend Rog and was for shipment to Salford. I don't know who the buyer is yet, but Rog's off organizing another load at the moment. I'll try and find out later.'

'Good work, mate,' said Rob. 'Find out when it's coming over and who's picking it up if you can.'

'Oh, by the way, another lad, Mike, got a working over last night. He's probably in a bad way,' I told him.

'Yeah,' he replied, disinterested, 'that's the price of messing with the big boys.'

'See you later,' I said and hung up, wondering what Rob would comment if I received a similar treatment from unhappy drug dealers in the future. On that disquieting note I headed back into town and decided to have a drink before meeting Rog later.

43

Me and My Family

BORN IN 1956 and brought up in north Manchester I attended the Norman House preparatory school in New Moston followed by the Hulme Grammar School for Boys in Oldham. School was all right, but I couldn't conform to the string of petty and, to me, meaningless regulations. Having made a mess of most of my O levels I was slated to take the re-sits in the winter. Unhappy and suffering from a virulent form of adolescent rebellion I upped sticks and left school without any warning.

I also chose that inauspicious moment to leave home, and without any indication of my plans I left Failsworth and my long-suffering parents in the dark and caught a train to Truro in Cornwall, where I had holidayed two summers running on school surfing breaks. Looking back it is a surprise to me that at 16 I managed to survive for so long on my own. But survive I did, and I was feeling pretty good. I had a job in Truro in a hardware store and lived in a holiday cottage in St Agnes, which a friendly owner let me rent cheaply in the closed season.

For a while it was great. I learnt to smoke, beginning with Park Drive, and I discovered scrumpy, a particularly vicious type of cider. I quickly caught on to the benefits of a couple of aspirin and a greasy bacon and egg sandwich for quelling hangovers. I will also remember St Agnes as the place where I lost my virginity, or more accurately where I spent weeks desperately trying to throw it away. Finally I succeeded, with a rather well-built local lass, Sue, who seemed to think that a couple or three afternoon romps on the clifftops amongst the heather and the screaming seagulls meant we were going to get married.

Nothing was further from my mind, and an invitation from my father to join him at work in Manchester seemed like a godsend. I quickly packed my meagre belongings and hightailed back to Failsworth to venture into the dirt and grime of an engineering apprenticeship. Luckily for me my dad had convinced his rather naïve boss that having benefited from a private education I was an ideal candidate as a trainee combustion engineer. Thus I was spared the indignities forced upon many of my mates during their first year of apprenticeship.

So I entered the employ of Associated Heat Services, a company part-owned by the National Coal Board and specializing in operating district heating schemes. These were large, usually coalfired boilers located in central boiler-rooms and providing heating and hot water to massive council-home estates by a complex web of underground water mains. My dad was the manager for the Lancashire region of Associated Heat Services, which meant I could move around the county at will. Wielding my dad's name and vicariously imbued with his power I thought I would be impervious to threats and be able to dodge anything that smacked of real work.

The first thing I had to do was to learn to drive and pass a driving test. Unfortunately my dad had accurately sized up my intentions with regard to work and killed two birds with one stone by placing me into the care of Joe Philbin, an ex-miner of small stature. Recruited by my dad as a general factotum, he had free reign on all the company sites and was a well-respected 'hard man', guaranteed to enforce the company's will. What he may have lacked in physical size he made up for in brute strength. Not many people crossed Joe.

Driving an old ice-cream van he was always threatening to

convert into a camper van, Joe spoke in a broad Lancashire dialect that I could scarcely understand as English. Especially when he lost his temper, and his mouth started running away with him. He was the original motormouth. Quick to anger and always ready to cuff me playfully if I answered back, he was also quick to smile, displaying startlingly white teeth in a broad grin. He always reminded me of a grown-up street urchin.

Joe was pleased with his new role of baby-sitter cum driving instructor, mainly because my dad provided him with an old company Morris 1000 van. The vehicle was knackered and should have been traded in years ago. But it had been retained as a site runabout. Joe set me to cleaning out years of accumulated filth from the van, and then sporting a new set of L-plates we were off. The insignificant fact that I had never before driven a vehicle on a road didn't deter Joe in the slightest.

He threw me the ignition keys and said, 'Don't go on them motorways yet, but drive me up to Oldham St Mary's.' Having been brought up near to an M62 motorway access link all journeys of any length had involved a motorway trip. Other than an occasional bus ride into Manchester city centre I hadn't got a clue how to navigate around Manchester or the city. But I became a quick learner, encouraged by Joe leaning back in the passenger seat and commenting on girl pedestrians and drivers, wolf-whistling and generally pratting about, seemingly uncaring about the ominous grinding noises emanating from the gearbox and engine.

Joe showed me the techniques necessary to drive a van with its own idiosyncrasies. I quickly mastered the rudiments of double de-clutching, signalling, overtaking women drivers, flicking a V to other drivers and the like, continually coached by an ever observant Joe who would cuff me if I made the same mistake more than twice.

We must have looked a sight in a rusty white van lurching and kangarooing around the city with me trying to read street signs and Joe turning the air blue with his choicest pit language. It is a testament to him that I passed my driving test on the first attempt, soon after my 17th birthday.

Under Joe's guiding hand I learnt about the dark mysteries of boiler engineering and soon discovered I had a natural bent for things mechanical. Drilling, burning, welding, turning and milling all revealed their secrets to me, and I became proficient in reading technical drawings, repairing conveyors, scapers, drive shafts and the myriad devices that comprise a modern industrial plant. Bonuses were paid by way of attendance at manufacturers' technical courses, and slowly but surely I became a proper trainee combustion engineer. I was well on the way to being self-sufficient in the complex world of boilers, burners, steam pipes and controls that supply the motive power for most industrial processes.

I revelled in the order and logic apparent everywhere in engineering; at last things around me seemed to make sense. Problems could be solved by application of practical learning, which to me was streets ahead of the abstract world of learning at school. I thrived and prospered, eventually taking the plunge and attending Openshaw Technical College, where I mastered the mix of technical training and practical skills. I never could handle technical drawing, the shapes and patterns of my doggy-looking papers were far away from the pristine accurate drawings of my classmates. Still, I never said I was perfect.

After a couple of years my father left his secure job and started his own engineering firm. Perhaps unsurprisingly Associated Heat Services decided shortly thereafter they no longer needed my services, and I was invited to leave, with a three-month payment in lieu of notice. It took me all of one minute to consider their proposal. The next week I started working for my dad. The formal training schedule was binned, and I was straight on to the tools; it was great.

After a couple of months we were making some money, and in 1974 my dad ordered a brand new minivan for me from the local Austin Rover dealership. I loved it; I fixed a massive pair of spotlights on the front bumper and installed a below dash Motorola stereo of dubious former ownership that I bought for a few quid in a local pub. A big whip antenna sprouting from the roof completed the picture.

At the time I had a girlfriend called Gill, a blonde Irish girl who lived in Birkdale near Southport, about 40 miles away from our house. I couldn't wait to show her the new van, which I did, nearly every night. We cruised forever up and down Lord Street in Southport, posing outside the Wimpy bar and the amusement arcades on Bath Street. I consoled my faintly troubled conscience by convincing myself I was running the van in nicely and steadily by the motorway driving between Manchester and Southport.

Of course, it all went wrong when I fell asleep at the wheel about four o'clock in the morning on the M63 motorway, following a late-night tryst on a Southport beach. Entirely unaided I managed to drive up an embankment, tumble back down and roll backwards into the central reservation.

Strike one minivan. It was just three weeks old and had covered more than 1000 miles a week. I was picked up by a police Range Rover, and after a Breathalyzer test and a lecture from a stern-faced sergeant in Eccles police station I was released into the cold, uncompromising dawn light, to explain to my mum and dad how it had happened. I treated the replacement van with a good deal more respect.

The small foundling business prospered by dint of hard work, long hours and some well overdue good luck. More contracts came in, and the scope of our work increased month by month. I discovered that in addition to understanding things mechanical I could cope fairly easily with business correspondence, preparation of estimates, quotations, reports and the like.

This was a great boon for my dad who hadn't had a formal education. He was drafted into the coal mines as a Bevin Boy during the Second World War, where he served his time as a mechanical fitter. He lifted himself out of a rough working-class start by attending night school and passing some City and Guilds exams. Having learnt the theoretical side of engineering his career blossomed, and he climbed the ladder of success. But he never did relish report writing and was more than happy to leave it to me.

Gradually I spent less time on the tools and more and more time in the office, where I found the commercial side of a business needs the same steady hand as the turner on the lathe or milling machine. As the business progressed the family wealth steadily mounted. When I was 20 I bought a 3-litre Capri complete with a first-generation carphone, whilst my dad had a new Granada Ghia. We thought we were the bollocks. With plenty of cash swishing around life was good. We held large parties, inviting friends and works' associates from miles around.

As I turned 21 I moved into my own place. Dolled up in my mohair suit and black James Bond polo-neck I drove around town on a weekend in my new Capri. I was sure I cut a dash, especially in the local pubs. Probably I looked a pretentious little pillock.

A good engineer friend of mine introduced me to his wife's girlfriend Kath, a local midwife. She had blonde hair, a petite frame and a charming smile. Older than me, she seemed very sophisticated. I was smitten from our first meeting. The fact that she was recently separated with three young sons all under six didn't bother me at all. Needless to say the family weren't too happy with this turn of events. They had me slated for more suitable suitors.

I chased Kath for ages, always rebuffed as being a toy boy. My charm was wasted; she looked through me as if I wasn't there. Of course the truth of the matter is that chat-up lines that work the oracle on teenage girls fall completely flat on a married woman with three kids. One night I met her and her friends having a few drinks out. She wasn't too well, and I offered to drive her home. As we sat outside her small semi-detached in Failsworth, she gave me her phone number. That was it, I had to get to know her better. I plagued her for weeks, phoning at all hours, dreaming up the wildest excuses to convince her that she should go out with me. I didn't know it at the time but she was depressed by the sudden departure of her husband, and she didn't need some young jerk mooning about and trying to get into her knickers.

Eventually she relented and invited me round to hers for some cheese and wine, provided that I supplied the wine. I whizzed into the local off-licence and bought a selection of the most expensive wines in the shop, as well as nuts, crisps of every flavour and the world's supply of cigarettes. We had some good laughs that night as she admitted she had asked me over because she was fed up with me mithering her and because she thought my persistence deserved some recognition. Personally I think she was just a lonely and isolated young lady, up to her ears in debt with a full-time job as a community midwife, an old banger of a car and three bread snatchers who were driving her insane.

The next morning I awoke with a mother of a hangover and noticed a pair of round eyes peering at me. Focusing hard I realized that the eyes belonged to a little kid, a sector of society I had always been nicely distanced from since I was at prep school. Oh, boy, was I about to have another education.

I soon left my own house empty and moved in with Kath, much to the disgust of her neighbours and work colleagues. Neither of our families was ecstatic at the match. Still we were in heaven on earth, at least for the first few months until the grim reality of bringing up kids set in.

Things were progressing nicely at work and a large industrial manufacturing group made an irresistible offer to buy us out. My dad hadn't been too well of late, and it seemed like the ideal time to get out and reap a good profit.

We sold out to the Hargreaves Group from Wetherby in 1983, and both my mum and dad retired on the proceeds of their shares sale. Meanwhile I was contracted to work as a manager for the new owners. It was goodbye to the Capri and hello to a Cortina Crusader, and the writing was there on the wall from the outset, but I just didn't see it. After a few months I knew it wouldn't work out. Work had become a ghastly re-run of life at school, where petty rules and regulations were the order of the day again. Every day there seemed to be another meeting, with bods appearing from head office to tell us how to run a business that had worked perfectly well before they got involved. Pettifogging accountants, planners, safety officers, union negotiators, we had the lot; the place was drowning in paperwork and procedures.

Of course the extra administrative load meant that more staff had to be recruited, and the additional overheads meant more sales had to be achieved. We were caught in the spiralling budget trap, and some of the staff were too busy fiddling expenses to have much company loyalty and involvement. Sales dropped because overheads increased our quotation prices, and everybody lacked commitment. It was a downhill race to oblivion. I jumped off before I was swallowed up whole and disappeared down the plughole with the rest of the business.

By this time Kath and I had married and set up home in Saddleworth, a stockbroker belt north of Manchester, a picturesque rural community nestling in the foothills of the Pennine Range. On the days when it didn't rain and the ever present mist cleared momentarily it was beautiful. The trouble was that the sky didn't clear for long; I think Saddleworth has a shorter summer than Reykjavik.

We lived in a large stone house set in a couple of acres of rough meadow. Though we were both still working full time we found time to raise pigs, cows, goats, chickens and a family of ducklings. In between fighting rising damp and galloping dry rot in our old house we recklessly decided to breed from our Great Dane bitch. A few weeks later a local farmer friend sat in the kitchen drinking tea and surrounded by barking and yelping puppies. He looked around in amazement and pithily remarked, 'Definitely a fuck too far, John.' He was right, but still it was fun.

Faced with the demise of the old family firm and disillusioned by the machinations of big business we decided to get out of the rat race and sample the Good Life. We made seemingly endless trips to Wales and Scotland to inspect farms and smallholdings. That period has left me with a lifelong mistrust of anything spewing forth from an estate agent's brochure. We drove hundred of miles to visit 'an idyllic retreat set in five acres with its own fresh water', where the reality we often found was a tumbledown cottage, surrounded by near vertically inclined hills and an access road that demanded a Land Rover or army half-track.

Eventually we decided to try abroad. We had holidayed in Spain, which at the time was all the rage amongst those British who wanted an alternative lifestyle. After further inspection visits we made our minds up; Spain it was to be. We sold everything and in 1984 set off in our Toyota Carina estate car – me, Kath, three boys and a great Dane – for the trip of a lifetime to Benidorm.

Passport and immigration control in the northern Spanish port of Santander were a riot. We didn't speak a word of Spanish, and the guards reciprocated by not speaking any English. We looked like the Beverly Hillbillies; all we were missing was a shotgun-toting grandma sat in a rocking chair on the car roof. All our papers were carefully scrutinized; the dog and her papers subjected to a separate scrutiny by a pompous little vet. Customs officers made ready to examine the car, but when they opened the doors and looked inside, the smell and detritus of the imprisoned kids and dog wafted out over them. Reeling back they nodded and decided we were safe enough to enter the country, and so we were in. We left the port and started the long road journey, for which we didn't even have an up-to-date roadmap.

A nightmare journey to Benidorm ensued, which involved a three-hour circular tour of Madrid's motorway ring road and a near miss with a suicidal horse-pulled cart in Burgos. We arrived in Benidorm in the early morning before dawn broke. Tired to death we crawled up to our apartment, and only realized after a sleep that we had left all the suitcases on top of the car. We could have saved ourselves the wasted energy in rushing down the seven flights of stairs because the suitcases and all our newly bought clothes were long gone. Another of life's little knocks. Hello, Spain.

We bought a small cocktail bar, complete with bronze wall-to-wall mirrors, a massive bar, seductive lighting and ceiling fans. It was in the old town area of Benidorm, a rabbit warren of narrow, sometimes cobbled streets leading down to a small cove, where old-fashioned fishing boats were still pulled on to the beach by hand each day. It seemed a different world to the concrete jungle, high-rise infested new Benidorm on the far side of the headland.

The bar was situated in a long narrow street, the Calle de Palmas. Proud of our new purchase we couldn't understand why the locals were cynical and embittered. We soon learnt why. Unaccustomed to the mind-slowing heat, bureaucratic officials endlessly demanding money in return for stamped scraps of paper, a lack of tourists and almost permanently pissed neighbours our enthusiasm evaporated like spit on a hot stove.

We should have sat down and analysed our position, abandoned the bar and the car and caught the next flight home to civilization. Instead we decided to stick at it, a decision that still ranks as one of the worst moves I have made since my birth. The bar was like a bottomless pit, and our not insubstantial savings haemorrhaged into the pit within months. Everything was either unavailable or expensive, except for the beer, which we, like other hapless and desperate bar owners, were selling at cost price just to attract trade.

At the time there were only two available brands of beer, Mahou and San Miguel. The two beer sales reps provided a constant source of light relief, attacking each other as they rode their little mopeds down the streets, legs flying, wielding clipboards and biros like bizarre modern-day chariot racers doing battle, all to secure the next meagre order from a bar owner who probably couldn't afford to pay them.

We stuck it for about a year before we returned home broken

spiritually, mentally and financially. Meanwhile, just after we'd taken over the bar, my parents had bought a villa in a beautiful location overlooking the town. At night Benidorm was lit up and looked just like a fairytale, the distance hiding the grim reality within.

Having escaped back to England and Oldham Kath quickly secured her old job as a midwife, delivering babies in the largely Asian community, centred around the now declining cotton industry. I replied to every advert in the *Daily Telegraph* that remotely called for my skills. I secured an interview in Bletchley with Energy Equipment, a subsidiary of the Brussels-based giant oil company, Petrofina.

I travelled down by train and was interviewed by a retired naval officer who seemed suitably impressed with my schooling and ability to talk technically about the merits of modern boilers. I got a job as a self-employed technical writer, paid at the dizzy rate of £8 per hour. I quickly found digs in a local pub and set to work with a will, writing technical manuals, travelling home just for weekends.

· Over the next year life improved, and we had the satisfaction of watching our bank balance grow again. I was promoted several times and eventually ended up with a roving commission troubleshooting and managing sites ready for handover to clients.

In 1987 I was seconded into another Petrofina subsidiary, which manufactured prison security systems and did high-tech security work at military establishments around Britain. I soon became familiar with the inside of various prisons: Full Sutton, Winson Green, Guernsey, Dumfries and the like. Petrofina had the same problem with its subsidiary that we had suffered with our Spanish bar: it was costing too much to operate and was losing money hand over fist. The business was discreetly offered for sale, but because most businessmen had at least a modicum of common sense no buyers came forward.

By this time the business was being managed by a golden-boy accountant from head office. Driving a new Golf GTi and sporting a chalk-stripe three-piece over his corpulent frame he dearly wanted to be seen as a corporate hit man, a saviour who rescued the company from its failing subsidiary. He was an ideal vehicle for my ambitions.

Over a few beers in a local pub in Olney, Buckinghamshire, I put a proposal to him that was calculated to make his career, he thought. I would buy the business contracts for a nominal sum if I could have the benefits left in the contracts and the payments currently due from the contractors. I offered him a lifeline, which he accepted with all the business flair and panache of a baby grabbing a biscuit. A month later, in September 1988, I bought the business from Petrofina.

I immediately called in all the debts and stopped any further work on the sites. All the staff had previously been absorbed into Petrofina, so contract engineers were laid off, and the company ceased working. This was a complicated form of asset-stripping or corporate piracy, and a very profitable operation it was too, although it took me two years to finalize.

In the meantime, in February 1987, Kath gave birth to her fourth child and first daughter whom we named Natalie Kate. A beautiful little girl sound, as they say, in wind and limb. This was a milestone event in my life, and overnight changed my outlook, giving me an unhitherto profound sense of responsibility.

By now we had moved to another small rural community in Humberside, to a locally famous village where they still practised farming in the medieval style. Now we had a farmhouse, a few more acres of land and felt we were finally getting closer to our goal of financial security, contentment and peace and quiet.

Using and developing my business contacts I opened a specialist employment agency. From a small start in a Scunthorpe office we developed within two years into greater things. Supplying technical staff to the petrochemical, steel and other heavy industries we had engineers placed throughout the UK and

Europe, including Italy, Greece, Turkey, and Eire, as well as in Saudi Arabia and Libya. The business was rolling along excellently, picking up momentum and surely destined for a successful and profitable future.

I was content, living in a beautiful location, where I could drive to work daily from home for the first time in seven years. My daughter was at private school and growing well; the boys were making friends and acquiring girlfriends; Kath was again developing her all embracing passion in animals and had recently taken up horse riding again, one of her childhood loves.

Then on the car radio on the way into work I heard that Saddam Hussein, the Iraqi dictator, had invaded his neighbour, the sovereign oil-rich country of Kuwait and was taking Westerners as hostages. I watched the situation develop with dismay, as each day brought worse news. Iraq was using Western hostages as a human shield, while the United Nations was going to defend and liberate Kuwait. The TV started showing footage of soldiers trooping into cargo planes carrying their kitbags, and lines of sand-coloured army vehicles could be seen waiting on docks to be loaded on to troop carriers. These scenes, evocative of the Falklands conflict, convinced me that the dispute would not be settled quickly or diplomatically.

At the office we had seen promised orders for oil personnel dry up overnight. Now British companies were pulling out their overseas-based personnel; GEC Turbines, Rolls-Royce, NEI and other core businesses were taking stock and cancelling orders. The writing was on the wall in big bloody lettering. No company supplying personnel overseas would receive any more orders until the Middle East had settled down, and with half the Western nations teetering on the brink of an all out war with the Moslem states who could say when that would be.

At work the situation was becoming drastic. Money was being paid out, and we were no longer earning anything. I moved quickly to stop the rot. After a week of heavy sessions with lawyers, accountants and bankers I decided the only way forward was to wind up the company. With a heavy heart I phoned a liquidator and arranged a meeting. Within a month the company was gone, closed down and in voluntary liquidation; it would take more than twelve months for its affairs to be completely finalized.

Caught up in world events completely outside our control we had seen a good viable business go down the tubes and sink without trace because some raghead megalomaniac had let his ego and greed get out of control. I was sorry when after invading Iraq Stormin' Norman's boys stopped on the main highway and didn't go all the way to Baghdad and shoot the bastard.

So now there I was skilled in business management but out of a job and disillusioned. Fortunately we had a reasonable amount of money tucked away. I cut down our expenses, sold off the horses, sent back my BMW to the dealers and prepared for the leaner times ahead. Compared with some we were lucky: we still had our family close by, our health and some of our wealth intact. We'd taken another knock, but we were still in the ring and raring to go.

After hours and hours talking and looking at other business prospects we decided to give it a try overseas again. There followed some months of planning, after which I finally left the UK in an elderly Mercedes van in 1993. I headed for the south of Spain, this time intending to set up a business in the tourist area of the Costa del Sol.

After their seven-year idyllic sojourn there my parents had now returned to the UK from Spain following my father's second heart attack. They were comfortably ensconced in a bungalow we had built for them in the grounds of the farm. I departed for Spain alone, leaving the family together as best I could to offer each other mutual support while I investigated the opportunities available. I had ideas about the form a business could take, but I just needed to check it out for myself before committing the family again. My first trip to the Costa del Sol was made with just that intention in mind.

44

Costa del Crime

MY SECOND DRIVE into Spain was more auspicious than the first journey in 1984 had been when we drove for a new life in Benidorm. This time I elected to take the Portsmouth to St Malo car ferry, drive through France and enter Spain via the Hendaye border crossing. I would continue along the Bilbao coastal road and then cut inland over the mountains into Burgos. From there the route was straightforward enough: Burgos to Madrid and then south past Toledo until I hit Granada. It was then a relative skip and jump to the Costa del Sol coastal road. I didn't have a firm destination in mind at that time, but I wanted to arrive on the Costa del Sol within the week.

We knew from our experiences in Spain that domestic electrical products were very expensive, especially when compared with UK second-hand prices. I had reasoned that it would be worth purchasing bulk loads of electrical equipment and retailing them with warranties in Spain. I spent a week buying up goods, intending to sell them as a pilot scheme to dealers and domestic buyers alike to test out the market and my theory. So after tearful farewells from the family I set off on the long journey loaded up with domestic white goods, second-hand microwaves, Baby Belling cookers, Burco boilers and small freezers.

The journey through France was uneventful, except that my failure to master French at school was revealed as a mistake: I couldn't even order a sandwich and coffee in a roadside cafe without looking a complete moron. The first night near Bordeaux was a disaster, but after much finger-wagging and hand-waving I somehow secured the bridal suite in a hotel. Why they thought I wanted a bridal suite I never did discover, but the coffee and croissants for breakfast were heavenly.

By the second evening I was near to the Franco-Spanish border, and I knew that barring any accidents I should be in Spain before the day was out. I decided to make a small detour to travel through Biarritz, a beautiful picture postcard town, quaint, clean and expensive, and one of France's treasures hidden away from most foreign tourists. Late that night I arrived at the border and was surprised to find it unmanned on the French side. I cruised slowly past the closed guard kiosks and the open barriers towards Spain. Crossing the Spanish border I saw an officious-looking guard waving at me imperiously from a floodlit area ahead.

I pulled over and wound down the window.

'Buenas noches, señor,' he greeted me. I responded in kind and thereby used up nearly half my Spanish vocabulary. Unfortunately my ready and correctly delivered response made him think I was conversant in his tongue, and he launched into a barrage of rapid-fire Spanish.

I was flustered and said in my best British Raj voice, 'I'm sorry, I do not understand you, señor.' The guard was a little taken aback, and I could see he was thinking I was taking the piss.

Not to be outdone he waved at me saying, 'Papers, por favor.' I scrambled to the passenger side and collected all the paperwork: passport, driving licence, insurance papers and green card for European travel. He carefully perused them under the glare of the lights and then motioned me out of the van. One of his moustachioed mates joined us.

It was then I realized these weren't border guards but Guardia Civil. With their peculiar little pillbox-style hats the Civil Guard was formed by the dictator Franco as a paramilitary force to administer the country. They are definitely high up on the list of people with whom not to tangle. This one wasn't amused and pointed to the rear doors in the universal symbol of 'Open up'.

I did just that, and he stared impassively at an interior full of kitchen appliances, topped off with clothes, personal gear and a sleeping bag. A quick jabber between the two of them, and again he demanded 'Papers'. I understood immediately that he wanted to see the invoices for the goods, and I was prepared for this eventuality. Within a couple of minutes I had handed over a sheaf of invoices relating to all the goods in the van, but he obviously hadn't got a clue what they were. Nevertheless he scrutinized them carefully, and after tut-tutting a couple of times he handed them back to me. With a minuscule nod thrown over his shoulder he marched away into the darkness, and I took this as a sign that my entrance into Spain had been sanctioned. I slammed shut the van doors and quickly jumped in and set off before he changed his mind and asked me to empty out all the goods and carry out an inventory. We would have been there all night.

As I drove along in the darkness I decided I could understand them searching vehicles leaving Spain, but what on earth would anybody smuggle into Spain? Try as I might I could only think of pirated video tapes and some decent reading material. I hadn't got a clue that such searches and the reasons for them would be a major part of my life in the next few months.

Other than a tyre blow-out on the Madrid ring road, which gave me an interesting insight into Spanish driving habits, the rest of the journey passed relatively peacefully. Two days later I followed the route over the mountains and through the two vast tunnels that drop the road on to the Costa del Sol, where I arrived hot, dusty and tired in the well-known concrete jungle of Torremolinos.

Lingering long enough for a quick drink and to buy a local large-scale road map I headed down the infamous coastal road, passing above Benalmadena. I knew the highway was nicknamed the street of death because of the inordinately high number of fatal accidents that occur on it during each of the summer tourist-infested months. I drove south towards Marbella, in search of accommodation in one of the smaller towns just off the coastal highway.

Approaching Fuengirola I marvelled at the majestic sweep of this multilaned super highway, paid for with European Community money. Obviously no expense had been spared in creating this monument to tourism. Bridges are made of beautifully sculpted concrete sections, footbridge ironwork is ornate rather than workman-like, and the tarmac contrasts blindingly with the white concrete rain guttering that shimmers in the bright Mediterranean sun.

Things move a little down-market when passing through the urban sprawl of Fuengirola town. There low-rise painted buildings, scrapyards and the debris of car crashes that litter the hard shoulder combine to give a feeling that you're driving in downtown Mexico. Rounding the long right-hander out and away from Fuengirola, however, there is a panoramic view of the sea that knocks the breath out of you. Passing the old castle ruins on the crest of a small hill overlooking the sea and the camp site on the inland side of the road, things start to improve again.

Suddenly the scent of pine trees wafts through the open windows, and the crisp clean aroma drives away any lingering sewer-like smell emanating from the back streets of Fuengirola. This is a reminder of Spain as it must have been before the tourist boom gave rise to the proliferation of tacky 'urbanizations' of identical white-stucco walled villas clamouring for space on the rise of every little crest.

When granting planning consent for the myriad of exotically named estates the urban planners obviously hadn't heard of visual pollution. A helicopter ride shows how the rash of creeping development has spread up and down the coast over the past decade. Now, years later, the developments are filled with expatriates suffering from the crippling water shortages caused partly by ever increasing domestic demands and the construction of massive world-class golf courses. The housing estates and the golf courses all feed from a system of natural underground wells. The problems are exacerbated by the fact that water is being withdrawn faster than mother nature can replenish stocks; the inevitable result is an ever worsening water supply with no solution in sight.

Pondering on the uncertain future of one of Europe's natural beauty spots I pulled off the road into a small beach area on the southern outskirts of Fuengirola in search of accommodation. This I soon found in a small family-run pension, which was clean, comfortable and modestly priced. The Spanish proprietor was not in evidence so I had the pleas-ure of dealing with Carmen, his wife. She was a beautiful, doelike creature with jet-black shiny hair held in place by a white hair band, a drop-dead gorgeous face and a beautifully turned and trim body. She looked stunning in a cropped white tee shirt and pink shorts. Definitely a woman to lust after. Carlos the boss was a lucky man.

Following the wondrous globes wobbling provocatively in Carmen's shorts I limped along the corridor to a well-proportioned room complete with a *cama matrimonial* and an en suite bathroom.

'Very nice, I'll take it,' I assured her. Carmen smiled. She instinctively knew what I was thinking. Though she may not have understood what a double entendre was, she certainly got my meaning. I paid a week's rent in cash and watched her as she waltzed out of the room and went back to sunning herself on the porch.

I caught sight of myself in the wall mirror and took a good look at my reflection. Pale skinned with white legs poking out below my shorts, a slight paunch and tired bags under my eyes, at 39 years old who was I kidding? Carmen and her ilk were only a watching activity for me and thousands of other middle-aged Romeos. I was quickly skidding towards being a dirty old man. So what? I could always join the club of the loose-change jiggling bar-goers, but I didn't intend to buy a gold chain in an effort to become the oldest swinger in town.

I unpacked and showered, feeling sorry for myself. Later I headed back into Fuengirola town and had a walk around the promenade whilst deciding in which café to eat. It wasn't an easy choice for there are hundreds of eating houses there displaying tempting cuisine from virtually every corner of the world.

Over the next few weeks I was kept busy making the first moves to get a business off the ground. First I needed an office with typing and fax services, a Post Office box number, a bank account, mobile phone and all the other trappings of modern commerce. Having established all that I retained a firm of lawyers and another of accountants, and finally placed adverts in the local English-language newspapers.

Business was brisk, and all the electrical goods I had brought from the UK sold in double-quick time, leaving the interior of the van as clean as whistle with not a microwave in sight. Encouraged by the successful start I put phase two of the business plan into gear. Scouring antique shops for suitable bargains I came across a giant-size Castilian-style reproduction sideboard. After a mammoth bargaining session I bought the piece of furniture from a 90-year-old gimlet-eyed geezer whose tongue had been honed on thousands of bargain-hunting tourists.

With the sideboard loaded into the van and protected by old blankets I set out again for home.

Everything went smoothly until I reached Hendaye. At the border this time French Customs had a proper go at me. Whilst one official checked my passport details, another examined all the van documents and my driving licence; a third poked around under the van with a probe and a mirror. I noticed they paid special attention to the diesel tank and spare wheel. In a final flurry of determined bad will they brought in a dog and encouraged it to jump all over the interior of the van, sniffing, I supposed, for concealed drugs. Apart from wagging its tail and trying to piss up one corner of the sideboard it did nothing productive. With apparent regret the French Customs guys returned my documents and signalled that I was free to continue my journey.

Including the border inspection I was stopped by French police four times during that journey from the Spanish border up to the Channel port of Cherbourg. Then, to add insult to injury, the police there carefully examined everything again before letting me board the ferry.

By now I was becoming something of an expert in searches and the techniques thereof. Strange, I thought, how these guys always seemed to stop single male drivers. This only shows my naivety at that time. What I didn't understand was that I was driving up the Hash Highway, the most notorious trade route for the shipment of illegal drugs from Spain into northern Europe.

Safely back in the UK the sideboard was entered into a local fine-arts auction and later realized a 100 per cent profit. I was pleased that I had proved to myself, if not to the rest of the family, that white kitchen goods could be exported to Spain. Return loads with carefully chosen pieces of furniture for the UK market completed the picture and reduced the travelling expenses to virtually nothing. I could look forward to the hard but enjoyable work of building up a business from scratch, a job that was right up my street.

On my next journey to Spain a few weeks later I took Nick along with me. He is the youngest of Kath's sons and at that time was 18 years old. Never a scholarly type he was good with his hands and a hard worker but was struggling to get a decent start in the rural area where we lived. He was unemployed for the moment and fancied the idea of a complete change of scene. Personally I liked the idea of some company and of somebody else to do the lifting and carrying instead of me.

During the next two months things progressed pretty well. We soon discovered which goods sold and which didn't. Second-hand microwaves, table-top washers, fridges and freezers are sought-after commodities in southern Spain. Back in the UK the English will apparently buy anything that has an old-fashioned Spanish look about it, and in my experience the darker the wood the easier it will sell.

For entertainment I was having fun watching Nick's antics with the local girls. An attractively lithe lad with a pleasant personality, he seemed to have an almost magnetic attraction for females of all ages. As the youngest boy he had always been fussed over by neighbours and relatives. Now he was being fussed over by women who had more basic designs on him, and he was loving every minute of it.

Most nights after work we would shower and set off into town to eat and grab a beer. As the winter gave way to spring tourists started to arrive in ever greater numbers, like blossom appearing on a tree. This was manna from heaven for Nick; it was as if he had access to his own private harem. He would swagger around posing, brazenly going from table to table and bar to bar chatting up girls indiscriminately. Clearly I was out of touch with how the scene works because as obvious as he was he inevitably stayed behind when I returned at night to the pension. I could sometimes hear him creeping in as dawn was breaking.

Carmen realized what he was up to, but this didn't make her impervious to his cheeky charms. It's never been confirmed, but a couple of times I noticed that particular eye contact and knowing looks passing between them that always signals carnal knowledge. The dirty, lucky bastard.

Being in a place like Fuengirola ensures it isn't long before you come face to face with drugs and the drug scene. Pushers are easy to spot, and we often used to sit outside bars watching their activities as they plied their trade more or less openly outside the discos and nightclubs.

They would target small groups of teenage tourists, approach them and engage them in short, whispered conversations, usually followed by head shaking or a surreptitious handover. Ecstasy, speed and hash were sold relatively freely on the street. Coke was not popular with tourists because they couldn't afford it, and it wasn't a drug with which they were familiar on the UK nightclub scene.

The results of the trade could be viewed from about midnight onwards. Couples or groups would wander into the road, falling over, staggering or skipping like children in a park, completely oblivious to traffic, the stares of passers-by or the presence of the police. If you have ever sat outside a disco in southern Spain and watched the young revellers then you certainly understand the terms 'off your face' and 'out of your head'. When on a high or tripping they have no sense of danger or responsibility to themselves or anyone else, and it is surprising to me that so few of these people are killed or injured.

I've seen scantily clad girls jump in the sea still drinking or smoking, with their shoes on and their handbags swinging from their shoulders. I've witnessed teenage lads running at full pelt down the middle of the road screaming blood-curdling threats and insults to passing cars and taxis, contemptuous of the dangers of moving vehicles only inches away from them. Voyeurs can have the time of their life wandering the beach in the early-morning hours. Frenetic fumbling and humping seems to be everywhere, with occasional muffled screams as yet another holiday-maker seals the romance of the day. A late-night walk on the beach is instructive and provides an insight into the permissive society of today. Forget the swinging 60s. It's all happening on Spanish beaches with the 90s' nightly love-ins.

During the wee small hours is when the dealers appear in their shiny BMW cabriolets or astride chromed Harley Davidson motorcycles. Cruising the streets with their sycophants, stereos blasting reggae beats, they smoke and chat with their pavement-treading minions as they crawl along, ignored by the police in their dark-blue Seat patrol cars.

The police just seem to sit like neutral observers in their cars parked on street corners. Windows open, they smoke and watch the activities going on before them. An occasional burst of car horns or a prolonged scream will draw their attention momentarily. They might look in the direction of the noise, but after a couple of seconds unconcernedly turn back round, laugh and continue smoking. Sometimes they climb from their cars, stretch and walk over to a bar, where they chew the fat with the owner or a waiter and drink a coffee or a *cerveza* before wandering back to the car, the epitome of boredom.

From time to time they rush off down the road, lights blazing and tyres squealing in response to a radio call. Considering the number of arrestable offences being enacted in front of them I always wondered what type of major event must be in progress to require such a display of energy. Later I would find out for myself.

The police on the Costa del Sol have a declared softly-softly policy towards tourists. This is understandable, because it is ultimately holiday-makers who keep the whole community ticking over. Remove them, and the whole economy would collapse within a year. Unfortunately by not policing firmly the authorities are perhaps seen to condone open drug abuse.

Belatedly the police have begun to realize the problems they have created, as family groups now tend to avoid the older Spanish resorts. These are increasingly populated only by property-owning expatriate pensioners who share the bars with beer-swilling lager louts of both sexes desperately seeking a couple of weeks' sun, booze and sex. It's like dying and going to heaven for the pissheads and druggies.

Further evidence of the drug trade can be found in the darkened corners of back alleys. There teenagers of both sexes who have followed the lure of a good time and travelled to Spain for work can often be found selling their bodies for a few hundred pesetas a time.

The summer travellers seeking work find a job in a bar, cafe or disco. But then they need visas or work permits, which they can't easily obtain, and so they jump from bar to bar in an effort to stay one step ahead of the local police. The downside of this existence is that the bar owners know their plight and some pay pitifully inadequate wages. There are many casual workers who work a 12-hour day for 2000 pesetas, about £10.00. They work in the kitchens in unbearable temperatures or end up serving tables, constantly with a weather eye out for the police.

Still in search of a dream these youngsters visit the discos after work, but they haven't the money to buy drinks at the exorbitant prices charged in the clubs. So they buy an ecstasy tablet for a few hundred pesetas, believing the effects are the same. Get out of your head, forget your problems for a few hours, that's the Costa philosophy in a nutshell.

Many don't realize they are on the slippery slope until it's too late. Spending their money on drugs and fags they party all night. When they then can't perform well at work, or they start to look pasty, ill nourished and used up, the charitable bar owners kick them out and offer their job to the next appealing bright young thing to appear on the doorstep.

Some of this black-market abused labour is processed further and appears on street corners selling time shares or working as 'proppers'. Everyone who has been on holiday to Spain has at some time been approached by a bright youngster bearing an armful of cheap invitation flyers. Whether a young provocatively dressed girl targeting the male punters or a tall, tanned Gladiator-type for the women pedestrians, they invite you to a club or bar and promise a wild night of enjoyment complete with a free drink on entry. They are propositioning you, hence the term 'proppers'. Successful proppers can earn good commission, depending on how many luckless punters they can entice into their employers' bar. These jobs are much sought after, and I have witnessed many a street scuffle as proppers fight to protect their turf on a busy street corner.

If they can't get a time share or propping job many disillusioned and broke youngsters drag their sorry butts home, no doubt spouting to their mates about what a great time they've had in Spain. The really unlucky ones progress further down the spiral and end up selling themselves, or, worse, acting as pushers for the more established peddlers and dealers.

Unwittingly they form the vanguard of the drug world. They are the infantry, sent out in large numbers as cannon fodder. If they succeed they sell drugs to other similar-aged tourists; if they are caught by the police they are quickly tried and summarily condemned to prison sentences of anything up to five years.

Rival pushers often fight both inside and outside clubs. The fights are short and brutal. A 20 year old from Britain is not normally mentally or physically equipped for a street brawl with another desperate youth from a *barrio* in South America. A flash of a knife or a broken glass, and it's all over; another casualty of the drug war at its lowest level will traipse home, whimpering, carrying a scar for the rest of their sorry lives as a constant reminder that the school of life can be a bastard for the unprepared.

The dealers, like the generals of old, stand back and watch as their infantry take the fall, either in a police raid or to a rival pusher. Each pusher only carries a small quantity of drugs at any time in an effort to reduce losses if they are nicked or mugged. This encourages the pushers in the belief that the dealer has their interests at heart. So the investment in each pusher is minimal and the risk to the dealer insignificant. If a pusher falls it's no big deal. There's always some other poor bugger desperate for a few quid who will rush to fill the shoes of a luckless predecessor.

The rewards for a successful pusher are excellent when compared with the wages paid in the bars. On a good night they can make upwards of 25,000 pesetas or £125. With no taxes and working every night, they are making reasonable money, and of course, another spin-off is that they can then buy drugs for themselves at discounted rates.

Suddenly with spare cash in their pockets they reappear on the streets wearing expensive Nike trainers and sporting clothes carrying inordinately large manufacturers' logos, thereby advertising their street credibility and selling prowess. Apparently they don't stop to think that the police can recognize all the symbols of their newly acquired wealth and thus know exactly who to target during one of their periodic purges.

I bet the drug peddlers and dealers don't tell the newly recruited pushers that the Spanish have built a new prison at the small inland town of Alhaurin el Grande. This jail has one large wing dedicated to holding only foreign prisoners, which is full to overflowing. Living in the intolerable heat and cramped conditions are many young Britons of both sexes who thought they had the system beaten.

This sad comment on modern life is not confined to the British youngsters. I have met Irish, Swedish and Dutch beauties, Germans, French and many South American cuties all swimming in the same sewer. Strangely enough most of the bigger dealers are Spanish or British, and there is a pretty large Dutch contingent on the Costa too, but other nationalities are few in number. Maybe the British are either the most gullible or the most greedy, but I don't know which is correct because I've met many of both categories.

I didn't know it at the time, but I was about to drop out of the safe, comfortable world I had always inhabited and jump headlong into this pool of amoral sharks who display all the human sensibilities of decency, honour and kindness of an Auschwitz guard.

With the onset of the full tourist season the roads were becoming busier by the day, and many of the smaller streets and back ways were blocked with hire cars. Driving the Mercedes van was thus becoming more of a problem. It was too big to be handled comfortably, and of course, being a right-hand drive model, I was seated on the wrong side of the road. I decided to hunt around for a more suitable left-hand-drive car or van.

Enquiries amongst the British expats whom I knew led to Colin Benson, a man who bought and sold second-hand cars. I eventually got hold of his phone number and called him. I expressed my interest in buying a car, and we arranged to meet later that week at the home of Doug, a mutual acquaintance.

Doug was from an upper-class family, and he came complete with a plummy voice and a charming air of culture despite his pathetic lifestyle. He reminded me of one of the seedy lead characters from the cult film *Withnail and I*. He was in his mid-30s, as gay as they come and with a witty and humorous camp attitude that endeared him to older women and caused him to be ridiculed by macho men. He made a basic living selling china and porcelain figurines and poor-quality prints at car boot sales. It was good fun to stand in the markets with him watching as he whistled at the shorts-clad younger male tourists and the ever present Spanish gays – although I noticed that I did develop a deeper voice when out with him.

Doug lived about 20 miles inland amongst the solitary goat herders. His family had bought him a few acres of upland scrub upon which stood a small cottage. Though prettily decorated, and incorporating a beautiful Spanish tiled floor, it had only three rooms. The modern necessities of running water, electricity and access roads were things non-existent, to which Doug always claimed he would attend when he had the time and the money. Sometime never, I thought, looking around. It took him all his efforts just to scrape together enough money to feed himself and his menagerie of dogs.

So I made the first move along the route to meeting Benson. The Chinese must have a meaningful phrase for such a start on a path of fate, but I don't know what it is.

Colin Benson is British born, from Lancashire, and was then in his late 40s. He is not very tall but broad and heavily built with a chest and arms that look oddly out of place on his short frame. An ex-boxer, the good life and a thirst for whisky have given him a rounded, comical appearance that belies his true nature. He looks like a butterball, but he is a hardball. The years haven't been too friendly to him, and he looks older than he is. With his well-coiffured head of thinning grey hair and affable, self-deprecating smile, his Benny Hill glasses give him a comical look. A broad Lancashire accent and a big cigar in his mouth convey a first impression of a moderately well-off semi-retired businessman, a look he cultivates with exquisite care.

Benson claims to be a dealer in second-hand cars and caravans, occasionally selling boats or other expensive, glitzy toys. Well known in the British expat community he also operates as moneylender to other expats who have need of a quick loan. He doesn't use written contracts but rather agrees a date for repayment with an arbitrary sum of interest. Defaulters have been known to suffer beatings; their cars have mysteriously vanished or been set on fire or their apartments or villas burgled.

I know many people who wouldn't argue with Colin Benson, and I recognize him now as a hardened criminal already with a long prison sentence behind him. But like most professional criminals he can wear the mask. His street cunning guides and protects him, and he can be the life and soul of a party and an affable friend when he wants. However, his disguise of geniality can drop in an instant chameleon-like to reveal the darker, truer side of his personality.

When I first met him he was, of course, Mr Affability himself. He offered me a diesel-engine Land-Rover Discovery, left-hand drive on English plates, complete with a current tax disc on the windscreen. The car was ridiculously cheap at £7000, which he justified by spinning a yarn about a bar owner in another resort whose wife had left him. The man was quickly cashing in and selling up, and he knew a 'left hooker' was not worth much in the UK.

Colin professed he was organizing the sale without profit to himself. He was merely doing a favour for a mate who was struggling. Obviously I thought, Oh, oh, a stolen car, but Benson showed me the DVLA Vehicle Registration Document for the Land-Rover. I inspected it carefully and compared it with the one belonging to the van. It was not a copy. I held the paper up to the sunlight and could clearly see it bore the same watermark and the correct typeface. Everything seemed perfectly in order.

Swayed by the price I became the proud owner of a Discovery. Benson seemed a charming guy, and I had no hesitation in accepting his invitation to a weekend barbecue at his villa. On Saturday afternoon Nick and I drove up to Cartama, the village where he lived in a beautiful villa, built on the crest of a small hill with a private drive that led to tall wrought-iron gates and the villa itself beyond. It was set in a couple of acres of land built up in a form of wide terracing. The lawned garden included a tiled swimming pool, barbecue, sweeping gravel drive and a large carport.

Brick-built kennels were ranged along the lower terrace area. They apparently also ran a hotel for dogs. It was an impressive array of about 20 large kennels divided into two blocks, each with its own private run and separated one from the other by galvanized fencing. This was no rickety, slipshod construction common to the inland villages. It had obviously been carefully designed and built and was now well tended. On the lowest terrace level, adjacent to the road frontage, was a storage and display area for caravans and the odd speedboat. Served by another set of iron gates the whole area was enclosed by quality chain-link fencing and covered by mast-set floodlights. It was a very imposing set-up.

Up the hill at the villa we were given a quick tour by Susan, introduced to me as Colin's wife. Later I discovered she was in fact his long-term, live-in girlfriend. Their home was tastefully furnished with a pine bar, an imposing local stone fireplace and marble-tile flooring. Not bad for a Lancashire lad I remember thinking as I sat down on a patio chair. The barbecue itself was well attended with neighbours and friends coming and going throughout the afternoon. We had good food, and there was beer and wine on tap. All in all it was a pleasant way to spend a Saturday afternoon.

Later when the eating was over and most of the guests had departed Colin sat down with me to share a few drinks. In expansive mood he told me how he operated as a dealer in cars, caravans and boats. He would trade locally, as in the case of my Discovery, or he would buy from the UK and sell into the expatriate community in Spain. He said he frequently travelled backwards and forwards to the UK tying up deals and spent a lot of time going up and down the Spanish Costas. He certainly seemed to know his way around Alicante, Benidorm and Javea on the Costa Blanca.

He expressed a deal of interest in my fledgling business, and driving back to the coast later that evening Nick and I reflected upon what a good contact we had made. Benson seemed to know everyone and certainly had fingers in a lot of different pies. Obviously life on the Costa was working well for him as his large house and apparently relaxed lifestyle bore witness.

A week or so later I was due to return to the UK to collect another load of goods. A couple of nights before we were ready to leave Colin telephoned me and asked if I could do him a favour when I was in the UK. He had sold a car to a guy on the coast near Nerja, he said. The customer was from Manchester and wanted to pay in sterling. Colin didn't want the money to go through a bank account because, as he said, the less the tax man knew the better. He said that if I could call into Manchester and collect the money, about £8000, then he would pay me for my expenses and trouble. OK, I thought, this isn't a problem. I could do him a favour and get paid for it.

So when we got back to the UK I dropped Nick off at home and phoned the number Colin had given me. I made arrangements to meet a man called Mark in Harry Ramsden's fish and chip restaurant near Granada Studios in Manchester. I duly arrived and found Mark in the reception area, who handed me a sealed padded Jiffy-bag-type envelope addressed to Colin Benson, Malaga. Everything was very relaxed and friendly, but I declined fish and chips and left after a quick chat to return home. I thought no more of the matter until I returned to Spain.

On the business front matters were still going well, and I was negotiating to buy a container load of second-hand fridges, freezers and washers. These were trade-in appliances from various electricity-board shops around the country. The prices were ridiculously cheap per item, and each appliance was tested and came complete with an electrical test certificate. I could easily view this as the springboard we needed to really make the business take off. I decided to make enquiries about renting a warehouse with a loading dock when I returned to Spain.

Nick and I drove back to Spain again, and after our arrival I visited Colin and gave him the envelope, exactly as it was given to me. He opened it and counted out the money, apparently it was correct. I was surprised when he gave me £200 for my trouble. I thanked him, and, after making arrangements to see him later for a drink in town, I left.

One day later Nick came storming in madly waving around a 2000 peseta note. Normally equivalent to around £10, this one was in fact worth nothing. It was a forgery, and he had just tried to hand it over in a local shop, where quite rightly they had refused to accept it. We decided it must have been passed to him in his change in a bar the previous night. Upon inspection I could see it was obviously a poor-quality counterfeit. There was no watermarking, the colours were blurred, and one edge was very ragged. Nick put it back in his pocket, and after a good laugh about it I forgot about the matter.

Later that week we were having a drink with Colin in a bar in

Benalmadena when Nick pulled out the note and showed it to Colin. He inspected it and laughed, telling Nick he was a dickhead for being tricked into taking such a poor forgery. Without more ado he took out his wallet and showed Nick another 2000 peseta note. 'That's the real McCoy,' he declared proudly.

On the table top we could easily distinguish the fake from the real note. Then he pulled out another note, indistinguishable from the previous one, so now there were two real notes and one fake on the table.

'Now then, lads,' he said, 'which is genuine and which is fake?' I didn't know it then, but we were about to hit a watershed in our dealings with Mr Benson. Nick and I both pointed to Nick's poor-quality forgery, but Benson only smiled and pointed instead to the original note he had placed on the table.

'That's a proper bit of hooky money,' he said, 'not that bit of old tat,' indicating Nick's fake. I stared at him, and in the words of Bertie Wooster, 'The scales had fallen from our eyes.'

Benson looked over and could see me grappling with the situation. I will always remember him relaxing in the chair and smiling smugly at my discomfiture. I should have just shot the bastard there and then, and if I had known what was to come I probably would have. But not having a crystal ball to reveal the dangers ahead, I just sat there and listened as he told us both the story of counterfeit money operations on the Costa del Sol. He did so by distancing himself and telling the story as a third party. He told us he had a mate 'up the coast' who made a living in 'hooky' money. But neither of us believed him. He knew too much about the job not to be involved himself in some way.

The way it works is this. Medium-value foreign denomination notes are produced in south London. The big operators are active in Spain, Portugal, the Greek Islands and Malta. They move from country to country dependent on the seriousness of police hassle. If a government issues a new design of note to beat the forgers, the counterfeiters move in immediately. They quickly obtain forgeries of the new notes and hit the designated country before the shop and bar merchants are themselves familiar with the new design.

At that time they were working Spain with 2000 and 5000 peseta denomination notes. These are shipped down in bulk by couriers in camper vans, touring caravans and cars. That is what the Guardia Civil guys had been looking for at the border crossing all those months before when they had wanted to check out my van contents.

In Spain the organizer rents a couple of cheap apartments in different run-down tourist areas, always paying in cash in advance. Next small-time petty thieves are recruited from the UK, usually from the foyers of magistrates' courts up and down the country. The organizers sit in court and listen to the cases until they see someone they fancy. They proposition them outside and offer them a couple of weeks in the sun, wages and an aeroplane ticket. Not surprisingly they don't have any trouble recruiting staff, especially in the deprived inner-city areas of Liverpool, Birmingham, Manchester and London.

Life has been made slightly harder for the organizers now. In the early days anyone could obtain a 12-month British Visitor's Passport on demand at a main post office. Now British Visitor's Passports are obsolete, so they have to obtain full ten-year ones. These cost more, more stringent checks are made before their issue, and they generally take a few weeks to obtain.

Still, having recruited a team of up to 10 or 15 staff, they are shipped as tourists in groups of five or so down to Spain. Briefed in their apartments they are told they will work in units of two or three for up to eight hours each day. One of them sits on a hired motor scooter wearing a sports shoulder bag and the other two work the bars, cafes, shops and kiosks up and down the town. Markets and night-time bars are their favourite spots.

The techniques used are easy to spot if you know what to look for. A teenager enters a bar and asks for a Coke or Fanta (never a beer or they would be pissed as rats after a few hours) and tenders a 2000 peseta note. If pushed, he or she will frantically search through shorts pockets and come up with loose change that is a few coppers short.

The greedy shopkeeper won't sell a drink cheap, so he takes the offered note and gives about 1900 pesetas change. The whole deal takes less than two minutes. The teenager nods his thanks, sips his drink and coolly walks out of the bar back to his mate on the scooter just around the corner, where he collects another note and tries his luck at the next bar. They continue to work at that rate for a couple of hours before having a break and switching to a different area or town or another village.

It is an easy business. If a shopkeeper spots the fake then the teenager, who is still pale and obviously a newly arrived tourist on his holidays, pleads ignorance. If the police are called he is searched, but obviously he has no other fake notes on his person. Sophisticated gangs operate by ensuring each operator has another genuine 2000 peseta note and a 5000 peseta note in his pocket, thereby indicating to a policeman that he hasn't pulled a scam on purpose and that in fact he tendered the fake by chance. At that time he starts objecting and claims that someone must have passed the fake note to him. This is usually enough to swing the argument, and the brazen operator moves off. He will be back at work a few hours later with a change of clothing in a different area.

The profits that can be obtained in a planned operation after a two-week period are astronomical. Imagine fifteen teenagers working in five gangs with ten scamming every five or ten minutes or so for eight hours every day. Giving them a couple of days off for a rest and some sunbathing time the organizers stand to make a gross profit of between £20,000 and £30,000 in a two-week period.

The cost of the counterfeit notes varies according to quality. Good fakes that will pass an ultraviolet lamp detector can sell, at the height of the season, for nearly half their face value. The organizers clear at least £5000 per week on that scam. Who said crime doesn't pay? These criminals are making big money whilst taking very little personal risk.

At the end of the fortnight the teenage villains are flown home, a few hundred pounds better off and having enjoyed a working holiday. If they are caught they can usually talk their way out of a tricky situation, but even if they are arrested the worst they can look forward to is being thrown out of the country. So there is virtually no deterrent to either the petty criminals at the sharp end of the operation or to the organizers who reap their ill-gotten gains with apparent impunity.

After his discourse Benson sat back again in his chair looking like the cat that had got the cream. He went on to tell us that he was a middleman operating between the London counterfeiters and the organizers based in Spain. He himself did not operate the gangs of youths, but he claimed he made a profit by handling the bulk packages of notes that were delivered from the UK, splitting down the packages and passing them on to the local organizers. Presumably he must have known where the main consignment of notes was stored, which I thought was quite a heavy responsibility.

After unburdening himself Benson began to play down his role, saying that he had only a minor involvement. His main business was dealing in cars and caravans, but he saw this as an opportunity to make a few pounds on the side. Looking at him, he didn't appear to be the archetypal villain. He was a businessman with a family and a large circle of friends, and it was easy to believe he was just playing on the edges of the counterfeiting racket and was not one of its prime movers and shakers.

I didn't want to give the impression that we were shocked by Benson's revelations, and that afternoon we had a few more drinks and a bite to eat with him. I finished off the meeting by telling him that we were travelling back to the UK within a week. Quick as a flash he asked if I would pick up the proceeds of another car deal for him, this time from the London area.

Thinking of the expenses money, I agreed. He told me I was to collect £10,000 from a man called Jim, and he gave me Jim's telephone number and asked me to call him and make specific arrangements when I was back in the UK.

I didn't know it then, but Benson had just asked me to contact directly a man who was on every policing agency's wanted list. He was a priority target, a known heavy with drug and firearms connections that spread deep into the London criminal underworld. I was going to meet him like a lamb to the slaughter.

45

HM Customs & Excise
Drugbusters

THE TOURIST SEASON was by now well under way in Europe. The roads were busy, and there were many touring caravans, camper vans and motorbikes in evidence up and down the highways, clogging service areas and cross-Channel ferries alike. Arriving in Portsmouth again we disembarked from the ferry, and I decided to ring Colin's mate Jim so that I could collect the money on the drive up north. I telephoned him from the ferry port, and Jim was very accommodating. We made arrangements to meet the same day at the South Mimms service area on the M25. I phoned Kath and told her we would be home in time for tea.

The interior of the van was like an oven as we motored up the M3 and on to the M25 in brilliant sunshine. We did the long crawling swing through the widening scheme road works up to the M25 services, and when I got out there I soon spotted Jim in the small specialist coffee shop inside.

He was sitting with a very attractive and expensively dressed young lady. Jim himself was short and slim with a receding head of hair, and he spoke with a thick London accent. He told me he was an electrician and had an interest in a second-hand car dealership, selling 'prestige motors, Jags, Beamers, Rollers and all that'. He added that he had known Colin for a few years and did a few deals with him. I tried to imagine Jim as a counterfeiter, but to my mind he didn't fit the image. I collected the money from him, wrapped in an unsealed Sainsbury's plastic carrier bag, and promised to deliver it as soon as I got back to Spain.

Jim was an interesting guy, and we sat through a couple of cups of coffee whilst I told him about my export and import business. I thought he seemed genuinely interested. Driving up the M1 later I felt more at ease. I must admit I had been slightly concerned about meeting Jim and had decided on the way up from Spain that if I thought he was dodgy then I wouldn't have anything more to do with Benson or his cohorts.

Nick and I sold more furniture at auctions and loaded up again with white goods we headed off to Spain. Whilst at home I had bought myself a Honda Goldwing motorbike. It was a beauty, nearly three years old with low mileage, and it had previously been owned by an older biker who had obviously treated it with loving care. There wasn't a mark on it. I planned to drive it down to Spain as soon as I could and use it for the summer.

A few weeks later back in Spain Benson asked me if I would deliver some packages for an old friend in Manchester on my next run home to the UK. Subject to having enough room in the van I agreed, and subsequently he delivered two sealed boxes. These were well wrapped, and each had an inventory fastened to the side. The lists claimed that the contents were business papers and stationery. As we loaded the boxes into the van Benson offered me £500 to deliver them into London.

Stop, I thought, this wasn't right. Nobody pays £500 for a delivery of two tea-chest size boxes. Any international removal company would deliver them both for £100 maximum. I jumped from the van and set about Benson. It was only when I threatened to open the boxes to check out the contents that he relented. He told me that each contained 10 kg of cannabis, or 'gear' as it is called. I went wild, but Benson just stood there looking at me as if it was the most normal thing in the world to inveigle someone into carrying drugs across international borders. He upped the offer to £1000 and said if I brought down the cash payment too then he would pay me £1500.

I was stunned. This guy was unreal. I backed off a little and calmed down. Sensing victory Benson said that I should think about £1500 profit and give him a call, after which he loaded the boxes back into his car, told me to call him later and then drove off. He seemed supremely confident. In his mind I suppose he had been testing me out by asking me to collect money, introducing me to his friends and then telling Nick and me about the counterfeit money operation.

I hadn't been too concerned about the counterfeit money. To my mind it didn't hurt anyone. You never saw a newspaper report about someone dying after spending it or because they had been given some in their change at a shop. Like many people I equated counterfeiting as a 'bit of a con' and not too important. Drugs were a different thing altogether. I'd never taken them myself – I get my kicks from a bottle – but I'd seen the effects they can have on the lives of ordinary folk. You could see ruined people every day in Benidorm, Alicante, Torremolinos and Fuengirola, in fact in any town on the Spanish Costas, and much of it was down to drugs.

Drugs are destructive. The effects are bad, and the penalties for people mixed up with them are very serious. No, sir, I did not want to get mixed up with drugs at any price. Benson obviously thought the offer of a couple of thousand pounds or so would be enough to buy off my initial fright. He had only seen one side of my life: a family man struggling to get a business off the ground by buying and selling second-hand equipment. He had not seen our home in the UK and didn't know anything of our history. We had never been involved in anything like this. Like many people I could look the other way if I were offered something cheap occasionally, but that was all.

I wouldn't say I had a strong social conscience or was a great moral crusader, but we all have our own values, and when we are put up against it, then we have to make a decision. I made mine right there and then.

I felt weak at the knees after Benson had left and quickly packed up the van, collected all the paperwork and drove into town to find Nick. Having spotted him chatting up a young hopeful I nearly dragged him into the van, and we then promptly set off towards Granada, our first route marker on the road back to the UK. During the first part of the journey I told Nick about what had transpired with Benson.

It was obvious to me now that I was in trouble here because to my mind all the money I had brought down for him was money for drugs. I had been used as a 'mule'. Things started to drop into place. Benson's interest in my business and the number of trips I was making between the UK and Spain; routes I was taking; what happened when I was stopped. All these questions now seemed to make sense to me. It was a pretty pensive time during that journey back to the UK. Funnily enough we weren't stopped once for a check during the entire run.

Back home Kath and I sat down for some serious talking. As a mother and a nurse Kath has always been totally against drugs, although it wasn't something we had come up against as a family. We had seen plenty of people smoking hash in Benidorm years earlier, and we were familiar with the unique aroma that is given off from burning hash in a joint. Drugs were something other people did. We were distanced from them, and we had never been involved with any drug users, let alone drug dealers, as far as we knew. Now the situation had changed dramatically. We talked for hours and hours, far into the night. Finally we decided to call the police and tell them what had happened.

The next day I phoned the Manchester police drug squad. I spoke for a while with Helen, a policewoman, and explained to her my predicament. I soon realized she wasn't very interested and asked her why. She told me that drugs outside the country and their importation into the UK was a matter for Customs & Excise and not a police affair. So she gave me a London telephone number, and we left it at that.

I called the number in London, but there was no answer. As it was a Sunday, I decided to leave it until the following day. On Monday I called the London number again and had a long talk with the Customs officer who answered the phone. He was very interested in what I had to say, and the upshot of the conversation was that I should phone the Manchester number he gave me for the Northern Area Drug Investigation Unit.

When I called there, I spoke with a man called Rob. This was not like a regular civil-service line. For a start the phone was answered with 'Hello, can I help you?' There was no announcement of department or any other information. It all seemed a little spylike right from the outset.

Rob and I spoke on the phone at great length. I gave him my number, and he called me back at home. He said he would like to meet, and that he would bring along a colleague too. That was OK with me, and we made arrangements to meet up at the Hartshead services on the M62 the next day. Both Kath and I felt more relaxed about the situation now, and we continued throughout the day to make plans for the next trip to Spain. Naively I had thought that when I told the Customs guys what I knew they would arrest Benson and his mates, and that would be that. With the situation normal again I would be able to carry on with developing the business both in Spain and the UK.

In the middle of the afternoon the phone rang, and Kath answered it. After saying hello a few times and listening for a reply she hung up. 'Strange,' she said, 'I could hear breathing, but nobody spoke. How weird.'

About half an hour later both the dogs started barking, and a car drew part way up our long drive, blocking it completely. Two men got out and stood in the driveway behind the five-bar gate that led into the garden and house area. I noticed one of them had his hand in his pocket.

Not acquainted with either of them I said, 'Hello, can I help you?'

'You owe us ten grand, and we've come to collect,' one of them

273

said. As soon as he spoke I recognized a London accent and thought to myself, This is trouble. The situation immediately crystallized for me. Benson's drug deals, carrying cash to Spain, London accents, car blocking the exit. Boy, we were in the shit.

'Just a minute,' I said and quickly turned round and went back into the house, shutting the door behind me. Outside our two German Shepherds continued barking furiously.

I rushed into the kitchen, picked up the phone and dialled 999. It seemed for ever before the operator answered. I asked for the police, and after quickly giving my number and so on they finally answered.

'There are some men in my driveway, and they're armed. They're Londoners, and they are demanding £10,000. You'd better get someone round here quickly,' I hissed urgently into the phone.

The operator was very calm and collected. 'Who are they? Do you know their names? Are they in a vehicle? What is its registration number?' I could answer none of this series of quick-fire questions. He must have realized then he was dealing with a dickhead and said calmly, 'Officers are on the way, sir. Try to remain calm and stay inside your house until they arrive.' I hung up.

It was too late, though, because Kath had gone out of the back door and was shouting at the men. 'Who do you think you are? What do you want? We don't owe you any money. You're a bunch of gangsters! Well, you can sod off. We've called the police and they're on their way now.' Brilliant, Kath! I thought, now they might shoot us just out of spite.

Instead the slightly bemused exchange they shared during Kath's tirade of abuse at them quickly changed to looks of concern. At this point they walked back towards the car. Belatedly I noted it was a big, burgundy Rover saloon. They climbed in shouting, 'We'll be back for our money, you bastards!' and underlining their threat by waving what looked like a shotgun in my direction, they reversed out of the drive at great speed and raced off, tyres squealing, down the road.

'Come on, Kath,' I urged, 'we're getting out of here.' Kath grabbed Natalie, and they quickly pulled on their coats and shoes whilst I called 999 again. I was quickly put through and got the same police operator again. 'It's OK. We told them the police were on the way, and they headed off in their car towards Gainsborough. They are driving a burgundy-coloured Rover saloon, and there seem to be four people in it. I'm sorry I didn't get the registration number, but they definitely have a shotgun.'

I could hear the operator relaying the car's description to someone else. 'We're getting out of here. I'll speak to you later,' I said and hung up again before he could reply.

With that Kath, Natalie and I jumped into Kath's car and hightailed it out of the drive. I took a back-lane route I knew, weaving circuitously between potato and sugar-beet fields, and headed for the motorway. One of the problems with living in a remote location is that you are isolated in the event of an emergency. Stories abound in the village pubs of the length of time it takes for the emergency services to arrive. The problem isn't helped by the lack of road- and street-name signs and the almost total lack of streetlighting. I knew it would take the police at least ten or fifteen minutes to arrive in the area and find our farm. By that time we were on the M180 motorway heading towards Leeds.

After a calming cigarette we assessed the situation. Natalie was crying, more with the shock of sudden events than with fear. Kath was shaking like a leaf and desperately trying not to cry herself. I myself was alternating between fear and a great tide of anger that was building up in my chest.

'Right, I've had enough of this shit,' I said, and I pulled off the motorway at the next exit and found a payphone. I called the Customs number in Manchester. 'Let me speak with Rob,' I said brusquely. Rob came to the phone almost immediately.

'Hi, Rob,' I said and went on to introduce myself. 'Listen, things are moving pretty damn fast here,' I announced, and I went on to relate to him the afternoon's events. 'I want to see you now, so that you can nail these bastards before someone gets seriously hurt.' By this time I was fuming.

'OK, John, calm down,' he urged. 'I can meet you about six o'clock tonight, where we agreed before. We will arrive in a dark-blue Orion, and we'll wait for you in the café area. See you then. Meanwhile I'll make some calls and check up on what's happening.'

With a curt 'Bye' I hung up. Back in the car I related the conversation to Kath, and we set off back towards the motorway. We arrived at the services rendezvous about an hour later and decided to book ourselves into the Travel Lodge motel on the site overnight. Luckily Kath had her credit cards with her.

We checked in, and Kath bathed Natalie. Then we visited the cafeteria and had some food. The resilience of children to adapt to new and strange situations amazed me. Natalie seemed completely recovered from the ordeal and showed more interest in playing in the amusement arcade at the side of the café than in the afternoon's events. After the meal Natalie took herself off to the arcade, and Kath and I had another talk, whilst keeping a watchful eye on the arcade entrance for Natalie. We agreed that the day's turn of events were awful, and that I should assist the Customs, and as a consequence the police, in every way possible to have these criminals tracked down, arrested and taken off the streets.

Just before 6 pm Kath took Natalie to the motel room, and I went outside to watch out for the blue Orion. I waited for ages outside. After about half an hour it still hadn't arrived, and I was becoming increasingly pissed off. I went back into the café and had a look at all the new arrivals again as they sat there eating and drinking. No obvious contenders stood out. I went outside again and continued my vigil.

After a few minutes a guy in jeans and a black leather jacket walked up to me and said quietly, 'Hi, John, I'm Rob. Why don't we go for a chat in my car?'

I was amazed. I had noticed the same guy walking into the phone box from the car park, but he certainly hadn't arrived in a blue

Orion. Now he walked me over to a red Sierra and opened the back door. I saw there was another man in the passenger seat. I hesitated. 'It's OK, John, this is my partner Steve. Sorry about the car thing. We just wanted to have a look at you. Make sure you were on the level, and that you weren't being followed by anyone. Everything seems OK so you can get in the car, and we'll try and sort things out.' He smiled encouragingly at me.

I climbed numbly into the rear seat. Steve introduced himself and flashed a wallet at me, just like the cops do in American films. But, other than seeing his photo on a card, I didn't have a clue what it said. Steve seemed to understand, and he smiled and said, 'We're the good guys, John. Listen, rather than talk all squeezed together in the car, why don't we go into the café and grab a coffee? It'll be more relaxing all round.' Steve with his modulated public-school accent somehow immediately put me at ease, while Rob hadn't endeared himself to me in the first few minutes of conversation.

So off we went into the café where we sat down with steaming mugs of coffee. Rob pulled out a pad, and looking like three men just having a chat after work we started talking in earnest.

Apart from reading Len Deighton spy thrillers and watching the occasional TV film about undercover cops I had not had any contact with any semi-secret organizations before in my life. Nor had I known anyone else who had any experience of dealing with the police or Customs. The nearest I had been to a Customs officer was at Manchester airport in the days when the personal cigarettes and booze duty-free allowances were strictly enforced, and my baggage had been checked over late one night by a bored counter jockey.

I instinctively believed this was the real thing. These guys were pros; it was obvious from their demeanour and bearing. They were quietly spoken, confident and seemed to understand everything I was telling them. They nodded together in an almost hypnotic rhythm as if it were a story they had heard many times before. Rob took copious notes, while Steve kept the conversation rolling.

I developed a quick rapport with Steve, and in an almost good cop/bad cop routine Rob left the talking to him whilst I unburdened myself. I told them everything. From the failure of the staff agency because of the Gulf War up to the latest events of that day. I missed out nothing, occasionally stopping to light a cigarette whilst Rob caught up with his note-taking.

They told me I had done the right thing by contacting them. They confirmed the police wouldn't be interested in drug smuggling overseas, but that the Customs and police often worked together on jobs involving narcotics in the UK when it could be shown that the drugs had come from abroad. This seemed a bit daft to me. Everyone knows that most narcotics crops are grown in hot tropical climates, and so they surely had to be imported at some point in the chain. To me the obvious exception would be chemically manufactured drugs such as LSD or speed, and of course Ecstasy tablets. Rob just smiled knowingly at my comments. God! he was a dark horse all right.

After a couple of hours Rob went to the payphones. He was there for ages, talking and checking his notes and occasionally glancing over at Steve and me. When he returned he picked up on the conversation again.

'Right, John, I just need to confirm some of the names and addresses you have given me.'

We talked about Benson – his appearance, distinguishing marks, tattoos, his lifestyle, friends, contacts I had met, cars he drove – it was like an observation game that you play at parties. I warmed to my task, and I'm sure I gave a good account of myself. Later Rob mentioned some other names and asked me if I knew them. I didn't. They then asked me what I knew about the drugs trade.

I told them about all I had seen years before in Benidorm and more recently my observations in Fuengirola as I'd sit watching the late-night antics of the tourists and drug pushers. That was the sum total of all my knowledge. Over the next two hours they increased what I knew by 100 per cent as they explained about the complex structures of the cannabis trade, from where it was grown in the Rif range of the Atlas mountains of Morocco through to its sale as cannabis resin in the towns and cities of Great Britain.

They advised me that I had become involved with a gang unknown to them but displaying nevertheless some of the classic dealing practices. Engendering trust, dummy runs, carrying small sums of money, big payments for the little work done and a gradual exposure of other criminal activities are the stock-in-trade tactics of the drug dealers' recruiting new staff.

They also told me that the car I was driving was almost certainly stolen, a conclusion I had reached myself earlier in the evening when mentally reviewing the day's events. The vehicle documents were in Spain, but I gave them the registration number, which Rob dutifully recorded. Bye, bye £7000, I thought, and I felt the knife of hatred for Benson turn a little deeper in my guts.

We discussed cigarette smuggling from Gibraltar, but they weren't too interested in that. They were after drug dealers. Rob and Steve weren't judgmental at all – that wasn't their job – they just wanted names, dates and facts. They left the moralizing and judging to others.

The methods employed by the drug dealers to get their product into the UK are ingenious and successful. They make the running, and the Customs agents are constantly trailing behind, trying to catch up. The best weapon in the Customs armoury is the undercover informant. He or she is the person closest to the action and is usually up to date on the latest smuggling methods and routes. Sometimes the agents are members of a smuggling gang and as such ideally placed to provide up-to-the-minute information about a gang's activities and plans to their Customs 'handlers'.

We talked about informers and drug dealers, and I confirmed that subject to Kath's approval I would certainly help them, if I could, to obtain information about Benson and his operations. By now it was nearly eleven o'clock at night, and after the day's traumatic events and the lengthy meeting with the Customs I was exhausted. We agreed to knock it on the head and meet later the next day at the farm. I dragged my weary bones to the motel room aiming for some much needed shuteye.

Not able to sleep properly, Kath and I sat talking until the early hours of the morning. Whilst I was in discussion with the two Customs officers Kath had spoken by telephone to her son Anthony, who was at that time a butcher in a nearby village. Travelling home from work on the main road past the farm he had noticed the police activity there and naturally had called in to see what was happening.

Undaunted by my cancellation call the police had arrived at the house in force, and not able to raise an answer to their knocking they had used their discretionary powers to break into the house and conduct a thorough search of the farm and its outbuildings. Not finding any bodies they had then scoured the area of the surrounding fields. Later receiving a call from Customs & Excise updating them on the situation they decided it best to leave police officers at the farm all night in case of a return visit by the gun-toting gang. It was a waste of time because nobody showed up.

The next morning after a café breakfast we all travelled home again. I arranged for a joiner to fix the broken door, and we sat down to await the call from Customs. Rob phoned me at about 10 am and said they wanted to see me urgently, so I gave him directions to the farm and invited them to visit us later that day. Both Rob and Steve turned up at about 1 pm. Kath fixed sandwiches and drinks for us all, and we sat down for my induction into the world of Customs informants.

Steve opened the batting, whilst Rob again took notes. He told me that if I agreed to become an informant I would be involved in work for the public good, but my efforts would never be publicly acknowledged. I would, however, be paid if criminal convictions were obtained against people about whom I supplied information. Equally, if drugs were seized I would also receive a reward.

Payments for drug seizures were not as high though as those for information that lead to arrests and subsequent convictions.

For my own protection I would be given a codename. It would be used in all my future dealings with HM Customs, and no one, including any superior officers, would have access to my true identity. That was a sacrosanct rule within the organization, obviously one put in place to protect informers for whom revelation of their real identity could open them up to threats or worse. The idea was also that an informant's true identity could never be disclosed by accident or through negligence.

I was to select my own codename because then I wouldn't forget it, and it would remain with me even under intense pressure. I thought about it for a while and finally decided to use the nickname that I'd been given at school. 'Benjy', I said. 'It's short, easily remembered and not likely to be used by anyone else.' OK. That was agreed. The name was adopted, and from that moment on both Rob and Steve called me by it, as if trying to impress upon me the seriousness of the situation.

Rob gave me a central London telephone number dedicated to a Customs hotline that was answered 24 hours a day by special operators who understood the problems that agents had to handle and with which they had to live. I could call the number any time and use my codename to obtain immediate contact with one of my 'handlers' or to leave a message for a later response. He told me never to write it down, even though it was ex-directory. Customs were aware that the big dealers had paid contacts in the police, and very possibly BT; these people could check out any telephone number or indeed any other information. To combat problems that might develop from this all the unlisted Customs phone numbers were registered to businesses unconnected to HM Customs & Excise. Steve gave me his bleeper number too, which I was permitted to write down. If it were to be investigated, this number also came back as registered to a business with no links to Customs & Excise.

That meeting with Rob and Steve lasted for more than four hours. We talked about everything to do with drugs and intelligence-gathering. Apparently they had checked out my story overnight and received confirmation that the names I had given them were genuine, indeed some of them were known to other agencies, such as the police.

They told me that I should try and get as close as possible to the drug gang leaders. They were not interested in the mules or carriers because they were catching them at the UK ports of entry every day. They were after the main dealers – the buyers and the sellers who paid for and organized the drug-smuggling runs. These were the guys who ultimately made fantastic profits from the illegal trade; all the others were just minions, who might earn a lot of money and were partaking in illegal activities but who were not making the vast sums accumulated by the organizers and buyers.

We agreed that I was to become a 'Confidential Informant'. That is an undercover agent who provides intelligence about drug-smuggling activities but only actively participates to a minor degree in any criminal activity. I was not to handle any drugs personally, and I wasn't to act as an *agent provocateur* which is to say that I wasn't allowed to provoke any person into committing an illegal act. Furthermore I had to report anything that seemed important, bearing in mind the prime objective of capturing the big boys. I was also supposed to relay to them any other illegal activity that I came across – counterfeit money operations and stolen car rings were activities that came immediately to mind.

In return for my assistance Customs & Excise would ensure that I did not have to appear in public court to give evidence for the prosecution against any dealers. This was very important to me. Having experienced a mild threat of potential violence I could all too easily imagine what would happen if I helped put dealers behind bars and they found out that it was my evidence that had helped to nail them. Their anger and subsequent retribution would know no limits, and they would simply kill me out of hand.

I had already read reports in Spanish newspapers of people disappearing only to be found washed up on a beach some weeks later, and of folk trapped in burning villas under questionable circumstances. More than one corpse had been found dumped in the hills overlooking Malaga. It didn't take a great leap of imagination to believe that these were the bodies of drug dealers or participants in the drug trade. That these were the men or women who had paid the ultimate price for deals gone wrong, or for rip-offs between rival gangs.

The Customs officers told me that there was also another policy in place to protect informants from exposure in the courts. If an informer's evidence were put before the court and the defence called for confirmation or the agent's cross-examination, Customs prosecutors would first discuss the matter in chambers with the trial judge. Usually the judge would rule that the informant did not have to be named. However, as sometimes happened, the judge might rule that the agent should appear in person, in which case Customs would offer no prosecution evidence, and the case against the defendants would be dropped. This was an expensive policy to implement in terms of finances and time, but to me it was the ultimate guarantee that I wouldn't be forced to appear in a criminal trial as a prosecution witness.

As I sat in the lounge of our home talking with Rob and Steve these risks seemed distant. The Customs guys were experts and knew exactly what they were doing. If it became necessary they had the power to protect not only me but also my family from any revenge attacks. If by chance anything went wrong and I were arrested whilst on an operation then I could rest assured that HM Customs would sort it out. This was normally done by a technical defect in the arresting procedure, placed there to enable any defending solicitor to get the charges against me dropped and allow me to walk away. The benefit of this technique was that the dealers wouldn't consider my release suspicious, but rather the result of police error. Apparently these knockouts over a technicality were not uncommon and would be accepted without any reservations by the drug gangs.

I was also told that I should not contact my handlers in any regular pattern, that I should vary the time and the place. When 'on the ground' in Spain I should only call when I had something important to say. They appreciated that active informants could be placed in difficult situations, and stressed that I should never risk compromising myself just to make a report. If I got into any major difficulties then no matter where I was at the time, whether in the UK or abroad, I should get along as quickly as possible to the nearest police station. If I were compromised by then working with the police, steps would be taken to protect my family, including our relocation and help with new identities.

During a natural break in the discussions Kath and I had a private chat in the kitchen. We both agreed that although the situation wasn't good – and certainly wasn't one that we would have wished for – there could be no doubt that Steve and Rob seemed to know exactly what they were doing and appeared to be dependable, stand-up guys. We decided that for the time being at least I would go ahead and work for them as an informant.

Later that afternoon we talked about what could have prompted the goons to turn up at the farm the day before, and Steve explained how a typical deal was done. A buyer, or a group of buyers, would send a 'tester' to Spain, usually to a known contact with whom there had been previous dealings. The tester was given some small samples of cannabis, which he would test carefully and give his opinion, usually by phone to his boss, over the next few days.

If the cannabis or 'gear' made the grade an order would be placed and agreed, and then the money, always in cash sterling, would be sent by courier to Spain. With a small outfit the head of the gang would travel to Spain and complete the deal to buy anything from 50 to 500 kg of gear. After paying for it the buyer had then to fork out for local storage, a wrapping service and transport back to the UK. These oncosts would be paid when the service was provided.

So, having bought the gear, it would be wrapped in layer upon layer of clingfilm or sealed in vacuum packets to defeat sniffer dogs. Then, depending on the buyer's preference, it would either be transported to the UK by a hired transport contractor or by the buyer's own transport and routing.

It was not unusual for a buyer to try and ship gear himself. If he proved successful he would increase his profits tremendously. But, if he were to fail, and the drugs were seized at a border crossing, the highest point of risk, then he stood to lose all his gear as well as the money already invested. In that scenario, using known contacts, the buyer would probably lose someone he knew personally with the attendant risk that they might tip off the police in order to negotiate a lower sentence.

Overall it was better for a buyer to use a third-party transport company. That way he didn't make as much on a shipment, but the risks to him and his gang members were minimal. Furthermore, because the competition for transport jobs was so fierce, the buyer could dictate payment terms.

The going rate for bulk shipments was £100 per kilo of drugs delivered within the UK, half paid up front as a deposit and the balance due on safe delivery. The downside of this transportation method is that the buyer hands over control of the goods previously guaranteed by his own trusted tester. Now there are other people involved – the storers and the baby-sitters, the wrappers and the couriers who do the actual smuggling.

Tampering with shipments is not uncommon. Partial loads might be stolen, or good quality cannabis swapped for something inferior, usually for gear contaminated with diesel fuel or 'let down', or mixed with wax, in the blending process. Sometimes the bars of hash, called 'soaps' and each weighing 250 gm, would be filed down slightly and 20 or so grams taken from each one. In this way the inside operator will steal about 20 per cent of the load. All in all there are many ways for a buyer to be ripped off.

When such shortages or losses occur the established buyer's revenge is extracted in a remarkably short space of time. If he knows who has ripped him off then he will arrange either through his own resources or by way of a hired team to hit back as soon as possible. This has two purposes. First, if the thief is hit fast and hard then the buyer may recover the goods or money, and the word on the street would make any other potential rip-off merchants think very carefully before making a move on that buyer. Second, if the buyer doesn't react swiftly then he may as well jack in drug dealing because everybody will rip him off all the time. So the jungle wars are swift and usually sure. Retribution is harsh, and the weakest fail.

It was more than likely that the money I had agreed to collect for Benson was the balance due following safe deliveries for Jim and his gang. But, when the gear had been sampled, it was possible that the quantity was short of the agreed load or the quality inferior, that is to say that all or some of the gear had been swapped.

Now Jim knew that I was only a mule carrying the money, but it made no difference to him. I was his last contact with the Benson gang, and he had handed me £10,000. I was the logical choice to squeeze first. If I came up with the money, all well and good; he could ignore the little difficulty with Benson and carry on business as usual. After all Benson could always get another mule. If I screamed when squeezed then Benson would hear and instigate a search for the real thief, either in his wrapping or delivery gang, or further back up the line among the storage boys.

Either way Jim was sending a message to Benson via me. What he couldn't and didn't know was that his squeeze operation had coincided with me contacting Customs about Benson anyway. All he had done was to convince both Kath and me that we weren't going to be walked over by those bastards. We were going to fight back and see them go down, one way or another.

Kath, Steve, Rob and I talked through every ramification. I even suggested they might let me have some gear seized elsewhere to replace that delivered by Benson's gang. This might lull them into a false sense of security. Rob laughed and said no, they could not allow such things to happen.

After several hours the meeting broke up amicably. I had agreed to work with HM Customs, not as a long-term informant but only so long as to ensnare Benson, his gang and other contacts. After a quick run-through of the business and a thumbnail training seminar we agreed that I should contact Benson to see how the land lay. No doubt he would have heard by now that I had phoned the police.

If the situation was still OK then I would travel back to Spain and go to work as an informer. But if he were frightened off then the matter was dead in the water, and I would continue to develop the import and export business and simply stay away from Benson and his cronies. Just before they left I told Rob I would phone him the next day. We all shook hands and as they drove away I noticed it was about six o'clock in the evening. We had been hard at it all afternoon.

Once again Kath and I sat up burning the midnight oil, discussing the various options and possible consequences. We decided I should have to go through with it, certainly for the time being until I managed to extricate myself from the invisible web that Benson had contrived to weave around me. We decided that the situation was now potentially too risky to involve Nick. He would be a liability in Spain, so I would leave him at home where he could help Kath. He could still go out and buy white goods ready for the next trip. I would leave the van at the farm and travel to Spain on the Goldwing.

It meant that the business plan was on hold for the moment, but I didn't mind too much about that. We could always take up the reins again when we were ready. It wasn't yet the type of business that depended on repeat orders or customer loyalty; it was still a young, fledgling operation. No, I had no doubts about my priorities: look after my family, remove the threats, make some money and strive for a peaceful coexistence with my neighbours. Surely, I thought, that wasn't too much to ask.

We also had to look at how we should best adapt to events that might happen in our lives as a result of my new role as an undercover agent. Kath could forget travelling to Spain with Natalie, certainly for the time being. There would be a great deal of stress to be encountered and overcome, possibly with only moral support and the odd, brief telephone call. I could hardly say, 'Sorry, lads, Kath's upset so I'm shooting off home for a week or so.' That seemed a sure-fire way of arousing suspicion. We decided the risks were too great to tell the family what I was doing, just in case anything slipped out by accident. So Kath would have to cope with the strain of it all herself without a shoulder to cry on when things got rough.

As we were talking that night I looked over towards Kath in the dimly lit lounge. I could see she was upset, that tears weren't far away, but the angle at which she held her head, with her chin jutting out defiantly, revealed to me her complete determination. She was generally more passive than me, but I could tell she wouldn't allow these fuckers to break our dreams or threaten our lives. We would get through all right. Like they say, the female of the species is more deadly than the male. She would do for Benson and his mates if it came down to it.

We went to bed eventually, and both of us slept soundly. We had made our decision and had the resolve to see it through. Now it was time to go to work. Early the next morning I phoned Benson feeling hyper alert and ready for any comments he might make. He was very calm and listened to my story. I explained angrily about the visit from the Londoners and told him I believed they were connected with Jim and the money I had collected from him. I demanded to know what was going on.

In turn Benson himself wanted to know what happened with the police. I responded furiously that it wasn't every day that we had a visit from men with guns threatening us, but that I told the police it was a domestic dispute, and we had the matter in hand. He seemed a bit wary about this, but it was the best I could do under the circumstances.

I wound up the conversation by saying I would be down in Spain during the next week, and he had better square up the matter with Jim. I didn't want a repeat performance at the farm. What I didn't tell Benson was that Kath and I had agreed that she and Natalie would fly out to Spain the next week to be with me. That way if the issue weren't resolved then at least there would be nobody at the farm for them to have a go at.

Benson seemed happy that I had taken such a stance, and he said he would contact Jim straight away. I called Rob at the Manchester Customs office later that morning and told him what had transpired during my conversation with Benson. He agreed that it was probably safe to go back to Spain, and that the operation was on. I left it at that and promised to be in touch.

Two days later I set off on the Goldwing, loaded down to capacity. I remember it was glorious weather, the sun shining down from a bright blue, almost cloudless sky. Kath and Natalie waved me off from the farm drive. It was a tearful parting even though I already had their flight details tucked safely in my wallet, and we knew we would meet up again at Malaga airport in six days' time.

Now it was official, I was an informant for Her Majesty's Customs & Excise. I felt great. Wrapped in their protective armour I was about to lay waste all the scum drug dealers I could get my hands on. I felt tremendously invigorated, and a sense of peace washed over me. I would show the fuckers. I knew I would succeed. It was the only way to protect my family and put the crazy, law-ignoring bastards behind bars.

46

Living as a Smuggler

THE TRIP DOWN to Spain driving my Honda Goldwing was one of the best journeys I have ever made. The sun shone all the way. I sat bang in the middle of the road, wrapped in a cocoon of taped music, courtesy of the powerful stereo. It was superb. Other vehicles moved over for me, and at junctions they allowed me to cut in front of them.

Whenever I stopped for fuel, to take a leak or grab a cold drink a small group of admirers would wander over and gather round, smiling and gesticulating, I'm sure no one noticed me; it was the Goldwing they were all interested in. The bike seemed to engender warmth and friendliness from everyone. Or was it just my euphoria at the task in hand? I don't know, but it was a bloody good feeling.

When I reached the by now familiar Hendaye border crossing between France and Spain there was an almighty queue of tourist traffic awaiting entry into Spain. No problem! I passed slowly up the line and waited until another driver waved me into the line in front of him. At the guard kiosk I stopped, took out my passport and handed it to the guard. He waved me on and commented, 'Formidable, monsieur! Bonnes vacances.' He was such a nice guy. Similarly at the Spanish border a couple of hundred metres ahead the guard was more interested in looking at the bike than inspecting my documents. I was across in no time at all with no hint of a check on me or my papers.

The trip through the heartland of Spain was hot with daytime temperatures soaring into the mid-40s. I stopped a couple of times at garage forecourts and bought a bottle of mineral water from cooled dispensers. I would drink my fill and then pour a great dollop of icy water over my head, face and neck, pausing only to thoroughly wet the inside of my helmet before I was off again. It was no good, though, because within ten minutes the coolness from the impromptu shower had evaporated, and beads of sweat were running again into my eyes and making my sunglasses slip down my nose.

Meanwhile my legs, crotch and back were bathed in sweat, and my flesh was chafing with every little movement. I pulled off the road and took a bag of clothes from a side pannier. Ducking behind a bush I stripped off and changed into a tee shirt, shorts and trainers. Re-stowing the bag I set off again. Oh, heaven! I felt great. The sun was beating down, but the passage of air cooled me just enough. Riding a powerful bike along motorways in the afternoon sun for hour after hour ranks as a must-do experience.

In the distance I could see the heat haze and the black tarmac shimmering, while eagles swooped lazily overhead. Other drivers gave me a thumbs up, wagons hooted, and even police motorbikers dropped their customary disdainful expressions to smile and wave at me.

As is the way of all good things this all came to an end, and after a great journey I arrived back on the Costa del Sol. I drove straight to Carmen's pension in Fuengirola and checked in. Carmen was surprised to see me without Nick; she kept glancing behind me to the open doorway as we were talking. She was even more surprised when I showed her the bike. I think all the Latin women love their men to be macho. I could almost hear her changing gear and reappraising my potential in the new light of a superbike. Later, darling, I thought to myself, right now I've got work to do.

I showered and changed again, gave Carmen my dirty laundry for washing and drove into town to phone Kath and grab a bite to eat. As I suspected the bike drew lots of attention, especially from English tourists, many of whom shouted as I cruised posing down the seafront boulevard. Feigning ignorance of their envious glances I parked the bike right in front of a bar and nonchalantly locking the helmet on board I adjusted my shades and walked inside. After talking on the phone with Kath for a while I wasted the rest of the day just relaxing and gathering my thoughts.

I thought I knew what I was up against. I was sure that after thinking about it intensely over the past few days of my solitary journey I was more than ready for it and eager to begin.

The next morning I phoned Benson to check out the lie of the land.

'Hi, Colin, it's John. I've just got back, how's it going?' I asked lightly.

'OK,' he responded. 'I'm sorry about that bit of bother you had, but I've squared it up now. Why don't you come up later on, and we'll have a chat?' he suggested.

'Okey-dokey, I'll see you about threeish. Cheers,' I said and hung up. Yes, the game was on. I phoned Rob in the Manchester office, and he sounded pleased to hear from me. I told him I was intending to visit Benson that afternoon. Rob warned me to be careful and not to take any chances.

That afternoon I drove up to Benson's villa in Cartama. Of course everyone came out and had a good look at the bike. Benson wanted to take it for a quick spin, and I let him, just to demonstrate there were no hard feelings. Later we sat alone on the shaded porch, a cold beer in front of each of us.

'Well, Colin, it seems like we have to get a few things straightened out between us,' I began, opening the discussion. He looked over at me, squinting against the glare behind me, and so we began to talk for more than an hour about the situation. I told him that he should have trusted me. I wasn't stupid, and I had realized how he made his money, which certainly wasn't from renting out kennels or selling the odd car and caravan. Besides people who had bought and sold cars didn't send round goons with guns to get their money back, they sent solicitors' letters and used the courts.

'No,' I said, 'you're involved in hooky money or drugs. Personally I'm not bothered which, but I wouldn't mind a piece of the action. Selling microwaves is a hard way to make a living.

'Besides I've got a good business head and could be a great organizer. I know the roads across Spain and France really well, and I'm used to the travelling. I know where the police hang out, and where they have roadside checks. Maybe, most importantly, I am totally clean – a good citizen without a record – I can stand up to any checks.'

'That's not such a good thing,' he temporized. 'Lot's of people prefer to work with known cons, someone who they can check up on easily.'

'Yeah,' I replied, 'so they have cons checking cons, and then you end with the sorts of problems you've obviously had with Jim. One of your trusted cons drives off into the sunset with your gear or your money. You need somebody straight who will work from the outside, sort of like a subcontractor.'

We also discussed the Land-Rover Discovery I had bought from him. When pushed Benson admitted it was stolen. In fact it had been stolen in France and put on to English plates by a gang operating out of a town near Salou on the Costa Brava. A printer in the UK turned out the fake Vehicle Registration Documents, and they really were indistinguishable from the real thing. Benson was proud of them and said they were the best available. As for the tax discs, they were original, stolen from various post offices in raids up and down the UK. Similarly MOT certificates were available for older cars, stolen from testing centres the length and breadth of the country.

So it went on for a couple of hours, but I didn't want to push it too far with him. I'd planted the seed, and that was enough for starters. As I stood up ready to leave he said to give him a few days, and then he would be in touch. No problem, I had plenty with which to occupy myself. I left and drove pensively over the hills down to the coast.

During the rest of the week I hung around likely haunts of drug dealers, shady Spanish bars and some of the rougher British ones. I made a few contacts and got on to nodding terms with a few dodgy-looking individuals.

A couple of days later Benson left a message for me at the pension. I phoned him and arranged to meet for a drink in Torremolinos. When we met he looked wary and couldn't settle. He told me that he had another hooky car for sale, a Ford Escort on English 'K' registration plates. He said I could have it for £1500 as it stood or £2000 with paperwork, logbook and tax disc. He obviously didn't want to talk about anything else, and so again I didn't push it. He looked like a man with problems.

I used that Escort as my ticket into the criminal fraternity. I talked to everyone who looked as if they might be the slightest bit interested, and it's a wonder I wasn't pulled in myself considering how I flaunted that knocked-off car. A few people mentioned that I might try a bar in Gibraltar, where hot items of property and other things were traded. Excellent, I thought, I'm finally making a bit of progress. The next morning I set off there.

Gibraltar is a strange place. A self-governed British dependency, the size of a small English market town, it holds a curious mixture of those of Italian, British, north African and Spanish origin as well as other generally cosmopolitan people who live cramped together in an atmosphere of repressed hysteria on what is effectively a small rocky peninsula at the southern tip of Spain. Its chief value is its strategic position on the Straits of Gibraltar, which makes it the gateway between the

Mediterranean and the North Atlantic Ocean. The seas of the Straits are notoriously dangerous at this point where two great bodies of water smash together through the narrow gap between two continents.

Gibraltar is famous for its British-style bobbies and circular red post boxes. It also has English money and English-style shopping centres. Woolworths and Marks & Spencer department stores stand in the main shopping street cheek by jowl with cheap tourist novelty shops selling china mugs, linen cloths and aprons decorated with blurred images of the Royal Family and Ye Olde English Tea Shoppes abound. There is a general air of seediness, of a place long past its prime. To my mind Gibraltar should have been closed down and handed back to the Spanish after the Second World War ended, though there is a strong pro-British lobby there.

Gibraltar's main asset now apart from its location is its duty-free shopping facilities. Tourists arrive in droves to buy 200 Silk Cut or Benson & Hedges cigarettes for less than the duty-free prices in international airports. Perfume, clothes, video cameras and electronic goods are all available at some of the cheapest prices to be found in Europe.

High on the small list of other things for which Gib has become famous is the well-kept tradition of smuggling, which the populace continue with vigour. Everyone does their bit. Tourists try to smuggle more than the tobacco or bottle allowance back on to mainland Spain, past the ever vigilant Spanish Customs guards, whilst the locals smuggle cigarettes by the speedboat load from Gibraltar to the beaches of nearby La Linea. They do so in a crazy game of cat and mouse with the local Guardia Civil, who ceaselessly patrol the area.

It is difficult to obtain a permit to reside in Gibraltar, and in any case property prices are sky high. Most of the better apartment blocks house the bankers and accountants that work in the Gibraltar-based offshore banking industry. Ordinary working-class people who are not in company-subsidized property live in La Linea, the Spanish border town that abuts the frontier with Gibraltar.

La Linea is a dirty, smelly run-down place. The roads are worn out, cratered and potholed with great mounds of sun-swollen tarmac that look like surreal fermenting dough. The streets seem largely to be populated by mangy-looking dogs, screaming, dirty kids and old women dressed in black who sit in shaded doorways. It's a hellhole with a pointless existence.

When I got to Gibraltar I headed straight for the bar to which I'd been recommended. Nearby there were other commercial units commonly known to be rented for storage by cigarette smugglers. Gibraltarian police and Customs officials know many of the smugglers by name and often stand by benignly to watch the nightly operations as the small black-hulled speedboats are fuelled up and loaded with boxes of duty-free cigarettes.

The smugglers are well organized and have accomplices in La Linea equipped with night-sight scopes and walkie-talkies. They sit around the beach and watch the roads, and when the coast is clear of police they radio the boats that have been hovering just around a blind corner of the cove. The drivers zip up the speedboats' throttle to maximum and zoom towards the beach at fantastic speeds. Once there the crew quickly throw their loads overboard to an awaiting group of perhaps 15 or 20 teenagers, who have materialized apparently from nowhere. They spirit away contraband up the beach, across the main road and into the warren of dirty little back streets to a safe house. It is all over and done with within five minutes of the boats' departure from La Linea harbour.

The contraband cigarettes are sold for £12 a carton for British-brand and Marlboro, and consequently hardly any of the locals buy cigarettes in the shops. It is in fact hard to purchase them in a shop in La Linea. Most shopkeepers just don't bother stocking them because they are so easy to obtain on the black market. Furthermore the Gibraltarian authorities don't much concern themselves with the tobacco smugglers. After all they are smuggling out of Gibraltar and not into it. Similarly there is a healthy trade in Scotch whisky, brandy and rum.

Obviously the Spanish are exceedingly unhappy with the nightly smuggling operations, which occur like clockwork unless there is an offshore wind that makes the sea too rough and stops the light speedboats from getting up and on to the beaches. The Spanish police try to stop the smugglers, but it is like trying to halt the tide. The rewards are just too good, and the risks minor. If caught the smugglers face a large fine or a small jail term, and the contraband and boat are confiscated.

Big deal! I know smugglers who treat the cigarette and alcohol smuggling as a proper business, even declaring the sales for tax in Gib and paying a levy on the profits. I have seen them fill up with gas at the small fuelling jetty and demand a receipt for the cost. This is then submitted as a legitimate expenses claim. This may seem to be turning smuggling into a fine art, but against this level of smuggling gall and expertise and Gibraltarian indifference the Spanish are fighting a losing battle. This is part of the reason why the Spanish are so tight on the land border and insist on stopping and searching every vehicle, which in summer can be a ballbreaker. It is no fun queuing up for two hours in the hot sun waiting to clear the Spanish checkpoint.

Once smuggled into La Linea the contraband cigarettes are either sold in the major Spanish holiday resorts, or bigger loads, concealed in packed container lorries, are shipped out to the rest of Europe and the UK. These are big operations with more than a million cigarettes smuggled out each time. I know that ocean-going yachts and small cruisers lie just off Gibraltar filled to capacity with cigarettes. When a cash price is paid in a local bar, the cigarettes are taken by boat to southern Ireland or Scotland. The carrying boat lies in international waters off a small harbour or deserted beach until rubber inflatables arrive to transport the light but bulky boxes to awaiting onshore vehicles. These milk runs are sophisticated smuggling operations that deal with millions of pounds worth of tobacco.

It was into this environment that I arrived hoping to sell the Escort that evening. I discovered the bar to which I'd been directed to be a strange establishment, populated by locals in denim shorts and flip-flops. Its atmosphere was noisy and crude, and the place was dirty and stank of stale beer. English beer adverts covered the walls, and the price list was in English with English prices, something of a shock after Spain. The bar was in no way pretentious and obviously did not seek to attract the tourist trade, although it is only a five-minute walk from the centre of the main shopping areas.

I settled myself in at the bar and ordered a pint of Fosters. All around me there was the quiet, conspiratorial purr of deals being done. Before long I began a conversation with a guy about bikes. The pavement and small parking lot outside was filled with Gib-registered motorbikes of varying makes and vintages. Inside the atmosphere was highly charged, and within an hour I was told that a lad called Peter was after a new car and directed to one of the lock-up units further along the block, facing the jetty. This turned out to be my entry point into the whole game.

Strolling into the heartland of the smugglers' territory I tried to look unconcerned but inside I was shitting blood. I nodded at the few people who looked up at me from the boats just feet below. These were all filled up with contraband and ready to go, just awaiting the word from their mates in La Linea. It felt surreal to be in the thick of international smuggling operations and trying to sell a stolen car. I was giddy with excitement and hoped I could carry it through, because if I fucked up I would be lucky to escape with just a severe beating. These lads obviously played for keeps, and they were all young, slim and as fast as greyhounds.

I walked up to a unit with an open door. 'Hi, there, I'm looking for Peter,' I said to one of the older-looking guys inside. He just glanced at me before speaking quickly into a walkie-talkie that had been lying on top of a box of cigs. I heard him say the name Peter as he briefly stared at me again and listened distractedly to the tinny voice that came back to him.

'He's on the boat. He will be here in ten minutes,' he told me abruptly and turned away.

'OK, pal, thanks, I'll wait here,' I replied to his back. Feeling a bit like a spare wheel I turned and walked out of the storeroom and headed back to the jetty to watch the proceedings unfold. There were about eight boats against the jetty wall held there by lads hanging on to lengths of rope fastened to eyebolts in the jetty flooring. I noticed that all the boats were painted black, and each had two crew in the cockpit. The engines were turning over quietly, and little trails of bubbles popped regularly to the surface below each stern.

There was a sudden shout, and in unison the speedboat engines rose to scream pitch, and the boats lifted almost out of the water as they shot for the marina entrance, jockeying for position at high speed. Within seconds they were out of sight around the stone harbour wall and heading for the Spanish coves. I could just see the non-drivers waving and gesticulating at each other, and it all looked like a high-school prank to me as the echoes of the receding engines reverberated noisily around the marina. I looked upwards and saw observers with binoculars on the stone-built headlands, no doubt ensuring their loads were delivered safely.

Within five minutes the first of the boats were returning at high speed and slewing round expertly in tight U-turns to pull up at the jetty. Those on board were excited, shouting and jabbering madly at one another. Within ten minutes all the boats had returned safely, and the crews had jumped ship and on to the jetty, heading off for the storerooms. Young lads of about 14 or 15 now ran to and fro the boats with the next consignment of contraband to be stored, ready for the express delivery service.

I wandered back to the storeroom and asked again for Peter. In the half darkness a slim athletic-looking young man with blond hair and a sparkling white smile turned to me in response. 'I'm Peter, man,' he said. 'What do you want?'

I told him I had heard that he wanted a new car. I launched into my prepared spiel and offered him the car for sale as if it were an everyday event. He looked at me for a moment, weighing me up. 'Sure, man, I need a new car,' he said. 'Have you got it here?'

'No,' I replied, 'I don't drive it around because my name isn't on the Vehicle Registration Document. But I can bring it down to show you if you are interested,' I added helpfully.

Peter was thinking about this when the radio crackled into life again. He grabbed it and pointed in my direction. 'Can you swim?' he asked. Dumbly I nodded back at him. 'Come on then, let's see if you are a copper.' I could have died right there. This stupid bastard wanted me to go on the boat with him. 'Come on, man, let's go,' he shouted, already halfway back to his boat. All his mates were looking at me and watching my reaction. This, I felt, was it, shit or bust.

'OK, let's go,' I said and ran after him to the boat. He jumped in, and a young lad who was holding the steadying rope looked at me. Fuck, I thought, this is the way to do it. I jumped the couple of feet down into the boat and took the rope from the kid's hand. Peter looked across at me and smiled as he spoke into the radio.

'Hey, man, what's your name?' he asked across the noise of the engines.

'John,' I replied and smiled back at him. 'How many years do we get if we are stopped?'

He shrugged. 'It's not the prison, it's the way they stop us now,' he smiled and motioned a man firing a rifle. Great, I thought, I could get shot by the Spanish just for being in this poxy boat.

Before I could reply the radio started to transmit instructions again, and without any warning to me to let go of the rope he pushed the throttle levers wide open. It was like being in an express elevator. The boat took off from the jetty like a Porsche, and I was still holding on to the rope and steadying the boat. Now

I knew why everyone was wearing gloves, and so much for me thinking they didn't want to leave any fingerprints. It was more mundane than that. They just didn't want the skin burning off their hands.

I screamed into the dusk, but I'm still not sure whether or not it was from searing pain or the sheer exhilaration of riding in that ultrafast speedboat. It was like nothing on earth, a live thing, bucking and jumping over what looked from the shore like small waves but close up were too big for comfort. The boat took off and landed with a bone-jarring jump into every crest. Water shipped on board in chilling scoopfuls, and within seconds I was wet through.

We were about third in a line of boats, the propellers of those in front roiled up the sea behind them in turbulent little cross waves. I snatched a look at Peter, who was standing up and steering with one hand and trying to talk into the walkie-talkie with the other. What a dickhead! I was holding on to the steel grab handle fastened to the front bulkhead for dear life.

They tell me a good run is to be in and out within five or six minutes, but to me it seemed we were travelling for ever. Suddenly, without warning, the engines cut, and the boat seemed to stagger in the water. A large wave sloshed over the side, and sea water gurgled around my feet in the footwell. There was a crunching noise from underneath as we beached.

'Quick, come on,' Peter yelled. I turned and saw him heaving boxes overboard like a madman. I jumped into the back of the boat and stood amongst the cargo and started throwing it out on to the beach. A crowd of youngsters had gathered and stood holding out their arms for a box. We both worked like crazies, and in no time the back of the boat was empty.

'OK, man, let's go,' shouted Peter. I just nodded weakly, now knackered by the sudden exertion.

The boat had been lightened by the loss of cargo, and we were semi-floating on the incoming waves. Peter gunned the engine, and with a groan and squeak the boat backed into the water. He spun the wheel and turned the engine to full throttle again. We were off bucking, jumping and writhing across the surf and into the bay. Not too bad, I thought, as we careered towards Gibraltar.

The return trip was more of the same, with conversation an impossibility. I was cold and wet and frightened half to death. This was nothing like a sedate water-skiing cruise up a lake or in the lazy offshore swells in the sunshine. It was hard, fast and dangerous. The stakes went up by a factor of ten when Peter pointed back behind us towards the beach. I couldn't see anything until a blindingly bright searchlight cut in from the sky and danced over the water to connect with one of the boats behind us. The light dipped and swooped but held fast on the fleeing boat.

We obviously hadn't been travelling at full throttle for Peter immediately gave it everything, and the boat jumped in the water like a hot-rod car. We were literally travelling over the wavetops. I could feel the water tugging under the boat as if it were trying to grab it and pull us back down into the sea. The engines screamed like banshees as we veered into the marina entrance. Abruptly the searchlight was cut off, and the other boats followed us in, screaming towards the harbour wall through the silent port. Peter cut the engine at the right moment, and we slewed in to a perfect berthing. Nicely done, this guy should have been driving in the world championships. He could handle a boat like nobody else on earth.

Another youngster passed me the rope and leapt into the boat behind me. He was dressed like an urchin and laughing at me like a nutter. Peter slapped me on the back and boosted me up on to the harbour wall. I reeled a bit before I could walk in a straight line. Peter and his mates gathered round and laughed approvingly. 'Hey, John, grande cojones' he said, and some of his gang clapped. 'That's pretty good, eh?' he asked. 'A free ride and a profit too.'

I was too fucked to answer him, and it took me all my time not to throw up on to the jetty. We headed back to his storeroom. The other members of the team looked up when we entered and gathered round us, one of them throwing me a towel, which I used to rub my hair dry. An open can of beer was thrust at me, and I drank it greedily. I hadn't realized how thirsty I was.

Later Peter and I sat on the steps near the harbour entrance and discussed things. He told me they liked to test out new people in boats, giving them no chance of backing out once they were in. No police would take the chance of being a target in a smuggling boat. Little did he know that if I'd known I could get shot at then nothing on earth would got me into that boat. So I'd passed his test by default.

Peter said he often made five trips a night, but that night he was finished because the Guardia Civil had turned up in a helicopter, something they did from time to time. He explained they were really after the drug boats from Morocco, but while awaiting the druggies they would chase the tobacco smugglers. A few months earlier they had fired rubber bullets at a boat, one of which had hit a fuel tank. The resultant explosion wrecked the boat and killed the driver; the other crew member had been rescued by police helicopter but was immediately arrested and sentenced to six months in the local prison.

Finally we got on to the topic of the Escort. Peter liked the idea of a nearly new car for £1500, and he was keen to buy it. He offered to pay me in cigarettes, which I didn't really fancy though he said he would let me have them at trade price. This was £8 a carton, which I could sell on for £15, and he would introduce me to people who would take them off me in Marbella. That seemed like a good deal to me because it would allow me to make further contacts, and sooner or later I would come across drug dealers rather than cottage-industry tobacco smugglers.

After we swapped phone numbers I left Gib in the late evening and drove sedately up the road to the Marbella area. It had been interesting, and I had made some initial inroads into the drug-smuggling fraternity.

I collected the stolen Escort from Benson the next day and drove it down to La Linea. I parked on the roadway outside the Anglo-Spanish frontier amongst all the other vehicles of those who prefer to walk across the border rather than risk getting caught up in the interminable traffic queues. I followed the crowds across the road and the airstrip and went into a burger bar near the walled entrance to the old fortress town to telephone Peter.

Five minutes later an old Mercedes pulled up outside, and from it Peter shouted at me to jump in. The car was crowded with his mates; an older man who turned out to be his father, Henry, was driving. Peter introduced me to everyone. They all appeared to have heard about my boat trip the previous night, and there were smiles all around.

We drove off and up to the border, where on production of British-style passports we were quickly waved through. More surprisingly, Peter's father started chatting in Spanish with the border guards. He was obviously well known to them. After a cursory look inside the boot we were off again.

Peter loved the Escort. He and his mates piled in and drove it around La Linea with the windows rolled down and the radio blaring. I waited by the Mercedes, trying to look cool as I chatted with his father. When they returned about 20 minutes later Peter confirmed he would take it. Without more ado we jumped back into the Mercedes and drove into a labyrinth of small streets. Parking up finally they gestured me inside a nearby house. The place was wall-to-wall cigarettes. There was hardly any furniture, just box upon box of Marlboro and Winston. It was an amazing sight.

'OK, John, you bring down some transport, and we'll load it with eight boxes of cigarettes. We can arrange for a friend called Ernesto to buy them off you at 4000 pesetas a carton. That will give you a good profit and help us with a transport problem we have at the moment,' said Henry. I noticed how Peter had slipped into the background, and the business dealings were being handled by the father. Family ties here were strong and deeply instilled. It was like dealing with the Mafia. I wasn't about to argue.

'What if we get stopped on the road from here to Marbella?' I asked.

'That is the risk you take if you want to make big profits, my friend. But if you plan carefully you can move all the cigarettes you want. All these boxes will be sent up the same road within two days. They will be sold in Malaga near the airport by the weekend,' Henry said and smiled knowingly at me, tapping the side of his nose. The crafty old goat knew how to move the tobacco without getting caught because he was more than likely paying bribes to the police. I would make a nice little offering to the police in return for a bit more peace and quiet for Henry and his family gang. Talk about cheeky, it was written on his face.

'Right,' I replied, 'I can supply transport, but I'll need you to lend me a driver for the van, because I'll be in front further up the road looking for Guardia patrols.' A nice answer, I thought. Henry couldn't refuse to help me, but he wasn't about to sacrifice one of his own gang.

He smiled at me shrewdly and said, 'OK, John, you call me when you have the transport ready in La Linea.' We shook hands and walked outside; suddenly everyone was all smiles again. These guys worked on the principle that their business offers weren't to be refused. I didn't like to dwell on what would have happened in that house if I hadn't agreed to the proposed deal.

I handed over the Escort's keys to Peter, and after he gave his name and address for the Vehicle Registration Document they arranged for one of the cousins to drive me back to Marbella. We all shook hands and wished each other well. I said I would be in contact very soon.

Later that day I sat at Benson's house telling a very different story. I made out that these were guys I had known for months through the motorbiking fraternity and that I was selling the car for £2500 of cigarettes at trade price. I could see Benson was well impressed. We arranged he would have the logbook prepared, and I told him I would pay him for the car within the next two to three days. He congratulated me on getting a good deal and said that he would at some point like to meet my friends in Gibraltar, to which I agreed when this job was over.

That night I called Kath and told her about what was happening. She sounded doubtful about the deal and didn't want me to get mixed up further with another gang of smugglers.

'This is cigarettes, love. It's part of a small industry, and it's no big deal,' I told her. 'These guys are doing it every day and have done so for years. They have all the bases covered, so there is little risk. Most importantly it's my entry ticket to Benson and his mates.' Kath still wasn't convinced by the time we'd finished talking. From where she stood she could see me dropping into a circle of criminals and smugglers who traded stolen vehicles and smuggled contraband. It was a far cry from anything else we'd ever done and was no doubt scary for her. As for me, I was hyper alert and living on my nerves. My stomach was in constant turmoil, and my appetite had dried up.

I called the Customs and gave Rob a précis of what had transpired. I had passed on the registration number of the stolen Escort and a description of Peter and his father, whose full names I had also clocked on their passports. Rob was noncommittal; he didn't say don't do it. He was pragmatic and accepted that I had to have some form of initiation into the smuggling fraternity to prove that I was *bona fide*. But with no encouragement from him I felt very down and sat late into the night musing on the situation.

I was in the middle, that was clear, and I could feel myself teetering on the edge of the smuggling pool. There was no doubt I was now a known man, and I couldn't walk away from this deal and maintain any credibility at all. I had to carry it through or just forget any ideas about living in Spain once the Benson gang was locked up and safely out of the way. No, I would continue and see it through to the end.

Early the next morning I breakfasted in Fuengirola and spent the morning recruiting some help. I visited the bars where I had tried to chip my way into the baddies' world, and in no time the offer of a 20,000 peseta cigarette-driving job soon had people interested. I picked Dave, a singlet-clad Welshman in his mid-20s. A friendly chap always with a ready smile he was rumoured to be lying low on the Costa after carrying out a few building-society robberies in the Cardiff area, topped off, he claimed, by one at a local Kwik Save supermarket on a Saturday. After that things had got too hot for him at home, and he was taking a few months off to enjoy the summer in Spain.

Dave was usually to be found lounging around the bars, or sitting on the terrace reading the *Sun* and drinking endless cups of coffee. He knew some of the local guys and sometimes disappeared for a couple of days, but I don't know if that was because he had pulled a bird, was nursing a hangover or was off on a 'job'. One thing was certain: he seemed to have lots of cash. As a result he wore the best designer clothes and had acquired a motor scooter, an inconspicuous mode of transport in the busy streets of the Costa.

Dave said he would drive my van, and we sat down outside as I laid out the deal. He would drive it down to Gib, count the cigarettes on board and accompany them to their dropping-off point in Marbella. He would also back me up when payment was being made, the point at which, it seemed to me, when the biggest risk might occur. Dave looked like he could take care of himself.

I called Peter on his mobile, and we guardedly made arrangements for the next day. Later I drove down to the builders' merchants in Marbella where the contraband was to be delivered. There I met Ernesto, a tall, hefty man of about 60, who was obviously the proprietor and who invited me into his office for a coffee. He had previously taken a call from Henry, who had informed him of our arrangements. It was a short, wary meeting in which we agreed the delivery would be made in the early evening. To accommodate any unforeseen delays Ernesto would wait until 10 pm for us to arrive; he would have the cash on him to pay me once the cigarettes were delivered into the yard. We swapped mobile numbers, and he wished me luck.

During the afternoon and early evening I again drove down towards La Linea and carefully observed the main road looking for police parking places and likely spots for roadblocks. By now I was feeling really tense and nervous. I wanted to get the job done and out of the way.

That night I met Dave in the London Bar in Fuengirola to make final plans. We decided to do the run in what passed for the rush-hour period when there was less likelihood of a roadblock, and the road would be busy with both commuter cars and tourist coaches heading back to the main resorts in time for tea. Dave had managed to borrow a mobile phone, and we agreed to stay in contact as much as possible so I could give him a running commentary on the state of play on the road ahead. I would drive the motorbike about a mile in front of him and hopefully give him enough advance warning to pull off the road if I saw a roadblock. If I was stopped there would be no problem because the motorbike and I were both legal, and I would have all my documents with me. The presence of a mobile phone marked me as a resident rather than a tourist, but that was of no real concern at that time.

In the morning we set off fairly early and travelled steadily down towards Gibraltar. Dave was driving my Mercedes van, which by now was back in Spain and empty of electrical goods, containing only some boxes and blankets to cover up the contraband. Once again it was a perfect day. The sun was high in a cloudless sky, and there was just a breath of wind off the sea. Driving along we were in constant communication, and I pointed out the various police checkpoints I had seen, and we checked for dead spots in the mobile's signal. Near to La Linea was a bad area for mobile phones, and reception was patchy at best. We would have to work through there as fast as we could. I had already shown

Dave the route we would be taking. He seemed altogether confident and just wanted to get the job over and done with.

I phoned Peter at about 2 pm and told him to meet us in La Linea. We drove there uneventfully and parked up in the car park adjacent to the large outside community swimming pool, a meeting place for camper vans and people on touring holidays. The majority of the vehicles were UK registered, and we blended in well.

A few minutes later Peter phoned to say they were ready, and we set off in the direction of the storage house. In the small lane near to it a young lad ran into the road in front of me and directed us into a yard off a small alley intersection. I swung in, and Dave closed up behind me. A corrugated sheet-metal gate clanged shut behind us, and Peter appeared from a ramshackle storage shed. He was all smiles and full of bonhomie.

'John, man,' he announced, 'your ciggies are all here, and we have put a guy on the top of the hill watching for the Guardia.' This was, I realized, to protect their driver and not for my benefit. We quickly loaded the boxes into the back of the Mercedes and covered them with blankets, but there was no way they would escape discovery if the van were stopped and searched. A young man introduced as Javier was to be our driver. I had seen him on the jetty during the night of my speedboat ride. He was pleasant enough, notable mostly for chain-smoking and just saying 'No problem' all the time. When we were ready to go Peter asked me to call him as soon as the cigs were delivered.

We set off in a convoy: a small motorbike in front to check the roads in town and to lead me a back route out of La Linea; then me on the Goldwing with the van as tail-end Charlie and Javier driving with Dave in the passenger seat looking as if he hadn't a care in the world. My heart, however, was in my mouth. If we were stopped I chanced losing my van to the police; the cigarettes would be confiscated and I would still owe Benson for the stolen Escort. This was the period of maximum exposure for me, and my body was letting me know it. I was quickly developing a banging headache.

Up through the hills, leaving La Linea in the valley below, we made it to the main road without incident. The scooter peeled off and waved goodbye as he shot back down to the coast in a puff of blue smoke. I was speaking to Dave who still seemed totally laid back. I drove easily ahead of the lumbering diesel-engine van to establish a safe distance between us. The road was busy with other traffic, and we were travelling at about 40 mph, which was slow, but the van blended in nicely with the other traffic.

Sure enough, though, as we drove down a long gradient, I spotted a couple of police cars ahead parked on either side of the road, and I quickly warned Dave to be alert. As I got closer I noticed that there was no roadblock yet. The policemen were talking and smoking in a small circle, obviously preparing to set one up. I could see traffic cones piled in little heaps at the side of one of the cars.

I relayed this information to Dave, and they decided to continue rather than pull off the road for maybe an hour or more until the police removed the roadblock. Further up the road I parked up and watched as the white van drove serenely past the police who still hadn't made a move to establish the block. That was too close for comfort for me, and as I picked up the pace again, I asked myself for the thousandth time what was I doing here? This was a far cry from the safe world of contracts and subcontracts in the oil business. I must have been mad.

The rest of the journey was just as tense, but despite the presence of a few police jeeps on the road the trip passed without any problems. We reached Marbella about two hours after leaving Gibraltar, and I called Ernesto. As we drove around the final corner I saw with relief that the yard was clear, and a garage door was wide open for us. I parked over to one side, and the van drove into the gloomy interior.

We quickly unloaded the boxes into a rear storage area.

Ernesto was happy to see us, and he and Javier launched into a conversation in Spanish. When we'd finished we all wandered into the inner office, and Ernesto produced a bottle of local 103 brandy. It was like firewater, but it helped stop the churning low down in my guts.

'Now, my amigo, the money,' said Ernesto, pulling out an old petty-cash box from his desk drawer. He took out an envelope and handed it over. I counted the money. It was dead right. We all said we would do it again next week because it had been so easy, and after a few minutes of chat we left. Dave was to drive the van back to the Fuengirola car park, and Javier climbed on to the Goldwing behind me. He loved the ride back to La Linea as we shot down between the traffic like two maniacs; the radio was blasting, and we waved at all the girls, pretty or otherwise. When I stopped just near the Gibraltar border post he jumped off and thanked me for the ride before disappearing into the throng crossing the frontier. I called Peter and told him everything was OK and promised to visit him again soon when the Vehicle Registration Document was ready for delivery. He was in good spirits and said he looked forward to doing more business with me.

Feeling much more relaxed I turned the bike once again to the north and headed for home at Carmen's. Later that night after a shower and change of clothes I met Dave in the London Bar again. I paid him his wages and was pleased to discover that he had been spreading the word about our little job to his mates. Suddenly the other locals seemed more friendly and had started to nod at me. It was great. I was being accepted into their circle, although I had no doubt they would have turned on me like a pack of wild animals if they had suspected for one minute that I was an informant for HM Customs & Excise and was setting them up for a big sting operation that was calculated to put them all behind bars for a long, long time.

Before a late supper of cheese, bread and tuna and a few glasses of red wine in the 24-hour bar on the front I took time out to phone Kath, who had been patiently waiting at home for me to call her. She was worried that something had gone wrong, and her nervousness and anxiety flooded down the phone at me disguised as shouts of anger. I tried to pacify her, explaining I had been busy and in company all day and could not have phoned her earlier. She wasn't to be put off, though, and gave me a good tongue-lashing. Although I was dejected by her attitude, I could understand how very difficult it was for her at home, kept in the dark and dependent on calls from me at odd hours to enlighten her of my progress. But I felt she didn't understand my position either, mixing with smugglers and criminals and on constant guard every minute of the day, trying to juggle between good and evil whilst knowing that one mistake could well be my last.

Little did I know then that the stress and tension were only just beginning to play a part in the plan, and their combined effects would conspire to nearly wreck our marriage in the ensuing months. It was with a heavy heart that I crawled into bed that night, exhausted by the events of the day: the hours of driving in the relentless heat, the constant vigilance not only over police movements but also of people whom I didn't know and trusted not a whit.

But at the bottom of all the dejection I could feel a little glow of satisfaction. I had done it. Albeit by breaking the law a little, I had nevertheless taken the first step into the world of the drug smuggler. Now I could only go forward and do my level best to stuff every last one of them with whom I came into contact.

47

Secret Agent

WITHIN A COUPLE of weeks I was on the way to becoming established as a free agent in the group of smugglers centred around Fuengirola. I made great efforts to be seen as reliable, sure and not too greedy, with a good knowledge of both the local roads and the main arterial routes up and down Europe.

The work started off with a request to ride shotgun in front of a shipment of tobacco, after which I was asked if I would do the same for a consignment of cannabis resin. The gear was being moved from La Linea to a storage villa just south of Marbella. That job went without a hitch, and I was paid £500 for half a day's work, which just goes to demonstrate the profits made by the drug barons who trade in any commodity so long as it is illegal, and there is money to be made.

They don't handle the goods themselves but just sit in the background organizing deals and shipments whilst their workers on the ground do the actual smuggling and take the risks. That way the barons can't get caught with their hands on any illicit gear and thereby ensure they are almost impervious to prosecution should any of their gangs get caught and turn against them to become prosecution witnesses.

I put myself about more and more, making sure that I kept in close contact with Benson. Every time we met I would drop a name into the conversation just to let him know I was dealing with the right crowd. It seemed I was on the go 24 hours a day, calling in at the different bars from Torremolinos down to Gibraltar during the day and doing the round of the bars, clubs and restaurants that served the night scene.

I quickly learnt a lot about drug smuggling: who was doing what, what the risks were, how packages were wrapped and prepared for shipment to the UK and all the rumours about who had been busted. I noticed that the professional smugglers had commercial vacuum-packing machines and used vast quantities of heavy food-grade plastic bags of varying sizes, of the type in which frozen meat joints are packed in supermarkets. These were the smugglers' main weapon against the sniffer dogs.

First two cannabis soaps are wrapped together in several layers of clingfilm. Then other layers are added, one of black pepper and another of coffee grains. After a final wrap of clingfilm the whole soap is placed in a plastic bag and sealed in a vacuum machine. The air is sucked out, and the bag shrink-wrapped around the contents in that familiar squashed-up look. The sealed bag is then cut to size and the open edge heat-sealed by the wrapping machine. The entire process takes about two or three minutes per soap for the experienced wrapper.

A consignment of a hundred kilos of cannabis contains on average 400 soaps, and the whole lot will be wrapped and stored within a full day. Cannabis resin is a dense product and doesn't take up much room; 50 kg can easily be hidden in an average family saloon such as a Ford Sierra.

The packers and wrappers are masters of misdirection and deceit. The wrapped cannabis is secreted under the back seat and in the door panels, not too much there though as the windows need room in the well of the doorframe to retract when wound open.

More product is hidden within the spare wheel itself and sometimes under the front bulkhead up in the heater area. The heaters are removed, the pipes sealed off, and the hot-air blower motors are taken out. At a casual glance the bulkhead looks identical to any other car, but it is only a metal and plastic shell covering. Cannabis replaces the guts of the heating system.

I have even seen cannabis placed in windscreen-washer bottles and air-filter boxes. Storing it in the engine compartment is tricky, though, because if the car breaks down then the drug could well be unearthed by a mechanic. There are the tales, jokingly passed around, of smugglers whose car engines have overheated and ignited the slow-burning resin. The resultant clouds of blue smoke have passed through the ventilation ducts and into the passenger compartment, affecting everyone in the car. Pleasantly stoned presumably no one cared about being arrested until the next day's sober realization of their predicament.

There are specialists who live on the Costas who professionally fix up cars just for the smugglers. The way in which they work is to obtain a vehicle, usually one on UK plates that hasn't been stolen, and doctor it. They remove the rear seats and sometimes the front ones too, the cloth facings and the padding, and fit in as much cannabis as possible into the seat frames. The padding is cut down and refitted, and then the facing material is also refitted and stitched back in place. It is a professional job, and it is hard to distinguish a cannabis-laden seat from one that has not been tampered with.

If the model of car has a steel partition between the boot and the rear-seat back then that steelwork is carefully cut away. This reveals an open space, which is filled with cannabis. Later the steel is welded back into place and then resprayed in a colour match. Finally the joints are sealed with mastic that exactly replicates the manufacturer's so as to end up with a perfect-looking concealment job. Sometimes a fire-extinguisher or first-aid kit is screwed on to the steelwork to add a touch of authenticity.

These cars are driven back to the UK by experienced operators who charge anything up to £10,000 per trip. The drivers apply for new papers for the car from DVLA in Swansea, take out motor insurance and buy a green card for European travel. Their documents are complete and accurate in every detail and will stand up to any check. Then they recruit passengers for the journey. There are husband and wife teams who, along with their children, regularly do the run between the Spanish Costas and the Channel ports.

In 1994 I heard about an English man and woman in their late 50s who were stopped and searched by French Customs officers on the Hash Highway in the south of France. They had their two young grandchildren in the back of the car who were found to be sitting on 40 kilos of high-quality cannabis resin. The grandparents were arrested, and the children taken into state care, until their parents travelled down from England to collect them. The grandparents are still in prison, serving a six-year sentence in addition to a massive Customs fine or the option of another two years inside.

I do not feel sorry for such people. They are not just naive old grannies caught up in a web of deceit but professional and experienced smugglers who carefully weigh up the risks before getting involved. They don't just walk into a bar in Spain and say, 'Hi, does anybody want me to smuggle some cannabis back to England for them?' That's an unlikely scenario. No, these people make a career of it and have probably already successfully netted thousands of pounds from previous trips.

For the experienced packer other great concealment opportunities are offered by camper vans and towed caravans. Cassette toilets are emptied, and the heavy plastic waste receptacles cut in half. They are filled with cannabis and sealed with plastic welding machines. This effectively forms a tank within a tank, after which the chemical toilet fluids are poured into the top tank. The cannabis-charged cassette unit is refitted into the caravan, and hey presto! there is both a useable toilet and a cache of hidden drugs. It's a brave Customs officer who rakes around in the shit tank just for a quick look-see. The only way to be sure whether or not there are concealed drugs is to weigh the empty cassette unit and measure the depth of the cassette from the exterior as opposed to the interior. This is a nasty, smelly job that, for obvious reasons, will not be undertaken unless the authorities have a very strong suspicion that there are drugs on board the caravan.

Calor gas and propane gas bottles are also used for concealment purposes. A bottle is completely emptied of gas and carefully cut around the middle seam weld into its two component halves. The bottom half of the bottle is filled with 10 kilo of cannabis and then a sheet of light-gauge tin is welded over the top. Finally the two halves of the tank are welded together again and spray-painted before the gas bottle is refilled.

The useable and partly filled bottle is placed in the caravan stowage compartment and connected up to the gas supply. The bottle now functions correctly, and if a Customs officer were to light the gas stove it would work. Alternatively if the official were to disconnect the gas bottle from the small regulator and open the handwheel valve he would get a blast of high-pressure butane gas in his face, another classic trick that is frequently used.

In touring caravans the whole of an interior wall may well be stripped out and the interior foam and polystyrene-type insulation removed. Packets of wrapped cannabis are carefully packed inside the outer skin and secured by tapes stapled to the wooden strengthening supports. The inner wood-grain or pastel-shade veneers are refitted very carefully, and all the accessories wired back into place. Both sides of a caravan receive the same treatment so that it sits levelly on the suspension. If experienced interior fitters are used it is impossible to tell that the walls have been disturbed in any way, although there can easily be 100kg of cannabis, worth £300,000, concealed within an average family-size caravan.

Professionals don't stash cannabis in cupboards or on shelves under clothes or in biscuit tins or coffee or sugar jars. They hide the gear in such a way that no casual check could ever uncover it.

These packers secrete the gear in such a fashion that damage must be done to the fabric of the storage vehicle, be it car, van or caravan, before the cannabis is revealed.

Bear in mind that the gear is wrapped so carefully no sniffer dog would discover the cache and lead his handler to a location. It is a brave Customs officer therefore who would systematically remove the wall from a caravan or cut open a toilet cassette or remove the welded plastic fascia of a caravan fridge or the plastic panelling in a shower enclosure just on a suspicion that there may be drugs stored on board. A normal border or port inspection consists of a sniffer dog inspection of the interior whilst a couple of Customs men open drawers and check shelves and cupboards.

A classic piece of misdirection is to secrete ten or so cartons of cigarettes in a remote, inaccessible cupboard, which are invariably found during an inspection. The surprised smugglers then offer to pay duty on their uncovered tax-free haul of tobacco, whilst the Customs men are satisfied they have found a family bringing back some extra duty-free goods. The offenders either pay the extra duty or escape with a stern lecture about the correct use of green and red Customs zones before shamefacedly driving through the inspection sheds and out to deliver the caravan full of cannabis a couple of days later to their colleagues in crime.

The Customs drugs units work mainly from information from registered informants or tip-offs from the public. They can't start dismantling every vehicle going through the various Channel entry ports into the UK. Abroad in France and Spain there are temporary roadblocks set up along the Hash Highway. These often discover the cannabis hidden by amateurs in the obvious hidey-holes, but they are not equipped to start taking vehicles apart. Any contraband that will pass the sniffer dogs and is well secreted will get past them, assuming of course that the roadblocks actually stop the smugglers in the first place. Most consignments travelling up the Hash Highway are minded by baby-sitters at the front, who are in constant contact with the loaded vehicle. Sometimes there is another vehicle behind providing a rear security screen and acting as overwatch for the main men back in Spain. Every effort is made to ensure that nobody has any clever ideas about taking a wrong turn and making off with maybe half a million pounds worth of easily saleable merchandise.

In 1994 and 1995 there was a growing trend to use motorbikes to carry cannabis. The ever vigilant smugglers had discovered that they were rarely stopped at border crossing points or by roadblocks. By their very nature there cannot be any large quantities of drugs concealed on a bike, unless the gear is stowed in the side panniers or back box, but either way it would be uncovered very quickly.

The smugglers quickly exploited this apparently laissez-faire policy towards motorcycles and put their carriers on to cruising bikes, and thereby sending hundreds of kilos of cannabis over to the UK during the following two summers. The sight of half a dozen bikers, not long-haired yobbos but more mature, respectable citizens riding quality motorcycles such as BMWs, Yamahas, Hondas and the like, does not attract a lot of attention from police or Customs officers. Furthermore, at the British entry ports bikers are the first group of travellers to be disembarked from the ferries, quickly let through immigration and Customs with no more than a cursory glance at the driver's passport.

There are more and more lone operators who regularly smuggle small amounts of gear for themselves. These guys and girls are usually successful because nobody is going to tip off the authorities about them. They keep their departure dates and itineraries to themselves and travel by constantly varying the routes and modes of transport. If they are caught it is usually by chance. Sniffer dogs may catch them because they don't have access to the vacuum-packing machines that are the foolproof method used by the professional gangs.

I knew several lone operators, each of whom did well from

their illegal trade, and as far as I know they are still in business. One young couple, Andy and Jane, were very, very good. When I knew them they had been bang at it for two years. It was their stated intention to carry on until they had sufficient money to buy a house in Wales. In their mid-20s they weren't saving up for a deposit and a white wedding, they were actually going to buy a place for cash.

Andy was smallish and wiry. Fair skinned, he coloured up like a lobster in the sun and was always to be seen wearing a hat. He wore jeans, cut-offs in summer, a Granddad-vest tee shirt and tennis shoes. He was amiable enough in a distant sort of way. Personally I thought there was a lot going on behind his dopey-looking mask.

Jane looked just the opposite. Slightly taller than Andy, she was bubbly and vivacious, always on the go. She had dark skin and tanned to a really good colour under the Mediterranean sun. She looked a real goer and flirted shamelessly with everyone in sight, all part of a carefully contrived image.

With the looks and the body she used both shamelessly to disarm people, effortlessly deflecting questions by 'accidentally' showing off her well-developed tits as she bent down to take a pack of cigarettes from her bag conveniently located on the floor near her feet. She would bend down and fiddle around and then look up with big, innocent green eyes, as if to say, 'Yes, I know what you've been looking at.' She was a bloody good actress who played Jeff to Andy's Mutt, and I'd hear them later, laughing about it.

Andy and Jane appeared quite hippie-ish but not at all rough. They were certainly well spoken, though she had a tinge of a Geordie accent when she was especially animated. They both smoked and drank a tad too much, but with all the stress in their lives that was probably no wonder. They were an ambitious couple who knew what they wanted and were apparently well on their way to achieving it.

I first met them in a known smugglers' bar in Fuengirola. When

I'd been seen to prove my credentials by consorting with some of the local hard men they started warming to me, and we began to talk. Once again the Goldwing was something of an icebreaker, and we chatted for a while about bikes. This led inevitably to a discussion about routes from the UK to Spain and then turned to the pros and cons of different border crossings, the best days and times to try the crossings and so forth.

Over time I had many such conversations with lots of different people in all sorts of strange and exotic locations. Although often drugs were not discussed specifically it would be unreal to think that ordinary people could be so preoccupied with frontier crossings and roadblock locations if they were only carrying an extra bottle of brandy or carton of cigarettes.

Andy and Jane became quite chatty once we had made friends. They didn't discuss their supplier or where they sold the gear, but they openly traded information about the different itineraries they had used, and they were interested in learning more about new and to them untried routes and methods of smuggling. They lived for a month or so at a time in a Dodge camper van based on a little site near Marbella. They were well prepared for their chosen money-making venture: they owned the van outright and had genuine paperwork, green cards, Caravan Club travel dockets and every bit of paper you could want.

The van itself was a diesel-engine professional camper-van conversion. The double-wheel high-top was old but in good condition with very little rust and obviously well cared for with an American-style shiny alloy spare-wheel cover and a chrome ladder leading up to a safari-type luggage rack. Alloy wheels and caged spotlights completed the picture.

During the spring, through summer and up to the middle of September the pair would travel monthly between Spain and England smuggling cannabis-resin soaps. They claimed they always bought from the same dealer and paid top money for the best product. They packed the gear themselves, and their concealment method was apparently always successful. The van's luggage rack held a windsurf board and sail and two Malibu surfboards. The drugs were hidden in one of the boards, which was split lengthways down the fibreglass-moulded side seam. The interior polystyrene was carefully cut away in sections, sized to accept the cannabis soaps, 20 or so of which filled up just over half the length of the board.

When the soaps were wrapped and packed they were sprayed with an aerosol can of cavity-wall fire-retardant spray, the stuff that is used by plumbers to fill holes in walls where pipes pass through. This spray held the soaps in place and stopped any rattles from inside the board. Finally the two halves of the board were put back together and sealed with a fibreglass car-body repair kit. Andy would sit outside the camper van under the awning, a glass of beer at his side as he repaired his damaged surfboard, and nobody paid him the slightest interest.

When the board was 'repaired' he would carefully paint over the newly sealed area. It would then be waxed and left in wet sand overnight prior to being fastened on to the luggage rack with bungee cords. For all the world it looked as if the board had been loaded up without being washed, with grains of sand still in evidence in the cracks and around the protruding skeg.

If they were unlucky and got pulled the van would of course be searched, but there was not even so much as a joint there, and a search of the interior would come up dry. Likewise the spare-wheel stowage, which cried out to be examined, was clean. If the surfboards were taken off and checked the repair was bang on, allowing for the different lengths and thicknesses the board weights were more or less the same. It was a perfect method of concealment. Again it would have to be a brave Customs officer or copper who started cutting up surfboards at random on a chance he might discover some illicit drugs.

On the other hand if they were caught they wouldn't receive such a heavy penalty: first offence, no previous record, of good character and only five kilos of product. Hardly *News at Ten* stuff, so they probably wouldn't even get a custodial sentence the first time around. They would make a profit of £10,000–£12,000 a trip, and that meant that with roughly six trips a year they weren't doing badly. They were also enjoying a hell of a lifestyle while they were doing their work. That young couple, Andy and Jane, were a classic example of how drug dealers make crime pay. They weren't big time, but they were breaking exactly the same laws as the drug barons, and they had carefully weighed up all the odds before getting involved in the business. They'll probably end up as Conservative MPs in a few years' time.

Andy and Jane were independent operators who received some respect from the bigger-known dealers. But they were only two of the many smaller operators, some of whom were successful while others got caught. It was all down to ingenuity, skill and a little bit of luck.

There were lots of wannabe smugglers. Some were dope heads who asked around to find out who had some product for sale, as if it were hard to come by. They wanted a couple of kilos as a first-time run to make enough to get a good start as proper smugglers.

It was obvious they only had a few grand to spend, and they behaved as if they were shopping in a supermarket, always hunting around to try and shave off a couple of hundred pounds from the sale price. If they'd had any experience they would have known it isn't the buying price that is important. The trick is to get hold of good-quality uncontaminated gear, have it properly wrapped and then smuggle it back into the UK. The profits per kilo far outweigh any small differential in buying price. By asking around continually for cheap gear and hanging about for days or weeks on end they marked themselves as amateurs. Then they became easy prey for the hustlers who worked the bars.

A couple of hard-looking men had come from a village in Wales, near Cardiff, to buy a few kilos of gear. They were ex-miners, redundant, thanks to an uncaring and short-sighted Tory government policy. They didn't fancy retraining as sole proprietors of a decorating business or taxi company, so they decided to invest some of their redundancy money in the drug game. Like most newcomers they were tempted by the fantastic profits that could be snatched by the successful smuggler.

These two were a joke. Aged about 40ish they couldn't get over the availability of cheap booze and all the young female flesh on offer in the tourist areas and drug zones of Spain. Most of the time they were either half pissed and swaggering around with a young big-titted girl on their arm or sitting in cafes nursing hangovers and a coffee. They were a desperate, comical pair, who reminded me of characters from *Boys from the Blackstuff*.

I spoke with them several times, and they were friendly in their blunt rural way, used to life down a coal mine and drinking in village union social clubs. They were hard men in their own fashion and would have no doubt been good one-on-one fighters. They were no match, however, for some of the hard-eyed youngsters roaming the Costa del Sol, as they were destined to find to their cost.

The hangers-on and hustlers who infest the Costa del Sol are the bottom of the human pile. With their backs constantly against the wall, they would glass a tourist, casually walk away and eat a McDonald's burger without any thought of the carnage they had left behind them. The miners were from a different school altogether and just weren't equipped to deal with the scum of the earth gathered from all the cesspools of Europe. It was an accident waiting to happen, and I had the misfortune to see it all develop like a bizarre cabaret in front of me.

The two miners, I never did get their real names, used to hang around a few different bars touting for ideas and waiting to bump into 'Mr Big' so that they could do a deal. What dickheads! The bigger of the two constantly carried a beach bag with him. I later learnt he carried a few thousand pounds in it, presumably in readiness to do a deal on a street corner. How daft can you get?

Well, the accident happened one quiet weekend. They had arranged to buy a few kilos from a street dealer, a gypsy-type with a horrible gap in his front teeth who spoke with a lisp. Spanish and broken English spoken thus is something hard to understand or to take seriously. They agreed to meet in a late-night bar in Torremolinos. There Manolo the gypsy was to introduce the miners to his friend who would supply a sample of gear for quality control.

Things went to plan until the sample was handed over for testing. Unused to smoking cannabis the miners had hired a local guy to test the gear for them, rolling him a joint from the sample. That in itself was a remarkable display of stupidity on their part, because obviously the local would declare the product to be of good quality, whatever its true state, so that he would get a kickback from the guys selling the drugs.

The sample was pronounced OK, and the miners agreed to buy a few kilos of cannabis to smuggle home. The most dangerous time in drug dealing is when the money and the drugs are in the same room. That deal fell apart at that juncture. Having taken the money and handed over a few kilos of cannabis soaps in an apartment in the rougher area of Torremolinos I heard the buyers and their new mates the miners had a bit of a party whilst they talked about future business deals. The miners no doubt fantasized about the road to super riches, egged on by a couple of dolly birds, the exotic, erotic location and the booze.

When they left the apartment block late in the night they were jumped by a waiting gang of hoodlums who promptly relieved them of the bag containing the gear. In the ensuing fight one of the miners was knifed in the stomach. The muggers departed with the drugs, and the Guardia Civil duly arrived to pick up the pieces.

The two miners claimed they had been mugged, but they were well off the tourist trail, and the police must have been suspicious. The injured miner was taken off to hospital and his pal for questioning. He must have been seething, but he kept his cool and was released the next day. By this time everyone in town was talking about the hold-up; it certainly made the next edition of the local English-language newspaper.

The miner who had been knifed had a damaged spleen and was in intensive care. Later that night his uninjured mate, who had by then put two and two together and realized the mugging was no casual attack, was making a nuisance of himself going from bar to bar looking for the dealers. Unsuccessful in searching out his enemies he started drinking hard. He claimed he was going to the apartment to get the money back.

I sat in the bar and listened to his impassioned ravings to a little Irish girl serving drinks. She tried to talk him out of it, but she could have saved her breath for it was obvious his mind was made up. When I left the bar he was still working himself up and fuelling his anger by drinking tequila slammers. Nobody had ever told him in his local pub at home that alcohol affected the sensibilities, and in that rage was similar to sex: the spirit might be willing, but the flesh was weakened by too much booze.

Sure enough the drunken miner returned to the apartment looking for revenge and his money. Unfortunately rage and alcohol combine as sweetly seductive but unholy bed sisters, and the Spanish have a beautiful phrase: 'Revenge is a dish best served cold.' The macho bit is OK in the cinema, but in real life it's a good way to get yourself killed.

The next morning as I sat eating bacon and eggs in a pavement cafe I learnt that a drunken tourist had fallen to his death in Torremolinos. The stupid fool, he should have slept on his ire for a few days. Instead he went home in a coffin and his mate in a wheelchair. They had lost several thousand pounds and stuffed their families' chances of getting out of an impending life of grinding poverty in a Welsh pit village, where the only source of work had closed its doors.

They would have been better off starting a decorating business or a taxi company in their mining community. Instead one family is now without a father, and one man has a damaged spleen and no money. This sad tale has a moral behind it somewhere. It is a harsh demonstration of what can really happen in the high-rolling world of illegal narcotics at its most basic level. I took it to heart as a lesson. If I were found out as a Customs informant I too would be going home in a coffin, that was if they ever recovered my body.

* * *

The miners' episode wasn't an isolated story. In the summer it was happening almost weekly. The place was full of hustlers, peddlers of dodgy gear, informers, robbers and, according to rumour, undercover cops. But still the dealers arrived with bags bulging with buying money, ready to take their chances in the drug-smuggling lottery.

A favourite trick of the established well-known and well-heeled smugglers was to climb down from their pedestals and sell a smallish quantity of gear to a new wannabe, usually by using a locally known dealer as an intermediary. The new buyers would be pleased that such and such a body was dealing with them. The dealer would be solicitous and advise them how best to get the drugs back into the UK, sometimes even supplying vacuum-packing services for them. The buyers would swagger around for a few days mouthing off about their business prowess in dealing with one of the bigger dealers.

Off they would go, dutifully following the route set out for them by the nice Mr Big. Meanwhile Mr Big had sent a bigger delivery up the same route, a few miles behind the new guys. When they were safely in the queue awaiting their turn to board the cross-Channel ferry a phone call would be made to either the British police or the Customs.

The new guys were about to be sacrificed to the authorities by Mr Big to increase the chances that his own delivery was not intercepted on the same ferry. Can you imagine the surprise and gut-wrenching fear as the new guys pulled up in the Customs shed at Dover or Portsmouth? They didn't know it but their car registration number was already logged on the Customs officers clipboard. 'Good afternoon, can you pull into that bay over there please, sir?' They must have shit themselves.

Of course the new guys didn't have access to the professional vehicle packers, and so the drugs would be uncovered stashed in the spare-wheel housing or under the seats. Bingo! Go straight to jail, do not pass Go and do not collect your drug profits. Another set of losers in the lottery. Meanwhile Mr Big's load of drugs has headed safely up the motorway to the delivery drop-off point. Who cares about the sacrifice suckers? They were lucky. At least they are still alive.

I passed details of many amateur runs on to the Customs, but they weren't really interested. They were more concerned with netting the major suppliers, the barons. One 500-plus kilo snatch would equal more than 50 of the smaller amateurish-size drug runners. So they were usually left to chance inspections at the ferry ports. It became obvious to me that I should concentrate on getting close to and dealing with the longer established dealers who had access to the barons.

The bigger loads of cannabis, 500 kilos and more, are handled in a completely different and more professional style. These quantities are the province of the really big players, drugs barons and overlords, all dangerous men who have millions of pounds invested in their illegal businesses. Because of the sheer volume of product carried they cannot afford the time or trouble to split loads and secrete everything carefully in cars and caravans. They are in the bulk transportation business, and they need a fast, reliable service shuttling back and forth to the UK on a regular basis.

These guys use the fruit and vegetable packing houses in the Barcelona and Alicante regions. Open wagons containing 20 tonnes or more of fruit and vegetables, usually oranges, are their preferred method of transport. Some massive bribes are paid to stash say 500 kilos of cannabis in the loading bed of a steel tipper truck. Oranges are poured on top, and the gear is concealed under 20 tonnes of fresh fruit. The wagons, with two crew on board, drive for 24 hours nonstop and arrive at the French Channel ports after stopping only to refuel and for calls of nature. The lorries are given priority at the ports because of their fresh-produce cargo. They are rarely detained by the Customs who have to process literally millions of shipments of foodstuffs, chemicals, household products and manufactured items of every type during a year.

Each 500-kilo load successfully delivered by the smugglers represents £1.85 million in sales. Taking into account a purchase price of £300,000 and delivery costs of about £50,000 the drug barons stand to make a profit of nearly £1.5 million per delivery. In 1996 Customs & Excise seized 46,000 kilos of cannabis resin in the UK, mainly at the point of entry, yet they acknowledge that figure represents a seizure rate estimated at only ten per cent of the total amount of the drug entering the country. It is easy to imagine the sheer volume of drugs and the profits made thereon arriving in Great Britain each week.

Another route the big boys use is the tourist coach. Drivers are suborned by offers of large cash payments. The coaches, owned sometimes by major tour operators, drop off their loads of tourists at their holiday destinations and then have a couple of spare days waiting to return to the UK with other homeward-bound, sunburned tourists. The coaches travel to local coach parks, where they are overhauled, washed, cleaned internally, restocked with drinks and so forth. During that time a nondescript van draws up and overall-clad workers transfer a number of suitcases and holdalls into the cavernous cargo and baggage holds located under the aisleway and passenger seating areas.

Days later when the coach collects the home-bound tourists no one would ever question that there are already some ten or twelve suitcases and bags already loaded. The driver heads home knowing that as a tour coach they are unlikely to be stopped and searched by Customs. At frontier crossing points immigration officers may enter the coach to check passports, but they are very unlikely to insist that all baggage is unpacked and checked. Of course all the drugs are carefully wrapped and sealed and so would be undetectable by the sniffer dogs.

At the English entry ports some work a system whereby coaches arrive and pass through the Customs with the passengers and baggage still on board. So the illegal shipment sails straight through the checking area, and another 400 or 500 kilos enters the country with nobody any the wiser. Except the smugglers and the driver.

The driver may be paid up to £20,000 for his part in the operation, which he may split with his co-driver, and there is little risk for either of them. If the drugs are discovered they can simply claim that they didn't see the bags loaded; that they were loaded at the coach park by a local courier firm. They're in the clear and are very unlikely to be successfully prosecuted. Meanwhile if the drugs do pass into the country then the smugglers have made another million pounds or so.

An alternative route used by the big boys is one with which I quickly became closely involved. I was asked to baby-sit a load of drugs being moved from a villa located in the hills outside La Linea to a small working harbour further down the main coastal road, south of Gibraltar.

The drugs were concealed in an old-looking Seat panel van, and I led them down the hour-long journey there without any problems. I drove into the harbour and as per instructions went into a small bar inside the marina. It was a cheap little place with a scarred counter and cracked tile flooring. Sitting at a small side table were two Brits. I recognized them from a British pub in Gibraltar, also frequented by drug dealers. I bought a Coke and sat down with them. One of them, Gerry, was openly rolling a joint, whilst his mate looked on. They seemed quite unconcerned and obviously felt secure in their surroundings.

We chatted for a few minutes while Gerry got his joint going. He told me he was from Northamptonshire, and his mate Vince was from Sheffield. Vince looked a real nutter. Gerry pointed out through the dirty window overlooking the harbour to a pretty sail boat.

'That's the baby, the *Ocean Spray*,' he said. 'She'll sail us back to the UK in no time, and then we drop off the gear and return home for a nice quiet year after so much hard work.' Both he and Vince fell about laughing at this. Whether it was a private joke or they were stoned I don't know, but it amused them no end.

After a while I reminded them there was a van parked around the corner and that the driver was probably having kittens by now.

'No sweat, John boy,' said Gerry. 'Come on, then, let's do it,' and with that he gathered together his bits and pieces and sauntered towards the door. The barman watched us leave with an impassive, blank look on his face. I could just imagine him picking up the phone immediately after we left his bar. I mentioned this to Gerry who laughed out loud.

'No way, Johnny, he's well paid for watching the boat for us,' he said. So the barman was a part of the gang too. It seemed to me that wherever I turned I tripped over a drug dealer or someone in their pay. No wonder these guys were so unconcerned. They had their arses covered on every side.

We climbed on to the boat, and I had a good look around. It was very pretty and clean both inside and out. I know nothing to speak of about sailing boats, but I noticed it had a sturdy rubber boat with a powerful outboard fastened to some bright steel davits on the stern. All the deck ropes were neatly coiled and tidy looking; all in all it appeared a functional, businesslike piece of kit. I surreptitiously paced its length at about 18 metres and noted that it was made of wood, had two masts and seemed to have all brass or steel fittings. It was not unlike another hundred boats lying in the marinas up and down each holiday resort on the Spanish Costas.

I called the Seat driver on the mobile, and shortly afterwards the van crept quietly up the concrete jetty to the boat and stopped alongside. The driver and two passengers got out and stretched. They obviously knew their way around and sauntered off casually to the bar for a drink and a piss.

My job was now done, but I hung around for a while talking with Gerry and Vince, who, it transpired, had jumped Crown Court bail whilst awaiting trial on possession and trafficking charges. For this, he claimed, he would have gone down for a couple of years. 'It's far better to be here in Spain with all the birds and booze,' was his philosophy.

Gerry told me the boat would leave within the next two or three days. They were waiting for a replacement part for the autopilot and would sail as soon as that was delivered and fitted by a marine engineer. By this time the sun was starting to go down, and I took my leave of them as they contemplated loading the drugs on to the boat under cover of darkness.

This opportunity was too good to pass up. It was my chance to land a really good catch for Customs. I had already discussed it with Rob and Steve, and now I had all the information I needed to pass along to them. I knew sufficient details: the name of the boat, her description, port of origin, destination and the amount of drugs on board. The names of the crew were incidental to the operation; the main objective was to stop 2000 kg of cannabis resin from hitting the streets and to catch the organizers.

Everything was set, and I flew back to England to discuss the situation with Customs. We met up at Hartshead services on the M62 again. I bought a copy of a boating magazine at the shop there and searched out a photograph of a boat like the *Ocean Spray* for the lads. I gave them all the information I had and advised them the boat was due to leave as soon as the autopilot was repaired and would probably depart within the week.

Customs were very happy with what I told them and asked me to return to Spain and report back to them as soon as the boat left. I had time for a quick overnight visit home, a meal and a few drinks in a local restaurant, and then off to Manchester airport for Malaga, from where I immediately drove down to the port. It was early afternoon when I pulled in to the harbour, and the boat was still there, glistening in the baking sunshine. By this time the boys were getting really pissed off with hanging about waiting for the repair to be completed.

Gerry seemed a bit suspicious of my interest, and I did not want to push it too far or appear too obvious, so I made up a story of having left a special Zippo lighter there last week. Driving in the area I had thought to call in and see if they had it. Later Gerry gave me his mobile number, and I promised to call him and visit with some beers the next night if they were still there.

That evening I called the Customs 24-hour number and asked for Rob. I had to give my codename to the male operator, who took my message and told me it would be passed on within the hour. It all seemed very James Bond-ish. I confirmed the boat was still in the harbour.

That night I stayed in a small pension nearby, a few miles off the main road. I took no chances and parked the Goldwing well back and away from the road behind some ramshackle outbuildings. I didn't want Gerry or his mates spotting the bike and putting two and two together. I had a solitary meal of ham, cheese and an olive and tomato salad and a few beers. The pension was clean, cheap and restful. After all the running about over the last few days I was knackered so I slept really well.

The next day I phoned Gerry on the mobile number he had given me, but there was no answer. I drove down to the harbour and stopped at a garage to buy a couple of packs of beer. Driving into the port I was surprised that the boat had gone. There was no sign she had ever been there, just an empty berth, the oily harbour water moving listlessly in the bright sunlight.

The guys in the bar were a bit reluctant to talk and would not be drawn into conversation. I sat around outside for a while and drank a few of the beers I had brought with me so that I didn't seem in too much of a hurry to leave. I remembered that the bar owner was in the firm and might well put in a call back to Marbella after I left. A couple of hot hours in the sun drinking beer seemed to me to be a small price to pay for security and peace of mind.

Driving back up to Carmen's pension in Fuengirola I called Customs again and advised them that the boat had left, that the operation was on. I could detect a quickening of interest over the phone. Steve double-checked the description again with me and told me I had done a good job. He suggested I should forget it for now, and they would let me know of any definite developments. I was only too happy to move on. I was a busy boy, and I had a lot more work yet to do.

48

Life in the Fast Lane

THE DRUG DEALERS on the Spanish Costas live in a manner that cannot be likened to anything akin to normal existence. Initially it is important to understand they are mostly from the criminal classes and consequently operate by a different set of rules to other, more law-abiding members of society. These people are human predators, and they cruise through different levels of society like sharks in the ocean. Similar to their marine counterparts they are ruthless, amoral, efficient machines. They feel no loyalty, have no regrets and display no real emotion other than anger when things don't run on track.

If the bigger players are caught and convicted they are rarely rehabilitated as full members of society. They often remain outcasts and will never conform; almost like serial killers they have to reoffend. They are in fact serial drug dealers, and no sooner are they released from prison than they slip back into the netherworld of drugs, sex and violence. They find themselves drawn to the massive illegal profits to be made there like moths to a flame.

They know society cannot really harm them and feel themselves safe from any meaningful retribution that would be a proper deterrent. They certainly don't fear policemen, Customs officers, judges or any judicial process. If caught or informed upon and charged with conspiracy they simply divert funds from overseas banks into the accounts of the best legal minds they can buy. State prosecutors, the Director of Public Prosecutions (DPP) and the Crown Prosecution Service (CPS), are only ordinary, workaday solicitors; these guys employ the best defendants money can buy. Unless they are caught with their hands on the drugs, which happens very very rarely, they usually walk free.

There is no effective deterrent that will stop them from buying, shipping and selling drugs. The only thing they fear are others of their ilk. Drug wars flare up and die away with monotonous regularity, like armies skirmishing along a disputed border. It may be over an imagined slight or a clash between two opposing dealers when buying or selling. Sometimes money carriers are ripped off, or they may tip off the police about each other either out of spite or for gain. It's a classic, capitalist world model, where battles are fought without rules, and any tactics are acceptable. The barons display all the moral attributes of Attila the Hun.

One day after I had been working freelance for a couple of months Colin Benson asked me to meet his son, also called Colin. I had heard a lot about this guy, most of which added up to what I can only describe as a really nasty piece of work. He was 28 years old, unmarried and looked like his father except for his rather feminine-looking mouth and bright pink lips and tongue. Short, fat and prematurely balding, he had black, greasy hair that lay thin and flat against his shiny scalp.

Ostensibly a dealer in the luxury used-car market he was every corpulent inch a successful-looking spiv. With a big diamond signet ring, a gold diamond-encrusted Rolex and top-quality leisure clothes he looked the part. He spoke with a gratingly nasal voice that complemented his image perfectly. Not one for social niceties he talked loudly and used gutter language continually, no matter in whose company or where he was. He would mouth off, belch or fart just as the mood took him, in a bar or restaurant or just walking down the street. He was a Lancashire version of a 1930s' Chicago street hoodlum.

I learnt from his proud father that Colin Jr was deeply mixed up with a London Greek gang heavily into heroin and cocaine dealing; he was a northern England connection for them. He was known to the police and had several minor busts behind him. Early one morning they raided him again after having had him under surveillance for some time and discovered a holdall containing several kilos of cocaine in his wardrobe. Caught bang to rights, he had been arrested and was refused police bail; the local magistrates' court jailed him on remand pending trial.

I was told that his London associates put up a substantial sum of cash for a rather dumb villain to tell the police the bag didn't belong to Benson but to him. Unsurprisingly the police were not taken in by this rather flimsy story, but it was enough of an argument when advanced by Benson's top-flight barrister to convince a judge in a private meeting in chambers that Benson Jr should be granted bail.

Although on bail he continued trading as before until the week of his trial. In the middle of the proceedings, when his barrister told him he would probably be convicted and go to prison for a considerable time, he decided to abscond. One day he just didn't turn up for court. On the run, he headed down to Spain's infamous Costa del Crime. By this time he had acquired some cash, a false passport and some contact phone numbers.

Young Benson arrived on the Costa del Sol looking for somewhere discreet to hide out. Because of my contacts with a couple of estate agents from when I was seeking industrial units for the import business, Benson phoned me and asked if I could locate a quiet, out-of-the-way place, not known to anyone, in which his son could lay low for a while. I told him I would think about it and get back to him. Of course I immediately told the Customs what I then knew about Benson Jr. They were interested and asked me to get closer to him.

I soon met up with both the Bensons. They really were like two peas in a pod. In the three or four days since I had spoken to Colin

Benson his son had established himself in a luxury apartment near Puerto Banus, an upmarket development of high-quality shops, villas and apartments centred around a millionaires' boating marina south of Marbella. Puerto Banus is where the megarich go out to play whilst staying on the Costa del Sol. Several movie icons and pop stars, Adnan Khashoggi the gun dealer and Arab oil playboys use the marine as a base. The value of the yachts in the small harbour would pay off a large portion of the Spanish national debt.

It was in this centre of ostentatious wealth that young Benson had picked a ground-floor luxury apartment for himself, a three-bedroom apartment for £1500 per month, with a two-month deposit. The place was tremendous. A large ornate front door led to a neo-Roman lounge complete with black and white marble tiles and floor-to-ceiling fluted columns. The lounge contained a pond with a fountain, a posh bar with an ice-making machine and a small disco-style dance floor. The furniture was old and heavy with an array of white leather chairs and settees around a massive coffee table with a solid crystal glass top. There was also a space-age kitchen, four bathrooms, a games room with a pool table and large French windows opening on to a tile patio overlooking a kidney-shaped community pool.

It really was quite incredible, and all that was missing was a drawer full of gold chains and a condom machine. As is customary in Spain the apartment was furnished down to the last detail, and all Colin Jr needed to do was to move in his clothing. Everything else came with the property: bed linen, table napkins, towels and his and hers bath sheets were all provided.

This was living millionaire style, and it was beyond the reach of most people. Yet this bloke had jumped bail, driven through Europe in a nicked car and less than a week later was luxuriating in a superrich lifestyle. But it had to be paid for, and he was the lad to organize the money-gathering. When I was first introduced to him by his father he wanted me to escort a shipment of 100 kilos of cannabis from Malaga up to a mate of his in Benidorm. He offered me £3000 for the trip and pulled a thousand out of his pocket there and then. I thought this was a good one for the Customs, and so I nodded at him in agreement.

'Right, well, you'll be going tomorrow night, so you can stay here with me tonight, and we'll have a few drinks together,' he said. So much for me immediately tipping off the Customs. I quickly found out that dealing with this guy was not like playing around with his father or any of the others in Fuengirola. This boy meant business, and he was as paranoid as a nun at a whores' convention. I immediately sensed a feeling of mistrust in him, and I resolved to tread very carefully.

I told him I would go out for a drink that night, but first I would have to return to my digs to shower and change my clothes. He smiled and offered to drive me there so that we could chat. There was no way I could refuse without it seeming suspicious. So we all piled into his car, a nearly new Mercedes with air conditioning, leather seats and dark-tinted windows, and went off to collect my kit.

It was always the same with Benson Jr: instant decisions, immediate action and sod the consequences. He should have been a City trader, and he certainly lived the lifestyle of a well-born and moneyed young executive. But because he was the new boy on the block he had to do some of the dirty work himself, and he would turn up unannounced at the sharp end from time to time.

After he had been in Spain for only a few weeks already he had acquired a small circle of friends, one of whom always carried a small automatic gun. It wasn't a Dirty Harry magnum-size showstopper, but it was enough to put a few holes in anyone who ripped off Benson or any of his mates. The frightening thing was not only that the gun was so easily available but also that he was probably stupid enough to use it. I didn't want any target practice on me.

* * *

I had visited Benidorm and the general area of the Costa Blanca many times in my life. Since living there during the abortive period when we had owned a bar in the old town we had returned frequently to visit my parents and on quick-break holidays. Whilst we hadn't formed any firm friendships in that town with its largely transient population we did know plenty of the old-timers, that is the people who have lived there for more than two or three years.

I certainly knew some of the dodgier hang-outs frequented by drug users, and it didn't take a great leap of the imagination to work out that the drug dealers were located in the same locales. I had used my Benidorm knowledge as part of my credibility-building factor with Benson, and now it was being called upon by his son.

The day of the Malaga–Benidorm run I met some English guys at Benson's apartment, and we planned out a route up to Benidorm. Really it was simple: follow the coast road towards Almeria, branch inland to pick up the motorway and carry straight on towards Alicante. It was a hell of a run, but actually safe enough. The Guardia were more likely to be looking for drug shipments heading towards the French border than any running along the coast roads.

The drugs were stashed in a butcher's van packed solid with trays of chicken, beef and so on. The vehicle was refri-gerated and bloody cold inside the rear compartment. Of course the idea was that the chill factor would defeat a casual search; no copper would make a driver and his mate empty out a full load of frozen but quickly melting foodstuffs at the roadside. That was the theory at any rate.

The van was based on a Seat diesel. A Seat is a Spanish-built Fiat, and like all Italian-bred vehicles it could really motor. The two English guys, George the driver and Alf his mate, were obviously well known to Benson, and I had the feeling I was going to be under scrutiny the whole trip. Anyway we all checked the batteries in our mobiles, agreed stopping points along the route, and then we were off.

It was a beautiful day, and we made good time along the road up past Fuengirola, Torremolinos and past the outskirts of Malaga itself. We swung inland for a while and then settled on to the motorway-like road through some stunning scenery, cliffs and coves that flew past at a good rate.

I arrived at the first stopping point a good ten minutes in front of the van and had a drink and a cigarette leaning against a wall as I watched the oncoming traffic. When the van pulled in the two lads disappeared inside the café cum garage without acknowledging me, though they had surely seen me and the Goldwing, both of us were in plain view. It seemed to me that for the first time I was working alongside a gang who seemed to have an idea of what they were about. I set off while they were still inside and motored further up the road in front of them.

Driving that motorbike around in a hot climate, with the sun shining down and not too much traffic, is better than riding in cold, wet England. There is no need for sets of leathers, scarves, gloves, boots and all the other warm and wet-weather paraphernalia. You can drive in shorts, shirt and trainers, though, of course, the safety purists argue that you need all the Kevlar protective gear whatever the weather. My view is that if you are dicing with death every day whilst acting as a drug informant the chances of being injured in a motorbike pile-up fade into insignificance. So there I was cruising up the road listening to a tape of Queen and Freddie Mercury singing 'Radio Ga Ga' and thinking that everything was pretty cool.

By now I was missing Kath and Natalie and wanted to get home for a few weeks to relax with my family. But I knew that by now I was deeply enmeshed in the drugs scene and that if I did anything so obviously out of step with the drug gangs' philosophy it would cause needless suspicion. So I resolved not to go back to the UK for a few more weeks at least. There was nothing for it but to continue on the road and try and find time to contact the Customs as soon as possible.

We drove for six hours that day, stopping every hour for a ten-minute break, mainly for my benefit. There's nothing like a thrumming bike seat to give you a numb bum. At first it's just uncomfortable, but if you ignore it the cramps set in, and it can be bloody dangerous. So we pulled over and had a cigarette and a drink from time to time and filled up with fuel. Other than a few words on the mobile there was no sign of recognition among us.

Towards tea time we passed through the sprawling town of Elche, and I knew we were on the last leg of the journey. On the bypass there I saw the first Guardia Civil car of the day travelling in our direction. The boys inside were smoking the inevitable Ducados and talking to each other, and they didn't seem like much of a threat to anyone. Up beyond Elche, then the area capital of Alicante, to Alicante airport, we kept to the motorway and didn't drive along the pretty, wide boulevards of the town. Then past Villajoyosa and its squalid roadside brothels and the short jag up to Benidorm, one of those places, like Miami, that always look good in the distance; it's when you see it up close and smell it that the magic starts to break down fast.

The van drivers and I had a short meeting at the motorway services outside Benidorm and worked out where we were to leave the van for collection by the other gang. We decided on a supermarket car park near La Nucia. Back on the motorway we drove for about ten minutes until we hit the Benidorm exit. We could see the town twinkling off to our right, and it looked great in the evening twilight. Instead of turning off towards it we took the exit up towards La Nucia. I watched as the van passed safely by the exit toll booth manned by an elderly woman.

Near La Nucia we drove through the roadside lemon groves; the aroma was enchanting. Soon we came to a supermarket and small parade of shops on the right-hand side, which had only just closed. We pulled off separately into the car park, the boys parking the van discreetly at the rear amongst the rubbish skips and empty pallets. It looked innocuous there, as if it were waiting till the next morning to make a delivery.

We got out, and the boys tossed to see who was sleeping with the van. George won, and after a quick call to young Benson we left Alf sulking with a cold pack of beer and some sandwiches before setting off on the Goldwing for the lights of Benidorm. We headed for town over the bumpy Lemon Express train lines and drove into the Ruzafa, one of the main streets in the old town.

We parked the bike alongside a million mopeds and some go-faster 125cc screamers, locked up the helmets, set the alarm, collected our mobiles, and we were off. I said we should check out the accommodation situation and visit some of the bars I knew.

Near the headland in the small pedestrian precinct of Calle La Palma, known more accurately by the locals as the Street of 1000 Arseholes, is the Playboy Bar. From the outside it resembles an old sweetshop, inside it is all dark wood and red upholstery with a spotlit bar and heavy Andalusian furniture. Tourists are encouraged and provide a welcome diversion from the locals bemoaning their lack of funds. The Playboy specializes in mixing weird and exotic cocktail drinks: the Banana Cow is a house speciality. The music is rock à la Jimi Hendrix and Bruce Springsteen. Eddie the bar owner, a tall, slim ex-Brummie, is discreet; a part of the old Benidorm establishment set, he is a good friend and drinking partner of Ray the Chippy, Benidorm's original fish and chip shop proprietor.

Eddie doesn't do drugs, but he watches the cavorting and shuffling throngs in his bar and sticks to offering a sympathetic ear to the never ending tales of woe. He learnt his bar trade in New Orleans and copies the Swiss style of management, knowing what goes on but happy to be a neutral observer and pocket the profits of selling drinks to winners and losers alike. Eddie is ageing now, with a few grey hairs creeping into his immaculate black pelt. He is respected in the town, and there is never any trouble in the bar; you get the feeling that it wouln't be a good move to argue with Eddie: he has presence.

The Playboy has the best-stocked bar in Benidorm, offering more varieties of whisky than can be found anywhere else in the town. The up-market locals meet in Eddie's for a few drinks and a gossip on Saturday afternoons and on Sundays before taking their families for Sunday lunch at the Broadway or whichever other eating joint is in vogue that season.

When we walked into the Playboy that night it was as if I had only been there earlier in the week. Eddie didn't raise an eyebrow, he just nodded and said, 'You look a bit thirsty. What'll it be? San Miguel or Mahou?' We settled for a bottle of Mahou each; no glasses, thanks, we're locals and eschew such niceties. It was close and hot inside, and Eddie was obviously econom-izing with the air con again, so we wandered outside and leaned against the wall watching the street activity.

Not far from the Playboy is The Castilian. A Spanish bar not for the faint-hearted, there are never many tourists in The Castilian. Years ago it was a small open-all-hours walk-in establishment with a minuscule bar area and a large grill where Carlos would cook a wicked *pincho* or burger with blue cheese and garlic filling.

Now after taking over and spreading into Harry's Bar next door, it is bigger and boasts separate male and female toilets, but the atmosphere is still overtly mid-80s, Spanish hippy. Walk in anytime after 10 pm and the noise will deafen you. Leather-jacketed locals use the place as their supply house. The whisky of choice is straight Ballantynes *con hielo*, and cannabis is available from a number of suppliers who frequent the place. As in most of Spain there is a regular supply of good-quality gear at good prices.

Generally a quiet, moody bar you can on occasion be treated to an impromptu flamenco show. But don't get upset if the dancer stumbles and crashes into your table – in keeping with the spirit of the place just shout a little, playfully, and offer the artiste a drink from your bottle, or you can always join in if you're so minded. The guy slouched at the end of the bar staring into the mirror behind the bar could be the local undercover narc. He won't bother the locals, but he has been known from time to time to pull a tourist and demand an on-the-spot 'fine', especially at the end of the month.

Brash, brassy Benidorm is like an old, careworn whore with a false smile and bleached hair, but I always feel comfortable there. I know all the nooks and crannies, the ups and downs and the places to avoid. That night though I was tired and just wanted a room, shower and bed. But it wasn't to be.

My mobile started ringing; it was young Benson. He wanted us to locate the guys who were collecting the van and hand it over to them. He told us he would be up in the morning to pick up his money for the delivery. This guy's arrogance was unbelievable. Everyone else was guarded in conversations when they were talking over open telephone lines, but he didn't seem to care a toss one way or the other. I kept the conversation as short and neutral as possible and promised to call him back later.

We walked to some phone boxes near the Plaza Triangular, near to where the Avenida Mediterraneo runs out of the narrow streets of the old town down the dual carriageway thoroughfare towards the Rincon de Loinx of the New Benidorm with its skyscrapers, McDonald's burger bars and night-club scene. We waited amongst the ETs – tourists phoning home – until a cabin came free. I stood outside whilst George called the local contact and made arrangements to meet. He grinned and gave me a thumbs up, and we returned to the bike and headed out of town back towards La Nucia and the parked van.

We found Alf fast asleep. We could have nicked the van from under him without him knowing what was happening. After a bit of piss-taking and another can of beer each an old-looking estate car on Alicante plates rolled into the car park. George and Alf seemed to recognize its two occupants and walked over towards them. Friendly nods and greetings were exchanged, and then the leader of the two newcomers looked over at me. He was about 35 years old with a broad Scots accent and wearing a baseball cap and blue jeans. A grubby-looking, baby-faced individual, he looked as if he were in need of a good tubbing with disinfectant and carbolic soap.

'Who are you then, friend?' he asked me. 'I'm showing these two the quietest routes and baby-sitting the van for Colin,' I replied, looking straight at him.

'I don't know you. You could be a narc for all I know,' he replied.

I knew he was just sounding off and couldn't possibly have a clue about my real role, but instinctively I felt my guts clench tight. This was just the kind of shit I didn't want.

'Well, mate,' I said, 'I don't know you either, but I'm not having kittens about it. You know Alf and George, and that's good enough for me.'

'Yeah, leave it, our Keith,' said George. 'John's OK. He's running with Colin now. He's just earning a few bob doing a little work on the side.'

Keith nodded, but I could sense a feeling of mistrust; he was obviously a careful man. We all walked over to the freezer van, and Keith said, 'Let's have a look at this gear then.' I thought he was joking, but George and Alf immediately opened the rear doors and started pulling out the trays of frozen food.

'What the fuck are you doing?' I almost shouted. 'We can't unload everything here. If the coppers drive past we'll all be busted.' George looked at me as if he hadn't considered the stupidity of unloading a freezer van full of frozen meat products in the dark at the back of a supermarket.

He nodded slowly. 'Yeah, John's right,' he said. 'We'll show you at your place.'

Keith nodded as if we'd just passed some sort of test, maybe it was a dope test. 'Yeah, OK, we'll take the van and see you boys in the morning.'

That seemed a better solution to me, because if anyone were going to get screwed it wasn't me. We quickly agreed to meet up at noon the next day, and Keith and his silent pal would drop George and Alf off down in Benidorm before shoving off to their hide-out. Quickly we mounted our respective rides and set off into town. I could feel my ears burning and could easily imagine the sort of conversation they were having in the estate car about me.

After the two Benidorm dealers had gone, Alf, George and I decided to have a last drink before finding a room. It was then I realized that the two of them seemed extraordinarily happy. The daft pillocks had both dropped an E courtesy of Keith and his mate during their short car ride. There was nothing I could do about it, they were set for a night on the town, dancing the night away. I made my excuses, pleading I was tired after the long drive from Malaga and slunk off to find a hotel. The boys weren't upset. I could see their feet itching as they jigged about impatient to be on with the night's entertainment. We said our goodbyes, and then I left them to it, silly idiots.

The next day Colin Benson arrived along with two more of his henchmen. He seemed to have an inexhaustible supply of them. They completed the final deal with Keith the Benidorm dealer, but by that time I was on the bike and headed back to the Costa del Sol. I had stopped at the first motorway services and put in a long call to my Customs handlers. Of course by then it was all after the event information, but it was of interest to them to have details of how the cannabis was moved between the coastal areas and the method of transport, as well as the names of the players involved.

I never did discover the final outcome, but a few months later I overheard that the regular shipment up to Benidorm had been busted. No one ever told me if that was a result of my information. Dealing with the Customs is rather like talking to a sponge: they take it all in, but never give back any information.

Benson Snr had been in discussions with a gang based in Liverpool.

His son effected the introductions to mates he had picked up during his time on remand. From conversations I heard it seems that remand prison is a form of employment bureau for villains; as soon as they are let out there is a job ready for them.

This gang were regular shippers of hundreds of kilos of cannabis and some cocaine. Recently they had lost a few loads, and because they weren't sure if it were either just dumb bad luck or the suppliers or shippers had an informer in their midst they wanted to try a new route and a new shipping contractor. Benson was ready made for this type of operation. I was in contact with my Customs handlers from day one on this shipment, and we were all set up and prepared.

The plan was that Benson would arrange to ship 65 kilos into Liverpool as a trial; if that were successful then he would organize 300 kilos a month along the same route for a six-month period. I don't know what he was due to be paid per kilo, but the thought of it was enough to make his eyes water. He spent thousands of pounds setting up his operation on the strength of profits to come.

Advertisements were placed in newspapers in the UK, the Costa Blanca and around the Malaga region offering furniture removal, shipping and export and import services. Offices were rented, letterheads produced and staff employed. A nearly new Mercedes box van was bought legally in England, sign written and driven to Spain.

There is a constant stream of people moving from England to live in Spain, and a line of folk returning in the opposite direction, of families beaten by the harsh economics of business, of lives ruined by booze or relationships shattered by infidelity. Spain is the absolute testing ground for partnerships and dreams. Many of these treks back and forth require an accompanying house move, and international furniture removers have, so I am told, a great and thriving business as a result.

Benson's idea was to graft a drug-smuggling organization on to an existing outfit. He started a business and got it off the ground very quickly. This was not as hard as it sounds because Benson succeeded by cutting prices to the absolute minimum and giving all sorts of guarantees about deliveries and free breakage insurance and so forth. His real competitors must have sat there scratching their heads and wondering how he could do it.

He dispatched several loads to England without any drugs on board just to test the Customs systems at frontiers and check out the roadblock inspections. I saw the consignments of furniture and household possessions leave. Everything was done properly: all the boxes were marked with collection and delivery addresses; there were typed inventories and multicopies of all paperwork. It was a dream to behold.

Eventually Benson and his paymasters deemed themselves satisfied and were ready to try a smuggling run. Furniture and household effects were collected from addresses in and around the Fuengirola area, all destined for the UK. The idea was that the drugs would be concealed in boxes in the middle of the household items. As insurance against the drugs being found the van driver would have an inventory that showed he had collected the boxes from an apartment in central Fuengirola.

This apartment actually existed, but it was a studio holiday-let for cash on a weekly basis. Two girls had rented it, had given false ID to the flat's caretaker who was really only interested in the proffered pile of pesetas he'd received from the skimpily clad young women. The pair just disappeared after the boxes were collected. I remember how the driver and labourer laughed about the fact that the caretaker had helped them load up. If questioned subsequently, however, he would not remember anything out of place or dubious about the exercise.

The boxes were inventoried and placed carefully amongst the genuine delivery. Each box was identified by a mark that confirmed it had been supplied closed and sealed by the customer, so the company were taking their client's word that the inventory was accurate. George, of the Benidorm run, was to be the driver again. I was to be paid £1000 cash to escort him as a baby-sitter to the Channel port.

A week before the operation was due to take off I returned to England. I met up with Rob and Steve, my Customs handlers, at another clandestine rendezvous in a motorway services, and we went through the operation in detail. I told them that I was to accompany the van carrying the cannabis up to the ferry port and then ring Benson to tell him it was on board. He would have another passenger on the ferry to check it went through British customs all right. Rob wanted me to phone him with the description and registration number of the van, which I said I would do as soon as the van was loaded. I had noticed, however, that Benson had become increasingly tense as the planned departure time approached. He was behaving in a very paranoid fashion and going to extreme lengths to keep the operation a secret, even from his normal circle of friends. Unbeknown to me he might arrange for a last-minute switch of vehicle. Nevertheless our tactics were agreed, and we parted. I returned to Spain, explaining my absence by the fact that Kath was ill and would have to go into hospital for treatment.

Two days later we set off. George drove the Mercedes van filled with furniture and the drug shipment, and I rode the Goldwing out front. We were in constant contact by way of mobile phones. From Malaga to Madrid the trip went like a dream. We stopped every two or so hours for the usual quick break, piss, drink and fuel up, then we were off again. The first night we reached a small town on the outskirts of the northern edge of Madrid. I pulled into a small motel just as dusk was falling and checked in and paid in advance for one night. Whilst unloading my overnight bag from the bike's panniers outside I called George and told him where I was.

A few minutes later he pulled into the car park and, ignoring me, walked in to the motel and booked himself in. After a shower I went into the bar cum restaurant and ordered a drink. George was sitting further up the bar nursing a beer, and we struck up a conversation and decided to have a meal together. To any observer we would have seemed just like two Brits travelling on the same road who after a chance meeting decided to chew the fat together. Outside on the patio drinking brandy and cokes we had a more private chat. I felt a little sorry for George, because if all went to plan he would be locked up the next night. Our drink together could very well be his last taste of brandy for a few years to come, if only he did but know it.

A few hundred yards up the road in what passes for next door on those Spanish international routes I could see the brightly lit, flashing neon signs of a Whiskeria. Ostensibly a late-night drinking club this is often a front for a brothel in Spain. I suggested to George that as he hadn't had a Spanish bird he should go along and try it out. Not speaking the language he was loath to go on his own and wanted me to accompany him.

So at about ten o'clock there we were walking into a brothel in northern Madrid. Inside it was dimly lit with red lights and spotlights on a small, raised stage area. Most of the customers were obviously transport drivers and local farmer types, a friendly enough bunch. We wandered over to the bar and ordered two beers from a bare-breasted girl behind the bar. Things were looking up.

Two beers and two whiskies of indeterminate manufacture were pushed across the bar. After much shouting back and forth over the loud 80s' dance music I learnt that every drink order had to include a whisky. The round of drinks cost 4000 pesetas, approximately £20, to include a free floorshow. A quick glance round the other patrons showed that they too all had small whisky shot glasses in front of them, so the rip-off was not just limited to us foreigners.

We made our way towards an empty table and chairs and within a minute of sitting down two 'ladies' wandered over and sat down too, smiling ingratiatingly at us. George beamed at me. Silly sod! he thought he'd pulled a bird already. I leaned across and explained the situation to him as directly as I could. These girls were workers, who would sit and entertain us, but we would be expected to buy a bottle of exorbitantly priced house champagne for the privilege. Later you could take the girl of your choice upstairs to one of the bedrooms for an agreed rate.

George seemed all for this but was badly hampered by his lack of Spanish: he was hard pressed to order a sandwich and a beer, so chat-up lines were way out of his vocabulary range. We were well off the normal tourist routes, and the girls, though willing, didn't speak much English. So I sat there like a big brother translating all sorts of shit whilst the women sat there grinning and drinking the £25-pound bottle of lookalike champagne as if they had been parched in a desert all day.

I was rapidly becoming pissed off with the situation and regretting I'd advised him to visit in the first place. I'm game for a laugh with the best of them, but I draw the line at screwing some roadhouse hooker who has probably been had by more men than I've had hot dinners. No, thanks, I wasn't that desperate.

I went for a piss, and when I returned George and his girl had disappeared, I couldn't see them dancing so unless they had gone outside for a walk they were no doubt upstairs making conversation. His lack of vocabulary hadn't slowed him down at all, still I suppose some subjects just cut right through the language barrier. I made my excuses to my intended and left.

The next morning George wasn't around for breakfast, but I couldn't really go and knock him up as we weren't supposed to know each other. No doubt he had been playing out till late with his new girlfriend and had overslept. I dawdled as much as I could with breakfast and then spent time ostensibly checking my route on a large map I spread over the breakfast table.

George appeared eventually. He looked bloody rough, his eyes screwed up against the sunlight streaming into the room, obviously nursing a daddy of a hangover. Over coffee he told me he had phoned Benson who had given him a change of plan. Rather than head up through France to the Channel ports we were to go to Santander or Bilbao. These are sea ports on the northern Spanish coast, both of which receive ferries directly from the UK. They have a longer sea crossing of 24 hours, and sailing the Bay of Biscay in winter can be a bit hairy. But these routes have the advantage of missing out France completely, thereby cutting out the risk of the Franco-Spanish border, the internal Customs checks, roadblocks and sometimes overvigilant police at the ferry ports.

On the other hand the Customs in Britain tend to concentrate on the Spanish-originated ferries as they know that all the vehicles have come directly from Spain. It was a risky decision for Benson to take and to me only a further demonstration of his paranoia. George had no idea about any of this and in his state was looking forward to the shorter drive.

We set off ten minutes apart and headed towards Santander. After we had passed Burgos and were in the high mountain passes that separate the northern coast from the great Spanish plains we stopped for a coffee. George was by now looking green around the gills. I was surprised when he pulled Brittany Ferries' Santander to Portsmouth timetable from his pocket. Maybe Benson was checking me out, and it had been their intention to take that route all the time. Now my paranoia kicked into overdrive.

George called the ferry terminal only to be told the next boat was fully booked, and there would be no room for him until a crossing in two days' time. He then tried P&O in Bilbao and learnt there was space for the four o'clock sailing. We would have to hustle but decided to go for it anyway. There was no sign of any police activity along even the busier routes. George drove as fast as the van was capable, while I just cruised nicely on the bike all the way into Bilbao.

At Bilbao we were late, but we parked up on the hill overlooking the port and watched the commercials being loaded on to the ferry. Benson's instructions had been explicit on this point: George was to wait until the last possible moment before boarding as Benson believed the Customs were less likely to check thoroughly a vehicle that was holding up departure. Maybe Benson was right, because as I sat alone later at the top of the hill I saw the Mercedes waved straight through the Spanish Customs checkpoint to join the last of the vehicles waiting to embark.

I drove into Bilbao and found a small bar, from where I phoned the Manchester Customs number. I quickly got put through to Rob. 'Hi, Rob, it's Benjy,' I said.

'Hi, Benjy, how's it going?' Rob's northern burr came back at me.

'OK. I've just watched our friend drive on to the P&O ferry at Bilbao. He'll be docking at Portsmouth sometime in the next 24 hours or so.' I gave him the van details and the registration number.

'Great work, Benjy,' said Rob and read the number back for checking, 'but I thought you said it would be Cherbourg,' he countered.

'Yeah, I know,' I replied, 'but Benson's been acting really strange over this one, and by pulling this change of route at the last minute he's really cut down the potential for anybody knowing where the shipment is going through. If anything happens he'll suspect me or George, and if George's been banged up he'll twig pretty quickly that it can't have been him.

'I suggest you let this load through. You can easily follow it into Liverpool and pull it there. But really, you know, this is only a trial run. If this gets through there are plans already made to send a 200- or 300-kilo shipment through in the next two weeks. Maybe it would be safer if you let this one go and grab the big prize next time.'

Rob was silent for a moment as he considered my proposal. 'I don't know, Benjy, it's not my decision. I'll tell my boss of your problem and see if we can't work out some solution that doesn't expose you to Benson,' he said.

'What do you mean, you'll try and work out a solution? This

isn't a game of chess. If you get it wrong, and Benson susses me out then I'm dead,' I said down the phone. I could feel my ire rising at Rob's seeming indifference to my plight. If Benson discovered what was going on I would have a very short career from here on.

'Leave it with me, John,' said Rob, forgetting my codename for the moment. 'We'll work something out. Call me back later tonight or tomorrow,' and he hung up before I could protest further.

I felt as if I had just been fucked over. There was a definite awareness that now they had the information they wanted I was on my own. I sat down heavily and ordered a coffee and brandy. I had some serious thinking to do before I made any more moves.

I phoned Benson's home, but he wasn't in, so I told his girlfriend, Susan, that I would phone back later. Then I called his son's mobile number, which was answered by Alf, a supposedly trusted gang member, with whom I'd done the Benidorm job.

'Hi, Alf, it's John the bike here,' I said, using my identifying name given because there were so many Johns involved in the gang and amongst their mates.

'Hi, Johnny, what do you want?' he answered.

'I'm looking for either of the two Colins,' I said. 'It's a bit urgent.'

'I'm in the bar playing pool with some of the lads. They're not here at the minute, mate. Do you want to leave a message?' Alf asked.

Sucker, I thought to myself. 'Yeah, tell Colin that I've just left our friend at Bilbao. Everything went as sweet as a nut. I'll speak to him later.'

I felt a bit better. By spreading the message I had lessened my own accountability by increasing the number of people who knew about the route. If push came to shove it might get me out of a sticky situation. If other people knew what was going on I could only be blamed for breaking security and not for being an informer. At least that was my theory. Wrapped in that weak protective armour I turned the bike and pointed south towards Malaga again.

It was a long, pensive drive back. I stopped for the night this time near the Toledo exit off the main highway and checked in at another hotel. I grabbed a handful of change and went off to find a call box to phone the Customs. I didn't want anybody checking my room phone later and finding a surprise on the telephone call register.

It was early evening and allowing for the time difference the Customs office would be closed, so I called the London emergency number. I identified myself, gave them the phone number and asked them to have Rob call me back as soon as possible. He rang me within five minutes.

'Hi, Benjy, how y'doing?' he asked, all bright and breezy.

'I'm really concerned, Rob,' I told him. 'Have you decided to play it straight up or are you going to stuff me?' I asked hastily. I was feeling really worked up by now.

'Well, we had a long meeting about it, and we've decided to take no action at this end; except to cover ourselves we've had to notify the Portsmouth office that a consignment is due in sometime soon. We weren't any more specific than that,' Rob explained.

'OK, I can live with that,' I said. 'If they pull the gear then it's more a question of bad luck rather than just targeting the wrong van.'

'Yeah, that's about the size of it,' said Rob, 'so you can stop worrying and go back there with an easy conscience. You are in the clear.'

'Thanks, Rob,' I said. 'You can always take out the next bigger load.'

With that I signed off, and after phoning Kath and updating her on the latest events I went back to the motel. I had a few drinks that night and went to bed half pissed to sleep fitfully dreaming of Benson and his mates attacking me with iron bars. The next morning I felt awful, with a raging headache and all the familiar symptoms of the high blood pressure that plagued me from time to time. I resolved to see the doctor when I returned to England.

After a long, hard drive I arrived back in Fuengirola late that night, tired, hot and dusty. I phoned Benson to check in. He sounded concerned and told me he hadn't yet heard from George. My heart dropped into my boots and then shot straight up to my throat.

'Oh, shit! You don't think he's been pulled do you?' I asked in a voice laden with dread.

'I fucking hope not,' he said menacingly. 'You'd better come up here in the morning.'

'Sure thing! I've just got back, and I'm knackered, so I'll see you about eleven,' I said.

'OK,' he grunted and hung up, obviously not a happy teddy.

I phoned the Customs and went through the usual rigmarole before asking for Rob to phone me. Ten minutes later the call-box phone rang, and I snatched up the receiver.

'Rob, it's Benjy. Listen, Benson has just told me that the van driver, George, hasn't called him. Did the van get pulled by the Customs in Portsmouth?' I gabbled.

'Relax, John. I've had no reports that the van was stopped. The driver's probably going to phone in the morning. If he's got any sense he'll be in bed or having a drink in a club. Leave it until tomorrow, and I'll check up then.'

Rob seemed so confident that I did relax. He was the professional, he could weigh up the risks in an operation. Yes, I'd leave it until tomorrow. George would ring then. I went to bed that night certain I was in safe hands, which just goes to show what a bad judge of character I am.

49

Feel the Pressure

THE NEXT FEW weeks of that long, hot summer were both busy and scary times for me. After the Bilbao operation when, despite my warnings and fears for my security, British Customs had busted George in Portsmouth, I was sure I was being watched carefully by many of the boys in the various gangs. George had been pulled at Portsmouth ferry port, and 65 kilos of cannabis were discovered by a sniffer dog. He, of course, had played the innocent claiming that he hadn't inspected the contents of each box before they were all loaded into the van.

His story was obviously not believed by Customs, because he was charged with importation of controlled substances and held on remand in Winchester prison. A few weeks later a Crown Court judge released him on bail.

Luckily for me his phone conversations with Benson convinced the Spanish end of the operation that his pull was the result of bad luck; he was sure that he hadn't been 'grassed up'. That conversation between Benson and George may have saved my life, because I know for certain that there was a palpable lifting of tension that everyone involved could feel. Still I was very careful around Benson and his mates for a few weeks after that.

I considered that it might be a good idea to lay low for a while. The school holidays were on us, and so I decided to bring Kath and Natalie out to Spain for a few weeks' break, especially as the continued prolonged tension had started to play on Kath's nerves, maybe more than on mine. She was pale and nervy looking and had developed a short temper that would flare up for no apparent reason, even trivial domestic problems were getting her down. By now we had dropped into a state of almost permanent cold war, and our telephone conversations were getting shorter, louder and more acidic each day that went by.

It was the moment for a bit of rest and relaxation. Time perhaps to switch off and enjoy the Costa del Sol as a holiday haven rather than view it solely as the drugs capital of southern Europe. So for three idyllic weeks we stayed at the beach-front hotel Las Palmeras in Fuengirola and lived quietly in a small suite overlooking the glorious Mediterranean. We swam in the hotel's pool, played on the beach, borrowed a fast speedboat from one of my new work colleagues and coast-hopped to Benalmadena, Torremolinos and back down as far as Puerto Banus. We took trips into the countryside and ate at small isolated restaurants.

By night we watched the hotel cabaret and sat having a few drinks whilst Natalie spent her time with the other holidaying children watching the flamenco, cabaret or magic shows. Later she would dance till she dropped at the hotel disco, and I had the job of leading her tearful, tired and sunburned from the dance floor and carrying her to our room.

Kath and I sat on the balcony each night talking about the situation and the unforeseen problems that had cropped up. We had many things to put to rights. You cannot sustain a relationship under constant pressure by a series of short, cryptic telephone conversations. There are too many things left unsaid, and we needed a period together to repair our relationship and pour balm on each other's damaged ego and character.

In many ways it was a blissful period, and time flew by all too quickly. From our hotel I had been able to keep a weather eye on the bars where the action was, and I spotted many of the dealers and carriers as we walked along the sea front and around the town.

One night Benson Snr and his live-in girlfriend, Susan, invited us for an evening meal. Kath didn't want to go to the house, and so we met them in central Torremolinos and dined in a mock Tudor-style restaurant. Luckily Benson was at his most affable and charming, and the evening passed without any major incidents, although I could feel Kath ticking like a time bomb, and I was seriously on edge, hoping that she wouln't sound off at him.

Sitting back and watching Benson perform it was hard to believe he was anything but a middle-aged semi-retired rough diamond who liked to tell tall stories and enjoy a few too many drinks. His benign smile hid his thoroughly vicious, bullying nature. I realized that night that I had passed through mere contempt and had begun actually to hate this evil man. Without both him and his son, the world would be a better place.

The night before Kath was due to return home to England with Natalie we sat up nearly all night talking and planning. Things were becoming good between us again, and we felt enough confidence to make plans for our future. We were both determined to move on and put the drugs, Customs, accompanying dangers and the rest behind us and settle down to the life we wanted in Spain. It was becoming time for someone else to pick up the torch, as we were growing tired of the constant stress, lies and crosschecking.

I had heard from Benson that two of his son's mates wanted him to move 300 kilos of cannabis from Spain to the UK by a new route. He was impatient to start the operation and made it obvious he wanted Kath out of the way so I would be free to help him. I agreed with Kath that I would help Customs out on that job, but if nothing came of it and Benson was still free at the end of it, then, sod it! – they could find someone else to do their dirty work.

The next day I drove my wife and daughter to Malaga airport and waited with them until their flight was called. I walked up to the chrome barrier in front of passport control and waved them all the way through the baggage check and into the departure lounge. I was sad to see them go and unaccountably felt extremely upset, as if I sensed that I wouldn't be seeing them for a long time, certainly not for a relaxing family holiday.

Alone again I went into the first-floor restaurant and bought a coffee and a large brandy, which I sat drinking while pondering on the situation in which we found ourselves. Finally after weighing up all the pros and cons for a while, I definitely decided that I would help Customs with this upcoming operation and then that would be it – I was getting out, retiring and getting back to and on with my own life.

So far I had given Customs & Excise a straight five months of my own life as well as my family's. We had put all our plans on hold, forfeited our dreams of starting a business and moving to Spain, placed ourselves under immeasurable amounts of pressure, and, up to now, we had nothing to show in return apart from promises of payments when and if the authorities successfully prosecuted anyone because of direct leads I had given them. This was a double-edge sword because as a Confidential Informant I operated on the basis that I would not be called into court as a prosecution witness. This could make a successful prosecution more difficult because Customs could only work with my information behind the scenes. They claimed they couldn't act overtly as I might be compromised.

To me it was a crock of shit. Benson and the other big operators would never be taken off the streets unless they were actually caught with their hands on the drugs. But that was something they never did. They had minions to do that work for them. So how, I wondered, could the drug barons ever be caught? Well, it wasn't my problem. I would honour my commitment, and then – stuff it! – I was getting off this crazy roundabout.

* * *

A few days after Kath had returned to England I went up to see Benson Snr at his villa. It was now getting towards the back end of the summer, and although the days were still hot, the nights were drawing in. It was a great time to sit on the patio with a drink listening to all the whistling and croaking wildlife that inhabited the garden shrubs and hedges.

Benson and I sat relaxing in cane easy chairs on his patio, each of us holding a tumbler of good malt whisky with the bottle on a table near to hand. The air was filled with the scent of nearby pine trees and the expensive aroma of Benson's big fat cigar. During the ensuing couple of hours Benson described how two of his son's mates, Paul and Tony, both big movers of gear, had recently lost a couple of loads in Irun, a town in northern Spain. They now wanted to use the Benson gang to transport their product up to the UK.

We talked about methods and routes and names of possible drivers. It was agreed that I would travel back to the UK and meet up with Paul and Tony to arrange the shipment. Benson had a novel idea that was supposed to defeat the army of informers that everyone suspected was operating in Spain. He was sure they noted details of departing suspicious vehicles and forwarded this information back to their paymasters in England. His strategy to overcome this obstacle was to change the carrier vehicle in France. He claimed to have discussed his proposals already with Paul and Tony.

The idea was to pack the gear in the Marbella area and then drive it as far as northern France. There the gear would be taken to a safe house and switched into another clean delivery vehicle brought over from England on a day-return ticket. The registration number of the second delivery vehicle would already be on a ferry manifest and would have been logged into the Customs' computer, therefore it would not excite suspicion as it re-entered England.

Benson said that he already had a place in mind for a safe house, that he would organize the delivery for the first leg of the trip and that his son would bring in a reliable driver. I was to check out the French delivery address and confirm the details of the operation with Paul and Tony. After that I was to return to Spain ready to act as baby-sitter for the shipment.

It all seemed feasible to me, and I couldn't wait to get back to the UK to talk about it with Customs. We parted late that night on good terms, and I drove a little unsteadily over the hills back to Carmen's pension in Fuengirola.

Nursing a hangover, I called the Customs in Manchester the next morning and had a long chat with them, laying out the gist of my discussions with Benson. I concluded by advising him I would be returning to the UK later that week. By now it was the first week of October, and I wanted to get back home before the weather broke and winter paraded its wet and windy wares across Europe.

My trip home was awful. It rained almost nonstop from just north of Madrid to Bayonne over the border in France. There aren't many activities that rate as low as driving a motorbike for hour after interminable hour in those conditions, and when I stopped for an early-evening meal and a shower I was wet through and chilled to the bone. The motorbike looked as though it had been washed down with a muddy hosepipe, its chrome and bright trimmings dull and dirty looking. I decided to turn in for the night and hope the weather improved the next day.

The following morning dawned bright and clear with a strong wind that had set in and blown the clouds across to the horizon. It was blustery and cold, but at least I would be dry. I pulled on my warm leathers and set off for Cherbourg. The journey was uneventful, and I caught the late-afternoon ferry. I arrived home the following morning to a joyful if wary family reunion; I hadn't warned Kath I was returning as I'd wanted to surprise her. Surprise her I did, as she immediately thought something had gone wrong and went into a flat-spin panic.

Her reaction demonstrated the kind of pressure we were both living under, and it increased my resolve to get out of this crazy situation as soon as possible. After I'd explained to Kath what was happening I had a long shower and then spent the rest of the day in bed cementing relationships.

Early the next morning Benson called me at home. There had been a change of plan, and he now asked me to travel to France to meet Paul and Tony at Nantes airport. I was to go with them to check out the suitability of an address for receipt and storage of the shipment there until its collection by the second van for the UK.

It was obvious to me that Benson had been thinking about his contacts in France and about how he could get the operation under way as quickly as possible whilst keeping his costs down, thereby maximizing his profit from the job. Using me for recce purposes meant that he could sit safely at home, well away from the scene of operations if anything went wrong later.

He reminded me about Eric and Jill, a British couple who lived in France and whom I had met twice before at his villa in Spain. This was a surprise to me, because I had thought of them merely as users of hash; I had them marked down as overage hippies. I didn't think they took part in smuggling activities.

Benson laughed when I voiced my doubts. 'I've known Eric a long time,' he told me. 'Just go and have a chat with him and see if it will be OK to move the gear up to his place.' He gave me their address, which was somewhere south of Nantes, and so I made arrangements to travel to France.

The next day I took the Honda and travelled down to Southampton, where I bought a day return on the Brittany Ferries' crossing to St Malo in Brittany. The voyage passed uneventfully until the ferry had docked and I was on the car deck unfastening the bike strapping. Feeling I was being watched I looked up. Bloody hell! You could have knocked me down with a feather, because there, right in front of me, stood Eric and Jill.

My paranoia kicked into hyper drive. How the hell could they have known I was going to be travelling on that particular ferry that day? The odds of meeting by chance were astronomical. Again

I felt a flash of fear. Just how much did these jokers know about what was really going on? Who exactly was watching who?

Putting on the social mask we all said what a surprise it was to see each other. After some other friendly exchanges we agreed to meet after disembarkation. I rolled off the ferry and quickly passed straight through the unmanned French immigration and Customs post.

I met Eric and Jill in the ferry-terminal car park, and we had a chat. I told them I was on my way to visit them at their house, and I noticed they didn't seem too surprised. They explained that they had been to Britain to sort out a problem with Eric's pension, and I had caught them on their return journey. Yeah, I thought, pull the other one it's got bells on. I explained what Benson had proposed and that I would need to visit their home in the company of two major players called Paul and Tony. I was watching them very carefully for their reactions.

If someone whom I knew vaguely from a couple of summer barbecues had asked me to accept and store 300 kilos of drugs at my place of residence I would have been damn more surprised than that pair seemed to be. They accepted the deal with such equanimity that I was sure they had been in contact with Benson and had been expecting me. I wondered if this was another example of how dealers kept a close eye on their minions, checking constantly for any signs of disloyalty.

In any event it made by job easier, and that was my main interest. I left Eric and Jill in the car park at St Malo and headed south past Rennes to pick up the N137 towards Nantes airport. In overcast weather I drove rapidly down through Brittany, stopping only for a quickly eaten baguette at a roadside cafe near a Second World War museum. It was hard to believe that towards the end of the war this area of France had been contested so fiercely by the Germans when the Allies were advancing. Now it just seemed peaceful, green countryside populated by lazy-looking cows chewing the cud in the watery late-morning sunlight.

It was lunchtime before I had negotiated the Nantes ring road and found my way into the airport, a futuristic tinted-glass and concrete structure surrounded by acres of car-parking space. Eschewing it I parked right outside the arrivals hall sliding doors, and after locking up the bike I went inside.

Two hours later the last plane due that day from England had landed, and all its incoming passengers had departed. The arrivals hall was almost deserted, and I was standing out like a nun in a sex shop. Obviously Paul and Tony weren't coming today. Angry and frustrated, I called Benson's home in Spain, from where his girlfriend told me he was out and not expected home until late that night.

I then called his son, who despite the hour was still in bed, no doubt with another bimbo keeping him warm. The ensuing, rather cryptic conversation wasn't helpful, and I decided to check out the Eric and Jill location on my own. I left the airport at a rate of knots and headed down the Route Nationale 137. It was a busy road with road works seemingly every couple of miles. I persevered and made good time by driving down the middle of the trunk road between the oncoming vehicles and the slow-moving southbound traffic.

I followed the instructions Eric had given me and turned off the main route on to a small back road. This was rural France, just like the movies. I almost expected to see a German tank appear from behind one of the hedgerows, but all I saw were fields and duckponds.

Eric and Jill's house appeared, and I quickly pulled into their driveway and parked at the side of their old camper van. After the second round of introductions that day they seemed as upset as I was that Paul and Tony hadn't arrived at the airport. We had a quick cup of tea, and I had a look around the outbuildings to check out their suitability. Everything seemed OK, and wishing to catch the ferry home that night I didn't hang around chewing the fat. I told them that the operation would be on within the month, and the next time they saw me I would arrive with the gear. To my mind they seemed incredibly laid back about the whole matter.

It was by now early evening, and I burned some rubber as I headed back up the N137 towards the Channel coast. I missed the St Malo ferry, though, and so headed to Caen where I caught the midnight boat departing for Portsmouth. When I eventually arrived home late the next morning I was completely knackered.

There had to be easier ways to live.

Two days later I met with Rob and Steve, my Customs handlers, at Hartshead services again. After some preliminary chat over a cup of coffee we left the cafeteria and sat in their dark-blue Orion for more privacy. Rob produced some photos of dodgy-looking individuals and asked me if I recognized any of them. I pointed out to them a man whom I knew as Garry, an ecstasy dealer whom I had met earlier in the summer during a visit to England with Benson.

It wasn't an operation that was of great concern to me as it had been a deal done by Benson and his son, and I had really only gone along for the ride and to be nosy. Benson had arranged for 10,000 ecstasy tablets manufactured in Holland to be smuggled into England. Garry was apparently a well-known northern-based dealer and a 'face' in the north of England nightclub scene. I had reported the whole matter to the Customs, who had passed it on to the police, but they had decided to take no action in the interests of public security.

Now that Customs were showing me his photograph it became obvious he was a high-profile target of theirs, and I wished I had taken more interest in the ecstasy operation. Rob confirmed they knew him and that he was a major player, but there was little further I could offer them on that subject. I could confirm that Garry had agreed to pay £4 per tablet, which meant he'd paid Benson £40,000 for the shipment.

I told them about the Benson plan for the French operation and his request that I arrange a meeting with Paul and Tony in Nantes.

I told them that the two dealers hadn't shown and that I had visited the proposed delivery address alone. By now I had told Benson that his buddies had failed to show up at Nantes airport, and he had given me a mobile phone number for Paul, which I gave to Rob and Steve. They agreed I should set up a meeting with Paul and Tony. They said they would use the opportunity to organize a covert surveillance operation to obtain photographs and check out the car they arrived in.

I made the call on my mobile phone and got hold of Tony. He apologized for missing the rendezvous at Nantes airport but didn't seem cut up about it. I arranged a meeting with him and Paul at Hartshead services for three days later. Customs were happy with the arrangements and promised they would be in touch to give me instructions beforehand.

We then spent some time talking about the stolen car operations that were becoming ever more popular in southern Spain. I was able to identify more than 20 such cars circulating in the Malaga area alone, with more cars arriving weekly. Most of the vehicles were 'ringed' or 'twinned up', in that their identity was concealed, and they were nearly all luxury-market motors: Mercedes, Jaguars, Volvos, BMWs and the larger Fords were the most popular. Hardly a day went by but I would be offered a 5-series BMW or a Granada for a couple of thousand pounds.

These cars were invariably delivered with a complete DVLA registration certificate and a tax disc bearing an official-looking post-office stamp and the false vehicle registration number. I noticed a distinct lack of interest by the Customs in relation to stolen vehicles and the gangs who were delivering them to order. I rationalized this to myself with the knowledge that Customs were only interested in the illegal importation of drugs; stolen cars were a police matter and nothing to do with them. In my view it was a classic example of interagency non-cooperation.

The day before the meeting with Paul and Tony was due to take place, Rob phoned me at home to give me precise instructions about what to do. He wanted me to sit outside the café in a picnic area overlooking the main car park. I was to position myself side on to the car park, reading a newspaper. When the two drug dealers arrived I should stand up and shake hands with each of them. He told me Customs would be waiting in a parked vehicle from where they would take their photographs. Everything was organized so he advised me to relax and try to act as naturally as possible. I agreed with him and resolved to give a good performance.

The next day I arrived early at the motorway services, and after buying a coffee and a newspaper I sat down as instructed. I was feeling intensely nervous. These guys were really hard men and potential killers, and if they suspected any funny business they would have no hesitation in bumping me off. While I was committed and prepared to do my bit, I just hoped my back-up was armed and watching carefully.

The plan hadn't taken account of the weather, though, and when I arrived the sky was leaden with low cloud. Just before the meeting was timed to begin it started raining pretty hard. Paul and Tony were late, and I was sitting outside in the rain with a newspaper that was quickly turning to pulp. Anybody with any sense would have been inside the nice warm cafe, so how could I sit here steaming in the pouring rain and try to look natural? I looked like a fucking idiot, so much for planning by the professionals.

Paul and Tony eventually arrived. They looked as hard as I'd feared, and I felt nothing but loathing for these two lowlifes. I was pleased to be of help in putting them away. They wanted to know why I was sat outside in the rain, which seemed a pretty fair question. I explained that it was more private here and that we wouldn't be overheard. Paul just said, 'Bollocks, we'll get piss wet through,' and that was that, inside we went. I hoped the Customs had taken all the photographs they needed.

Inside the cafe the meeting lasted for the duration of a couple of cups of coffee and a few cigarettes. They explained that the proposed French operation would be the first on a new route, which if it went to plan would be used for about six trips. They had heavy goods transport that travelled from England to France regularly on a weekly basis. They claimed this transport was good and legitimate and had never been stopped. Benson's job was to collect the gear from Malaga and then ship it to the French farm. They would pay him £100 per kilo delivered, so I knew Benson stood to make £30,000 for his part in the operation.

They asked me what role I would play, and I told them I would be the baby-sitter on a motorbike in front of the load. They seemed pleased by this. After warning me of the consequences for all concerned if anything went wrong, they wished me luck and said they would soon be in touch with Colin in Spain.

I left the café, and as previously agreed with my handlers I climbed into my car and drove home without making any calls or seeing anybody else. The next day I had an extensive debrief with Rob over the phone. I related everything that had transpired, and for his part he confirmed they had taken some good photographs. I was very pleased with the operation, and that night Kath and I went out for a little private celebration to a Chinese restaurant in Retford.

Over the next few days I received at home a series of phone calls from Benson, Paul and Tony. In effect I became the linkman, coordinating the shipment. Therefore I was privy to most of the planning details, even down to knowing the name of the van driver. I spoke several times to Customs, and we decided to have one final meeting, which we set for the last day of October 1994 at Birch services on the M62 near to Heywood in north Manchester. The three of us met there late in the afternoon.

It was looking as if this job were shaping up to be the big one, the operation that would net both Bensons and two major north of England dealers as well as remove 300 kilos of drugs from the streets. This operation, I decided, was to be my swan song. With Benson out of the way we could get on with our own lives and move a little nearer to achieving our own ambitions.

It had been raining hard on my trip over the Pennines, and I was very wet when I joined Rob and Steve, who were already seated and drinking coffee. We got right down to business. Rob had brought along a map of northern France for me to pinpoint the exact location of the delivery address, but it didn't cover a sufficiently large area, so I went into the services shop and bought a road map of France.

We sat in the cafe poring over the map, and I showed them exactly where the farmhouse was to be found. I also sketched out the proposed route we would be taking across Spain and up through France to the drop-off point. I described the layout of the farm and gave them its full postal address including the postcode.

By now Customs had everything they needed for the operation. They knew the names of the buyers, the Spanish-based organizers and shippers, the type and volume of drugs to be smuggled and a timescale for the operation. Obviously they were aware that my intended role was to drive in front of the shipment on my motorbike acting as a front-runner escort and baby-sitter. For this Benson had promised me £10,000. Most importantly they knew that the intended plan included an exchange of carrying vehicles. This was where my input was critical, because I was the only one who could identify the second vehicle coming from England and report its details and registration number back to the Customs.

Rob and Steve appeared pleased with my assistance and offered me £500 to help with my 'running expenses'. I had to sign a receipt in the name of 'Benjy' for the cash. They warned me to be careful and not to break the law. This was delivered straightfaced by Rob, but I just sat there and looked at them incredulously. What a farce! Here we were, discussing the ways and means of smuggling 300 kilos of illegal drugs worth £1 million across at least two international frontiers and over nearly 1500 miles of roadways, yet he had the nerve to sit there and tell me not to do anything illegal.

I was so incensed by the transparent naivety of his statement that I said straight out that this was to be my last job for Customs.

I let rip a little and told them what I really thought of their operations, how the drug dealers were laughing at their attempts to stem the tide of drugs being smuggled into the country. The smugglers are ruthlessly efficient operators backed up by well-paid organizations that can quickly adapt to changing circumstance and move the goalposts at will. On the other hand Customs were constantly playing catch up with the smugglers, hamstrung by policies and outdated policing methods that had never been designed to deal with international drug trafficking on such a major scale.

The dealers and barons could move about freely, crossing borders with ease as many as five times per smuggling trip. Customs, however, had to liaise with several different policing authorities. Each subject to their own internal agendas and local politics, the competition between the policing agencies was fierce. The interservice cooperation promulgated by the politicians and media spokesmen was a joke that wasn't taken seriously by either the authorities or the smugglers, it was just so much hot air.

I recall that Rob and Steve sat there in silence as I continued with my diatribe, but they certainly didn't disagree with me. After I had finished I gave them the last titbit of information I had about the upcoming operation. Benson had told me that the first carrier vehicle to be used on the Spanish–French leg of the operation was a Mercedes van stolen from a Hertz rent-a-van depot in Britain. Hertz's corporate livery was a distinctive bright yellow, and I thought it would stand out like a spare prick at a nun's wedding. To me there didn't seem much future in using a vehicle that was begging to be stopped and checked by every passing police car.

We agreed that the next time I would make contact with them would be when the drugs had arrived safely in France, and I had the details of the van coming from England to collect them. It was a cordial parting, but I felt that much of the earlier friendliness had dissipated. This I put down to my criticism of their employers.

Kath and I decided to move our plans forward a piece. I was so convinced that Benson and his cohorts would soon be out of the way, she was going to travel out to Spain and start searching out a property for us. We decided to all fly out together as soon as possible.

I contacted a local guy I knew in Sheffield who had previously organised a driver for Benson and asked him to fix me up with a driver. The idea was to put the motorbike in the back of a trailer and have it driven down to Spain. This would allow me to travel to Malaga with Kath and Natalie, and I would be there quicker to keep an eye on developments. The weather was really shitty and I didn't facing spending three days driving to Spain when I could travel it in three hours. I had done a lot of travelling around Europe in the last couple of months, and I was getting really tired and worn down. A nice warm trip in an aeroplane drinking wine and looking down on the snowy mountain tops seemed just right to me at that moment.

The next day I took a call from a guy called Barry, who had been put up for the driving job. I invited him to our farm, and he seemed all right. He was an ex-army cook, single and looked as if he could handle himself. He came highly recommended by our mutual contact, and I was told he was trustworthy enough to drive a trailer down to Malaga. We agreed terms, and the next day we loaded the motorbike and some other bits and pieces into the back of a covered trailer, and he set off in his Orion towing the trailer, destination Spain. Meanwhile Kath, Natalie and I set off for Birmingham airport, from where he had booked tickets for the flight to Malaga.

The following day we checked in again at the hotel Las Palmeras in Fuengirola, and Kath and Natalie started to renew their acquaintances with the local shops and cafes. It was now early November, and the weather had turned, but it was still warm compared with the late English autumn we had left behind us, so much so that young Natalie spent an hour or so each day in the hotel pool.

Meanwhile I was busy with Benson, making sure that everything was ready for the forthcoming trip. I inspected the Hertz van and expressed my reservations over its vivid colour, which Benson ignored. Of course he wasn't the sucker who was going to be driving it, so his concern was limited to financial aspects.

A couple of days later Barry arrived on the coast with the trailer. I met him near the brewery adjacent to Malaga airport and escorted him up to Benson's villa, where the trailer was to be stored temporarily until Barry returned to the UK. By now I had learnt that Barry was unhappy with his lot as proprietor of a small cafe and intended to look around in Torremolinos and Fuengirola for some winter work in one of the hotels, restaurants or bars.

As we drove into Benson's villa Barry's eyes were popping. It is easy to become inured to ostentatious luxury and grandiose lifestyles, because after a while you take it for granted, and it doesn't really register any more. But a newcomer introduced into the circle always stepped back in amazement. It was rather like walking on to the set of *Dallas*, and these surroundings seemed to imbue Benson with a sense of potency and enhance his charisma. It's really no wonder he was such a success with women.

We unloaded the bike, and Barry, with Jack, one of Benson's handymen, parked the trailer away with the caravans on the lower patch of ground. Benson took me aside and told me quietly that we would be on for the operation within two or three days. Then, because we were lacking a spare motorbike helmet, he volunteered to drive Barry down to the coast.

I saw the glint in Benson's eye and knew that he was going to sound out Barry for future use. That was how all the dealers worked. They cultivated an ever increasing circle of contacts hoping that one day one of them would come in useful. Still I wasn't Barry's keeper, so I left them to it and drove back to Fuengirola to have my evening meal with my family. That night we sat again and watched the hotel cabaret until Natalie was too tired to keep her eyes open, then it was a quick supper of ham and cheese at the 24-hour bar and off to bed and more relationship cementing. I was starting to feel like a bloody builder.

The next afternoon we were walking around the shops in Malaga's main shopping area when Benson called me on my mobile phone. He was in a right state and insisted he wanted to see me as soon as possible. I agreed to meet him after dinner. Later at his villa he told me that the van driver they had organized had failed to turn up there as agreed. So what? I thought. It wasn't my man or my arrangement, and it meant little or nothing to me. But the problem went deeper. The driver had taken the Hertz van the previous day to fuel it up and check tyre pressures and so on. He had parked it up, but now he had disappeared, and so had the van keys, which presumably were in his pocket.

This was a problem because it is not so easy to obtain spare keys for Mercedes vehicles. Apparently each one is tagged into a central computer and can be linked back to a specific vehicle. The risk was that if one of Benson's men called into Mercedes' main dealership in Marbella then they would soon know he was trying to obtain keys for a stolen vehicle. For obvious reasons this was a chance Benson didn't want to take.

I could see all my plans evaporating in front of me, as I thought about the problem for a while. If Benson didn't go ahead with the scheduled delivery then he would escape the elaborate net that was now set for him. All my own and Kath's dreams would come to nought again as we couldn't countenance moving into the area with the two Bensons hanging around free as birds.

I offered him the use of my old Mercedes van, which I had used for the import and export trials in what seemed a couple of centuries ago. Parked up nearby it was still in good nick and had the advantage of being white, a less conspicuous colour than the Hertz bright yellow. Another big bonus from Benson's viewpoint was that, although old, the van was legal, and all the papers were authentic.

I felt there was no material risk posed to me or to my van by this change in detail. The main players remained the same, we were still smuggling the same amount of drugs to the same address in France, in effect all that had changed was that I'd allowed my vehicle to be used.

Benson then told me that he had done a deal with Barry, who would now be driving the van. Even if the original driver turned up he would not be going with the shipment. Instead he would be lucky to escape with an assortment of broken limbs to show him that he couldn't piss about with Benson and his gang. A sort of grisly example to keep the minions in line.

Barry must have figured something pretty strange was going on when he first saw all the opulence around him, and no doubt he had readily understood when Benson explained the secret of the source of all the cash. Using Barry as a replacement driver wasn't a problem for me. He had said he was looking for a job, and I supposed this seemed an easy way for him to get some quick cash. I heard that he had been offered £4000 to drive the van up to France, but I don't know if that was an accurate figure.

Barry was a minor player in the operation, and I had previously reported many such small fry to Customs, who had taken no action against them, declaring their prime interest was in catching the main men. Therefore I couldn't see there was going to be any problem with the change of the driver, and I certainly didn't think it was up to me to report such a detail to Customs at this late stage. In a way it was a typical piece of drug smuggling, more like organized chaos than anything else. The smugglers were making absolute fortunes, but most of them couldn't organize a piss up in a brewery.

Later during that meeting Benson told us he had decided to load the drugs into the van the next day in readiness for departure. He asked me to help in the collection of the drugs from Fuengirola and to take them up to the packing house. At last, I thought, we can get this bloody show on the road. It was a good move as the constant strain was by now really telling on me. I was short tempered, irritable and often my blood pressure was giving me blinding headaches. Most of the time I had a nagging sort of background headache, which I had learnt to live with.

I invited Barry to join us at the cabaret session that night in Fuengirola. He seemed pleased to get the offer and have a valid excuse to leave Benson behind. I took Benson off to one side and told him I would keep an eye on Barry, giving Benson the nod to impart a special insiders' meaning to my words. It was little asides like this that made Benson feel he was in command of a situation. He was always happier thinking he had people watching each other for signs of disloyalty.

We played happy families again that night, Kath, Natalie, Barry and I laughing and joking at the comedian. Barry was warily swigging lager from a bottle of San Miguel whilst his eyes kept scanning the audience. I didn't know if he was looking for a bird to try his luck with or if he was expecting a horde of policemen to jump out of the crowd. He looked decidedly unhappy, and I figured he hadn't been involved in anything remotely like this before.

The next day Barry and I spent a few hours getting my van ready for the trip, fuelling up, checking oil and tyre pressures and so on. Later in the afternoon I delivered Barry up to Mijas Jardins where the drugs were to be wrapped by Benson's man Jack and someone else supplied by Paul and Tony's organization, who was no doubt keeping his eye on his master's drugs. He would be ensuring that there was no switching of product and that none of the 1200 soaps of cannabis disappeared into the wrong hands.

I knew we would be going sometime the next day, and so that night the three of us went out for a special peaceful meal on our own. It was the calm before the storm and was to be the last time I would sit down with my family for more than half a year.

The next morning it was all go, packing clothes, bike leathers, wet-weather gear, toothbrush, razor and other personal kit. Considering it was the first week in November the weather was fine with a watery sun just hot enough to dispel the sea mist and break up the high clouds. Barry came down and joined us for a massive English breakfast at one of my favourite bars. After eating we sat around drinking coffee and making small talk while Natalie wandered about in one of the nearby gift shops, watched by an eagle-eyed shop assistant.

Barry confided that he was going to use his pay-off this run to start a café or bar in one of the coastal resorts. I choked back a splutter of laughter. What was it with people? They could see the evidence of failing businesses all around them, intense competition was driving even the moderately successful bars out of business, and yet newcomers kept coming and plonking their money down, determined to show all the others how it should be done. It was like watching a tide of lemmings dropping off the edge of a cliff. Still who was I to laugh? I'd been convinced I could do just the same in Benidorm all those years ago.

About noon Benson called me on the mobile, and I knew the show was on. Barry went to collect his bag from his room. Kath was going out to meet a firm of estate agents that afternoon and intended to visit some properties to see what was on the market. I promised to phone her as soon as I could and let her know how we were doing. Just in case anything went wrong I made her repeat the Customs emergency number back to me a couple of times, I didn't want her to write it down anywhere. By now we were both running in a constant state of high tension, and no precautions seemed too outrageous to us.

Barry arrived back, and we all walked up to the Honda. I turned the engine over, and Barry and I climbed aboard. We waved our goodbyes, and with the throbbing beat of a Rod Stewart hit dancing behind us we swung up the road and headed towards Cartama village and Benson's villa again.

We set off on the journey at roughly three o'clock that afternoon. Me in the front leading the way, and Barry driving my Mercedes-Benz van at a steady 55 miles per hour. I was covering twice as much distance as Barry, powering three or four miles up the road and then doubling back to check he was OK. At the first agreed stopping point I had to tell him not to flash his lights whenever he saw me, a dead giveaway to any cops who might see him. Powerful bikes and old diesel vans were not conventional fellow travellers, and it would certainly arouse suspicion and a degree of interest that we wouldn't like.

We continued onwards, heading up the excellent N321 road through Antequera, climbing continually to the ancient city of Granada perched high up in the Sierra Nevada mountains. After playing cat and mouse with the congested traffic around the city we were headed dead north through Jaen and the beautiful countryside to Bailen, one of the main junction towns in southern Spain. There are always plenty of Guardia Civil around that area, watching the traffic and pulling both cars and commercial vehicles over for spot checks, seemingly at random.

I stayed close in front of Barry, and sure enough I could see a couple of jeeps used by the Guardia near the Repsol garage in the centre of the route interchange. I drove over towards them and made a big show of climbing off the bike and pulling a road map from the rear box. Engaging them in a mimelike conversation I checked I was on the right road for Madrid, the coppers were only too pleased to help me and pointed vigorously to the north saying, 'Madrid, Madrid'. I thanked them and tinkered with the stereo on the bike as Barry swung past, I could see him gaping at me through the windscreen. He obviously thought I'd been pulled up, but he did the right thing by driving on and ignoring the little sideshow being played out at the roadside.

I climbed aboard the bike, and waving at my new friends I pulled off smoothly towards Madrid. I easily passed Barry within a couple of minutes, the relief on his face as I roared past giving him the finger was clear to see. We settled down for the next leg of the long journey. On the large three-lane dual carriageway European E5 route we passed through Valdepenas, home of some excellent Spanish wine, and ploughed on steadily towards Ocana, where the main road forks back off towards Cartegena and Murcia.

We hit the Madrid ring-road system just after darkness had fallen, but at least we missed most of the traffic. Barry was sticking to the job faithfully, and we circumvented Madrid without taking any wrong turns, a memorable feat late at night. An hour north of the capital we pulled off the road and checked into a motel for the night. We were not far away from where I'd stayed with George during the Bilbao operation earlier that summer, but I wasn't interested in brothels and hookers. I'd been in the saddle for a long time and was suffering from a severely numb bum.

We didn't bother with the pretence of not knowing each other, because the place was crowded with travellers, and it was obvious that nobody gave a shit about two more weary souls crawling in from the dark. I left Barry downstairs in the bar trying to order a beer and went to my room, where I took a long hot shower. Later we ate a good meal with lots of crusty bread and copious amounts of beer before retiring early for a good sleep.

The next morning we were up and off early. I was feeling as stiff as a board and wasn't looking forward to another ten-hour stretch on the bike, but it had to be done. By mid-morning we were on the outskirts of Burgos, a large commercial town nestling in the middle of a mountain chain that runs all the way up to the northern coast near to Bilbao. We ran along the top of the range heading towards the Vitoria pass. By now it had turned really cold, and snow lay on the hills. There was a cold, stinging rain, and I was feeling wet and miserable and envious of Barry nice and dry and warm in the Mercedes behind me.

Dropping down the appalling road through Vitoria was always hazardous, but now the route was wet and slick with oil and diesel and especially tricky and treacherous. A heavy mist came down, and hairpin bends loomed up without any warning. I had to take it slowly and steadily, and by now I was becoming really pissed off by this because we needed to get a move on to cross the French border before darkness fell. Like cockroaches the French Customs came out to prey on commercial vehicles after dark.

We headed for the dirty industrial town of Irun just next to the border. This area was thick with police like fleas, they seemed to be on every corner. The only thing to do was to keep on and tough it out, but I could imagine Barry was crapping himself by now.

Eventually we passed through Irun and headed the couple of miles up to the small town of Hendaye. The main motorway was on a causeway high above our heads, and we could hear the constant roar of traffic passing by. I had plenty of butterflies batting about in my stomach now, and the tension was giving me a headache. It was little comfort to think that UK Customs should have OK'd the route with the Spanish and the French, this was major bottle-twitching time. I wouldn't have been surprised if Barry had pulled up and left the van before catching the next bus home.

I saw the small border crossing ahead and drove up for a look-see. Unbelievably it was unmanned, except for one guard on the Spanish side who was sitting in his glass kiosk reading a newspaper. I about turned quickly and went back to spread the good word to Barry. I discovered him creeping up the road as slowly as he could, obviously working up his courage to attempt the crossing. I swung round in front of him and gave him a big thumbs up whilst waving him on. I could hear the old van accelerate gamely behind me.

I drove slowly across the frontier, and it was definitely unmanned. Safely in France I pulled to the roadside parking area and watched as Barry negotiated his way round the series of barriers and chicanes. It was now gloomy dusk, but I could clearly see a big grin stretched across his face from ear to ear. He was through.

Without hanging about we headed up the small coast road to St Jean-de-Luz, a seaside resort. The place was too small for our needs, and we continued now in the pitch darkness towards the upmarket resort of Biarritz. We passed a local airport full of parked-up millionaires' toys and found a small chain motel on the outskirts of the town that was admirable for our purposes. We quickly checked in, changed clothes and hit the bar. The border-crossing tension surge on top of the long drive had left us both tired, but managed to sink a good few beers and brandy chasers before devouring a plate of sandwiches made up for us by a kindly night porter. That night we eventually turned in completely tired out and the worse for drink.

I was looking forward to the next day. I knew we would arrive at the farmhouse drop-off at about teatime, and then hopefully the day after the van would arrive from England. A quick phone call to Rob or Steve at the Customs and the show would be over, in more ways than one. Well, the show was about to be over all right, I just didn't realize how it was going to end.

50

The French Connection

THE TRIP UP from Biarritz was largely uneventful. We travelled north up the N137 passing through several small towns in the Cognac region. Driving all day with breaks for fuel when we would grab a cigarette, a drink and a sandwich bought from petrol-station shops we arrived at our departure point from the Route Nationale at about six o'clock in the evening.

I had gradually increased my distance in front of Barry in the van as I began to search for a suitable place to leave him parked up whilst I checked out the farmhouse refuge. Not far from the main crossroads where our route turned off the main road I saw a deserted garage. There were no lights in the building, and the car park seemed to be full of broken-down cars, some of which, minus wheels, were perched on blocks. This seemed an ideal location to me. As a bonus, in between the car park and the pavement, there was a telephone kiosk.

I quickly doubled back and soon saw Barry ploughing steadily up towards me. I U-turned and overtook him and pulling to the roadside told him my plan. I led him to the garage, and he pulled into a corner and switched off his engine and lights. I instructed him to await my return and walked over to the phone box. Once inside I dialled Manchester Customs' number but received only a buzzing noise from the handset. I tried again with the London contact number but got the same result.

This was getting beyond a joke, obviously the poxy French phone wasn't working. Tired out with concentrating after the long journey I decided to try again the next day, after we'd dropped off the van and got a good night's sleep. By this time I was knackered, I had been in the driving seat for nearly 14 hours already, and the day wasn't yet over.

Leaving Barry behind at the garage I continued up the road to the traffic lights where I would turn off. The junction was obviously the centre of town, and there were various local shops cheek by jowl with a new school, a community car park and some sort of public building flying the French flag. I quickly passed through the town and turned off into the country down a D-category road. I passed through a copse with a large lake on the right-hand side. A flight of ducks disturbed by the echoing sound of the bike's exhaust took flight, squawking their annoyance at the unwarranted disturbance.

I knew I was in the close vicinity of the safe-house rendezvous and carefully scanned the hedges for the concealed driveway. Concentrating on finding the farm I didn't see the cow dung dropped from a farmer's trailer until I was on top of it. I felt the squelch of a six-inch pile of shit at the same time as the front wheel started to slide into a skid. Quickly I decelerated and hauling the front wheel back upright I managed to regain control, shouting a curse that must have been heard everywhere.

Still recovering from the near accident and wobbling a little I saw the farmhouse ahead. I pulled around the side road and parked the bike at the side of a muddy path, and I remember emitting a long, relieved sigh; we had made it. To have got so far and then nearly come to grief just outside the delivery point was a bit much. I dismounted and noticed that my legs were trembling with effort and fatigue. I realized I was more tired than I thought as I pulled off my helmet and gloves. My movements seemed disjointed and slightly out of synch, like being tipsy without drinking any alcohol.

I opened the little wrought-iron gate and walked up the drive past the kitchen window. Before I could knock at the old stained front door it was pulled open, and I was blinded by the bright light pouring through.

'Hey, Jill, look what the cat's dragged in,' a man shouted over his shoulder back into the kitchen. No problem, it was Eric, and he waved me in.

'Hi, Eric,' I said. 'Any chance of a cup of tea?'

'Course there is, me cock sparrer,' Eric replied. 'Come in, and Jill'll put the kettle on.'

Inside the heat of the kitchen hit me like a blow. After travelling all day in the cold November weather I was tired out and chilled to the bone. It wasn't long though before I was sitting cradling a mug of steaming hot tea. I noticed that Eric and Jill didn't seem very surprised to see me, maybe I was correct in assuming they had a direct line back to Colin. They had been expecting me, but I felt that they needed reminding of the quantity we were carrying. Despite their previous agreement, Jill didn't seem too happy at the thought of 300 kilos of cannabis being parked overnight in her driveway. Eric was up for it, but he wanted payment in kind, straight away that night.

After a bit of haggling for effect we agreed that he would be paid one kilo of gear, worth about £3000, for minding the storage van overnight and until the pick-up vehicle arrived from the UK, supposedly early the next day. Having sorted out the storage details I left to collect Barry and the van. As I climbed wearily back on to the bike, I noticed my back and thigh muscles were starting to complain. Back at the garage I found Barry asleep in the driver's seat. What a dickhead! I woke him, and he started the van up and made to follow me into the dark countryside.

So that he could keep up I drove back at a snail's pace towards the farm. I noticed a car with yellow headlights behind the van that made no attempt to overtake even though we were travelling so slowly. I put the driver's reluctance to pass down to the narrowness of the country lanes and the tight bends along the route. When we reached the farm I saw Eric had opened the drive gates and moved both his car and his camper van out of the way. I parked up and watched as Barry reversed into the driveway right up to the garage door, leaving the van at the top of the drive next to the camper van. It seemed safe enough to me.

In the house I made the introductions and dropped it on Barry that Eric wanted a kilo of gear that night before he would allow us to leave the van on his premises. After a lot of moaning about the dark and the fact that all the gear was concealed in the middle of the load Barry agreed to fetch it. Meanwhile in the kitchen Jill was warming some homemade soup.

Amid a lot of banging, crashing and swearing Barry finally located the cannabis in the van. He emerged to ask for a knife and eventually resurfaced nursing a nasty cut on his hand and four blocks of cannabis. 'There you go, mate,' he said, 'don't smoke it all at once.' He gave the soaps to Eric who inspected them individually and then took them into the house.

Barry and I closed up the van and went into the kitchen. Jill offered us some soup and lovely crispy bread she hacked off a long French stick. The meal was excellent, both Barry and I were starving. Soon Eric returned and sat down to his soup; he asked us about the trip through Spain and France and when we would be leaving. I noticed he seemed very cool about the whole deal and that he didn't mention Benson particularly, which I thought more than a little suspicious.

As we talked I became more confident that he had been in touch with Benson and knew more about our plans than he was letting on. It would have been typical of Benson to have let Eric, who was a buddy of his, know what was going on without my knowledge. These sort of built-in security details are important in the world of drug smuggling for they allow the organizers or buyers to monitor the movement of shipments and maintain security whilst not being close to the product at any time.

Eric told us we couldn't stay at the farm as they had no spare beds, but he directed us to a hotel in a town a few miles away. We did not suggest that we might sleep on the settees or the floor, because it seemed to me that Eric wanted us out of the way. Perhaps he was intending to make a few phone calls of his own after we had gone. Barry borrowed a spare bike helmet, and soon after we both left for town on the motorbike.

The hotel was old fashioned but clean and warm. We had missed the evening meal hours ago, but they made us a large plate of cheese and ham sandwiches, which we quickly demolished along with a couple of beers. After a coffee we returned to our separate rooms for a shower and a change of clothes. I put a call through to Benson and confirmed our safe arrival. I told him the van had been left with Eric and Jill, and advised him of the payment terms I'd agreed with them, all of which he seemed to think were OK. I added that we would be at the farm tomorrow ready for the switch over.

'The collection van will be there about 11 am,' Benson said. 'They have bang-on directions, I gave them myself this afternoon,' OK, I thought, the job's a goer. I was pleased because I was sure that Benson and the English buyers would all soon be in the bag.

After speaking to Benson I put a call through to Kath at her hotel in Fuengirola, but there was no answer. I decided, she was probably watching the nightly cabaret show with Natalie in the lounge, so I thought I'd catch her the next day. I briefly contemplated phoning the Customs in the UK, but the hour was late, and I would have to ring the London number and wait for them to call me back, which could have been a bit tricky with Barry hanging around. Besides I had nothing new to tell them yet. The Customs part of the operation would start tomorrow when I got the number of the collection van.

I returned to the bar where Barry was now waiting. It was very quiet there, and we couldn't talk without being overheard so we decided to go for a drink in the town. Many French small towns seem to die when the sun goes down, and this one was no exception. We walked around for ages, but the whole place looked deserted, with shutters closed on all the houses and shops. We had almost given up trying to find anywhere when we heard the sound of a jukebox playing on the night breeze. We tracked back and discovered a tiny open bar in an alleyway.

Inside it reeked of strong French tobacco and beer. The bar was a students' haunt, full of leather-jacketed youths and fresh-faced large-breasted girls who all seemed to be wearing tight-fitting woollen sweaters that reminded me of the beatnik scene of the 60s. We sat at the counter, and after pantomiming our need for two beers we turned to watch the scenery whilst enjoying our drink.

Some lads were playing pool on a massive table, while their mates were enjoying old-fashioned bar football, the sort of wooden box game with two teams of players fastened to shafts and operated by handles, a machine found now usually in old greasy-spoon transport cafes. It was obviously all the rage there, and the players and onlookers were laughing and joking and whooping loudly when one of the teams scored a goal. All good stuff. Barry and I turned back to our drinks and surveyed the talent.

The jukebox kicked in with a French version of a heavy metal hit, which to our ears was absolute crap, but the French kids seemed to like it. Soon fed up with the watery beer, the smell and the overwhelming noise, the idea of another drink waned quickly, so I paid the tab, and we left. After the noise of the bar the streets seemed as silent as the grave. Back at our hotel we went straight to bed. During the walk back to the hotel I had said to Barry that tomorrow would be a long day. I didn't know how right I was.

The next morning was cold, bright and clear with a cutting wind. After a breakfast of croissants and coffee we set off on the bike for the farm. I could feel Barry shivering in his thin jacket. The wind was buffeting the bike pretty badly, and each gust had him gripping me harder. I'd end up with bruised hips if he carried on.

We arrived at the farm about ten o'clock. Barry jumped off the bike quickly. 'Bloody hell, that was cold,' he complained. His nose was red and his eyes were watering with the wind. Without gloves his hands were frozen. After a lot of knocking on the door Eric finally arrived. 'Morning, lads,' he said, 'that's a good bit of shit you've got there.' He looked wrecked with eyes like pissholes in the snow, he'd obviously had a good sampling session last night.

'Morning, Eric,' I said, 'get the coffee on before Barry kicks the bucket. He's bloody freezing.'

We went into the old-fashioned kitchen, and Eric filled a kettle and placed it on top of the Aga hotplate. He opened the firedoor and raked about inside before adding a log from a wicker basket. 'It won't be long boiling,' he informed us. 'What's the plan today then?'

'It all depends what time the van arrives,' I said. 'As soon as it gets here we'll swap the gear over, and that's it, we're off back to Spain, where it's a damn sight warmer than it is here.'

Just then Jill walked in wearing a long woollen dressing gown and heavy slippers; she too looked like she'd had a night on the tiles. She nodded a good morning to us and sat down at the kitchen table. Over a mug of coffee Eric explained that they grew their own marijuana and offered to show us his plants, I wasn't bothered but went with him anyway just to have a look and a nosey. He had several marijuana plants each over six foot tall growing in a little coalshed at the far end of the garden. He had removed the old tiled roof and installed clear plastic sheeting so that the sunlight shone directly on to the plants, it was like a greenhouse in there. The plants certainly looked healthy enough and the atmosphere in the small room smelled sweet and heavy. Eric showed us how he collected the younger leaves because they made the strongest smoke when dried out.

The farmhouse itself was very old and full of strange hippie-type objets d'art. Pine furniture and woven rugs were the order of the day, with wicker baskets occupying many table tops and odd corners. Dried flower arrangements gave an air of Laura Ashley's Rural Collection. The folksy image was at odds with a large poster tacked to a door depicting a faintly-smiling Mona Lisa smoking a joint as big as a carrot. I had noticed a similar picture of the Queen appearing to be smoking a joint in ceremonial dress behind the bathroom door. Overgrown hippies, I thought to myself.

As the time approached 1 pm I became restless, the van should have arrived by now. I walked out into the lane and wandered in the direction of the main road. I strained my ears but couldn't detect the sound of a commercial engine. I would have to phone Benson to get an update. I hoped there were no problems with the second van, the whole operation hinged on its arrival. Eric and Jill didn't have a phone in the house, and my mobile didn't work in France, so I clothed up and drove down the road into the village. I located a phone box in the market square and called Benson. He sounded as frustrated as me.

'There's been a delay,' he told me. 'Can you get Barry or Eric to drive the van further up towards the coast?'

'No chance,' I told him. 'Barry wants to get back off to Spain, and Eric is scared of his own shadow.'

'Tell Eric, it's worth another kilo to him,' said Benson.

'Look, Colin, what time's the van going to arrive?' I asked him. 'If it's going to be much longer there's going to be some serious bottling here.'

'Just hang on, and if it hasn't arrived by three o'clock give me a call,' he said.

'OK,' I said and hung up. Shit, I could feel the operation starting to slip away. I knew I had to ring the Customs at some stage today, hopefully before they all buggered off home.

I returned to the farm and asked Barry and Eric if either of them would be prepared to drive the van towards the French Channel ports. They both knew that security increased closer to the coast with roving Custom patrols stopping vehicles at random. They were not interested in moving the gear another inch.

Barry said he wanted to return to Spain. I thought he was looking frightened by now. I've noticed before that action of any kind is OK, it's during periods of inactivity that people seem really to think about what they're doing, and that's when they lose their bottle. Barry's part in the job was finished, so I agreed that we would get him off as soon as possible. Before he could go we would have to unload all the gear into the garage, but this didn't seem to be a problem to me as we would have to move it from the van it was now in to the one coming from the UK anyway. It would save us time later.

Eric agreed we could use his garage, so the three of us set out to unload the gear. When the job was under way I left them to ring Benson again and spring the news on him that the van wouldn't be going anywhere nearer the Channel coast. By now I was really concerned about the delays and told Benson that unless the second van arrived soon both Barry and I would leave the gear on the garage floor and return to Spain, leaving him to sort out the mess himself.

Benson went apeshit, he threatened me with a beating and said if the gear was lost he would have me shot. What a stiff! He was over a 1000 miles away and still shouting the odds, but I knew that nothing would induce him to travel up here where the action was. He wanted to sit in his villa and rake in the profits from his illegal trade whilst other suckers carried out the dirty work. There was no way I was going to leave the gear and return to Spain because I needed the registration number of the van coming from the UK, but I hoped that my putting pressure on Benson might hurry the situation along a little. Eventually he promised to get an update on the van and said I should phone him back at four o'clock.

When I returned to the farm all the gear was stacked in the garage. In the process of unloading some of the packages had split open, and there were cannabis soaps strewn all over the floor. The air was redolent with the heavy, spicy aroma of the drug. Eric dreamily surveyed the nearly half a ton of cannabis. I could see his mind ticking over: that amount of gear would bring in about a million pounds' cash when it was sold at street value and in a city or big town it would disappear within a week. We were looking at a tremendous tax-free retirement bundle.

His face clouded, and I knew that reality had set in. If he tried to get the gear himself he would be dead within the week, such is the threat of violence in the subculture of the world of drugs. Almost as bad was the thought of the crippling jail sentence he would receive if the police became aware of its presence at his farmhouse. I knew it was a sobering thought for him, I could read it clearly all over his face. He shook his head and walked back into the farm kitchen. Barry and I left him and Jill alone for a few minutes, but it was too cold just hanging around in an unheated garage so we went back into the kitchen.

Eric made yet another cup of tea, and we discussed the situation. Jill had disappeared into the lounge where she was ironing clothes, she seemed to be adopting an ostrich-like strategy of ignoring the situation and pretending that we weren't there. We agreed that I should phone Benson again, and then we would wait until five o'clock before Barry and I left. I intended to phone the Customs at that point and tell them something had gone wrong; the van hadn't arrived as planned, they could make the final decision as to what to do. I had a suspicion that there wasn't going to be a van arriving at all, the arrangements about the collection seemed too loose. It was not the way of things to leave 300 kilos of gear lying around awaiting collection. I thought that maybe Benson had contracted with the owners to have the gear shipped directly into the UK and had decided to wait until we were committed to the run before telling us of the final phase of his plans.

I came to a decision and decided to phone Benson back early. I put on my jacket and helmet and went outside. Barry was in the garage, Eric was talking to me as I walked up the driveway, and Jill was still ironing. As I sat on the bike in the drive talking to Eric I heard the noise of a car engine screaming along the lane outside. A dark-blue car skidded to a halt across the driveway in a spray of mud and soil.

Before we could react four men dressed in black bulky jackets and ski masks jumped out of the car and ran towards us, leaping the garden gate. I was stunned to see they were pointing big pistols at us. Just then a helicopter descended from the sky and a loudspeaker cut in shouting something deafening and unintelligible in French. More black-suited men vaulted the hedge, and rolling in the grass and mud they jerked upright and pointed guns at us. It was a bladder-leaking moment. There was a crash of breaking glass, and Jill screamed loudly; a thump of metal hitting the floor told me she had dropped the iron.

Everything seemed to drop into slow motion as the first guy, his face all covered by his mask, reached us; he dropped Eric with a shoulder charge to his belly. Eric crumpled like a paper bag and went down with the guy kneeling on his chest. I saw the silvery glitter of handcuffs as the guy reached into his back pocket with one hand whilst pointing his gun at Eric's head with the other. The attacker stood up and rolled an unresisting Eric over into the mud. In a flash the handcuffs clicked onto his wrists, and he was a prisoner. The whole process had taken less than 20 seconds.

The second masked man who had targeted me couldn't knock me over as I was sat on the bike. He contented himself with shoving his gun into my chest and trying to pull my helmet off one handedly, but it was fastened by the chinstrap. I reached up to unfasten it and received a pistol slap across the back of my hands; he snarled something to me and unfastened the strap. He pulled the helmet off roughly, nearly taking my ears off in the process and immediately rammed the pistol against my forehead saying something directly in my face. I felt the spray of his spittle.

He gestured with his free hand, and following his sign language I climbed slowly and carefully off the bike, all the time the pistol pressed closely to my head. As soon as I was off the bike he transferred the gun and thumped me hard on the shoulder pushing me face down on to the ground. I quickly dropped down and felt his knee dig into the small of my back as he reached for my arms.

He pulled them down behind me, and I felt the click of handcuffs being fastened; he squeezed the ratchet and the cuffs bit tightly on my wrists. I was a prisoner now too.

I lifted my face from the gravel and mud and looked around. Eric was lying face down about six feet away sobbing quietly into the mud with a guy standing over him still pointing a gun at his back. Jill was still screaming, although the sound had now subsided to a sort of long, shuddering sobbing interspersed with an intermittent scream. There were loud crashes and bangs, and the sound of breaking furniture from inside the house. Barry was still in the garage behind the closed door. He obviously thought he would hide in there rather than take a chance outside.

I realized then we had been busted by a police squad. That was a relief! At first I thought we were being held up by another gang, but I quickly decided they wouldn't have a helicopter hovering overhead. The tinny noise of chattering police radios forced its way into my consciousness even above the deafening roar of the chopper. Bits of gravel, leaves and paper were blowing around in crazy circles, it was an incredible, unreal scene.

Amid the confusion, shouting and crying the police seemed to realize they were one man short. They ran up to the garage and pulled open the door pointing their guns into the gloomy interior. Barry shot out like a greyhound from a trap. He was either crazy or hadn't seen the guns, because these guys were pros. Barry reached as far as the edge of the field next to the drive when the two policemen who had given chase landed on him. He went down with a whooshing noise as the breath was knocked from his lungs. They sat on his back as they handcuffed his arms and legs, and he was trussed up like a chicken.

The helicopter moved away, and suddenly there seemed to be hundreds of police milling around the garden and roadway. The ones dressed in black pulled down Velcro patches on their jackets to reveal large police badges; on the back of their jackets the word

POLICE was similarly exposed in bright orange lettering; others had donned plastic armbands.

We all lay on the ground whilst the search of the house continued noisily for about 15 minutes. A photographer walked up and started snapping away at everything in sight, including us on the floor, the vehicles and endless pictures of the van from every possible angle. Finally a tall middle-aged copper who seemed to be the one in charge walked over and stood in front of us.

On his command, as we lay looking up at him, we were picked up and taken, each of us between two coppers, to look at the cannabis lying on the floor of the garage. He started shouting at us in French, but I didn't have a clue what he was saying and could make out only the words, stupéfiants, cannabis and prison. He was ranting and shouting at the top of his lungs. Oh, shit, I thought this guy is really pissed with us. Barry looked across at me and winked, which drew him a sharp cuff across the face from a black-clothed copper. 'No contact,' he shouted.

The photographer came in and took a further series of snaps of each of us stood in front of the pile of cannabis. Then a few of the boss coppers posed there too, smiling in front of the gear. That's one for the family album, I thought. Incongruously it reminded me of an old sepia-tone American cowboy photograph, the sheriff standing over the body of the vanquished criminal. I smiled at the thought, a mistake not to be repeated, when a baton appeared from nowhere and hit me straight in the solar plexus. Fucking hell, that hurt! I doubled over and gasped, trying to get some air back into my body.

After the viewing the gear and photographing charade was over we were taken into the farm kitchen, which by this time had been thoroughly trashed. Cupboards and drawers were open, and all the contents thrown on to the floor: broken plates, cups and glasses were strewn everywhere. There was a constant sound of scrunching glass underfoot whenever anybody moved. Some of the kitchen windows were broken, and the curtains were blowing into the room. As Eric and Jill looked at the mess of their home, Jill set off crying again. At this a policeman snapped at her, presumably telling her to stop. Eric gave him a murderous look but wisely kept his mouth shut. The atmosphere was very tense and threatening. I saw Eric, Jill and Barry were by now really dejected and fed up. I suppose I looked the same way too.

After a few minutes a copper came in, plonked a large portable cassette recorder on the kitchen table and switched it on to record. He spoke clearly into the mike, presumably giving his name and basic details of the operation, then thrust it towards each of us in turn and in basic and hard to understand English demanded our names. We duly announced them to the machine.

A whoop and laughing outside signalled a new find. Two coppers came in with mud on their fatigues. Eric was dragged outside again, doubtless to view his attempts at growing marijuana in the coalshed. When he came back he was crying, tears streaming unchecked down his face. 'I'm fucked,' he said to no one in particular. 'Yes, you are fucked, mister,' said one of the coppers in a voice sounding remarkably like Peter Sellers' Inspector Clouseau. At least one of them could speak English, I thought.

The police left us in the kitchen with a couple of armed guards whilst they began to examine every piece of paper in the house; even old newspapers Jill had used to line shelves were inspected. We weren't allowed to talk to one another, although there was much glaring and shrugging of shoulders going on, it was a conversation by signals.

At the first opportunity I would inform the police of my undercover role in this smuggling operation. I wanted to let the police know who I was before the wheels of bureaucracy started turning. It was bad enough being arrested, but I didn't want to make any statements and be indicted by the French. I knew that once charges became more formal they would have to be processed, and then lawyers would be involved before my release on the intervention of the UK Customs. That would completely blow my cover, of course, and Kath and Natalie were sitting patiently in Spain, right in the middle of Benson's area, awaiting my return. Besides having guns pointed at my head wasn't covered by any agreement with Customs. Maybe it was a hazard that could be expected from the bad guys, but these were the good guys.

The coppers decided to hold initial interviews with us at the farm. We were all questioned together. Rather like a bizarre game show, it went like this:

'What is you name, smuggler?'

'John Lightfoot.'

'Is that your real name?'

'Yes, it's the name I was christened with.'

'Where are you from?'

'Great Britain and Spain.'

'Where are your guns?'

'I don't have any guns.'

'You must think we are fools, we know perfectly well all smugglers carry guns.'

'Maybe that's so, but I don't have a gun.'

'What is your name?'

'I've just told you, John Lightfoot.'

'And what is his name?' pointing towards Eric.

'Eric.'

'And his family name?'

'I don't know.'

'Salope! Do you think we are stupid? It will be hard for you if you do not cooperate with us.'

'I'm sorry, I don't know his full name, but if I'm under arrest I wish you to notify my embassy please.'

And so it went on for ages. All this was delivered by the copper in a stunning Inspector Clouseau accent, which obviously he did not realize sounded comical to our ears. Because of the language difficulties the whole interview had an aura of farce, which if it hadn't been so serious would have been funny.

Eventually they gave up on questioning us and opted to move us to police headquarters. After a brief consultation they decided that Barry and I should be taken back to our hotel so that our rooms could be searched.

They put us in separate cars with three coppers in each, and we set off. They were obviously not familiar with the local topography, and I had to try and direct them. After nearly an hour of wrong turns and difficulties in communication we finally reached the town, and I directed them to the hotel. We all went in together, six coppers with guns surrounding Barry and me. The receptionist, a pretty girl of about 20, looked as if she might faint when we marched through the doorway. The senior copper explained in rapid-fire French what was going on and quickly obtained our room keys.

We went straight upstairs, where the police started a thorough search, looking under the beds in each room, even though they had obviously been cleaned, and between the sheets, despite the fact the bed had been made by the chambermaid. They checked my holdall containing clothes and washing kit very thoroughly. Eventually they knew they had drawn a blank, which they seemed pretty pissed about.

'Where are your guns, monsieur?' asked the senior copper for about the tenth time.

'We don't have any guns,' I repeated yet again, and we carried on this argument down the stairs back into the entrance lobby. More fast French to the receptionist and a bill was quickly made up and handed to the copper. He indicated to me to take some money from my wallet and pay it. Then leaving the hotel staff and clients standing agog in the open lounge area we climbed into the cars again and drove off.

By now it was pitch dark and raining heavily. The car windows were all steamed up, and there was the constant twitter of police radios. I was hungry, not having eaten all day, and had a raging headache. Worst of all was my desperate need for a cigarette, even a foul-smelling Gitanes that the coppers were chain-smoking would have been good at that moment.

'May I have a cigarette, please?' I asked. The guy sat at my side looked at me. 'Cigarette, tobacco, please?' I repeated. He grinned, one smoker to another and put his cigarette to my lips. I inhaled deeply and promptly coughed. God, that tobacco was awful, it tasted like old sweaty socks. He laughed and pulled the cigarette away.

During the nearly two-hour-long ride some of the tension leaked away, and their command of English gradually improved along with their more relaxed manner.

'Why do you smuggle narcotics?' one of them asked.

'I am not a smuggler,' I replied. 'I am an agent for British Customs & Excise, *Les Douanes*. When we reach your base I want to talk privately with a senior officer,' I added slowly, carefully enunciating my words. The effect of my remarks was as remarkable as if I had casually lobbed a hand grenade into the car.

There was a ten-second silence, and then they all began chattering at once. The boss copper in the front passenger seat picked up the radio handset and started talking earnestly to somebody. At last, I thought, now maybe I'll get a little sense out of them.

The one with the best English said to me, 'Why did you not confess you are a Customs agent at the farm?'

'Because I am an undercover agent. My role is confidential, it's a secret,' I said slowly, trying to make sure he understood. 'None of the others you have arrested knows I am an agent,' I added. The copper had turned round in his seat and was looking at me intently in the car's gloomy interior. I stared back into his eyes and nodded confirmation of my claims.

I was satisfied that when we reached the police station inquiries would be made, and my true role would soon be revealed. This was why I had been given a codename and had secret telephone numbers. As I sat there I drifted back to the conversations I'd had with Rob and Steve at our farm in England. It all seemed a long time ago, but I could recall our discussions vividly. I was sure the machinery would swing into action, and I would be 'released on a technicality'. Everything was going to be OK.

Once inside the police station we were all taken into the cells area at the rear of the building. Still handcuffed we were searched more thoroughly by uniformed police. They weren't just looking for knives or other weapons, they took all items from our pockets, including such things as paper tissues and small change. Jewellery, watches, belts and shoelaces were also taken from us, and everything inventoried on a big official list before being sealed into plastic bags.

Once we had been searched we were placed in individual cells. It was a depressing experience. They were small with tiled walls and a slatted wooden bench fixed into the wall. There were no washing facilities, and the toilet was a concrete pad set in the floor with a hole in the middle emptying straight into the sewer beneath, the stench rising from it was vile. From the graffiti covering the walls I gathered that some enterprising souls had managed to sneak pens into the cell. It was interesting trying to decipher it.

Suddenly I could hear voices: Eric and Jill were shouting to each other between the cells. I joined in, and so did Barry. Eric had just yelled, 'Tell them nothing, they can't prove it's our gear,' which I thought was a particularly crass thing to say. A guard stomped down the outer corridor. 'Tais-toi,' he shouted nastily and banged on one or two steel doors for effect. I didn't understand him, but I gathered he wanted us to shut up.

After what seemed like a couple of hours of just sitting around thinking I began to get cold – the cells weren't heated, and I had no jacket. There weren't any blankets on the bench, so it looked like a cold night ahead for us. I lay for hours looking up at the wire caged lamp high up on the ceiling. There were no windows, and the whole place was damp and claustrophobic. Exhausted by the day's events I eventually drifted off into an uncomfortable sleep.

The next morning I was taken for questioning. The police had arranged a local high-school teacher as translator, and we got off to a good start. We went through a basic question-and-answer session; they wanted my home address, family names, mother's maiden name plus all the information that was in my passport, which they now held. Later in the morning one of the senior guys from the arresting team joined us.

'We have contacted the Customs in England, and they tell us that they don't know you,' he began.

I was dumbfounded. 'It's a mistake, you obviously didn't speak to the right person,' I said and gave them the full names of my Customs handlers. 'Call them on the number I gave you and tell them Benjy needs some help. Benjy is my codename with Customs and Excise.'

'We telephoned them, and they don't know you,' repeated the copper.

'Look, if they don't know me how come I have their private phone numbers and the names of their investigation officers?' I demanded. This was getting silly, and I thought he was trying to wind me up.

The police and the interpreter talked amongst themselves for a few minutes before the one who had been questioning me said, 'OK, why don't you tell us about your work with the Customs?'

I could see no harm in that, they were after all on the same side as the Customs, so for the next hour or so I told them of the names, operations and anything else that came to mind about the Customs and drug dealing. They listened avidly and took copious notes. During this time there was a distinct easing of the atmosphere. I was given coffee and cigarettes, and attitudes became more relaxed and friendly. It was a case of carrot and stick by the cops, as long as I was cooperating they would be nice to me. But although aware of their obvious show of basic psychology I wasn't bothered by it.

The information I was giving them wasn't secret, much of it had been ignored by the Customs, and I could be talking my way out of a tricky situation now that the Customs seemed to have abandoned me to my fate. I gave them all the details of the French operation, right from the beginning. When I got to the part about the van coming from England they were very interested and alert. They went into a huddle again and held a whispered conversation.

'John,' said the younger cop who spoke some English, 'we want you to cooperate with us and help us to catch the van from England. We will allow you to make some phone calls to arrange a rendezvous, and it will be good for you when we tell the judge.'

Ah, I thought, here is the trade-off, if I assist them then the 'technical hitch' ploy will be brought in, and I'll be released. 'OK,' I agreed, 'first off I will have to phone Benson in Spain.'

A tape recorder was produced and connected to a telephone. They locked the door so that no one could interrupt, and we quickly prepared a story to tell Benson. Two minutes later I dialled his number.

'Hi, Colin,' I said when he answered, 'we've had a bit of a problem here. Yesterday afternoon I came off the motorbike on a back lane and ended up in a local clinic. I got out this morning and went back to the farm. Everyone there was just about shitting themselves, but no van has turned up. What the fuck is going on?'

Benson was surprised to hear from me and even more surprised that I had fallen off the bike. But he didn't know what had happened to the van.

'Well, I'm not in the mood to hang around here much longer,' I said. 'I'm OK, just a bit bruised and sore, and the bike isn't damaged badly. But we're all getting really pissed off with your English mates, and we are leaving here one way or the other today.'

'OK,' he said, 'why don't you phone Tony direct in England and see what's happening?', and he gave me a mobile phone number.

'Great, I'll speak to you later,' I replied and quickly hung up. That was the last time I ever spoke with Benson.

Tension drained out of the room like air escaping from a balloon. 'Well done, John,' said the copper whose English was adequate enough to follow the conversation. He explained what had transpired to the others and then told me to phone Tony. But when I did so there was no answer. By now it was lunchtime, and the cops wanted to eat. One of them gave me a pack of cigarettes and a book of matches before I was handed back to a uniformed cop and returned to the cells.

Considering the circumstances things were going pretty well, and I could see me being released in the near future. I sat in the cell for a few more hours, and then the English-speaking copper appeared to take me off for further questioning. Later I made further calls to Tony in England and finally managed to arrange a meeting with the driver who was coming to collect the drugs consignment destined for England.

OCTRIS, a specialist drug squad operating from Paris throughout France, staked out the meeting spot and late that evening arrested a man driving a British-registered vehicle that matched the description furnished by Tony. Various bits of incriminating evidence were found on him, and he was charged with conspiracy to smuggle drugs across France. I never saw the guy and didn't even know he had been arrested until the following day. The cops were very pleased with my efforts and told me that I would get a greatly reduced sentence because of my help in nailing another gang member. But I wasn't after a reduced sentence, I was after a no-sentence scenario.

For now I was photographed, proper mug shots just like you see on TV, holding a card with my name printed on it in front of my chest. Then I was fingerprinted by a taciturn old man who stank of booze. Back in my cell I began to feel a bit worried. What was the point in photographing and fingerprinting me if they intended to release me?

Other than a guard bringing me a plastic cup of coffee and a sandwich nothing else happened until late in the evening. A senior uniformed policeman and a few juniors collected me from the cells and led me to a storage room across an open courtyard. It was great to be outside, even so briefly, and so what if it was raining. Inside the storage room all the goodies seized during the farm raid were displayed on the floor, everything marked with small orange identification tags.

The interpreter was in full swing. 'Mr Lightfoot, do you recognize this contraband seized at the time of your arrest?' he asked. I think he was feeling more nervous than me judging how his voice had gone up a couple of octaves. I suppose he wanted to make a good impression on the chief who would no doubt be paying him. I noticed the photographer hovering on the edge of the group.

'No, I've never seen this lot before,' I said loudly. That really threw them. The chief shouted, 'Imbécile! at me and started ranting at his mates before he turned and quick timed back into the main building, leaving me standing there grinning. Back again in my cell I felt a flash of pleasure. What an arrogant bunch of dickheads! They had all the evidence they needed and plenty of statements to boot. All they had wanted with that little charade was the icing on the cake. What a great story it would have been for them.

Imagine the scene, an international drugs trafficker confronted with his misdeeds broke down and confessed to the chief of police and his band of arse lickers, all nicely recorded by camera, with the damning evidence forming a sinister backdrop. No doubt it had been timed to take place in the dark to increase the dramatic effect of the tableau. Well, bollocks to them. They could now work it out for themselves, I was going to look after number one for a change.

I got no food that evening and spent another cold night on the bench alone. As I lay there I could occasionally hear snatches of Barry singing 'Rule Britannia,' followed by a guard shouting at him. Barry responded with, 'Fuck off, you frogs. I want a cup of tea!'

A crazy feeling came over me as I realized there was nothing worse they could do to us. We were locked up, unwashed, unfed and without access to any lawyers. I joined in with Barry. We sang at the tops of our voices for a couple of hours to an accompaniment of French coppers shouting at us to be quiet, but they were powerless to stop us.

We pushed it as far as we could, encouraging each other to sing louder and louder. That night the French heard some wild renditions of 'Land of Hope and Glory', 'Rule Britannia', 'God Save the Queen' and so on; finally we moved on to some Queen songs before we petered out. It was a great demonstration of the good old British *Bridge on the River Kwai* spirit, and it boosted my morale tremendously, but now my voice was hoarse, and I was knackered out. I slept really well that night despite the cold and the stink of shit from the sewers.

* * *

The next morning everyone acted as if nothing had happened. I was given a coffee and questioned for several more hours. Repeated pettifogging questions and answers that became mind-numbingly boring as the hours ticked by.

After yet another bland, tasteless sandwich for lunch I was left alone and told that I was to see a lawyer appointed by the court. Shortly thereafter an important-looking middle-aged man walked into the office wearing a three-piece suit, floral bow tie and pince-nez glasses fastened to a cord around his neck. He was a sight, but he spoke perfect English.

He kicked off the short interview by saying, 'Good afternoon, Mr Lightfoot, I am your defence lawyer appointed by the court. During this period of the police investigation I cannot discuss the details of the case with you. I can check on your welfare and ensure that you are fed properly and allowed washing facilities. I can also check that a relative or your country's embassy is informed of your arrest and detention by the French police.' He smiled encouragingly as if he had just delivered some good news.

'Well, I can tell you that so far I've had a few cups of coffee, two sandwiches and not been allowed to wash. How does that fit in with the French rules for detaining prisoners?' I asked. 'Furthermore, I am an informant for the British Customs & Excise working on an operation to catch some drug smugglers. I have told the police officers who arrested me, but they claim the Customs don't know me. That is a ridiculous statement, and though I have cooperated in every way they still will not accept I am not a drug dealer, and that I am an informant for the Customs.'

Once I got into this area he started shaking his head and repeated, mantra-like, 'I am not allowed to discuss the criminal charges or their circumstances with you. You must take these matters up with the judge who you will see later when you are indicted.' In a wary tone of voice he finished, 'I will take up the matters of food and washing facilities with the police officer in charge of your detention, but that is all I can do. I am sorry for all the rest.'

He seemed more nervous than me. Perhaps he thought the conversation was being recorded, or he was expecting me, a desperado drug dealer, to jump at him. I don't know which, but he was definitely in a hurry to get out of the room. As legal advice went it was minimal. Within seconds the English-speaking copper had opened the door and reseated himself as the lawyer made a swift exit. The whole interview had taken less than ten minutes.

'Hell!' I said as the lawyer left, 'if that's all the law can do for me then I might as well represent myself.'

'You must understand the charges of international drug trafficking are very serious in France,' the young copper said. 'They are looked upon the same as terrorism. You will all face a maximum penalty of 30 years in prison when you are convicted, but you will be helped by your assistance in catching the other driver.' I just stared at him as he continued, 'It is in your interest to assist us to catch any other members of your gang, then your sentence will be reduced still further.'

'Just a minute,' I retorted finally, 'what about the small fact that you seem to forget that I am here with the permission of the UK Customs? This was a planned operation to catch the gang leaders in Britain, and it's not my fault you guys jumped in too early. You should be arresting Benson in Spain and Paul and Tony in England, they're the money men behind this operation.'

'We shall see. That is a matter for the judge,' he replied, in a similar vein to the lawyer. He then turned back to the prepared statements and starting asking the same set of questions over again.

As I answered him my mind was thinking, thirty years, bloody hell, I'm going to have to do something to make these jokers see sense, never mind a few years off for cooperation. But they had no intention of seeing sense. They were happy they had caught a gang of foreign drug smugglers with 300 kilos of cannabis. It was a major coup for them. I was merely an annoying side issue, a thread that needed tucking back into place so that they could present a nice clean picture of their efficiency to the judge. So they stitched me up properly.

Later that day they asked me to sign all the statements that had been taken. All together there were more than 20, each of which the translator went through with me. Although very detailed I noticed there wasn't a single reference to the UK Customs or my claims that I was an informant for them. I questioned them about this.

'We are trying to protect you, John,' said the young copper. 'All the other gang members and their lawyers will have access to these statements. If we put in that you are a Customs agent they will know, and you could be in great danger. We shall make a secret confidential report to the judge that will not be available to anyone else. We will tell the judge of your Customs connection in that document, but it is better that the statements are "clean'' and make no mention of the Customs.'

That seemed a reasonable deal to me. At that time I was in no hurry to have Barry or Eric and Jill know I was a Customs agent. If they knew it was only a matter of time before Benson found out, and Kath and Natalie were still down in Spain near to his vengeful hand. So I signed the prepared statements.

The next day, the fourth since our arrest, we were loaded into separate cars and each driven with a police escort to the criminal courts. There we were locked in individual holding cells under the main building. The cells were small, but at least they were warm. Before they handed us over one of the cops gave me another packet of cigarettes.

After an hour or so of kicking my heels in the cell I was handcuffed and led up a narrow staircase opening out into a public area. There was carpet on the floor and potted plants in a corner, which all looked very civilized. We then filed into an office filled with important-looking prosperous and overfed citizens. A man behind an impressively large desk introduced himself through a middle-aged female interpreter.

'Hello, Mr Lightfoot, I am examining magistrate Maurice Marlière. I am in charge of the criminal case and will be investigating the facts of this affair.' The translator spoke in a dry, schoolmarmish voice.

'Hello, judge, I would like to know why I have been held all this time without anyone formally acknowledging that I am an agent for HM Customs and Excise?' I started off hard, looking him straight in the eyes. From the surprise on the faces of the interpreter and the judge I could tell this was all news to them.

The senior OCTRIS guy immediately launched into a discourse with the judge telling him, I hoped, that I was an agent for the Customs. Whilst he was talking M Marlière was flicking through and reading various documents.

'Mr Lightfoot, if you are an agent for the Customs then why do you not say that in your statements?' he asked. The anger and frustration started to bite at me.

'This is ridiculous,' I said. 'There is no mention of my status because OCTRIS said it was better left out for my security. They also said they would report to you confidentially about my claims.' By now I was really indignant and nearly shouting. I could feel the policeman behind me twitching as he got ready to restrain me if my anger boiled over and I went for anyone.

The OCTRIS agent and the judge talked rapidly for a few more minutes before Marlière nodded his head in a satisfied manner.

'Well, Mr Lightfoot, it seems that OCTRIS have investigated your claim to be an informant and cannot get any confirmation from British Customs & Excise. They tell me you have cooperated well and assisted them to capture one other member of the gang. I will make my own inquiries into your position with the British authorities, and if what you say is true you should be released in the near future.'

'But now,' and he adopted a firm stentorian tone, 'you are charged with contravening several articles of the French criminal code in that you as a member of a gang imported a substantial quantity of illegal drugs across the French border. You will be held in prison until I have completed my inquiries.'

And that was it. I didn't get the chance to reply before I was being led out the door. I don't know what forced me, but I had to have a last word.

'So this is French justice, is it?' by now I was shouting back into the room. 'The fucking Common Market, it's a load of bollocks. You just do your own thing. What happened to European cooperation, eh?'

It was too late, the decisions were already made before I had even entered the room. There was no way they were going to release me on a 'technicality'. I had been lied to, and now I was hung out to dry on my own. I could tell instinctively that things weren't going to be easy. I would have to prove to this judge that I really was working for UK Customs or else I was going to be in deep shit for a long long time.

Oh, well, I thought, that was pretty good. Within the space of five minutes I'd insulted and probably pissed off the one man who could help me get out of this mess. I would have to wait and see what the future held for me now.

51

Prison Strife

MY INDUCTION into the French penal system took place one cold, wet night. Following my brief but fiery appearance in court I was hustled handcuffed past the stares of cleaning staff and outside. It was now very dark and raining in a steady, continuous downpour. I was dumped unceremoniously into the back of a closed van in the company of two large and armed gendarmes. They looked at me indifferently and talked quietly to one another.

Accompanied by a motorcycle escort lead squad with a back-up car behind I was driven through the quiet and near deserted town. After some slowing and jerking the van stopped, and I heard the driver talking and laughing with someone outside. We moved off again with another jerk for a few yards, then the van came to an abrupt halt. With my hands tied behind me and unable to hold myself upright during the irregular jolting motion I had rolled off the plastic bench seat and ended up lying on my side against the rear doors.

I was scrambling to sit up when the doors were suddenly thrown open. Unable to help myself I tumbled heavily out of the van and dropped on to a concrete floor at the feet of two prison guards. Disorientated and blinded by powerful arc lights I heard a grunted curse, and then my introduction proper started with a booted kick to my kidneys.

Not wanting another kick I quickly scrambled to my feet and

tried to see where I was. The dazzle of the lights and a searing wind were debilitating, and I felt a wave of anxiety and exhaustion wash over me. Hot bile rushed into my mouth, and before I could clench my teeth shut stinking vomit erupted down my front, spattering on to a guard. He cursed again, and I heard the gendarmes behind me laugh crudely. A hefty push in the direction of the prison gates helped me empty the rest of my stomach contents on to the yard floor. I couldn't wipe my mouth, and the residue dribbled down my chin and burned the back of my throat. I felt a complete arsehole.

Tiredness, vomiting and the pain of the kidney kick combined to force tears of pain, anger and frustration to my eyes. Embarrassed by my show of weakness I shook my head and said as coolly and unemotionally as I could, 'OK, so that's a demonstration of the French sense of fair play. Well done.' They didn't understand the words, but another shove told me they had read my tone of voice. As I fell heavily on my left knee I screamed involuntarily and collapsed on the ground with a searing pain in my leg that radiated up my thigh from the knee.

To more curses and shouting I was roughly hauled to my feet and dragged through a small arched doorway. Squinting against the light I looked up and saw the inscription AD 1810 carved into the weathered rock. Snatching a brief look around me I saw we were in a large yard surrounded by high stone walls. Great, I thought, a bloody Napoleonic nick is all I need.

In a brightly lit reception area the prison guards accepted me from the gendarmes with the minimum of formalities. I was roughly searched, and my small bag of personal belongings was emptied on to a table and checked over again. My cash was counted and placed into a zip-lock plastic bag. My watch, wedding ring, St Christopher and chain were all placed into another zipped bag.

A guard shouted me over and after releasing the cuffs gestured to me to sign my name in an old-fashioned ledger that immediately brought to mind a Dickensian accounts book. The ordinary biro he was thrusting at me seemed inappropriate, and in my exhaustion I thought a quill pen would have been more fitting. This irrational unbidden thought brought a smile to my lips, but the touchy guards seemed to think I was laughing at them. This earned me a sharp, menacing reprimand from the guard. His fetid, beery breath overlaid with garlic rolled over me as he moved closer and glared into my eyes. Nauseous I looked away, and with a deep sigh I signed my name. And so I became a prisoner of the French penal system.

I was led down a flagstone corridor through a pale-blue painted steel grillage that incorporated a sliding steel gate, operated electrically by an unseen hand, and into a holding area behind the reception desk. The door slid shut behind me and clanged with that special sound that is so evocative of prisons the world over. There is a grim finality to that clang, over time you learn to recognize the differing tones of each door in the prison. Now I am a connoisseur of the clang.

I was dumped on a wooden bench whilst the guards and the gendarmes discussed me and the case in general. I heard my name and the word 'stupéfiants' a few times as they kept glancing across at me and laughing. I must have looked a mess. Without a wash or shave for nearly five days, wearing crumpled and torn clothes and smelling strongly of vomit, I looked more like a drunk raked up from a gutter than an international narcotics trafficker. I couldn't have been a pretty sight, but I seemed to amuse the guards all right.

After about half an hour of their chatting, during which I studied a notice board and started to doze, an older guard appeared. He was comical looking, sporting a large, droopy mustache and dressed in regulation navy-blue uniform with an incongruous pair of tattered tartan house slippers. He was smoking an evil-smelling briar pipe, which he pointed in my direction and gestured for me to follow him. As I did so the gendarmes and the reception guards bade me a mocking good night, and my new guard grinned, showing nicotine-stained teeth. But somehow his grin didn't seem as menacing as the others, and his manner was not overtly threatening.

I started to feel more at ease. Later I found out that he was just an old boy working his way towards his pension by doing the night shift, which, after the final lockup, is the quietest time in prison. Barring any problems in the cells the night guard's duties only stretched to watching TV and drinking coffee. My late-night arrival provided a small but interesting diversion for the old timer.

He unlocked a steel door and took me into another brightly lit room smelling of cheap disinfectant, which contained only a tatty wall cupboard, a metal-frame chair and a rather disconcerting steel eyebolt protruding from the wall at shoulder height. This room was painted the same institutional mustard yellow as the reception area and had the same well-used, drab and impersonal feel to it. There was an overall impression of depression and dejection – or was that just my overtired mind?

The guard started talking to me in a conversational tone, but as I didn't have a clue what he meant I just stared back at him and shrugged my shoulders. He left me for a moment and returned with my original tormentor, whom I had mentally nicknamed Garlic Breath. After locking the door behind him Garlic Breath began yelling at me. He obviously wanted me to do something but I didn't know what he wanted. Shouting didn't help me understand any more, and Garlic Breath was becoming increasingly frustrated when he realized he wasn't getting anywhere. Eventually, though, I got the picture: they wanted me to undress.

I quickly complied and stripped down to my boxers, which Garlic Breath signalled he wanted off too. No problem, I pulled them off and handed them over. He then pointed between my legs and said something to the old timer, laughing crudely. Unsurprisingly my dick didn't appear a good testament to British manhood at that moment, it had shrunk for protection and looked as if I had been in a cold swimming pool for a couple of hours. I felt my balls tighten in anticipation of worse to come. How right I was.

It was body-search time. My sprits plunged into free fall as Garlic Breath took a pair of rubber gloves from the cupboard and pulled them on. I stood naked in the centre of the room whilst he minutely examined every part of my body. Between my toes, my scrotum, armpits, ears, hair, all were thoroughly investigated. He used a wooden spatula to check out my mouth and teeth and his fingers for every other orifice. He felt my shrivelled balls in their scrotal sack and laughed lewdly. His squeezing wasn't sexual, it was simply to let me know that he literally had me by the balls.

Psychologists talk about the fight-or-flight syndrome, but all those chemicals being pumped into the bloodstream to fuel those primitive impulses don't count for anything when you're overtired, emotionally worn down, naked, and your enemy holds your balls in his hand. You just stay quiet and take the shit as it's doled out.

After the body search the older guard passed me a pair of cotton pyjamas to wear; this was the next episode in my humiliation. Those pyjamas would have been too small for me when I was 14 years old. Try as I might there was no way I could get into them, but it was obvious there would not be a larger pair forthcoming. In desperation I forced one leg into the bottoms and then pulled on the jacket as best I could.

The two guards were joined by more of their mates, and I was taken from the reception and administration area into the prison accommodation wing. Marched through more steel gates and up a flight of worn stone stairs I ended up on the ground floor of a large block. Stone built with high walls that disappeared from view in the darkness, I could just make out three levels of cell doors, each reached by a painted metal staircase, and steel platforms running around the walls.

Catching nets strung below the landings and flagstone floors completed the living picture of an archetypal Victorian prison. Maybe it would have looked like home to Papillon, but it looked cold, stark and depressing to me. Illuminated only by low-wattage night-lights, it was grim and full of foreboding. The air smelt of damp, disinfectant and that dirty stale urine smell reminiscent of old council high-rise lifts.

The prison guards seemed to find it highly amusing to watch me hopping along barefoot in those ridiculous pyjamas, whilst holding on to a mattress and some sheets. Across the courtyard until we reached a cell door they catcalled and ribbed me just like a noisy gang of teenagers. As the guard opened the door to admit me I turned and said to the group, 'Goodnight, gentlemen, now bugger off like nice little frogs.' Instantly they became less amused, and I was roughly pushed across the threshold and into the cell. The door clanged shut behind me, and I listened for the first time as two shoot bolts were slammed home and a big lock squeaked as the tumblers turned. I was locked in. This was one of many occasions I would listen to that clanging and squeaking, and a great depression enveloped me like molten lead.

So here I was, many miles from home, lost to my loved ones for the foreseeable future. My heart weighed heavy in my chest, and I was filled with a soul-wrenching despair and loneliness. I had learnt a valuable first lesson that night as I lay in bed with a sore and bruised backside. The French sense of humour doesn't extend to laughing when the British poke fun at them. Deep down there is a well-hidden core of racism in the French psyche, much as there is in the British.

In the days to come I was to feel more lonely and isolated as well as having further lessons in racism, and I would discover what life could be like when you are in a minority of one on a playing field of hate and distrust. Eventually I fell into a troubled sleep.

I was awakened in the early morning by the sound of my cell door opening. A coalblack man whom I took to be a trustee prisoner, a longer-term, non-violent inmate working towards release, stood in the doorway, the smell of coffee wafting into the cell. I jumped out of bed on to the cold stone floor and limped over to him. He took one look at my pyjamas and burst out laughing, then he gestured towards a steaming bucket in his hand. I looked down and saw it was brimful of coffee. I didn't have any drinking utensils, and so I smiled and made a palms-out shoulder shrug towards him and said, 'Ah, coffee, oui, oui.'

The prisoner replied, 'English, eh? Manchester United? OK!' I was wondering how to advance further and get a coffee when a guard appeared who stopped our basic attempts at conversation by snarling something at the prisoner and without more ado swung the door shut. Obviously no coffee for me, a perfect start to the morning.

Dejected, I sat on the bed and wondered what the day held for me. It was cold in my cell, and I wrapped myself in an old blanket to keep warm. It was still dark, and I had no watch, but I estimated the time to be about 6 am. I could hear the sounds of the prison coming to life: cell doors clanging, a hosepipe splashing nearby, the sweeping of brushes in the block area and the overall background noise of men coughing and hawking. I felt unbearably tired; my knee and back were stiff with bruising.

Some time later the door opened again, and a younger-looking, smartly turned-out guard appeared and gestured me outside. I followed him across the courtyard to another cell door. Looking around I saw there were various prison parties cleaning, and the sight of me set all these guys off laughing, pointing and whistling as I hopped along behind the guard still wearing my ridiculous pyjamas. All I could manage in return was a sickly grin.

I was shown into a musty black-and-white tile shower room. There were no individual cubicles or stalls, just a plastic-moulded bench along one wall and five shower heads with some old, rusty-looking pipework. Water flow was controlled by a small nipple-like button on each shower-head feeder pipe. I quickly stripped off and pressed the button. The spray of icy water was exquisitely painful. I've always preferred a hot shower to the masochistic pleasure of a heart-stopping cold one, but this cold water blasted the tiredness and cobwebs away.

I noticed the guard had left me alone, but he returned some minutes later to toss me a bar of carbolic-like soap. I thanked him and vigorously soaped myself all over. The water started getting hotter, and with the simple act of becoming clean I began to feel almost human again.

When I finished the guard nodded to get dressed again, and without any towel I did so whilst still dripping wet. There were again catcalls as I passed the workers, but feeling more alive now I turned to them, grinned and gave them the finger. On the floor inside my cell was a steaming glass bowl of coffee. What luxury! Maybe the day wouldn't be too bad after all.

After I had drunk the coffee the door opened, and a guard tossed me a plastic bag. Things were definitely on the up, the bag contained a personal hygiene kit including a toothbrush and toothpaste, soap, shampoo sachets, plastic comb, and most surprisingly, a tube of shaving gel and three disposable Bic razors. I immediately set to work and had a really good clean-up. Shaving was a bit tricky without a mirror, but what the hell! I wasn't about to enter a beauty competition. Anyway now I was in the best frame of mind since my arrest five days previously.

After about an hour the guard appeared again and passed in all my clothes and my own bag of gear. Cheered up no end, I dressed quickly, ignoring the sweaty smells from dirty clothing and socks. Now I was washed, shaved and dressed normally again, I felt remarkably human. It shows how a little deprivation and humiliation can depress even the most ebullient of us; but then give us back a little dignity, and our spirits soar and return to normal.

Later that morning I was taken to the infirmary to see the prison doctor. The infirmary was in a small white room that contained a stretcher trolley, a dentist's chair and a large glass-front cabinet housing a wide variety of shiny medical implements. A jovial old country-style doctor weighed me, measured me and looked in my ears, eyes and mouth. He then fitted a needle to a new plastic syringe and signed for me to make a fist. I shook my head, if anyone was going to take blood from me I wanted to know what it was for. The guard stood up and hitched his belt meaningfully. 'OK, OK,' I said. 'You can have the blood if that's what you want.' I smiled and offered my left arm, the guard relaxed, and the doctor tied a rubber strip around my upper arm and found a vein. He filled two syringes and offered me a small sticking plaster for my arm.

Sensing the perfunctory medical was nearly over I told him I suffered from high blood pressure and needed the tablets taken from me by the police. To an onlooker this pantomime explanation must have looked like a bizarre game of charades. Making pumping motions with my hands and miming taking tablets didn't help the doctor understand; it was obvious he hadn't got a clue. He dispatched a guard who returned with a small French–English dictionary and a large plastic bag containing my belt, boots and all the other forbidden items.

I quickly showed him blood and pressure in the dictionary. He got the message and produced an ancient-looking sphygomanometer from the cabinet. He took a bloodpressure reading and seemed surprised that it was 170 over 120. He made some tutting noises and carefully examined the box of tablets found by the guard in my bag. 'Ah, Tenormin,' he exclaimed and then berated the guard, presumably for withholding medication. The doctor pressed a tablet from its bubble cap and handed it to me; without the offer of water I dry swallowed it quickly. He made a few notes on a medical card, and that was it. It was interesting to note that French doctors write in the same illegible scribble as their British counterparts.

Back in my cell I lay down and took stock of my position. Rumbling in my belly reminded me that I hadn't eaten since the previous day, when I'd had a salami sandwich whilst waiting my turn to see the judge. That was nearly 24 hours ago, and now I was feeling ravenous. The effects of the coffee had long gone. Of course thinking of food set off a craving for nicotine. I would have killed for a meal and a cigarette.

Hunger forced me into action. I kicked on the cell door, which rash action chased away my boldness as I awaited a response with some trepidation. Minutes later the door opened, and the same guard looked at me questioningly. I said, 'Sandwich, please,' and pointed towards my stomach. The guard laughed and pointed across the block where I could see two trustees pushing a trolley laden with food containers towards the cells. A few minutes later I was served up a large piece of crusty bread and a stew that seemed to be made of celery ends, green beans and a few potatoes. It wasn't very tasty, but it was hot, and I ate it ravenously. Best of all I was given an orange, which I ate complete with the skin.

Later that day two guards came to the cell and indicated that I should collect my scanty belongings and follow them. They took me up the first flight of steel stairs and opened the door to cell 43. I entered to find a room not much larger than the first cell, but this one was occupied by four other prisoners.

All the others began complaining when they saw me and my bedroll, and I must say that I agreed with them. The room was smaller than a Barratt-style domestic garage and included a set of steel bunks fastened to the wall, a single bed, two wall cabinets, a small toilet enclosure and a caravan-size chipped porcelain sink. Unperturbed the guard shrugged his shoulders, introduced me as 'the Englishman' and banged the door shut behind him. Now there were five of us locked in a small room with only three beds, a brutal introduction to the French prison overcrowding problem.

'Hi, I'm John', I said, summoning a friendly smile, only to receive blank looks. OK, I thought, try again, and calling up my best schoolboy French, I said, 'Je suis John. Bonjour.' This time I got a smile from one of them. 'Salut, John. Je m'appelle Stefi. Tu es une personnalité.' He pointed to a small portable TV mounted at high level on a shelf. They had seen the aftermath of the bust on the local TV channel news. They knew about the 300 kg of cannabis, and they seemed to look at me with a kind of grudging respect. Maybe they thought I was a kind of master criminal.

The tension broken, introductions were made all around. Soon I was sitting on one of the three stools smoking a roll-up cigarette and drinking a glass of strange-tasting black coffee. My cell mates were all French, two of them came from French territories, one from Algeria and one from the Seychelles. Two of them, Stefi and George, had been recently convicted and were awaiting transfer to a central jail in Rennes to complete their sentences, and two of them were remanded in custody awaiting trial.

Stefi was 32 years old and had been convicted of trafficking in cannabis for the second time. Caught with 1.5 kg in his possession he had been sentenced to four years. If I went to trial and was convicted and sentenced on the same ratio of weight of drug to sentence, I would go down for 800 years. Suddenly the 30-year maximum sentence bandied about by OCTRIS seemed reasonable. From the looks on the faces of my new cell mates I could see they thought I was in deep shit. This, I'm sure, prompted their sympathetic looks. It's always comforting when you have a problem to know that somebody else has a bigger problem than yourself.

George was a handsome, sun-tanned lad of 22 from the Seychelles. A crew member on an ocean-going tramp steamer, he had been involved in a fight with the local harbourmaster's son. A knife slash to the belly and a few grams of speed found in his pocket earned George a three-year sentence. He was a wild-looking lad who appeared as if he could handle himself in a situation. He was friendly enough, but there was a definite sense of reserve in his attitude to me.

Jacques was the oldest before I joined in. He was a 36-year-old lifelong felon who specialized in housebreaking. Getting somewhat ambitious he had been caught trying to rob the town's main post office in the early morning hours. As a recidivist he was expecting a sentence of about five years, his time spent on remand would be deducted from any sentence, so as he had a cushy job in the prison kitchen he wasn't in a hurry to go to trial and be transferred to a big central jail.

Yosef was a small weak-looking 18-year-old Algerian, accused of raping his young male cousin. I took an immediate dislike to this dangerous individual. He was treated with contempt by the other inmates, and I later discovered he rarely left the cell.

That first day passed fairly quickly and, tired by my experiences and the cumulative lack of sleep, shortly after the evening meal I made a bed of sorts and lay down under the table, the only space available. After bumming a last cigarette from Stef I had a contemplative smoke and soon drifted off to sleep.

I awoke once that night when one of them made his way to the toilet and trod on my outflung arm. Jumping up I hit the table overhead and knocked it over with a crash to the floor. Shouting curses I leapt to my feet rubbing my head. Everyone else woke up, and the light went on. I must have looked a strange sight stood in the middle of the room surrounded by broken glass and swearing like a madman. Nobody laughed. Later, when quiet was restored, and I was back on the mattress, I thought it was strange that no guard had come to investigate the shouting and noise of breaking glass.

'Bonjour, John,' said Stefi. I turned over and looked up at the battery-operated alarm clock; it showed 5.45 am.

'Shit,' I said, 'I'm going back to sleep.' I was dog tired and bad tempered, and in any case I'm pretty useless in the morning until I've had a cup of tea and a cigarette. The realization that I would get neither didn't please me any. Loneliness and depression came flooding back like a black tide. I groaned and rolled over again to bury my face in the pillow.

Soon the clanging of cell doors started. I could hear the guard coming inexorably along the passageway to our cell, opening doors along the way. Sure enough ours sprang open, admitting the bright light and a chilling draught.

'Bonjour, donnes-moi la poubelle,' the guard called cheerily. Not understanding, I just looked up at him from my prone position. 'Eh, rosbif, la poubelle maintenant!' he called. Clueless, I shook my head. He strode into the cell and picked up a plastic bag of rubbish from near the toilet door. He pointed to the bag and said, 'La poubelle, rosbif, comprends?' Cackling he backed out of the cell and slammed the door with a jovial bang. So ended my first French lesson: poubelle meant rubbish.

Now everyone was awake, and there was the usual cacophony of a group of men waking and getting up: hawking, coughing and farting. Everyone seemed to compete in making as much noise as possible whilst taking their first piss of the day. Five of us dressed to a concert of muffled curses as we constantly elbowed each other in the confined space between the beds and the table. What a carry on! Next on the agenda was the cigarette-rolling performance, and I bummed another from Stefi.

Just as the cigs were all ready the morning coffee arrived. We queued at the door for a ladleful of the steaming brew. I noticed everyone but me had glass tumblers or beakers, so I made do with a glass bowl. So there we sat at 6.15 am drinking coffee and smoking. Excellent.

After the morning ablutions the TV was switched on, and we all watched the morning news. There it was, the farmhouse looking deserted with open doors, broken windows and household debris scattered on the lawn. A couple of puffed-up gendarmes posed threateningly for the cameras. I think all the French have a keen sense of self-importance in front of a camera.

'Merde, t'as aucune chance, John,' said Stef sadly. This provoked a short conversation amongst my cell mates, and I noticed a few sad glances thrown in my direction. Suddenly their enthusiastic chatter drained away, and in the ensuing awkward silence I felt terribly distressed and isolated again.

Our reveries were broken by the guard opening the door and calling, 'Bon, messieurs, dehors.' Everyone jumped up and pulling on coats trailed outside. I had no coat to put on, but I followed anyway. All the cell doors on our side of the block were open, and many prisoners headed down the stairs. Crowding to a small exit after a cursory body search we passed through one at a time into an outside yard.

I tried to take my bearings, but there were no landmarks visible over the high stone walls. I followed the throng and started walking up and down the asphalt yard, which measured 54 paces lengthways and 41 paces across. A small oblong strip of muddy earth to one side was given over to prisoners playing boules. It immediately struck me as incongruous that in a prison full of dangerous inmates the authorities provided heavy steel balls for them to play with. Footballs I could understand, but steel balls, very strange.

During that first walk I was an object of scrutiny and curiosity. Some prisoners came up to me and thrust out a hand. Claude and Henri, Joel and Jacques and others all made their introductions that morning. A nod, a quick handshake, and they were gone back into the crowd. A big guy dressed in a grey shiny shell suit and Reeboks came up and stopped four square in front of me, blocking my path.

'Rosbif, je m'appelle Roget, le Chef,' he said and hawked a lump of phlegm on to the ground just in front of me. I put out my hand, which he ignored, and scowled at me. I was reminded of Paul Newman and Sylvester Stallone in all those prison films. I knew they would have kicked the shit out of him to take his place as the boss and hero of all the inmates. But that didn't seem on somehow. This guy was built like a brick shithouse and mean looking too, with a close-shaven head and an earring the size of a brass curtain ring in his ear, he would make mincemeat of me.

Discretion being the better part of valour I nodded to him and said, 'Bonjour, Monsieur le Chef,' with that I coolly walked on past him. Honour satisfied, he laughed and returned to his gang of mates in a far corner of the yard, where they held sway laughing and joking around.

Another, older guy sidled up to me. 'You are British, yes?' he asked in pretty good English. I looked at him amazed. These were the first friendly English words I had heard, other than the interpreter, since my arrest six days before. 'Yes, I'm English. My name is John. What's yours?'

We shook hands. 'My name is Jan. I'm from Holland,' he said grinning. 'You will not find many of the guards or prisoners here who speak any English, and those who do understand a little won't admit to it.'

Jan was a nice guy of about my age, on remand for a cheque scam. He had been travelling Europe using false chequebooks and identity papers. He told me that after serving his French sentence he expected to be sent to Germany to face similar charges there.

Having a common language we spent the next 15 minutes until the end of the exercise period talking intently about the prison and the rules. First on my list of priorities was the need to get my cash converted into francs and deposited in a prison account, to buy some essentials, such as cigarettes and toiletries, and to be able to contact my family. Jan explained to me that every request from remand prisoners had to be sent in writing via the prison director to the judge in charge of the case. All letters had to be written in French. He agreed to help me out in this regard.

Jan was fluent in four languages: Dutch, English, French and German. Why is it that many foreigners can speak so many languages, when most British people don't even have a rudimentary command of anything other than our mother tongue? Could it be our island mentality, or is it a hangover from the Empire period when English was the most important language in the world? Whatever the reason our language deficiencies affect our dealings with the rest of Europe.

When the exercise period was over we returned to the cell after a head count and further body search. Whilst we were out Yosef had completed the housework, tidied and swept out the cell. I noticed some clothes soaking in the sink, and after a while got through to Stef that I needed to wash my own clothes, which by now were pretty high, though, strangely, no one complained of the smell of stale sweat.

Stef lent me some washing powder, and I washed my jeans in a plastic bucket. There was only a cold-water tap in the cell, with no hot water at all for washing or laundry use. Prisoners in small French jails are almost exclusively local inhabitants, and they receive visits from family or friends nearly every day. During these visits they normally exchange a bag of dirty laundry for clean, but for prisoners like myself without family or visits there were no laundry facilities, so one had to wash clothes as best as possible in the cell.

Heating was provided by a length of three-inch steel hot-water pipe, which ran across the back wall of the cell at knee height. There was not enough surface area of pipework to give out sufficient heat, and during the day the winter temperature in the cell was cold. All the inmates wore jumpers or sweatshirts all day and in bed at night.

The heating pipe was the only place to dry wet clothing, and this caused a lot of condensation, giving rise to clammy walls and a streaming window. All books, newspapers, photographs tacked to the walls and bedding had a permanent damp feel; stored clothes developed spots of green mould. Because of the poor heating and ventilation arrangements my constant washing and drying of clothes made me unpopular, and many times I would find my clean but damp laundry thrown into a corner next to the toilet, where they lay stinking of piss.

Routine in the prison was fixed, and I soon fell in with the monotonous timetable. Reveille, rubbish and outgoing-mail collection at 6 am, followed by coffee delivery at 6.15 am. Morning exercise at 8 am for 30 to 40 minutes. Those lucky enough to have work went to the workshops from 9 to 11.30 am. Incoming mail was delivered at 11 am along with any prescribed medication. Lunch was served at noon, and, weather permitting, there was a second exercise period at 2.30 pm for 45 minutes. The evening meal was served at 5.30 pm, and after a final head count the cell doors were securely bolted for the night at 6 pm.

Twice each week we were allowed a ten-minute shower. Bed linen of dubious cleanliness was supplied on an exchange basis once a fortnight. Cell inspections were held at random intervals, and the integrity of the window bars was checked twice daily. The almost constant echoing clamour of a steel rod ringing on iron bars is a noise I will never forget. During the day the doors were kept locked closed at all times, and at night the shoot bolts were secured. There was no free movement or integration of prisoners, and you were only allowed out of the cell for a prescribed purpose.

Prisoners who didn't have any work were locked up for 22 hours each day, seven days a week. It isn't surprising that petty grievances and jealousies flared into brief but often spectacular fights between prisoners. Nerves were rubbed raw by the constant lack of privacy and noise. Many prisoners grouped together along ethnic lines and picked on minorities. As the only British prisoner I was subjected to a fair amount of anti-British feeling from inmates and guards alike, which on occasion flared into violence.

One wintry morning during the exercise period a guy I had never spoken with walked up to me and demanded a cigarette. This was a calculated threat on his part because tobacco was a form of prison currency, hoarded and only shared between cell mates or friends. I shook my head and explained as best I could that I only had a few left until my next ration. By now I had become an expert in reading body language and animal-like interpreting facial expressions, I often tried to express myself with a meaningful shrug, smile or grimace, but it was obvious from the guy's stance that he wanted a confrontation. In response to my refusal he gobbed a big lump of snot on to my shirt. Enough was enough, I was in a black mood that morning and not about to turn the other cheek.

I hit him, a good solid thump to his nose, which erupted into a great-looking nosebleed. Surprised and hurt he staggered back, and as if by magic a sharpened blade appeared in his fist. I kicked out at him, and my hard-soled prison boot connected with his hand and knocked the blade loose. At that moment I felt good; his attack had provided me an excuse to fight back, and all my frustrations against my arrest and the subsequent pettiness poured forth as blind rage. I remember roaring and going for him. His expression changed, and I saw a flash of fear in his eyes. Before I could continue and deliver a proper hammering two guards jumped on me, and a baton blow delivered with stunning force to my shoulder made me cry out in pain and finished the fight before it was properly under way. The show was over, but I bet matey was sore for a few days afterwards.

I didn't resist as they dragged me inside. Thrown into solitary I was back in the original cell where I'd spent my first night. Later that day the prison director reprimanded me and made notes in red ink in my prison file. I was kept in the solitary cell for a week without tobacco, books or personal kit. Nobody was interested that I hadn't started the fight or that my assailant had a blade, which, given the chance, he would have used. He was French, and I was a troublesome foreigner. I later discovered my new-found enemy was a real hard case, serving four years for grievous bodily harm after stabbing a nightclub bouncer.

When I was returned to my cell after a week my cigarettes, pens and postage stamps had disappeared, courtesy of Mr Nobody. On reflection maybe I should have given the bloke a cigarette, it would have been easier in the long run.

So life went on in the prison day after day with few breaks in the routine. With help from Dutch Jan I transferred my cash into a prison account and bought writing paper, envelopes and stamps. I used the interminable hours to write letter after letter to the judge, the police and my family. I spent time when I could in the library trying to discover the addresses of the British Embassy, the European Parliament and anybody else I could think of to whom to explain my plight.

I received my first letter in prison on 8 December 1994, 27 days after my arrest. It was from my wife, who, having learnt of my arrest and imprisonment, had left Spain and returned with our daughter to the UK. Getting no help from HM Customs she contacted the Foreign Office who had put her in touch with the London-based charity Prisoners Abroad.

They wrote to me and sent a batch of pamphlets containing all sorts of useful if depressing information for British prisoners in overseas jails. It made interesting reading, because, compared with the standards of jails in places like Thailand, Turkey and Egypt, it appeared I had it pretty easy. At least I was washed and fed on a regular basis. My heart went out to those British prisoners condemned to serve long sentences in cramped jails surrounded by intolerable cultural differences.

I felt a great outpouring of love and affection for my family, quickly followed by tremendous hate for the people who had condemned me to this private hell: I resolved there and then to get out of prison and make the guilty parties pay for their irresponsible and cavalier attitude with my liberty and life. I felt an overwhelming hatred for the people who were putting my family through such mental torture, and I planned all sorts of terrible vengeance against them.

On 12 December a guard called me out of the cell and took me for an unannounced visit. In a small side interview room a young woman of about 25 with a briefcase was waiting for me. She stood as I entered, and the guard locked the door behind me. I remember her watching me carefully as I entered the room. When she spoke it was in a neutral tone of voice.

'Good morning, Mr Lightfoot. I'm Madame Tardieu, Vice Consul with the British Embassy in Paris,' she introduced herself. 'I have come here at the invitation of the French authorities to check upon your welfare.' Young and arrogant looking with dark hair pulled severely back into a bun she wore a smart business suit and an expression that matched her small tight voice. She proffered a tiny smile and a nod as if to encourage me to speak. She reminded me of an uptight Sunday school teacher, but there again we were hardly meeting under normal circumstances, and I suppose she felt a little bit tense. I know I did.

'Good morning,' I replied. 'What is it specifically you wish to know?' I was immediately cagey, maybe it was jailhouse paranoia kicking in, but I expected British Embassy staff to have English names. With her French name and slight accent I was suspicious of some trickery; by this time I would have believed anything could happen.

'I can tell you that your wife Kathleen, daughter Natalie and mother Dorothy will be coming to visit you within the next few weeks,' she said. 'We have assisted them in applying to the French authorities for visiting permits.' This was said to put me at ease.

'OK. How can I help you, and how can you help me?' I asked, somewhat mollified.

'Firstly you should know that we cannot interfere with the process of law in a foreign country, and we cannot intercede on your behalf in any trial or convictions. Our job is to ensure that you are treated in the same manner as other prisoners, especially as national prisoners of the host country, and that you have adequate medical, dental and religious facilities.

'We're a very busy department of the embassy, and though we will monitor your stay in France we cannot visit you more than once each year. Nor can we offer you any advice relating to the criminal charges against you or provide funds for you to buy goods or to obtain the services of a lawyer.' She parroted by rote. She sounded like an upper-class holiday tour rep, the sort of bird who would work for Kuoni.

'Just a minute,' I said, 'I'm not planning on staying here for more than a year, so this will be your only visit to see me. I hear what you're saying, but surely the government can intercede on my behalf when I'm locked in here because of the actions of the government's own civil servants. I'm not a drug dealer, lady, I'm a recognized undercover informant for HM Customs & Excise. When I was arrested I was working on an operation for them.' That got her attention; she sat down and opened her briefcase.

'If you wish you can explain to me the circumstances leading to your arrest. I will take notes of your claims and have a word with my superiors,' she said smoothly, though I could see that my outburst had rattled her. There was no warmth or emotion in her face or voice, she sounded as human as a speak-your-weight machine.

'OK, let's start at the beginning,' I suggested. Before your visit here today did you know I am an informer for the Customs & Excise?' I asked.

'Mr Lightfoot, you shouldn't assume that I know anything. I haven't seen or discussed your case with anyone. All we know is that you were arrested by OCTRIS on 11 November, and that subsequently you were charged with international trafficking in narcotics. This is a serious crime in France as it is in Great Britain, and our role in the Foreign and Commonwealth Service is to check upon your physical welfare. I am visiting several British prisoners in jails this week, and it so happens that you are on my route. There is nothing more than that,' she said tartly.

I felt the cool wind of bureaucratic indifference. 'Right,' I said, 'I was working as an undercover informer for the Customs & Excise Investigation Unit, based on the 4th floor of Aldine House in Manchester.' I gave her the names of my contacts there, plus the name of the Drug Liaison Officer (DLO) at her embassy in Paris, Chris Martin, who should have some information on me. Then I went on to fill her in on everything that had happened so far. As I got into my stride, Tardieu took copious notes.

'To date,' I concluded, 'absolutely fuck all has happened except that I have had a yard fight and all my personal gear nicked. You are the first representative of the British Government to turn up, and you tell me that all you can do is to check that I get to see a dentist when I need to.

'Well, it's nowhere near an acceptable situation, and if you people are not prepared to help me then I'll fight this myself, and heaven help you when I get out.' I finished, but by now I had lost it again and was starting to shout.

'I can see you are upset,' Tardieu responded, looking a little nervous. 'Obviously your claims will be investigated by the examining magistrate, and if they are true then I have no doubt you will be released from prison. We cannot interfere with the judge's enquiries, but I will make a full report of this matter when I return to Paris.'

There was little more to be said, and after some further general enquiries and wishing me an early Merry Christmas she left. I returned to my cell and brooded quietly.

52

'Perfidious Albion'

JUST A FEW days before Christmas I received the promised visit from Kath, my mother and daughter Natalie. I had written to the prison director requesting extended visits on the grounds that I hadn't received any previously and that my family had travelled all the way from England to see me. I had received no response to my request.

Since arriving in prison I had started to grow a beard, and now with my hair long and shaggy I looked too much like a convict for comfort. I decided I needed a haircut. Getting one wasn't simple: I had to write a letter in French to the director to request it. Three times I wrote and still didn't get any response. Finally another prisoner cut my hair during an exercise period, for the cost of three cigarettes, and the result was not too bad.

The day of the visit eventually arrived. The guard had told me during the morning that it was imminent because a visit permit, complete with a passport-style photograph, had been authorized by the judge and a copy forwarded to the prison. It was a simple security device that enabled the prison to know exactly who to expect. I was allowed a shower that morning; afterwards I changed into my cleanest and least damp-smelling clothes and scrounged some aftershave from a cell mate.

At the appointed hour a guard took me downstairs, where I waited in line with the other prisoners. Most of them, lucky bastards, held plastic bags full of dirty linen, ready to exchange for nice clean clothes. The air was full of good-natured banter, and one or two of the prisoners I knew gave me a thumbs up; they seemed to realize it was my first visit.

We all filed one by one into a small, brightly lit anteroom. The guard told me to undress, a command with which I could now comply because by now I had learnt a basic French vocabulary, which was all I needed to get by from day to day. I hadn't thought about having to strip for the occasion, but what the hell! It seemed a small price to pay. I quickly dropped my clothes, and the guard searched me. At that time I couldn't imagine what anybody would want to smuggle out of prison; later I was to discover there was a thriving business in uncensored mail for onward posting.

After the search I was led into the visits room, a space with perhaps ten formica-top tables set out at various points around the perimeter of the room. At each table there were three plastic chairs. I picked a table at random and sat down facing the door through which the visitors would enter.

After about five minutes I could hear Natalie's voice echoing along a corridor. She came into the room shyly, and a few prisoners looked at her and said, 'Bonjour,' and smiled. Natalie stared back as if she was in a zoo, which I suppose she was really. I called her name, and she came over and jumped into my arms for a big bear hug from her dad. Mum and Kath followed her in, and we all had a hug, until a guard came over shook his head and wagged his finger at us. That was the sort of down-to-earth experience that set the tone of the initial meeting.

We all said our hellos and exchanged banter about how well we all looked considering the circumstances, until I pointed out that we only had 45 minutes, and that we should get down to business. There had been many things I didn't want to write in my letters to Kath, I could see no benefit in telling the judge all about my relationship with Customs, and what I intended to do about my predicament. After all he was the enemy, he was the reason I was still locked up.

Now I made up for lost time and quick fired questions to Kath whilst Natalie sat on her mum's knee watching me intently. I vividly remember stroking her hair whilst talking to Kath and my mum. From what we'd been told, we understood Customs were denying any responsibility for me being in prison and were claiming to Kath that the arrest was nothing to do with them. We'd heard that they had offered to assist the French, if they were asked formally to do so.

We decided that my current legal-aid French lawyer didn't appear to be doing as much as we thought he could to help me. We decided that the best way forward was to appoint someone else, and mum agreed to pay for a private lawyer to get the ball rolling a little faster.

I had made inquiries amongst the other prisoners, and the name Christian Traineau, a young, smart criminal defence lawyer, kept coming up as the best man to have on our side. I asked Kath and my mum to track him down and instruct him to start on the case immediately, which they promised to do that afternoon.

Then we talked of other events. It seemed that the day after I was arrested the English police had raided our farm in the UK looking for drugs. They had apparently been understanding but claimed to be acting on an anonymous tip-off. Obviously the search had proved negative. I had never had any drugs at our farm, or anywhere else for that matter.

Kath told me that because I had been arrested in France I was not entitled to legal aid in England, so once again my mum stepped into the breach and said she and my dad would pay for an English lawyer to approach Customs direct to request that they acknowledge I was working for them. A contact in the police had recommended a supposedly good firm of criminal lawyers based in Sheffield, whom she would instruct on my behalf.

We'd been talking nonstop when suddenly I noticed the

visiting period was over, and prisoners were saying their goodbyes to their families. I stood up and spoke to the guard, trying to explain that I was entitled to an extended visit. He shook his head and said something about see the director for permission. I was furious, but there was nothing I could do at that time: the guard had his instructions, it was pointless having a go at him.

Kath and my mum promised to visit the next day, and my mum told me she had brought some Christmas food: mince pies, Christmas cake, small pork pies and so on. From Kath there was a case full of paperback books, some clothes and a good English–French dictionary. I kissed them all goodbye, and off they went, looking very unhappy at leaving me behind.

I returned to the strip-search room and argued with the guard about the extended visit I was due; I might as well have talked to the wall for all the good it did me. I dropped my clothes on the deck ready for the search, and just to show me there were no hard feelings about our little argument the guard insisted on conducting an in-depth personal search. I wasn't into shoving cigarettes up my arse, that's a trick I'd rather leave to the French, but the guard felt he had to check anyway.

I made a complete pain of myself for the rest of the day, demanding to see the social assistant, the judge and the prison director. In the end they took me down to see the chief guard, who wasn't a bad stick really. We had no common language and spent half the time trying to understand each other. But I got my message across eventually by showing him copies of the letters I had sent to the director requesting extended visiting times.

The next day I was again called for a visit and went through the same procedure as before. This time the atmosphere among us all was a bit more relaxed, even so it was obvious we were all very much on edge, and we knew that if things didn't go right I could end up spending many, many years in a French prison.

If I was convicted of smuggling drugs over the French border then I would be in deep shit. So it was critical I got my liberty to allow me to clear my name before the trial. Afterwards would be too late because no one would believe me. It would just seem like the desperate claims of a convicted smuggler seeking a reduced sentence.

The best way forward seemed to be somehow to get Customs to confirm that I was working for them, or at least to acknowledge they knew that I was participating in the smuggling run from Spain to France and that I had taken part in it to assist them. This didn't seem at that time such a hard thing for them to concede, or so difficult for me to prove. Kath told me they had an appointment with the lawyer Traineau later that same afternoon, so I asked her to request that he visit me as soon as possible so that I could set him off on the right trail.

That day we got our extended visit and talked for nearly one and a half hours. Nevertheless the time seemed to fly by, and we were still deeply engrossed when the guard indicated time was up. The only jarring note had been when Natalie had offered me a toffee from a bag of sweets she had in her coat pocket. Without thinking I had taken the proffered toffee from her, unwrapped it and popped it into my mouth, just as the guard had turned around to see me do so.

I didn't know I couldn't accept a sweet from my own kid, but from all the fuss he made you'd have thought I was taking a speedball from her. He wasn't satisfied until I spat the offending remnant into a nearby wastebin. Natalie was upset by his intimidating mien and withdrew into her shell; she hardly spoke again during the entire visit.

That incident cast a shadow over our time together and broke the spell of hope that all this would soon be behind us. The guard's attitude demonstrated the lack of flexibility of the system. We all knew it was going to be an uphill battle, but it was one we knew that ultimately we could and must win, for if we failed then all our lives would change dramatically for ever, and that was something we couldn't countenance. We parted in a quiet and pensive mood, and I could sense that Kath and my mum were psyching themselves up for their important initial meeting with Christian Traineau later that day.

Christmas was for me a deadly dull and depressing event that year. There was no official acknowledgement that it was happening outside the grey concrete prison walls, and there was no break in the monotonous routine. It was a Christmas lived vicariously through glittery television shows and tinsel-laden adverts. We celebrated in our cold cell eating my mother's mince pies, a delicacy hitherto unknown to the palates of my cell mates.

I had received Christmas cards from immediate family and a handmade card from Natalie. They were little pools of light and cheer against the backdrop of the drab cell wall above my bed; I would lie on the bed looking up at them and transport myself away to other happier times.

On New Year's Eve we could hear the townspeople cheering in the main square not far away, the constant ringing of the church bells heralding the onset of another year. New Year's Day is not a happy time for any prisoner, they think about the time already served and then of the years left still on their sentence, waiting in line ahead of them, each one marked by yet another New Year's celebration.

If anything that miserable Christmas was a time of catharsis for me, and by the new year my resolve had hardened. I was still depressed by my day-to-day environment, but inside I was more sure it was going to be a transient stage. I knew I had the intelligence and the will to force a change in the tide of events surrounding me. Given a fair hearing and a little bit of luck I would be freed in the near future, and then I would be able to undo this great mistake and get on with my life. Buoyed up by this strong, welling rush of enthusiasm I turned with a will to kick-start my campaign for freedom.

The first meeting on a cold, rainy day in January with my new lawyer, Christian Traineau, set the format for our future relationship. We hit it off immediately and were soon chatting away like old pals. Traineau is well over six foot tall and heavily built with a swathe of jet-black shiny hair; he reminds me of a Russian dancing bear. His massive size and presence dominated the small private visiting room, and I could easily imagine him tearing a prosecutor limb from limb.

It soon became obvious that his size was matched by his formidable intelligence. He was married to a school teacher who taught English to teenagers in the local school. He too had a good command of English but had difficulty sometimes with his pronunciation. He spoke clearly, albeit with a strong French accent, which most women would call sexy, but which I thought sounded rather like John Cleese doing his French waiter act. But it was music to listen to him as he verbally destroyed the prosecution's case against me.

Throughout our relationship he was consistently truthful with me and laid out each position carefully and accurately. Not one to mince his words he would always tell me both good and bad news without any sugar coating. On this occasion, lighting yet another Philip Morris cigarette, he said, 'The first thing we have to do is to get you out of prison, and to achieve this we have to convince the judge that you really were working for HM Customs.'

The first thing I had to do was to write him a letter of authority appointing him as my defence lawyer so that he could go to the judge and buy a copy of the criminal file. In France they charge three francs a sheet for any part of the file required by the defence team. I was not allowed to have a copy of the file, or a translation, and I could only read it in the presence of my lawyer.

A week went by whilst Traineau got hold of the file and studied its contents. During that time I received a copy of a letter sent by Richard Crampton, my local Member of the European Parliament (MEP), to Valerie Strachan. I had never heard of her, but I soon enough learned that Strachan was the head honcho in HM Customs & Excise.

The MEP's letter was the opening shot in what was to become a series of misunderstandings between me and HM Customs. For whatever reason there was an alarming breakdown in communications. Perhaps I'd been misinformed myself, but it seemed they did not appear to be in possession of the full facts of my case; not one of them had actually met me since my arrest and heard my side of the story.

In France, Traineau was grappling with more down-to-earth problems. 'We need a letter of confirmation from Customs to say that you were working with their authority at the farm when you were arrested, John,' he said, spelling it out. 'Without such confirmation things are looking bad for you. This 300 kilos of cannabis is the biggest haul of drugs ever intercepted in the Vendée region of France, and all the protagonists are English, which inflames French feelings of sovereignty. It is a big news story and a high-profile case, and there will have to be a successful prosecution. I fear the sentences will be hard and result in many years in prison for you if we fail.'

Well, at least he was being honest with me, but I didn't fancy spending years rotting in a French jail when I had done nothing wrong. HM Customs were surely aware of what I was doing at the farmhouse, and why I was doing it. It didn't make any sense. I told Traineau to contact my English lawyers and liaise with them to set up a meeting with Customs as soon as possible.

Life in the prison continued with boring regularity. I spent much of my time reading about French criminal law and their different methods of investigation and criminal trials' procedures. It was heavy, boring stuff, all in French. I would sit up for hours at night reading the law books, assisted by my French to English dictionary.

Light relief was provided by cell inspections, and opportunity the guards used to upset us thoroughly and tramp over our meagre possessions. They were supposed to be looking for contraband, but it was just a good opportunity for them to rummage through the cells. Searches rarely turned up anything for the prisoners were experts at camouflage and concealment. Smuggling illicit goodies into the prison was something at which the prisoners and their visitors were particularly adept. Alcohol, money, porn mags and drugs were all forbidden by the authorities and consequently much sought after by the majority of the inmates.

One ingenious method of smuggling alcohol into the prison was demonstrated by one inmate, whose wife visited weekly and brought the lucky bugger a constant stream of clean laundry. One night after lockup he pulled down a towel she had delivered earlier that day. He filled the sink with two inches or so of cold water and dumped in the towel; we all watched as the water turned a milky colour. Amongst much laughter and back slapping he filled a glass with this dubious-looking liquid and took a tentative sip, then he coughed and smiled and declared the drink OK. The glass was passed around and I had a tiny taste. The mixture was Pernod and water, with an admixture of pine-smelling clothes softener, which left a strange but not-too-unpleasant aftertaste on the tongue.

The smuggling system worked thus. His wife would wash a towel and dry it normally, making sure all the washing powder was rinsed away. Then she would soak it in a bowl filled with Pernod or some other anise drink; the towel would then be dried again. Before it was taken back to the prison it would be lightly splashed with a *soupçon* of fabric softener to disguise the pungent smell of aniseed.

The towel was slipped into the middle of a batch of clean clothes and passed to a guard for checking. Generally the authorities were looking for knives and other metal objects. In any case I think most of them were too soaked in booze themselves to notice the smell of an alcohol-soaked towel, or at least if they did they turned a blind eye to this minor infraction of the strict rules of conduct.

Quite a few nights we sat watching TV, passing around glasses of Pernod and water. We had to ensure that all the anise and water mixture was drunk in the one session so that a snap inspection wouldn't discover our little enterprise, so the temptation was to use as little water as possible to release the dried-in booze.

I'm sure the fabric conditioner must have contributed to the terrible hangovers we all suffered, but it seemed to be worth it at the time. It's a wonder we didn't end up blind or with serious liver damage. Now I can't smell fabric softener without developing a headache, and the smell of Pernod always reminds me vividly of the nights sitting around getting pissed in prison.

Other prisoners went to great lengths to get hold of drugs. At night you could spot the cannabis smokers in the various cells. They puffed away with the windows open to help dispel the distinctive smell of burning hash and flicked the ash from their joints outside.

A couple of days after my birthday in late January 1995 I received another letter from my MEP enclosing a response he had received from Valerie Strachan. Although Strachan acknowledged they knew me, she claimed I had no authority for my actions. I considered its contents alarming to say the least, full of errors. She claimed, apparently, that one of her officers had visited me in December, and I had confessed my part in the failed smuggling attempt.

I hadn't had any visit from any British official, other than Mme Tardieu, the consular official from the British Embassy, so I could have hardly confessed my guilt to a nonexistent visitor. What worried me was that, though misinformed, the letter from the head of so powerful a British institution would automatically be given credence by anyone reading it.

All remand prisoners in French jails have each and every letter read by the judge in charge of their case. In my case Judge Maurice Marlière, the local examining magistrate, didn't understand much

English, so all my mail, both incoming and outgoing, was translated into French by the official court translator. I could just imagine his eyes popping when he read Valerie Strachan's letter to the MEP claiming that I had confessed to smuggling. I had to get this sorted out as soon as I could.

Without access to telephones as soon as possible meant within a couple of weeks. The only way to get mail out without it being censored was to write to your lawyer, or use the risky method of a prisoner passing a letter to a visitor for onward posting. This method was fraught with risks and was expensive, each letter so smuggled out cost at least five cigarettes. If the circuitous postal attempt was discovered you were in deep shit with the prison director.

I decided to write directly to the judge in an attempt to clear up this mess. I sent him a lengthy missive telling him I had not received any visit; this he could easily check from a quick perusal of the visitor permits. He never did reply to my letter. Christian Traineau told me later that the Strachan letter carried a lot of weight with the judge, and, as you might expect, it militated against my early release. Traineau wrote to Customs, but it seems they were not prepared to discuss the matter with him.

By now I had been in prison for 12 weeks. It was then that I heard a meeting had been organized in Manchester between Customs and my English solicitors, who took along with them a barrister. The minutes of the meeting were handed over to the judge, who continued to keep his own counsel and wouldn't be drawn into comment one way or another.

Three weeks after the Manchester meeting the Customs indicated in a very short letter they were prepared to answer questions about my status to the right authorities. Christian Traineau buttonholed the judge in his office and coerced him into getting his translator to telephone Customs and arrange an urgent meeting. Bearing in mind Traineau's size I can easily imagine how he convinced the judge to authorize that call. The translator phoned Manchester, and a meeting was set for the next week. Two Customs officers were coming over to explain the situation to the judge.

They arrived the night before, flying into Nantes airport and lodging overnight at the translator's home. I was dressed in my suit and was ready from early morning for the call to go to the judge's office. They came for me in the early afternoon. I was escorted to the holding block under the main court building and locked in a tiny cell. Shortly thereafter Christian Traineau arrived and told me the two Customs men had been with the judge all morning; they had also lunched in his office.

When finally we went up to the judge's office we were initially asked to remain outside in the foyer. A secretary passed a lengthy statement to my lawyer, which was the official Customs stance on the matter of my arrest. Before we had time to read their document properly we were ushered into the meeting. Rob Williams was waiting in there, and he came over and shook hands with me; behind him was an older man who introduced himself as Alan Smith. I'd never seen or heard of him before, but it transpired he was Williams' boss.

The meeting didn't go too well. I was feeling very angry, and I wanted some explanations from Customs as to why, so I'd heard, they had denied I was their informant, and why Valerie Strachan had written that letter that didn't help my case at all.

In fact, in my presence that day Customs confirmed I had been a good agent and had helped them with seizures of drugs worth several million of pounds. But when we got on to the specifics of the French operation they became less forthcoming. They claimed in formal statements that I hadn't kept them informed of changes in the plan and that by allowing the use of my own van I had crossed the line, and they had heard I had become a smuggler myself. Smith said that they had received information from another source in Spain that I had gone beyond my agreed brief and they suspected that I had in effect changed sides.

He claimed that because I was out of touch for nine days after the last meeting they didn't know where I was or what had become of me, so they arranged for NCIS, the National Crime Intelligence Service, to send a fax to Chris Martin, the Drug Liaison Office (DLO) based in the British Embassy in Paris. Martin had then phoned OCTRIS and told them to expect a drug-smuggling attempt centred around Eric and Jill's farm. OCTRIS had staked out the farm and had watched Barry and me drive up and park the van in the driveway there. The next day they had observed all our comings and goings before they busted us late in the afternoon.

Smith produced the fax that had been sent by Howard Leather of NCIS to the DLO for the judge to read. The judge insisted that a copy of the fax be entered into the evidence file, which was a useful move on his part for it meant that I could study it later with my lawyer.

We went on to talk about the surveillance operation at Hartshead services when at Customs' request, I had met with Paul and Tony to discuss the French operation. Rob Williams said that the photographs were not of a good enough quality for identification purposes; he also claimed that although they had identified the drug dealers' car they couldn't confirm that it belonged to either Paul or Tony.

This was becoming confusing. I was under the impression that the photos were acceptable. In any case what I did get Rob Williams to confirm was that it was agreed with him and Steve Brown that I wouldn't contact them again until I had the registration number of the van coming from England to collect the drugs.

By now it was past seven o'clock in the evening, and the judge started to wrap the meeting up. Christian Traineau submitted a typed bail application for me, after which the judge and I got into some good-natured wrangling about how much the bail sum should be. He wanted 100,000 francs, I offered 10,000. After five minutes or so we agreed, and bail was set at 50,000 francs.

Traineau used the telephone in the judge's office to telephone

Kath at home in England and told her the judge had agreed to bail and that he needed 50,000 francs to get me released. If the money were received quickly I could be out within five days.

Everyone in the office was smiling, although there was a definite air of discomfort around the two Customs officers. I went back to jail contentedly that night and slept well. I was certain my problems would be quickly sorted out as soon as I was out of prison.

*　*　*

A couple of days later I had to visit the judge again for a confrontation with Eric and Jill. They were now claiming that I had inveigled and threatened them into accepting and storing the drugs. Naturally they wanted to be seen as victims rather than as active participants.

This didn't equate with the soaps of cannabis OCTRIS had discovered in their house or the marijuana plants growing in the garden, but the judge was obliged to investigate their claims. I was not too bothered by the story they were putting forward. I always believed the purpose of the operation was to snare the drug barons not the minions who carried out the jobs at the sharp end. Besides I didn't think the French courts would have too much of a problem getting to the bottom of their story.

After the interviews were over, and we had all restated our positions yet again, I noticed that the judge had the suspicion of a smile hovering around his mouth.

'I think, Mr Lightfoot, you are possibly suffering from what we French call Perfidious Albion.' I was taken aback, I didn't think he could speak any English, and here he was demonstrating his fluency admirably.

As the five days following my bail application sped by I started giving some of the prison things I had acquired during my stay to my cell mates. I collected some addresses and promised to write to various people and their families. I was cool, anxious and ready to get out of this stinking cesspit.

On the Saturday morning I was expecting to be released the guard opened the cell door and called me out. As he directed me to the visiting room, I felt the cold hand of dread grip me. Christian Traineau was sitting there quietly, brooding like a sleeping giant in the middle of the room. As ever he cut to the chase.

'John, I have just come from Judge Marlière's office, and I have to tell you he has refused the bail application,' he said.

I couldn't believe my ears. 'But, but,' I stuttered, 'he agreed last week. We even agreed the bail cash. There must be some mistake.' I was shattered.

'No, there has been a development in the case, and the judge thinks you should stay in jail until the matter is cleared up,' said Christian. 'He took a call from the Foreign Ministry in Paris, and they informed him that Benson has been arrested in Spain and is to be extradited to France as soon as possible. So the judge wants you available in jail to have a confrontation with Benson when he arrives.'

I slumped heavily into a chair. 'But extradition can take months or years. Surely he doesn't want to keep me here all that time?' I was alternating between deep despair and terrible rage. I was also developing the world's worst headache and feeling nauseous.

Christian was as upset as I was. We sat for ages in that little room, supposed to be talking about strategy and tactics for mounting an appeal to the High Court in Poitiers but in reality dealing with the shocking body blow the judge had delivered.

I told Christian I had given away all my bits and pieces, including chocolate and cigarettes; the next time the shop was open was five days away, and there was no way I could survive until then without nicotine. When he left Christian gave me a couple of packs of cigarettes to keep me going and promised he would visit the judge again to make him see reason. If all else failed, he said, he would appeal to the European Court of Human Rights to get my release. He meant well, and I could see that he was upset at the thought of having to telephone Kath and pass the bad news on to her.

What a pisser of a weekend I had! I felt unbelievably depressed by the whole situation. Life in prison is a series of emotional roller-coaster rides. Up and down, up and down, there is no end to the switchback of feelings, but that weekend I felt as if I had a season ticket on an emotional big dipper. It's not difficult to figure out why so many prisoners take the easy way out and top themselves in jail rather than continually face the boring certainty of life there.

During the ensuing weeks I rode that roller coaster many times, sometimes with Christian sitting at my side. I carried on writing daily letters to Kath and the family and received their responses in dribs and drabs as the judge saw fit. We mounted several appeals and further applications for provisional release, all to no avail.

Finally, on 3 April a guard called me out of the cell just before noon. Great, I thought, another cold lunch when I get back. As I walked along the platform towards the open staircase I could see Christian waiting at the bottom. He was grinning broadly at me and waving his car keys.

'Come quickly, John,' he called up to me, 'we are going out for a meal.' I almost fell down the bloody stairs. We went into the visits room for the last time, both grinning like idiots. 'It's true, John. The judge has just signed your release papers. His secretary will fax them to the director, and you will be released immediately,' he beamed at me, stupidly we shook hands. A guard knocked politely at the closed door and gestured towards Christian. 'There it is, the fax has arrived. Now go quickly and collect your belongings, we have to go to a party.'

I was truly in a daze. I had been expecting to be released at some stage, but now it was suddenly a reality I was having trouble taking it in. I floated upstairs and back to my cell. Word was already out thanks to the grapevine, and I was surrounded by cell mates wishing me well. I grabbed my bag of clothes, files of documents and letters, and I left the rest of my belongings for the lads to share out and returned downstairs to the prison office.

The formalities were quickly sorted, and within minutes I was outside with Christian. Fucking hell! It felt good. Before we drove off I turned and stared for a moment at the façade of the prison. I had been in there for 108 days of my life, and I had never seen the main entrance in daylight. It looked rather like an old storage warehouse, its grey, lifeless exterior belied the hundreds of lives ticking away inside its grim walls. I turned and climbed into Christian's old car; it was party time, French style.

* * *

Driving across town Christian told me that to get bail granted it is necessary that a prisoner has a registered address in France where he lives and to where court documents can be sent to him. Obviously I was lacking this, so Christian had given the address of his sister, who lived in a nearby town. The judge had accepted Christian's proposal. He went on to explain that his sister couldn't accommodate me because she had a young family, but I was welcome to stay at his house in the town.

This was the other side of French culture, not seen by many foreigners. Here we had a prominent local lawyer giving shelter to a foreigner just bailed from prison, who was charged with international drug trafficking. For all he knew I could be an addict who would rob him blind, attack him or his wife and take off never to be seen again. I was amazed and couldn't think of the right words to thank him. He just laughed his great booming laugh and dismissed my attempts to do so.

'Everything will work out fine,' he said, driving and lighting a cigarette at the same time. This man was larger than life in every sense of the word.

Christian and his wife, Sylvie the teacher, lived in an old imposing townhouse a stone's throw from the Palais de Justice, the French court buildings and prosecutor's offices. When we arrived Sylvie was waiting inside, and Christian made the formal introductions in that typical French style. A sweet, petite woman, with high cheekbones and slim hips, Sylvie is like an immaculately dressed porcelain doll. She hangs on her husband's every word and willingly rushes to carry out every little task for him, like a butterfly hovering around a big almost bumbling bear.

That first day of my release was open house. First we had lunch with a journalist friend of theirs, Emanuel, a serious-looking individual. He reminded me of pictures of wartime French resistance agents, with flashing eyes and a stern demeanour. He is in a way a latter-day one for he writes some quite radical articles in the local newspapers. Throughout the afternoon and evening there was a constant stream of their friends and work colleagues, and I started to feel I had a type of celebrity status. With plenty of drink flowing, to combine with my soaring spirits, I felt as if I was floating on air.

I telephoned Kath and my parents in England, who were all overjoyed to hear me. Christian had tipped them off about my probable release, but he hadn't told me in case anything went wrong again. That was a downer he had correctly figured I could do without. I told Kath that I had to see the judge the next day, and he would set my bail conditions. My mum had sent Christian the bail money and an extra 2000 francs for me to pay my way.

Life felt great: I was free, amongst good company and had a wonderful, warm feeling of security in the happy household. Sylvie gave me a housekey and said I should come and go as I please, unbelievable charity from relative strangers. It would be easy for me to slag off the French as a race, as I suffered some degree of abuse during my time in prison with a lot of indignities heaped upon me simply because I was a foreigner. But here I was being offered a home, friendship and a tremendous amount of trust by two young people who only knew me through my criminal file and by way of professional prison visits. Without being aware of it, Christian and Sylvie went a long way to restoring my faith in human nature and showing me by their actions that there is good and bad in all nationalities.

The judge set some keen bail conditions for me to comply with, but he demonstrated he too had a human side. When I visited his office the day after my release his secretary gave me a cup of coffee and the judge passed over a couple of aspirins. I had a daddy of a hangover, and must have looked sorely in need of medication.

As well as paying the 50,000 franc bail money I had to sign in once a week at the local Gendarmerie. The judge held on to my passport, and I was restricted to movement within the Vendée region, unless I had his prior approval. That was no bother to me, there was nowhere I wanted to go except home.

I had to visit a panel of psychiatrists to be assessed as to my mental state, in other words to check if I understood the charges against me and if I could stand trial. They agreed I was sane. Bang went the idea of an insanity plea!

Life settled down into a pleasant rhythm for a while. I was allotted space in a file storage room in Christian's town-centre office. Kath sent me a word processor over, and I started collecting facts and figures, dates and receipts to justify my claims. By now I could read French pretty well fluently, and I spent many hours poring over the file, reading and cross-checking statements. I consulted Christian's law books at length, often burning the midnight oil in the office. We sat up into the early hours drinking our way through his excellent wine cellar, debating issues and strategies.

Christian introduced me to the world of politics and local ambitions as played out in the Palais de Justice, and it seemed that, as in Britain, justice in France is a fickle friend, depending largely on the whim or ambition of the local prosecutor or examining magistrate. I learnt that the judge in my case had a serious problem, unrelated to my case. Apparently he had been under suspicion of shoplifting in a local hypermarket. That really sealed his fate, and eventually other members of the bench refused to sit with him at trials. I don't know if he was guilty or not, but there was a lot of local unrest, and a couple of newspapers ran versions of the story. It all became too much to be ignored, and eventually he was transferred to the French dependency of Martinique, the Siberia of the French judiciary.

The weeks were quickly turning into months, and I was now chafing at what had become in my mind a sentence in an open prison. I was the proverbial canary in the gilded cage. It was a very nice one, but a cage nevertheless. Christian and I pushed the judge continually to allow me to return home. By now Eric and Jill had been released from prison on their own recognizance. Barry was still held in prison, and Benson was fighting extradition in Spain. The case was in a state of suspended animation, and there was little left to do to push forward any further. In a last desperate bid we made an application to the Appeal Court in Poitiers to have the travel restrictions against me lifted. On the day of the hearing we drove the couple of hours to Poitiers in Christian's Volvo.

It was a daunting experience, with three senior judges to hear the appeal. It was interesting to meet another court translator: she was thirtyish and looked like Farah Fawcett, a real doll. By this time my French was good enough to understand the proceedings, but I wasn't complaining when she sat down close beside me and whispered translations of the events taking place before us. It was quite a cosy meeting considering the circumstances.

The senior state prosecutor was there to argue against the appeal, but in fact he indirectly supported it by stating that never in all his experience of prosecuting drug trials had British officers ever turned up to give evidence on behalf of a defendant. The court's verdict was received three days later: the appeal court weren't able to interfere with the local judge's decision, but they suggested that I might wish to apply for acquittal against the charge on the grounds that I was working with 'legitimate authority' at the time of my arrest.

This was a ground-breaking decision in our favour. It meant that having looked at all the evidence in the file the three judges believed that I was working for Customs when we were busted. Despite any vagueness about the circumstances they were signalling that I would never be tried and convicted by them. This was great news, and me, Christian, Sylvie and all their pals held a big house party to celebrate. It was a pretty good bash, and I was surprised when another judge, a friend of Christian's, turned up to spend the evening socializing with us.

Armed with this strong decision we went back to Judge Marlière and asked for an acquittal. He replied that although he was sympathetic to my plea, he wasn't obliged to make a decision until the anniversary of the case being opened, which meant he would look at the issue in November. I was staggered. Nevertheless his refusal to act put the whole case in a new perspective for me. I was fed up now, the game had gone on too long, and I was stagnating. I was still charged with international drug trafficking and facing, if convicted, a very severe sentence.

The Customs continued to be less than helpful. I was now perceived as a dangerous, loose cannon to them. They had apparently closed the door and wouldn't respond to our letters or calls. It became obvious that I was impotent in France, and the judge wasn't going to assist me at that time .

By now it was early June and getting hotter each day. We heard that the judge was leaving the town during the court's two-month summer recess. A new judge would be appointed in the autumn. I hadn't seen my family for more than half a year, and I was surviving on the largesse sent by my parents, who were also keeping Kath's body and soul together. They had dug deeply into their retirement savings and had ended up funding my adventuring into the drug world. I felt it was time to move on and repay the debt.

Privately I contacted Kath and laid out my plans. I knew that I had to make my move without implicating Christian and Sylvie in any way. If I escaped the French might well look hard for accomplices to victimize. Everything was set up between me and Kath by phone and fax. One Friday, whilst Christian and Sylvie were at work, I packed my bags and left. Christian and I had never discussed the possibility of my returning to England, and clever as he was I was afraid my abrupt departure would be a great shock to him. I fervently hoped that I was not about to ruin a great friendship by walking out and returning to my family. I hoped he would understand my need for proper justice.

I bought a one-way train ticket and set out on the long journey home. Overnighting in Nantes I walked around the old town centre for hours. My French was passable, and I stopped at various street cafés for a beer. I whiled away the evening contemplating the last year's events. My experiences in France had been horrendous in some ways, but there had been good times too, both in prison and later with Christian and Sylvie. It was a shame that I was about to become an outcast from my new-found friends, but there was nothing else to be done: I had an overriding obligation to my family.

I reached the port of Cherbourg the next morning in time to watch the arrival of the ferry from England. It was full of tourists all heading south for the sun. A red car detached itself from the stream of traffic leaving the port gates and turned into the main terminal car park. I watched from a distance as Kath and my mum alighted and headed into the café and booking hall. Silently I sidled up behind them and put a hand on each of their shoulders. They were expecting me, but they still nearly jumped out of their skins.

'Hello, you two,' I said, smiling at them both, 'let's not make a scene here. We'll just go and grab a coffee over there.'

We walked to the hot drinks counter and then sat down to finalize the plan to smuggle me on to the ferry and into Britain without a passport. Kath had brought my birth and marriage certificate and electoral roll card. I had made enquiries and found out that a British citizen didn't require a passport to enter or leave Great Britain. All I had to prove was where I was born and show that I had a right of residence in theUK. Of course, if I were stopped by immigration officials in Britain it wouldn't be as easy as that, but once I was firmly stood on British soil they sure as hell couldn't deport me back to France.

By now the British newspapers had also picked up the story of my plight and had run articles questioning the Customs actions. If I were caught they were primed to create a big song and dance in the Sunday papers.

After a couple of calming coffees we ran through the escape plan one last time. Kath and my mum had bought two day-return tickets in England, and now Kath was to go to the ticket office and buy a single ticket as a foot passenger back to the UK. I was to drive the car with mum beside me as a passenger. I had no passport but held on to Kath's return ticket. I knew that there was only a passport check when buying a ticket and no police check when leaving France. It was all a bit tense. If the plan went wrong now I was going to be sent back to prison and held until the trial. There would be no second chance for me, not Christian or Perry Mason would get me bail a second time.

The plan in fact worked like a dream, and half an hour later I found myself standing in the queue to buy a duty-free drink at the ship's bar. We had made it so far; now it was just the British authorities I had to contend with. I took my drink and stood on the windy afterdeck watching the French coastline receding towards the horizon. I had the feeling I wouldn't be returning there for quite a while. I was ecstatic at the thought of returning home, but my elation was tinged with sadness at the friends I had deserted without so much as a goodbye. Still, I rationalized, you can't make an omelette without breaking eggs.

When we disembarked at Portsmouth we all did so together in the car and followed the line of traffic towards the Customs checkpoint. Immigration officers were passing down the row of parked cars checking passports. As a woman immigration official inspected the vehicle in front of us I tensed up: this was it, shit or bust.

Just then the line of cars lurched forward. I stuck ours close to the tail of the one immediately in front, and as the immigration officer approached my open window I waved at her and joked in a strong Manchester accent, 'It's OK, luv, we're all English. There's no hidden Pakis in here.' The woman laughed and waved us on towards the waiting Customs officials. As we drove up to the checkpoint we were all holding our breath. We must have looked rigid and as guilty as sin. Sure enough we were stopped.

'Where have you come from?' asked the Customs officer.

'We've been on a shopping trip to France,' I replied, 'but the prices were too high for us, so we just bought some wine.'

I jumped out of the car to open the boot, loaded up with a couple of cases of French wine and a few cartons of duty-free cigarettes. The Customs officer gave the contents and the inside of the car a cursory inspection.

'OK, sir, thank you. You can go now,' he said.

53

On the Run

RETURNING HOME SAFELY was a tremendously uplifting experience and if I had been of a religious bent I would have kissed the ground and offered a prayer of thanksgiving. I am not religious, but I knew I was the happiest man in England at that moment, and I knew things were going to get better and better. But it wasn't the end of my nightmare adventures in the world of drug smuggling and bureaucratic indifference. Rather it was the start of another phase, a phase we are all still living through today.

One of the consequences of the campaign to force my release from prison was that I had been forced to adopt a high profile campaign, both in England and France. Now it was a racing certainty that many of the drug dealers in Spain and Britain knew about my role as a successful informant for the Customs.

After my return the media were interested in my adventures, and various articles soon appeared in national and local newspapers and magazines, and later I was featured in a Granada Television *World in Action* production.

I had cost the dealers at least £6 million in lost drug revenue as well as exposing their names and operating methods to the Customs. There was no doubt I was now a target, it was a question of when, rather than if, they would arrive to claim their payback.

The local police were sympathetic to our problems and installed a radio-controlled panic alarm system in our house. All we had to do was press the button, and a radio signal automatically triggered a priority alarm in the main police station. The flaw in this system was that our farm was in a remote rural location, exposed on every side. If a hit-team despatched by the drug barons came to visit us, they would probably come about three o'clock in the morning. They wouldn't hang around, it would be a quick in and out operation, the job would be over and done with in a couple of minutes. Far quicker than any police unit could respond to our call for help.

The police were aware of this unavoidable shortcoming, and after hours of consultations and family meetings we decided we would all be safer living at a different, more secure address. Yet again the knock-on effects of my volunteering to help the Customs was having a definite impact upon all my family. We moved into rented accommodation in a large town about a hundred miles away from our own home, which we put up for rent via an agent.

I spent many hours in meetings with lawyers and barristers. The general consensus of the legal experts was that my shabby treatment by the Customs was actionable at law. I gave the necessary instructions, and the legal machinery creaked into operation. It took 18 months to get all the requisite pieces in place, but eventually a High Court writ was issued against the Customs & Excise, and that court case is still ongoing at the time of writing. The case seems destined to run the litigious process for at least another two years. Recently, applications from my lawyers to the French requesting copies of statements and interviews has fallen on deaf ears. Now it seems we must pursue the French judiciary in a battle through the European courts.

Through my lawyers, I made a formal complaint to HM Customs about my treatment, using their complaints procedure. After a brief, initial flurry of correspondence the complaints procedure ground to a halt. We are still waiting two years later for the first face-to-face meeting to be held.

Another consequence of the continued stress we had all

suffered so long manifested itself in the weeks following my return home. I couldn't establish a normal sleeping pattern. Frequently waking with a start and then unable to drop off back to sleep I would wander around the house in the small hours fidgeting and mithering about trivialities. The constant lack of sleep made me irritable, and eventually I consulted a doctor. After listening to my story he referred me to a psychiatric specialist. I travelled to Northampton and had an initial three-hour meeting with the consultant.

His report concluded that I was suffering from moderate to severe post-traumatic stress disorder, an illness I knew little about. I thought firemen and policemen who attended catastrophes and major accidents were obvious contenders for it, I was shocked to be told that I was suffering exactly the same symptoms and worse, I was told that there was no specific cure, no magic pill that I could swallow to alleviate my condition.

For many months I lived in a twilight world of my own. I developed a habit of scouring newspapers and television news for stories of drug busts, and would find myself reliving the experiences I had undergone in Spain and France. For a while I truly feared I was becoming unhinged, but time and family love are great healers. Luckily for my sanity those terrible, vivid recollections are now mostly confined to my memory and no longer keep me awake night after night.

From time to time something would happen that would throw me back in time to my previous experiences. One day I was walking down a main shopping street with Kath and Natalie when a car engine backfired with a loud crack. Quick as a flash I hit the ground and rolled towards the protective shelter of a parked car. Kath and Natalie screamed, and Kath later told me she thought I had been shot. I realized what had happened: my brain had picked up the noise and categorized it as a gunshot. Without any conscious thought on my part my instinctive reactions had taken over.

I stood up and brushed off my clothes before we walked quickly away from the small crowd of shoppers who had gathered around us. Such events were totally beyond my ability to control, and it was as if somebody else was in control of my body and pulling the strings, not a pleasant experience.

Events like that and our almost obsessive need for security and safety caused us to cut ourselves off from our friends, and our social life died a quick death. Others who had heard the rumours about me, drugs and being imprisoned in France distanced themselves from us. We noticed that Natalie no longer received invitations to her school chums' parties, and it became obvious that something was going on when only two kids from an invitation list of more than ten turned up to her birthday party at our home. By now the local rumour machine was in full swing, fuelled by malicious gossip from people who couldn't possibly have known the truth of the story.

Such ostracization didn't bother me but was deeply upsetting for my wife and daughter. A few of the parents of the children had obviously heard all the rumours, but not one came forward to ask us about the matter directly, preferring quietly to withdraw their offspring from any connection with the tainted family. A prime example of good old British middle-class hypocrisy in action. Eventually I changed my name, and we moved again to a new town away from the gossips.

The rumour-mongers are a persistent bunch of buggers though. Anonymous phone calls were made to Natalie's new school, and an embarrassed head teacher called me in to discuss the problem. He had been told that I was a drug dealer and not a fit parent to have a child in the school. I was incensed at having to justify my position in such a manner, but the headteacher put a call in to my solicitor who set his mind at ease, and the matter faded away. Such callous handling by a society that I had been trying to assist left a very bitter aftertaste.

* * *

Meanwhile back in France a new judge was appointed in the town. Barry was released by the Appeal Court on bail and allowed to return to his address in England two weeks before Christmas. I considered this a bit of a raw deal. I had been confined to live in France, but Barry, who had confessed his role in the smuggling, was allowed home. After he'd done so he contacted us, and after giving his proposal much thought I agreed to meet him. Feeling particularly cynical at that time I chose Hartshead services as the rendezvous spot, a location from which many of my unhappy experiences had begun.

Barry told me he was surprised when he had been taken to the Appeal Court in Poitiers and told that he would be released on bail. It had been decided it was unfair to hold him in prison on remand when Benson was still in Spain, and there was no date in sight when Benson would be extradited to France. No bail surety was required by the Appeal Court. Whilst I was not unhappy that Barry had been released it did seem iniquitous that he should get off with no bail money being deposited and be allowed to return to the UK. I didn't consider Barry a drug dealer, he was more of a down-on-his-luck opportunist who had grabbed the chance to make a few easy bob when the time was right.

He was pleased to see me, and we discussed French prison for a while. It was through him I learnt that Benson was still held in prison in Madrid. The extradition process was interminable, though it seemed it was temporarily stalled because Benson had been implicated in an international car theft ring. The extradition process would recommence when the outstanding Spanish investigations were completed. At least he was out of circulation for the time being, and we could all breathe a little easier because of that.

My lawyer Christian Traineau, who didn't hold any grudge that I had left without any warning, submitted another application that my bail conditions be relaxed. In an amazing *volte-face* the new judge claimed that, because I had jumped bail, I was obviously guilty of being a smuggler and promptly issued an International Arrest Warrant against me. This was an incredible step and flew in the face of the earlier Appeal Court verdict. The new judge, who had never met me, was obviously flexing his muscles and showing the Poitiers High Court that he would not brook any interference in the case he had inherited from Marlière.

This was a bad move and could have some serious implications for me. If implemented, the International Warrant would be effective in Britain, and the French judiciary could reach out their arm and try to snatch me back to France. I would be arrested and taken before Bow St Magistrates Court in London for an extradition hearing. Christian told me that if I were extradited to France then I would be held in prison until the trial. Worse, he claimed I would almost certainly be convicted of international drug smuggling and condemned to a lengthy prison sentence.

We were told that it took about two or three months to execute an International Arrest Warrant. In a high state of nervous tension I spent the next few weeks appointing and meeting with specialist extradition lawyers and blowing new life into the old 'Get John Home' campaigners.

The sword of Damocles didn't fall as expected. In fact, even after Benson was eventually extradited to France and spat all sorts of lies about me to the judge I heard nothing from officialdom. We have tried to find out, both in France and England, what happened to the warrant, but everywhere our inquiries meet with a wall of bureaucratic silence. We know it was issued and have seen a copy of it. The extradition office at New Scotland Yard have my solicitor's details and have promised to call as soon as it reaches their in-tray. It never did resurface from the bog of European bureaucracy.

The strain of living with an arrest warrant floating around with your name on it is awful. For weeks I had a holdall packed and ready for my arrest and removal. I went everywhere with emergency contact numbers for all my team of lawyers and media plotters in my pocket. Plans for the future were impossible, we lived in a perpetual state of dread of strangers knocking on the front door.

I am more determined than ever that the whole truth of the matter should be revealed, now I know I am not alone with my problem. I have learnt there are others who have suffered similarly poor treatment after volunteering their services as informants.

A Customs drug investigation officer came forward following a newspaper article about me. He wanted to remain anonymous but met me in the company of a Granada TV producer and investigative journalist. He told us unbelievable stories of a powerful government-backed investigation unit running out of control. According to him, there were informants languishing in foreign jails too scared of repercussions from the drug barons to come forward, no help in the background for them from HM Customs.

Customs & Excise will have to stand up and explain what really happened just before the ill-fated drug run. They cannot refuse to talk for ever; they must justify their actions. The general public and the courts are only too aware of the potential for error within Customs & Excise ranks. The Churchill Matrix affair demonstrated that they were capable of tampering with evidence and witnesses, and their interference with natural justice in that case was displayed to all. They have so far seen me imprisoned, supported damaging claims about me, refused to consider my demand for compensation and put my life and the lives of my family at risk. They admit I was a good informant who freely volunteered my services. Ultimately I assisted in stopping more than £6 million of drugs from hitting the streets of Great Britain, for which they paid me the princely sum of £500.

I believe they, more than the drug dealers, are partly responsible for the waking nightmare that both I and my family are constantly living.

The trial was finally held in France, more than 3 years after we were arrested. Benson stood alone in the dock. Barry and Eric were absent because the summonses issued to them were incorrectly dated, so they can look forward to their trial some time in the future.

Jill was acquitted of the charges against her at the end of the Judge's investigation, based on her insistent denials and lack of physical evidence against her. But in another court, Eric was convicted of growing marijuana in his garden, he has still to face a trial for the importation of drugs.

My trial was held in the main court in the Palais de Justice. It was all over and done with in one day. Three judges presided, there was no jury and I was not entitled to a defence lawyer. Christian sat through the trial, impotent, unable to speak up in my defence as the Prosecutor and later Benson attacked me, my motives and my character. Of course I could not be there; Christian told me how it had gone that evening.

The Prosecutor demanded that I should be found guilty and condemned to eight years' incarceration. The judges conferred and pronounced sentence. I was found guilty of importing 300kg of cannabis into France as a member of an organised gang – a serious offence. I was sentenced to three years in prison, with two-and-a-half years of that term suspended. My previous jail term was all I would have to serve to complete my sentence, so if I had been in court, then I would have walked from the courtroom a free man. Additionally, I was banned from France for 10 years, but I managed to avoid any financial penalty.

For his part in masterminding the smuggling operation, Benson was condemned to eight years in prison, he was banned for life from French territory and fined FF1 million, with an additional two years' imprisonment if the fine is not paid.

The immediate result of the trial was that the international arrest warrant would be halted – now it would never arrive. But I was now a convicted drug dealer. Christian and I discussed the matter for hours; we had achieved a practical result which meant I would retain my liberty, but in his opinion, the guilty verdict flew in the face of the evidence. We decided to appeal against the verdict, and Christian began the formal process.

We weren't the only party unhappy with the verdict – the Prosecutor thought my sentence too lenient, and submitted an appeal as well. Both appeals will ultimately be heard by the same Appeal Court in Poitiers, which had already indicated that I should be acquitted.

The appeals procedure in France is a long and murky process. We expect a full court hearing although we are unsure of the outcome; results can range from complete acquittal to an increase in sentence, along the lines of the Prosecutor's demands, or even greater. As Christian said, we have chosen to dance with the devil.

All bets are off once again, and the threat of an international arrest warrant is back to haunt us. Weary and tired of being harrassed, we have yet again been moved to a new location. We also knew that the drug barons in England would be able to locate our address from court records, and so, worried by the constant threat of their retribution, we thought another move might finally let us live in some kind of peace.

The story isn't yet finished. The civil proceedings against the Customs & Excise continue, my lawyers are now getting ready to travel to France to interview the senior OCTRIS officers in an attempt to discover just who was telling the truth about events leading up to my arrest. With the assistance of my lawyers and new-found friends in high places, we continue to unravel fiction from fact – those responsible for my untimely fall from grace should take this opportunity to rest easy while they can.

For them, the winged horsemen of the apocalypse can be heard approaching in the distance – they come for retribution.